When Men Murder Women

When Men Murder Women

R. EMERSON DOBASH

AND

RUSSELL P. DOBASH

UNIVERSITY PRESS

Oxford University Press is a department of the University of
Oxford. It furthers the University's objective of excellence in research,
scholarship, and education by publishing worldwide.

Oxford   New York
Auckland   Cape Town   Dar es Salaam   Hong Kong   Karachi
Kuala Lumpur   Madrid   Melbourne   Mexico City   Nairobi
New Delhi   Shanghai   Taipei   Toronto

With offices in
Argentina   Austria   Brazil   Chile   Czech Republic   France   Greece
Guatemala   Hungary   Italy   Japan   Poland   Portugal   Singapore
South Korea   Switzerland   Thailand   Turkey   Ukraine   Vietnam

Oxford is a registered trademark of Oxford University Press
in the UK and certain other countries.

Published in the United States of America by
Oxford University Press
198 Madison Avenue, New York, NY 10016

Library of Congress Cataloging-in-Publication Data
Dobash, R. Emerson.
When men murder women / R. Emerson Dobash and Russell P. Dobash.
    pages cm.—(Interpersonal violence)
Includes bibliographical references and index.
ISBN 978–0–19–991478–4 (alk. paper)
1. Women—Violence against.   2. Murder.   3. Violence in men.
4. Murderers—Psychology.   I. Dobash, Russell.   II. Title.
HV6250.4.W65D625 2015
364.152'3–dc23
2014038913

9 8 7 6 5 4 3 2 1
Printed in the United States of America
on acid-free paper

For Kate Cavanagh and Margo Wilson
In loving memory of lifelong friends, fellow researchers, and colleagues who were dedicated to doing research that mattered in the wider effort to understand violence and to improve the lives of all those affected by it.

CONTENTS

LIST OF FIGURES

FOUR TYPES OF MURDER (FOUR TYPES) (CHAPTER 11)

LIST OF TABLES

INTIMATE PARTNER MURDER (IPM) (APPENDIX.III FOR CHAPTERS 3–4)

SEXUAL MURDER (SexM) (APPENDIX.IV FOR CHAPTERS 6–7)

MURDER OF OLDER WOMEN (OWoM) (APPENDIX.V FOR CHAPTERS 9–10)

In 1979, we published *Violence Against Wives* based on our research into the topic of "wife beating" or "violence against wives," which was, at the time, just beginning to be discovered and to become a topic of public concern and a focus of emerging activism, research, and public policy.

Since then, the name of the problem has changed many times to reflect changing times, conventions, and focus, but the issue of violence against women remains central, even as the terminology has changed, and the topic is now familiar across the globe, with virtually tens of thousands of articles, research papers, and books now in press. At about the same time, or slightly earlier, the topic of rape and sexual assault was going through a similar process beginning with efforts to gain recognition of the problem along with those seeking to introduce changes in social and legal policies, practices, and interventions. To a somewhat lesser extent, violence against the elderly, which included older women but was not exclusively focused on them, began to be recognized. Early publications about family violence often included something about violence against older men and women, but this was likely to be conceptualized as an issue of conflicts across generations that related more to the age of the victim than to their gender. It was more a matter of being old than it was one of being a woman who was also of a certain age. Over several decades, we have continued to expand the arenas in which we have studied interpersonal violence with the dual aim of extending knowledge about the nature and dynamics of the various forms of violence and of doing so in a manner that might, in turn, be productively used by those who work in a myriad of ways to end the violence and the destruction associated with it. This study of the murder of women by men is a continuation of the ongoing efforts to expand knowledge and to seek changes that are both relevant and effective.

ACKNOWLEDGMENTS

- We thank the many unnamed individuals who facilitated our research in the prisons in which we examined casefiles and conducted interviews, to the men and women in prison who agreed to be interviewed, the Prison Services in England/Wales and Scotland, and the staff within each of the separate prisons who allowed access to their records and facilitated our research within the context of the many and varied demands of their daily routines.
- We thank the Economic and Social Research Council, ESRC, for funding the research.
- We thank Kate Cavanagh and Ruth Lewis, coresearchers who spent countless hours working with us as we developed the data collection instruments, collected data from the casefiles, conducted interviews, and prepared the quantitative and qualitative data for analysis. Their dedication and professional approach were invaluable in the process of conducting a very difficult and demanding piece of research, and their friendship, sense of humor, and optimism were equally valuable.
- We thank our friends and colleagues who took the time from their own busy schedules and lives to read and comment on drafts: Nancy Jurik and Gray Cavender, Monica Wilson, Fran Wasoff, and Martin Daly. We valued their comments and needed to hear what they had to say.
- Finally, we thank the many individuals at Oxford University Press who worked with us throughout the process of writing and producing this book, particularly Stefano Imbert, Devi Vaidyanathan, and Sylvia Cannizzaro.

TYPES OF MURDER:

IPM	Intimate Partner Murder/Murderer
M-M, MxM, MM	Male-Male Murder/Murderer
OWoM	Older Women Murder/Murderer
OWo	Older Women Murder
SexM	Sexual Murder/Murderer
Sex/Murder	[of older women]
Theft/Murder	[of older women]

ALSO:

IPH	Intimate Partner Homicide
IPV	Intimate Partner Violence (or abuse)

SOURCES OF DATA:

cf	Casefile/s
iv	Interview/s

SOFTWARE FOR DATA ANALYSIS:

Nud*ist/QSR	software for analysis of qualitative data
SPSS	software for analysis of quantitative data

When Men Murder Women

Homicide Across Time and Place

Expanding Knowledge and Refining Focus

Throughout the world, across time and place, men have murdered women in many different circumstances. In times of war and when groups are in conflict, men kill the women of their male enemies while at the same time they continue to murder women from their own group. In times of peace, men continue to murder women from their own community in the context of conflicts between intimate partners, as a part of a sexual attack, or during a robbery in a public place or a theft within the woman's home or place of residence. In some cultures, bride burning, dowry deaths, and acid attacks are used against women who, as wives or prospective wives, are deemed to have "failed" in some way to fulfill expectations set by the man and his supporters, often family members including women. Their "failure" is used to justify various acts of deprivation and violence including starving, beating, and burning that result in extensive injuries and even death.

Although such treatment may be viewed by some as brutal violence and/or torture, it may be viewed by others, particularly perpetrators and those who support them, as justified and acceptable particularly in the context of various cultural and/or religious beliefs and practices. There are various responses to those who object to the violent treatment of women. Objections from those outside the particular culture or religion may be defined as inappropriate, incorrect, interfering, or imperialist based on the notion that the critical outsider somehow fails to understand, appreciate, or respect the culture, traditions, or the people who perpetrate various types of violence against women as well as the beliefs and customs on which the violence is based and that provide the foundation for legitimizing even the most brutal treatment of women. In contrast, objections made by individuals who are "inside" the particular culture or religion may result in such individuals being repositioned as "outside" the group and therefore without the authority or remit to comment or criticize. Thus, "insiders" become "outsiders" whose critiques and objections do not count. When violence against women is deemed to be a valued cultural norm to be practiced by all and protected through social customs and practices as well as through institutional policies and legislation, the general position of women is bleak and the prospect of individual, social, or institutional change is similarly dire. In this respect, the efforts of those who work on behalf of women throughout the world are to be supported and applauded, and the enormity of the task is not to be underestimated. Efforts to end violence against women are confounded by conflicts of interest in which men with greater power and influence than women, no matter how limited these may be in some absolute sense, are allowed or even encouraged to use violence against women as a fundamental part of their position as men within the wider society as well as the varied and numerous smaller groupings within it.

Although we stress that the widest possible scope, scale, and understanding of the murder of women by men is global, our efforts here are more delimited and do not include the murder of women in times of war or in the full diversity of cultural or religious contexts. Instead, the focus is on the murder of women by men in the context of everyday life that is not punctuated by nations at war, gangs in conflict, natural disasters, or other such events that may, in various ways, alter the rates and patterns of such murders. Focusing on the murder of women by men in the ongoing contexts of everyday life rather than in the context of external or extraordinary events avoids the temptation to view the murder of women as solely or primarily a reaction to such circumstances. Instead, *When Men Murder Women* focuses on the murder of women by men in the context and activities of everyday life in the family, the community, and the wider society. It is set within the more general framework of wider social values, beliefs, and institutional policies and practices that, despite numerous important changes, continue to be deeply gendered and problematic.

Evidence about the murder of women by men is drawn from a wider, intensive study of all types of murder in Great Britain that will be referred to as the Murder Study. The specific focus is on three types of murder of women by men: intimate partner murder, sexual murder, and the murder of older women. It is about the murder events, the contexts in which the murders occur, the lifecourse of the men who perpetrate them, their relationships with the women they kill, and their subsequent reflections about the murders including rationalizations and justifications as well as their feelings of empathy and remorse. Each of the three types is examined in detail and compared with murders committed by men against other men. As will be seen, men's orientations to and relationships with women are fundamental to the explanation and understanding of these murders.

HOMICIDE PATTERNS WORLDWIDE AND FINDINGS
ABOUT MEN MURDERING MEN

Across the world, rates of homicide are driven by men killing other men. Men murder other men in a wide set of circumstances. They range from those that involve the most immediate and personal circumstances, such as possessiveness and jealousy of an intimate partner, to those driven by financial gain from businesses, both legal and illegal, such as conflicts over the ownership or profits from a company or struggles for control of illegal gains from international drug importing to dealing on the street. Men kill their friends in drunken fights after a night out together and in arguments about sporting events, debts, or girlfriends. Men kill other men more often than they kill women, and the circumstances would appear to be more diverse than when they kill women. Overwhelmingly, it is men and not women who commit murder, with individual countries reporting that men commit between 85% and 95% of all murders, and the United Nations reporting a global figure of 95%.[1]

In countries where homicide rates are extremely high, the figures are driven by men murdering other men in circumstances that often involve illegal activities such as drug trafficking or gang wars or as a result of civil strife between competing groups based on differences of religion or historical conflicts over land, property, or commerce. The men are usually, although not always, young and may be involved in behaviors that are contentious or extralegal in which groups of men compete for limited resources and depend on force to regulate their interactions, defend their gains, and obtain redress for their losses. Violence is common, and murder is sometimes the outcome. In such contexts, rates of homicide are usually high and sometimes extremely high. In nations that are *not* experiencing such extraordinary circumstances, the vast majority of murders are still between men and involve situations and circumstances such as robbery, drunkenness, and various forms of conflict including personal affronts and perceived offenses.

Homicide rates are usually based on one homicide for every 100,000 residents of a given nation, state, or city. Table 1.1 shows countries with the highest and lowest homicide rates reported by the United Nations for 2008–2010.[2] It should be noted that the lowest rates of homicide are in most European countries, Canada, and the United States, and the highest rates are in countries in Africa and Central and South America. The strikingly different homicide rates

Table 1.1. HOMICIDE 2011. UNODC (ORDERED FROM HIGHEST TO LOWEST COUNTRIES ONLY*)

Rate	Country	Rate	Country
66.0	El Salvador	5.0	United States of America
56.9	Cote d'Ivoire	4.6	Cuba
52.1	Jamaica	2.3	Finland
49.0	Venezuela (Bolivarian Rep.)	2.1	Israel
41.7	Belize	1.8	Canada
41.4	Guatemala	1.7	Belgium
39.2	United States Virgin Islands	1.5	New Zealand
38.2	St. Kitts & Nevis	1.4	France
36.3	Uganda	1.2	United Kingdom
35.2	Trinidad & Tobago	1.2	Ireland
33.8	South Africa	1.2	Australia
33.6	Lesotho	1.2	Portugal
33.4	Columbia	1.1	China
30.8	Congo	1.1	Croatia
29.3	Central African Republic	1.1	Netherlands
26.2	Puerto Rico	1.0	Italy
25.5	Ethiopia	1.0	Sweden
25.2	Saint Lucia	0.9	Spain
24.9	Dominican Republic	0.9	Denmark
24.5	United Republic of Tanzania	0.7	Switzerland
24.2	Sudan	0.6	Norway
22.7	Brazil	0.5	Japan
22.0	St. Vincent & the Grenadines	0.5	Singapore
21.6	Panama	0.3	Iceland

*original in alphabetical order, here reordered and reduced to only highest to lowest.
SOURCE: UNODC, United Nations, *Global Study on Homicide*, 2011.

around the world are, for the most part, attributed to male-male murders in countries experiencing internal conflicts between political and social groups and/or
in those with problems of smuggling or drug dealing. In such circumstances, the
murder of women might also be elevated in relation to "collateral" killings associated with these conditions, but the rates are still lower than those for murders
between men. It is easy to see how high homicide rates are driven by the killing of men by other men who are involved in activities where they compete for
resources and attempt to maintain control and/or to settle scores by killing other
men. Extremely high homicide rates have the effect of obscuring the murders of
women by men.

Even in countries with rates of homicide that are not extremely high, such
as those shown in the right column of Table 1.1, the majority of homicides are
still committed by men against other men. Whether the overall rates are high
or low, the rates of homicide of women remain unknown unless the data are
disaggregated. Veli Verkko was an early proponent of disaggregation based on
his extensive statistical research in Finland from the 1920s to the 1950s. He
"observed that the proportion of female homicide victims was higher when the
overall Homicide rate was low, and vice versa." This and other statistical patterns
in homicide became known as "Verkko's laws."[3] This pattern is evident across
European countries where the homicide rate is relatively low. For example, in
France approximately 40% of all victims of homicide were women from the
1970s onward, and in England/Wales women represented 31% of all victims of
homicide from 1998 to 2008.[4] In the United States, where homicide rates are
higher than in Europe, the figures for 2010 indicate that females represented 22%
of all victims of homicide.[5]

Although the disaggregation of homicide data by gender is essential if we are
to achieve a better understanding of the *rates* of homicide, it is also important if
we are to gain better knowledge about the *nature* of homicides committed against
women. A by-product of this is an enhanced knowledge about murders between
men. In 1957, Marvin Wolfgang published the classic American work on homicide. He focused broadly on the topic of homicide and noted that it was usually
committed by men against other men, but he also noted that the murder of women
was an important part of the overall examination of and concern about homicide.[6]
Although the murder of women was identified by this early influential scholar, it
was generally ignored for decades, data were not usually disaggregated by gender, and theoretical explanations were primarily shaped with male-male murder
in mind.

KNOWLEDGE ABOUT HOMICIDE—NATIONAL DATASETS,
ACADEMIC RESEARCH, AND POPULAR MEDIA

A number of countries hold a national dataset containing information about every
homicide known to have been committed during a given year, and the findings are
reported to the public on a regular basis, annually or at more infrequent intervals.
National figures about homicide are usually based on data collected by police
and provided to a central source for the purpose of collating and reporting on
crime, violence, and homicide in each nation. These data are usually descriptive

and limited to a fairly small number of variables about each case of homicide, such as the age, race, and gender of perpetrators and victims; location; and summary details about the circumstances. Adding to this knowledge, academics conduct research on homicide and present the findings in academic journals, books, government documents, and public reports. On another level, cases of murder that gain public interest or notoriety may be covered, sometimes in great detail, by newspapers, radio, television, and social media. Together, these sources of information provide different levels of knowledge, insights, and views about homicide in a given nation at a particular point in time. National datasets provide a broad overview that generally reflects what is occurring in the wider society. Other sources of information, such as the popular media, are more sensational in nature and serve to satisfy the seemingly insatiable public curiosity about the most extreme acts of murder but rarely provide insight into the nature and complexity of such events.

Most national datasets contain all homicides known to the police and hold a limited amount of information about each case, which is used to construct the overall patterns of homicide in a specific time period for an entire country, region, or city. While they can provide an overview of all murders committed in a given place over a given point in time, the very fact of gathering information about all such cases inevitably limits the amount of information that can be collected about each case. A well-constructed homicide dataset contains enough information to allow for the exploration of general patterns, but it is rarely possible to go beyond these patterns in order to reveal the complexity and dynamics of such events or to examine in any detail the different types of murder that occur such as the killing of children, older women, intimate partners, or others. Since the majority of homicides are usually committed by men who kill other men, it is the characterization of male-male homicide that predominates in any examination of homicide that does not disaggregate them into the other types that occur less frequently. Even when homicides are disaggregated into the different types of murder, the limited amount of data held about each case restricts what can be known about murder and about each of the different types of murder being examined.

NATIONAL DATASETS: WHAT THEY TELL US AND THEIR LIMITATIONS

Large, national homicide datasets have been the topic of various critiques. Although these data sources offer significant statistical information, they are subject to limitations that jeopardize both the validity and reliability of the information gathered and make national comparisons difficult, if not impossible. For example, a survey of homicide data in 36 European countries revealed important variations in a number of relevant areas, including the definition of homicide, which in many countries includes other violent crimes, such as "attempted homicide" and "missing persons," in the homicide statistics; variations in the sources of data (e.g., criminal justice or healthcare agencies); differences in data collection and recording; and a lack of standardized measures, with some jurisdictions counting a case as a homicide at the beginning of the police investigation while others count cases only after a conviction for homicide.[7] Comparisons across countries are difficult, if not impossible, because some European countries have no specialized national institutions or pro-cedures for collecting, collating, and recording homicides. Barely mentioned in this analysis of European datasets, but of considerable importance, is the problem of missing data. European homicide researchers have concluded that these and other problems make it difficult to make valid comparisons and that the safest approach is to compare trends over time using regional rather than country-specific patterns.[8]

In the United States, reports on homicides at a national level have mostly used information extracted from the Supplementary Homicide Reports (SHRs), which are gathered through the national Uniform Crime Reporting program of the FBI.[9] The collection, compilation, and analysis of these data suffer from a number of prob-lems, including missing data, limited information about specific homicides, and a scarcity of information about potentially relevant factors.[10] For example, in the late 1990s, an analysis of the SHRs found that victim-offender relationships were "not known" in 39% of the cases.[11] An examination of intimate partner homicides by Langford and colleagues found that as many as 29% of the SHRs for Massachusetts were not properly identified, with some described as homicides between "acquain-tances" when they were, in fact, intimate partner homicides.[12] For 2010, of the 12,664 homicides across the United States reported in the SHRs, the circumstances and type of relationship were not known or specified in 50% of the cases.[13] Similarly, when 7,542 homicides in England/Wales from 1998 to 2008 were classified by type, Soothill and Frances found that 2,503 cases were defined as "other homicides" (i.e., not defined) and for about 13% there was "no known suspect," which made it impos-sible to categorize them into any meaningful type.[14] Furthermore, the "circum-stances" of the homicide (e.g., arguments/altercations) could not be determined in 1,848 cases, and the relationship between the perpetrator and the victim was coded as "unknown" in 1,134 cases. In 2002, the U.S. Centers for Disease Control and Prevention (CDC) initiated a new surveillance system, the National Violent Death Reporting System (NVDRS), in order to address some of these problems by gather-ing additional data about violent deaths.[15] Over 270 data elements for each case of violent death are gathered from death certificates, coroner files, law enforcement agencies, and crime laboratories. By 2004, 13 state health departments were using this system. Although U.S. and European homicide data at a national level continue to reflect the problems outlined above, these data are among the most reliable mate-rial available, and ongoing developments continue to increase their utility in the expanding study of homicide. Despite these improvements, much of the informa-tion that is essential for the examination of the various types of murder considered here continues to be missing or unavailable.

CASE STUDIES: WHAT THEY TELL
US AND THEIR LIMITATIONS

By contrast, studies containing a small number of cases of homicide, such as "fatal-ity reviews," are designed to gather more comprehensive data about each case exam-ined, but this approach presents a different set of problems, particularly the ability to generalize about murder. While studies that contain in-depth information about one or a small number of cases may be able to provide detailed descriptions of the nature and dynamics of one or a few murders, the small numbers make it impossible to generalize to any wider group or population even though these single cases may contain extremely interesting and valuable insights particularly to agencies such as the police, social work, healthcare providers, and voluntary organizations. For example, the detailed information in a fatality review about a single case in which a child is murdered in the home by a parent or stepparent is designed to provide the maximum amount of information about that case in order that various agencies might learn lessons and possibly modify existing policies and practices. Although extensive knowledge about a single case is certainly valuable in developing intervention strategies based on lessons learned from such a "fingertip" examination, such knowledge cannot be used as the basis for drawing overall generalizations about the murder of children. Another example is that of the microscopic detail often provided in the examination of the very small number of cases of serial killers. While the presentation of almost every known facet of the several murders of a single serial killer is certainly interesting and not unimportant in gaining insight into the very small number of such cases, such knowledge, no matter how detailed and valid, cannot be generalized to the vast majority of murders, which rarely fit the pattern of this very small minority of murders.

THEORETICAL AND CONCEPTUAL FRAMEWORKS

Accompanying the empirical focus on the majority of homicides committed by and against men has been the theoretical and conceptual frameworks used to develop explanatory notions about who commits murder and when, where, and why it occurs. Various theoretical perspectives have focused on the individuals who kill, the immediate circumstances in which they do so, and the wider social, cultural, and historical contexts in which such events occur. While the domains vary in focus from the personal to the situational to various cultural and/or institutional contexts under examination, they share in common, either explicitly or implicitly, notions of a gendered dynamic that is basically male in nature. Some of the most common approaches in search of correlates and/or explanations of murder have focused on socioeconomic factors, culture and subcultures of violence and offending, interactions and relationships between perpetrators and victims, lifecourse of offenders, perceptions and cognitions of offenders, and psychological characteristics. Lifestyle, routine activities, education, employment, and problems of alcohol and substance abuse have frequently been the focus of research.[16] A brief overview of some of these approaches highlights the various explanatory frameworks commonly used in the study of homicide and illustrates the main focus, which is on violence and murder committed by and against men.

Sociostructural explanations rely on social class and ethnicity as markers of inequality and social deprivation associated with the weakening of social controls and increased levels of social strain within the community and society that result in increases in general crime as well as violence and homicide. More specifically, this body of research has shown that those who commit crime and homicide, and their victims, are disproportionately drawn from men who are poor, undereducated, and unemployed and, in the United States, those who are African Americans.[17]

Cultural explanations from anthropology and sociology focus on beliefs, values, and norms that support and justify violence in specific situations and circumstances.

The early work of Wolfgang stressed subcultures of violence and noted the relevance of notions of "male honor," courage, and manliness in encounters between men that end in violence and/or homicide. Other ethnographic and historical works have found similar cultural patterns in various countries.[18] The cultural perspective has also been used in efforts to explain higher rates of violence and homicide in the southern regions of the United States that are characterized by specific cultural beliefs and practices that are more likely to support the use of violence in disputes.[19]

Wolfgang also introduced the concept of "victim precipitation," which stressed the aggressive actions of the person who ultimately becomes the victim of violence or murder. Most of this work was about violence between men, but Wolfgang also included examples of women who killed male partners who had been assaulting them and, as such, whose actions might be defined as self-defense.[20] In much of the subsequent literature, the imagery that underpins the notion of "victim precipitation" is one of challenges, contests, and the willingness of two fairly evenly matched parties to engage in a fight in which either person might emerge the victor or the victim. A frequently cited example that integrates both the cultural and interactional perspectives is Luckenbill's notion of "victim precipitation," which contains various stages in the encounter between the perpetrator and victim that results in a homicide.[21] He proposed a sequence of events composed of six stages prior to the homicide including a stage in which both parties come to "a working agreement with the proffered definition of the situation as one suited to violence."[22] In this stage, the victim fails to comply with the challenges or commands of the perpetrator and, as such, accepts the situation as one suited to violence between them with an uncertain outcome in terms of who may become the victim of the encounter. This is primarily based on notions of male orientations to conflicts with other males and contains many implicit notions about such encounters. These notions are deeply gendered. The victor-vanquished outcome of mutual participants in a violent encounter does not always apply, even to encounters between men, but it certainly does not apply to the overwhelming majority of events in which a man attacks and murders a woman.[23]

The focus on male perpetrators of homicide usually includes demographic details such as age, employment, education, race, and previous offending, as well as life-style issues such as the abuse of alcohol and drugs. Many have a history of alcohol abuse and previous offending for all types of offenses including, but not restricted to, those involving violence. Evidence about previous offending suggests that 68% of those convicted of homicide in England/Wales, and 67% of those in the United States, had at least one previous conviction prior to committing the murder.[24]

Consumption of alcohol has been shown to be a reliable correlate of violence and homicide. An extensive review of North American research notes that alcohol consumption is a strong correlate of homicide rates, and estimates that about half of all homicides in the United States are alcohol and/or drug related, with particular emphasis on alcohol.[25] Similar patterns have been observed in Europe. In various European countries, violence and alcohol have been tracked in terms of price, availability, and consumption, and it has been concluded that there is an increase in violence and homicide when alcohol is cheap and widely available. Accordingly, both European researchers and policy makers have suggested that alcohol should be regulated in terms of price and availability.[26] It is not merely the amount of alcohol consumed but also the patterns associated with consumption that are related to violence and homicide. Although alcohol has psychopharmacological effects related to altered judgment and inhibitions, individual characteristics and sociocultural contexts are also important. In some European countries, homicide is associated with daily drinking, drinking in public, frequent drunkenness, drinking without meals, and particularly the cultural practice and acceptability of "drinking to intoxication."[27] This is in contrast to cultures where alcohol is usually consumed with meals and associated with "having a drink," rather than with drinking to "get drunk."

Although the lifecourse of offenders and onset of offending are of central importance in the field of developmental criminology, most of the research in this area focuses on those who commit nonlethal offenses, such as theft and assault, and not on those who commit murder. Within this tradition, particular attention is given to early childhood, the onset of offending in childhood or adolescence, and the persistence and/or desistance of offending in adolescence or adulthood.[28] In an earlier publication based on data from the Murder Study, we examined the onset of offending across the lifecourse of all the 786 men who were convicted of murder, whether their victims were men, women, or children. Three groups were identified: "early-onset offenders," who committed their first criminal offense before age thirteen (20%); "late-onset offenders," who committed their first criminal offense after age thirteen (67%); and those with no known history of offending prior to committing the murder (13%).[29] Overall, 87% of the 786 men in the Murder Study had at least one previous conviction prior to committing the murder. Comparing the three groups of men across the lifecourse, we found that male murderers who were "early-onset offenders" were more likely than the other two groups to experience adversity both in childhood and adulthood and that "late-onset offenders" were less likely than early-onset offenders to have had problems in childhood but just as likely to have had problems as adults. By contrast, the men in the "no offending" group stood out in two ways. Men with no previous convictions prior to the murder were much less likely than the other two groups of men to have experienced problems in childhood or adulthood, and they were more likely to have murdered an intimate partner. This seemed puzzling at the time but suggested that there might be a link between the absence of a record of previous offending among these men, the type of offense, and the nature of their relationship to the person they kill.[30] This will be developed more fully in the chapters about men who murder intimate partners and those who commit sexual murders.

Other conceptual frameworks focus on the nature of the relationships between the perpetrators and the victims, the contexts in which murders occur, and the views that perpetrators have about themselves and their victims. Relational distance, from strangers to intimates, is often used as a conceptual tool in considering the relationship between offenders and their victims.[31] For example, male-male murders usually involve strangers or acquaintances, and male-female murders usually involve intimates and men known to the woman victim. Polk notes that the classifications of victim-offender relationships are highly variable, that there is a minimal amount of consistency across studies, that they "are more diverse than they are consistent," and that most classifications "do not provide enough information to inform theoretical analysis of why people kill."[32] Polk also notes other problems of classification that concern important issues such as motives, circumstances, and rationales. Examples include a study with as many as 13 categories of "motives," another with 30 separate groupings of what is termed "homicide circumstances," and others that suggest "homicide syndromes" as "expressive," "instrumental" or a "mystery."[33] Questions of motives, intentions, rationales, and justifications include the orientations of perpetrators and what they might be thinking about various situations, circumstances, and the actions and intentions of others, including the victim. Perpetrators may define the behavior of victims as somehow culpable and deserving of the act of murder and, at the same time, view their own behavior as legitimate or righteous and accordingly see themselves as "moral enforcers."[34] Accordingly, the violence is excused, exculpatory accounts are given, and responsibility is denied and/or placed elsewhere. From this vantage point, there is no need to feel guilt or remorse about the murder or to have feelings of empathy with the victim.[35] In differing ways, the various explanatory frameworks traditionally used in the examination of homicide employ conceptualizations that primarily, although not exclusively, rest on the notion of male perpetrators in the context of encounters with victims who are also men. Even though there are numerous problems with these theoretical conceptions, particularly in relation to the murder of women by men, they nonetheless provide an initial framework from which to begin to explore more fully the murder of women by men.

KNOWLEDGE ABOUT THE MURDER OF WOMEN

In the early 1980s, after an extensive review of the literature, Wilbanks concluded that he could find no systematic investigation of the "patterns of homicide by or against women," and the general absence of literature focusing on the murder of women was noted a decade later.[36] Despite this, by the 1970s and 1980s, some notable exceptions had begun to reshape the field to include research on the murder of women by men, particularly the murder of intimate partners. In 1969, Toch included an analysis of the murder of a woman intimate partner in his book *Violent Men*, and in 1978, Chimbos published a small-scale study, *Marital Violence: A Study of Inter-Spousal Homicide*.[37] The pioneering research of Daly and Wilson (1988), *Homicide*, included a comprehensive examination of the murder of women in intimate relationships, and the murder of women was also examined by others including Block (1988), *Homicide in Chicago*; and Mercy and Saltzman (1989), "Fatal Violence Among Spouses in the United States."[38] In the 1990s, the area of research expanded with an increasing number of works including, but not limited to, those of Gartner (1990), "The Victims of Homicide: A Temporal and Cross-National Comparison"; Jurik and Winn (1990), "Gender and Homicide: A Comparison of Men and Women Who Kill"; Radford and Russell (1992), *Femicide: The Politics of Woman Killing*; Campbell (1992), "If I Can't Have You, No One Can"; Browne and Williams (1993), "Gender, Intimacy, and Lethal Violence: Trends from 1976 Through 1987"; Polk (1994), *When Men Kill*; and Websdale (1999), *Understanding Domestic Homicide*.[39] By the turn of the century, gender had clearly been identified as an important factor in the examination and explanation of homicide, and the disaggregation of homicide data became a more established part of this domain of research.[40] To date, the disaggregation of homicide data by gender and other relevant factors has proved to be a fruitful approach to gaining a fuller and more nuanced understanding of homicide, which should, in turn, provide additional insights into various efforts directed at prevention and intervention. In subsequent chapters, we explore more fully the relevant literature about intimate partner murder, sexual murder, and the murder of older women.

THE MURDER STUDY—RATIONALE, FOCUS, SCOPE, AND METHODS

Background and Rationale

Our interest in the study of murder, choice of research methods, and orientation to studying issues of wider importance came out of our earlier research about various forms of interpersonal violence. In our first study in the 1970s, we focused on "wife abuse," which was beginning to be identified by women activists as a social problem of importance about which something should be done. This was an issue that affected the lives of many, but there was a vacuum of knowledge about almost every aspect of it. Questions were asked about the nature of the violence, the predicaments of women who were abused, responses of the police and courts, and what policies or provisions might make a difference in effecting meaningful change. We thought research could assist in filling an important gap in knowledge about the nature and existence of the problem and the effectiveness of different responses to it. The resulting study included in-depth interviews with 104 women who fled to the refuges for abused women newly opened by Women's Aid in order to escape the violence they experienced at the hands of their male partners. In addition, we read over 34,000 police cases for a 1-year period in order to establish how much police work involved responding to violence against women by intimate partners.

The answers to these questions were stark. The interviews provided first-hand accounts of women who lived lives of constant fear and physical abuse at the hands of abusive male partners. The analysis of police records provided knowledge about the extent of this form of violence within the overall work of the police, and revealed that one-tenth of all police cases involved some form of violence, and that 25% of all cases of violence involved attacks on women partners. *Violence Against Wives*, published in 1979, detailed these and other findings about the nature and extent of this form of violence and placed it within the wider historical, social, and institutional contexts in which it occurred and in which it must be understood if it were to be addressed and changed.[41] Following this, we undertook studies, sometimes with other colleagues, on related topics including institutional responses to violence against women in Britain and the United States; women's responses to the depiction of violence against women on television; child sexual abusers; bodybuilding, steroids, and violence; and an evaluation of the effectiveness of programs for men convicted of using violence against women partners.[42]

Across all this research, we have used a combination of interviews and analysis of official records from agencies such as the police, courts, and social work. Findings are based on a combination of quantitative data that are used to delineate patterns and qualitative data that are used to illustrate these patterns and to give them meaning. We employ a context-specific approach, rather than abstract theories, in order to examine the different types of violence in the historical, social, and cultural contexts in which they occur in an effort to provide explanations that are based on human actions, beliefs, and orientations rather than on theories that are abstracted from them.[43]

This approach has deep roots in classical social science, particularly in the works of sociologists such as Max Weber. He proposed that efforts to describe and explain the complex and dynamic aspects of human action are more likely to be successful when they are located in the sociocultural settings in which they occur rather than placed within constructions of abstract general laws/theories about social phenomena that are detached from the sociocultural settings in which such behaviors actually take place.[44] While Weber thought that some general theories might be heuristically useful, he believed that they were too broad and general to provide explanations that are meaningful. Although some scholars still try to erect general theories that are intended to explain all types of violence from genocide to mothers who kill their babies,[45] we believe that more meaningful explanations may be achieved by focusing on specific types of violence and the contexts in which they occur. This approach to explanation requires a close engagement with the violence itself and with those who perpetrate it. In that regard, and based on the findings from our previous research, it is impossible to exaggerate the overwhelming importance of gender and the relationships between men and women in the general understanding of violence against women, and it is against this background that we embarked on the study of murder.

THE STUDY

The Murder Study was designed to examine all types of murder committed by and against men, women, and children. The overall aim was to expand and extend the amount of data gathered about each case well beyond the small number of variables contained within existing national datasets in order to enhance knowledge about the nature, complexity, and dynamics of all types of murder. This required the collection of more information about the murders; more about the situations and circumstances in which they occur; more about the individuals involved, especially the lifecourse of perpetrators and their relationships with their victims; more about subsequent reflections on the murder itself; and more about perpetrators' orientations to their victims.

Gathering more information across this wider range of issues presents the dual challenges of determining what information to gather and how many cases can be examined in this more expansive fashion. As suggested, a great deal of information can usually be gathered about a single case or a fairly small number of cases such as undertaken in case reviews, but there is a limit to how many cases can be examined in such an intensive fashion within the usual strictures of time and finance of any organization or research team. Other issues relate to obtaining a sample that is large enough to warrant drawing generalizations and, at the same time, specific enough to allow for the collection of an intensive amount of information about each case.

The Murder Study stands somewhere between national homicide datasets, with their limited amount of data about all known cases of homicide; the case study, with its exhaustive coverage of a single case; and the microscopic examination of the cases of serial killers, which are few in number. Increasing the amount and type of information known about each case of murder examined while at the same time including enough cases to be able to generalize from them cannot be satisfied either by what is now held in national datasets or by burrowing down into the exhaustive level of detail of a single homicide such as undertaken in a case study. Although each of these approaches fulfills an important role, neither can provide the type of information and knowledge that stands between them, which is the approach taken in the study as outlined below.

From Original Focus and Design to Modifications and Expansion

Here, we provide an overview of the design of the Murder Study, the type and content of data-collection instruments, the techniques used to gather information from the casefiles and the interviews, and other issues relating to the collection of data within the contexts of individual prisons and national prison records (for fuller details and technical specifications, see Appendix I). The research began with a major change in the initial design based on the unanticipated discovery of the value of the casefiles, which are held for every person convicted of murder (but not those convicted of manslaughter). The original intention was to conduct a study based on 200 in-depth interviews with men and women in prison for murder and to examine 100 individual casefiles, in order to inform the construction of the Interview Schedule and improve our readiness to conduct the interviews.

The interviews were to be conducted in depth in order to provide a much fuller understanding of murder events and the orientations of the men and women who commit them. After presenting the proposal to the funding body and obtaining all relevant permissions and protections necessary for obtaining access to the archive of casefiles and the various prisons where we planned to conduct the interviews, we began reading the casefiles and immediately realized that the material in them was far too rich to be used simply as a backdrop to the interviews but should, instead, become a major source of data in the study. Thus, the final design was changed dramatically. The original proposal to conduct 200 in-depth interviews was retained and resulted in interviews with 180 men and 20 women, but the original proposal to examine 100 casefiles was drastically increased to a total of 866, including 786 men and 80 women.

Casefiles

Before describing the overall design and data collection instruments, it is useful to consider why the casefiles exist, what they contain, and their place in the criminal justice system. With the abolition of the death penalty in Britain in 1965, every conviction for the offense of "Murder," but not "Manslaughter," resulted in what is termed a "life" sentence with a suggested "tariff" specifying the number of years to be served in prison before the individual might be considered for parole and possible release into the community.[46] Parole can only be granted upon satisfactory completion of special programs designed to focus on various aspects of the offending behavior such as alcohol, drugs, or violence, along with a positive assessment by the parole board of the person's suitability for release.[47] Even if the conditions are satisfied and parole is granted, those convicted of "murder" remain on what is referred to as a "life license," which means they remain within a nexus of supervision and surveillance by probation for the rest of their life and can always be returned to prison for violations of the conditions of their parole. The vast majority of those convicted of "murder" receive a "tariff" as described earlier. Very few receive what is called a "whole life" sentence, which means they will remain in prison for their entire life, will never be reviewed for parole, and will never be released. In England/Wales in 2012, about 60 individuals were serving a "whole life" sentence for murder.

The casefile is of particular importance for the overall operation of this system, and contains what is, in effect, a life history of each man or woman convicted of murder. It should be stressed again that this applies only to convictions for "murder" and not "manslaughter," which does not carry a mandatory "life sentence" but a "fixed term" sentence specifying a given number of years to be served in prison before release. It should also be noted that, in Britain, a conviction for "murder" does not require premeditation and the intention to kill but rather that the offender intended to use bodily violence and to cause grievous bodily harm.[48]

Casefiles are extensive and contain records, reports, and information from numerous sources about the individual before the murder and imprisonment, including reports from schools, social work, healthcare providers, mental health professionals, police, coroners, probation, and the trial judge. They also contain reports about the person after imprisonment from various prison professionals including governors, prison officers, psychologists, probation, chaplains, the parole board, and others. Casefiles contain information across the entire lifecourse of the offender before the murder and once in prison. Information about childhood includes reports of contacts with the family, school records, and reports of early offending. Information about adulthood includes employment history, previous offending, personal and family relations, previous partners, number of children, and contact with various agencies for problems such as alcohol and/or substance abuse. Information about the perpetrator at the time of the murder includes details of employment, housing, marital status, and contact with various agencies. Information about the relationship between the perpetrator and the victim includes details of police interviews with others who might have knowledge either about the perpetrator or the victim, such as family members, friends, neighbors, work colleagues, and various professionals. Specific information about the murder includes forensic evidence from crime-scene analysis and coroner's reports, police and probation reports, and "eye" and "ear" witnesses at the scene who may have seen or heard some or part of the murder itself or events preceding or following it. Reports of the trial judges provide an overview of each case and any additional information concerning the proposed length of the sentence—the "tariff." Information after imprisonment includes reports of conduct within the prison, discipline reports, and progress reports from prison staff and staff delivering prison programs. Other relevant information includes reports from periodic meetings with prison officers, probation officers, social workers, medical and mental health professionals, psychologists, psychiatrists, chaplains, members of the parole board, and others. While not every casefile contains all of this information, the majority of them are extremely detailed and comprehensive and contain numerous reports from various sources that cover a wide spectrum of the life of the perpetrator from childhood to the time of the murder and after imprisonment.

Sample, Data Collection, and Analysis—Casefiles and Interviews

Overall, a total of 866 casefiles were sampled, read, and coded at several locations. For each person convicted of murder, their casefile is held in Prison Headquarters in London (for prisons in England/Wales) and in Edinburgh (for prisons in Scotland), and a duplicate copy is held in the institution where they are imprisoned. The casefile dataset includes a systematic sample of casefiles selected from each of the universal archives (London and Edinburgh) and *all* the casefiles of those residing in the seven prisons identified as "strategic sites" where the interviews would eventually be conducted. Prisons were selected as strategic sites for several reasons: to ensure the inclusion of both men and women offenders, to include prisons located in different parts of the country, and to include prisons that held offenders convicted of different types of murder. The configuration of the resulting sample is very similar to that of the Homicide Index for England/Wales, which is the national database of all homicides during the relevant period.[49]

In order to capture the detailed material in the casefiles for quantitative analysis, an original data collection instrument was designed which was 52 pages in length and contained over 400 variables coded directly into SPSS (For data collection instruments for casefiles and interviews see Appendices I.1 and I.2). At the same time, a Word document was opened for each casefile in order to collect the rich textual material that would later be converted into Nud*ist/QSR for analysis of qualitative data.[50] The content focused on the lifecourse of the perpetrator from childhood through adulthood, as well as the murder event and subsequent reflections on it after imprisonment.[51]

The 200 interviews with the men and women serving a prison sentence for murder were conducted in order to obtain a first-person account about themselves, about the murder, and about their subsequent reflections. At each of the seven prisons selected as strategic sites for interviews, the researchers introduced the study to the relevant prisoners in various ways including a general letter, posters, and/ or an oral presentation. In seeking their willingness to participate, the researchers informed the men and women of the independence of the researchers and the nature and content of the research and that the interviews would be anonymous and confidential. The interviews were tape-recorded and guided by a structured Interview Schedule that was 23 pages in length and began with questions about their general background followed by questions about their childhood, adult lives, and relationships; the murder event; attitudes and perceptions of others; prison behavior and adjustment; offender programs; and overall progress. The cover page of the Interview Schedule contained a list of all the categories to be discussed in the interview, which was presented to the man or woman at the beginning of the interview in order to highlight the topics to be covered, to reconfirm their agreement to be interviewed, which had previously been obtained in advance of setting a date for the interview, and to request their agreement to have the interview tape-recorded (see Appendix I.2). The structured Interview Schedule allowed the interview to progress through all of the topics covered in the casefiles. For both the interviewer and interviewee, the writing of answers and turning of pages allowed for a sense of progression through the various topics and signaled that the end was in sight as the last of the 23 pages was turned.

The interviews usually lasted between 1 and 2 hours, and the tape recordings were first transcribed into Word documents before the qualitative data were "coded" by the researcher who conducted the interview and transferred to Nud*ist/ QSR for subsequent analysis. Analysis of the qualitative materials from the casefiles and interviews involved classifying textual material into various theoretically significant nodes (categories) for Nud*ist/QSR. The categories were similar to those used to examine the quantitative data in SPSS (see Appendix I.3, Variable Specifications for SPSS). Information of particular importance obtained from both the casefiles and interviews includes the lifecourse of the perpetrator from childhood to adulthood, the context and circumstances of the murder event, the murder event, adjustment to life in prison, participation in offender programs, and subsequent orientations to the murder and the victim, particularly relating to issues such as responsibility, empathy, and remorse (see nodes in Appendix I.4, Nud*ist/QSR Nodes for casefiles and interviews).

The qualitative dataset contains categories and subcategories (nodes) focused on childhood, including the early family of orientation, childhood carers, violence in the family, childhood discipline problems, and offending. The nodes associated with adulthood include employment history, relationships with others, general offending, criminal careers, substance abuse, and violence. For the murder event, the several nodes include the context, the day of the murder, and details of the murder including the nature of the assault and injuries. The use of alcohol and drugs and adult relationships with friends, partners, and children were also categorized. Several nodes were devoted to life in prison: behavioral problems, relationships with staff and other inmates, and participation in training (job skills) and treatment programs. A few nodes were unique to the interviews, with the offenders including their self-image at the time of the murder, after imprisonment, and at the time of the interview. Reflections on prison life, problems in prison, and first-person accounts of reactions to prison programs and counseling were also unique to the interviews. The Nud*ist/QSR dataset contained the complete version of the entire transcript of each interview and all of the qualitative information from each casefile. This made it possible to consult the transcript of an entire interview or the material compiled from a particular casefile, as well as to examine a specific node such as "Alcohol-drugs" for information about a single case or information about all cases in the dataset.

A team of four experienced researchers, including ourselves, conducted all of the 200 interviews and gathered all of the data from the 866 casefiles. Following the data collection, all of the quantitative and qualitative analysis presented here was carried out by the two authors. The quantitative data are presented in two ways, as graphics in the relevant chapters and in tables in the relevant appendices (NB—some additional figures are presented within relevant chapters). Chi-square and the odds ratio are used in all comparisons, and detailed results are presented in the tables. In the graphics, those that reach statistical significance are indicated by an asterisk. The qualitative materials presented are fairly lengthy in order to retain information about the overall context and the dynamic nature of the murder events. The quotes are organized conceptually and are structured to reflect the main patterns found in the qualitative data. They are usually ordered from the lowest to the highest levels of intensity or severity of the particular issue being examined but also to exemplify the conceptual development of the main patterns and the dynamic and complex nature of relevant factors.

All Murders

For the Murder Study, the achieved sample of 866 casefiles (786 men and 80 women) and 200 interviews (180 men and 20 women) provide the core of the following analysis (see Appendix II.1, Casefiles, Achieved Sample of All Murders). At the time of the study, the casefile sample for all men and women in prison for murder in England/Wales and in Scotland included slightly over 20% of all men imprisoned for murder in England/Wales (612/3000) and 35% of all men in prison for murder in Scotland (174/500). For the women in prison for murder, the achieved sample included 61% of those in prison in England/Wales (70/115) and 100% of those in prison in Scotland (10/10). It is relevant to pause here and again stress the finding that the overwhelming majority of those convicted of murder are men. The male perpetrators ranged in age from the youngest boy of 14 to the oldest man of 69, and their victims ranged in age from infants under 1 month to a 90-year-old man and an 88-year-old woman. Since the focus here is on the murder of adult women by adult men, the present analysis does not include murders committed by women nor does it include the murders of children under the age of 16.[52]

Focusing only on those murders committed by adult men (age 16 and over) against other adults, it can be seen in Figure 1.1 that men murdered other men in 61% of the cases (n = 424) and men murdered women in 39% of the cases (n = 271).

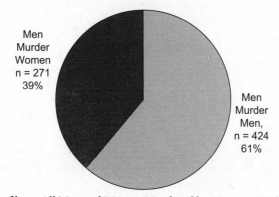

Men
Murder
Women
n = 271
39%

Men
Murder
Men,
n = 424
61%

Figure 1.1 Casefiles—All Men and Women Murdered by Men, n = 695*.

When Men Murder Women—Three Types

Men murder women of all ages, from the very young to the very old, and do so in many ways, including attacks that are short and intense to those that are sustained and excessively brutal. Motivations for murder are many, including anger and revenge, sexual desire, a wish to punish or humiliate, and/or to obtain financial gain. An act that may begin as a rape or a burglary may become a murder when the man attempts to avoid recognition and possible apprehension by killing the woman who is a witness to his initial crime of rape or burglary. Women may be murdered by men who have long histories of offending and sometimes by those with no known history of offending. Knowledge of the different contexts in which men murder women provides insight into the nature of such events and enhances the understanding of them.

Based on evidence from the casefiles and the interviews, the murders of women by men were classified into three main types that differentiate them in several important ways. Of the 271 women murdered by men, 90% (n = 243) could be classified into one of the three types shown in Figure 1.2. Of these murders of women by men, 105 (43%) were intimate partner murders, 98 (40%) were sexual murders, and 40 (17%) were murders of older women over the age of 65 (see Appendix II.3 for details of the 28 (10%) women who were not included in the analysis because they did not fit into any of the three types), Where overlaps occurred in the three types, such as the murder of an intimate partner who was sexually assaulted or of an older woman who was sexually assaulted, we categorized the type of murder based on the preponderance of evidence in the casefile.

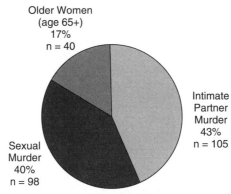

Figure 1.2 Casefiles—Three Types of Murder of Women by Men, n = 243.*

THE MURDER OF WOMEN—THREE TYPES—THREE PARTS

Each of the three types of murder of women by men will be examined in a separate part containing three chapters focused on the knowledge, the murder event, and the perpetrator. Knowledge about current research concerning each type of murder will be followed by a chapter focused on the murder event and another concentrating on the lifecourse of the perpetrators of the particular type of murder. Part I focuses on intimate partner murders (IPMs) (chapters 2–4), Part II on sexual murder (SexM) (chapters 5–7), and Part III on the murder of older women (OWoM) (chapters 8–10).

The Knowledge

Each part begins with a chapter reviewing relevant research about the particular type of murder. These chapters constitute the foundation of evidence to which the findings from the present study will be added (chapters 2, 5, and 8).

The Murder Event: Relationships, Contexts, and Circumstances

In chapters 3, 6, and 9 we examine the contexts, situations, and circumstances in which each of the three types of murder occurs. The nature of the relationship between the perpetrator and the victim, from strangers to intimates, is explored in terms of factors that are related to the murder. This is followed by specific issues

of conflict and previous violence to the woman victim. The lifestyle of the perpetrator at the time of the murder includes employment and alcohol and/or drug
use and abuse. These and other issues at the time of the murder are followed by a
close examination of the murder event itself, including the nature of the physical
attack, injuries and cause of death; whether the murder contained a sexual element
or attack; actions after the murder, including the treatment of the body; and subsequent actions to avoid detection.

The qualitative material from the casefiles and interviews is presented in considerable detail in order to extend current knowledge about each of the three types of
murder of women by examining the circumstances before, during, and after these
events. In addition, men's accounts provide insight into their thinking and rationales at the time they committed the murder and their later reflections about the
murder event and the woman they killed. These accounts range from total denial
to claims of self-defense and other justifications to various levels of acceptance
of responsibility for their actions. Across the three parts, comparisons are made
between the 424 male-male murders (MM) and each of the three types of murder
in which men murder women (IPM, SexM, and OWoM). The comparisons are presented in graphics at the end of each of the substantive chapters as well as in tables
in Appendices III–V.

Perpetrators: Lifecourse, Orientations, and Cognitions

In chapters 4, 7, and 10, the focus turns to the perpetrators—their backgrounds,
orientations, and cognitions. The focus on the lifecourse includes childhood, adulthood, behavior in prison, and subsequent reflections on the murder. Findings
about childhood include the family of orientation, carers, schooling, physical and
sexual abuse, alcohol and drug abuse, the use of violence, and the onset of offending. Findings about adulthood include education and employment, alcohol and
drug abuse, previous offending and convictions, and those about relationships
with women and previous physical and/or sexual violence against women, including women partners. Finally, the men are followed into prison, and evidence is presented about their behavior within the context of the prison regime as well as their
responses to various prison programs. Some men are defined as "model prisoners"
who adjust to routines, adhere to rules, and have few, if any, infractions of discipline. Others fail to adjust, have numerous problems with discipline, and may even
continue to be a danger to women staff within this highly controlled environment.
Findings are presented that reveal the assessments of various professionals about
numerous issues related to personal change and reform.

Within prison, the men have contact with numerous professionals from prison
officers to probation officers, psychologists, and others in relation to various aspects
of daily life as well as those relating to the murder. Everyone in prison for murder
must successfully complete various intervention programs aimed at altering their
offending behavior. Some are quite general, such as "Thinking Skills" and "Alcohol
Awareness," while others are more specific to certain types of offending, such as
"SOTP, Sex Offender Treatment Programs." These and other programs focus on
the offense and the offending behavior in an effort to address issues relating to the

murder in order to reduce the risk to the community when prisoners are released on parole. The programs are designed to work on notions used to rationalize or justify the murder, and, as such, the professional reports provide numerous insights into the life of the man, the context of the murder, modes of thinking at the time, and subsequent reflections on it. The materials regarding programs and behavior in prison are based on professional assessments recorded in the casefiles. The graphics illustrating the patterns associated with the lifecourse and imprisonment of the men are presented at the end of the relevant chapters and in the tables in Appendices III–V.

In the final chapter, we draw out some of the main findings about each of the three types of murder of women by men and compare them to the murders between men. The comparisons across all four types of murder are illustrated at the end of the chapter in Figures 11.1–11.5). Together, all of this illustrates the nature and complexity of gendered violence, which provides the background to the vast majority of murders in which women are the victims. With this enhanced and refined knowledge about the murder of women, we reflect on the implications for assessing and managing violent men and the risk they present to women along with a brief consideration of the various interventions focused on the prevention of such murders.

OVERVIEW

The focus of the analysis of the murder of women by men is both wide and narrow. It is wide in the examination of the lifecourse of men who murder women including early childhood, adulthood, circumstances at the time of the murder, and later reflections on the murder after conviction and imprisonment. It is narrow in the close attention to details about murder events and the contexts in which they occur. It is both static and dynamic, including the static biographical details of the men from childhood onward and the dynamic unfolding of contexts and events at the time of the murder. The focus is contextual, relational, and individual, including the contexts of the lives of the men who perpetrate the murder, the nature of relationships between perpetrators and their victims, and the orientations and perceptions of the men who murder. The analysis begins with a double disaggregation of murder based on the gender of victims who are first separated into men or women and with women victims then separation into the three main types found in the Murder Study: intimate partners, victims of sexual murder, and older women. Each type is examined separately and compared to male-male murders. In the last chapter, the comparisons across all four types of murder are presented and discussed in order to compare the three types and, in turn, to compare the murders of women to the murders of men. Overall, these findings add further depth and detail to what is now known about homicide in general, to what is known about the murder of women by men, and to what is known about each of the three types of murder examined. As will be seen across this analysis, men murder women in contexts that are usually underpinned by men's orientations to woman and gendered relations between men and women.

PART I

Intimate Partner Murder

2
—

The Knowledge
—Intimate Partner Murder

Murders involving women either as victims or as offenders attracted little research attention until the last quarter of the 20th century, and most of what did exist focused on women who committed murder rather than on the murder of women. Studies about why women murder found that it was usually in response to men's violence against them within an intimate relationship and that the women who responded by murdering their abuser were often convicted without due consideration of these circumstances and, as such, may have received sentences that were unjust.[1] With the rise of the battered women's movement, the initial focus was, quite correctly, on the women who were abused and various responses focused on assisting them.[2] At the same time, a few scholars began to investigate the murder of women by an intimate partner.

There are at least three strands of this research. The first is based on evidence from national or regional datasets that are collected continuously by government agencies and provide statistical trends in homicide and, more recently, evidence about different types of homicide including the murder of intimate partners. The second includes academic research of various types such as case studies, case-files, surveys, case controls, and interview studies that use known samples to focus on intimate partner homicides (IPHs). Based in disciplines such as criminology, sociology, and healthcare, these studies focus on the demographic characteristics of perpetrators and victims as well as the circumstances associated with the murder, and sometimes compare intimate partner murders (IPMs) with nonlethal violence and abuse in intimate relationships. The third focuses on the attributes of offenders with special attention to men's orientations, perceptions, and cognitions based on measurements using standardized psychological tests or on more qualitative data from interviews focused on men's attitudes, orientations, and "ways of thinking" about themselves, women, and women partners. Here, we review some of the main findings from these three strands of research about IPM before briefly considering some other types of murder that are related to intimate partner conflicts such as collateral murders, homicide-suicides, and familicides.

HOMICIDES OF WOMEN AND INTIMATE
PARTNER HOMICIDES IN THE UNITED STATES,
THE UNITED KINGDOM, AND EUROPE

In the United States, the Office of the Bureau of Justice Statistics data on violence and homicide for the 14-year period from 1993 to 2007 indicated that the overall rate of the murder of women almost halved during that period, from a rate of 4.18 to 2.38 per 100,000 females.[3] Using the FBI Supplementary Homicide Report (SHR), the Violence Policy Center analyzes the annual number and rates of IPMs of women across the United States. In 2009, there were 1,818 female victims of homicide (8% were under the age of 18); 93% were murdered by a male they knew, and 63% of those women were wives or "intimate acquaintances" of the men who murdered them (SHR figures include wives, common-law wives, ex-wives, and girlfriends, but do not include ex-girlfriends). The average age of women victims was 39, and female murder victims were much more likely than male murder victims to be killed by an intimate partner.[4] African American women were murdered at a rate almost two and one-half times higher than white women (2.62 vs. 1.12). While the rate of murder of women of Hispanic background, a large ethnic minority in the United States, could not be calculated for 2009, an earlier report for 1998 suggested the rate was slightly higher than that of white women.[5] A firearm, usually a handgun, was used in 52% of all murders of women and girls and in two-thirds of the murders of women intimate partners.[6]

Since 1976, systematic information about all homicides in the United Kingdom has been gathered from information provided by the police across the country and compiled into "Homicide Indexes" for the three distinct jurisdictions of England/Wales, Scotland, and Northern Ireland. In England/Wales, from 1998 to 2008 women represented 31% of all victims of homicide, and figures from 2009 indicated that 54% of all women victims were murdered by an intimate partner, most in their own home, while only 5% of all men who were murdered were killed by their woman partner.[7] In the United Kingdom, as in most other European countries, there is considerable consistency over time in the relative distributions of different types of homicide, with the murder of women in intimate relationships constituting a significant proportion of all women who are murdered.[8]

With some important exceptions, European studies of homicide have been rather scarce, although this began to change in the last quarter of the 20th century and particularly with the creation of the European Criminology group and a subgroup of researchers interested in homicide.[9] A few European countries, notably the Netherlands, Finland, Germany, Sweden, and Switzerland, have long had well-developed institutional systems for collecting national statistics on homicide and now report on specific types of homicide including those of intimate partners.[10] However, in many European countries IPHs are subsumed under a broad category such as "domestic" or "family" homicide, which may include the murder of a parent, sibling, or other relative. This makes it difficult, if not impossible, to examine the murder of women by an intimate partner. Despite this, some useful information can be gleaned from these databases, and that which is available in several European countries indicates that the murder of women represents a considerable proportion of all homicides, at least 30%, and the largest proportion of women victims, between one-half to three-quarters, are intimate partners.[11]

Asymmetry of Intimate Partner Murder

The World Health Organization analysis of global data reporting on 66 countries found that, on average, IPHs accounted for about 40% of all killings of women but only 6% of the murders of men.[12] Research in numerous countries reveals that the ratio of male to female IPM is around 1 to 5 or 6.[13] That is, for every six women killed by a male intimate partner only one man is killed by a female intimate partner, and in some societies there are no reports of women murdering their male partners.[14] Across the world, the pattern of IPH is asymmetrical, with more women than men being killed by an intimate partner. The only known exception is the United States, where until recently the ratio was almost 1 to 1.[15] This anomaly is mainly associated with the skewed pattern among African American couples with explanations that include cultural factors, racial oppression, abject poverty, and the failure of social and justice agencies to meaningfully intervene in domestic violence in African American communities that has the effect of leaving women in desperate and dangerous circumstances.[16] This ratio has recently begun to change with a dramatic reduction in the murder of African American men and women in intimate relationships,[17] and research suggests that this may be associated with improved responses from criminal justice and social agencies.[18] Across most of the world, the murder of women constitutes about one-third of all homicides, and women are more likely than men to be killed by someone they know, especially an intimate partner. Overall, the murder of intimate partners is usually perpetrated by men against women, and not the obverse, and this asymmetry underscores the importance of gender in understanding and explaining IPM.

Type of Relationship

The type of relationship between intimate partners—marital, common-law, boyfriend/girlfriend—has been shown to be associated with IPM. Examining the 18-year period from 1976 to 1994, Wilson, Johnson, and Daly used the national statistics for Canada and estimated that the risk of homicide was eight times greater for women in cohabiting relationships than for those in marital relationships[19]—a pattern found in other countries. An estimate from the United States suggested that women in cohabiting relationships were about nine times more likely than those in marital relationships to be killed by their intimate partner, and similar differences have been reported for Australia.[20] Research about girlfriend/boyfriend relationships and cohabitants revealed similar elevated risks when compared with those who were married.[21] In addition, a Canadian study of 703 cases of IPH found that a sexual attack was twice as likely within the murder of women who were cohabitants or girlfriends compared with those who were married to the male perpetrator, and that boyfriends were much more likely to be estranged from their woman victims and to be motivated by jealousy.[22] In our own earlier research using data from the Murder Study, we compared cases of IPM to cases of nonlethal violence against a woman intimate partner and found that the type of relationship between the victim and perpetrator revealed differences between those that resulted in murder and those that did not. Boyfriend/girlfriend relationships constituted only 4% of the cases of nonlethal violence but 26% of the cases of murder.[23]

Dating and cohabitating relationships have been linked to an elevated risk of homicide compared with marital relationships, and this has been explained in terms of the sociodemographic characteristics of the men and women in each type of relationship. There is evidence that some cohabiting relationships may be more "unstable" and tenuous and that the individuals in such relationships may differ in important ways from those in marital relationships.[24] Women and men in cohabiting relationships are usually younger, more disadvantaged, and more likely to be unemployed, which suggests a greater risk both for violence and for murder. Additionally, cohabiting and dating relationships may be less likely to "benefit" from the kinship networks associated with marital relationships. Networks that are more likely to provide various forms of social control and "legitimate" intervention in support of marital relationships in contrast to cohabiting or dating relationships, and in this respect marriage may act as a protective factor.[25] Debates and speculations about IPM and the different types of intimate relationships center on the question of whether the issue is the type of relationship per se or the attributes of individuals in the different types of relationships. These arguments are based on the assumption that there are different rates of murder in the different types of relationships as originally posited by Wilson, Johnson, and Daly in the 1990s.[26]

More recently, using the FBI reports and U.S. census data for 2005, James and Daly found no difference in the rates of IPH among those who were married and those who were cohabitating.[27] In asking what might explain why the rates no longer differ, James and Daly consider the possibility that the sociodemographic attributes of victims and offenders may be converging and, as such, the differences in the levels of disadvantage, class, age, and educational achievements may no longer be as relevant. However, they found that this is not the case and that, if anything, the differences among individuals in the two types of intimate relationships have increased. What else might explain this recent pattern? In their earlier work, Wilson and Daly speculated that the differences in the rates of homicide in the two types of intimate relationships might be a reflection of contextual factors in cohabiting relationships that increase instability and conflict, such as the presence of stepchildren, a greater likelihood of dissolution of the relationship, and the greater infidelity of women.[28] In the more recent work, James and Daly suggest that such notions have yet to be explored.[29]

CONTEXTUAL FACTORS

Possessiveness, Jealousy, Separation, and Previous Violence

Although the type of relationship may be important, the contextual and dynamic aspects of intimate relationships may be of equal or even greater importance in understanding IPMs. Whether a male partner is a husband, cohabitant, or boyfriend, his orientations to women, to intimate relationships, and to his partner would seem to be of great importance in how he conducts his daily affairs. There is a wealth of research indicating that men who abuse, coerce, and assault their partners do so within the context of conflicts common to daily life, including issues of domestic work, children, and money as well as those involving questions of male authority within the household along with possessiveness and jealousy, and various forms of

violence and controlling behaviors are linked to these orientations.[30] Intimate partner violence is clearly associated with men's attempts to control and punish women
for actions they deem inappropriate, and especially those that relate to associations
with other men, but the nature and level of such control varies across cultures and
seems to be particularly intense in some societies. Possessiveness and jealousy are
felt both by men and by women and exist within most, if not all, intimate relationships, but they would appear to be of particular importance in relationships that end
in the murder of a woman by her male partner.

In Daly and Wilson's early foundational work on IPH, they stressed the importance of male jealousy, possessiveness, and control in the murder of women
partners.[31] Their extensive and intensive analysis revealed that jealousy and possessiveness were apparent in all societies from small kinship-based cultures to modern,
urban industrial societies, albeit in varying levels.[32] They proposed the term "male
sexual proprietariness" to encapsulate the thinking and actions of men as reflecti-
in jealousy and possessiveness and argued that it is a manifestation of the biologi-
cally evolved psychology of all men.[33] At the same time, they noted that there is
considerable variation in the nature and extent of this thinking and the violence
associated with it across time and cultures, which suggests that sociocultural factors
must play a significant role in male possessiveness and the behaviors related to it.[34]
While it is possible to demonstrate the importance of sociocultural and individual
factors that relate to men's violence against women, it is difficult, if not impossible,
to establish the inferential evidentiary links to the supposed biological roots of
this thinking in some distant, evolutionary time. On this issue, Polk notes that it is
impossible to substantiate the evolutionary chain associated with male proprietariness.[35] Possessiveness and jealousy are relevant and important issues when men
murder an intimate partner whether the root source is social, cultural, psychological, and/or biological. The debate about the "ultimate" source of such thinking and
behavior cannot and need not be resolved here. Despite this, insights into the thinking, attitudes, and beliefs of men who murder their partner may be gained through
their own accounts and rationales, those of other observers, and evidence of the
context and circumstances at the time of the event.

Both qualitative and quantitative studies of IPmurderers have confirmed the
importance of possessiveness and separation in the thinking of men who murder.[36]
Campbell's intensive investigation of 28 men who murdered an intimate woman
partner revealed that two-thirds were jealous and had previously been physically
abusive to the victim. The vast majority were *not* intoxicated at the time they committed the murder and thus were *not* thinking or acting under the influence of alcohol.[37] Websdale's study of 67 cases of the murder of women intimate partners found
previous "woman battering" in 87%, and possessiveness and jealousy in 51% of the
cases.[38] Adams interviewed 31 men who killed an intimate partner, and identified
five types.[39] The largest group of men (78%) was identified as the "jealous type,"
and almost all of them were defined as "extremely jealous." The "jealous type" was
preoccupied by jealous thoughts, made jealous accusations (e.g., she was having sex
with other men), attempted to confirm jealous suspicions by "monitoring" and/or
stalking the woman, and committed at least one assault against the woman and/
or the person with whom he presumed she was having sex. Adams is skeptical of
the claims of men who attempted to justify their actions on the basis of a "jealous
rage" (i.e., out of control) because of their suspicions of the infidelity of their woman

partner. In many cases, relatives and friends reported that the supposed infidelities only existed in the "minds of the perpetrators," and that the killing was actually very calculated. Of the jealous men, 12 murdered their partner when she informed him that she was leaving, which lends support to the importance of the man's sense of possessiveness and to the elevated risk associated with the act of separation.

In our own comparison of 105 cases of murder (from the Murder Study) and 122 cases of nonlethal violence by men against a woman partner, we found that possessiveness and jealousy were significantly more prevalent among men who murdered (36%) than those who assaulted (10%) their woman partner. Separation was more likely in cases involving murder than those involving nonlethal assault (37% vs. 20%) with most of the murders occurring within the first 3 months after the woman left the relationship.[40] The relationship between separation and a subsequent murder, usually within a few months after the woman's departure, is supported by findings from several countries.[41] Using data from eleven U.S. states, Campbell and her colleagues compared 220 cases of IPH and 343 cases of domestic abuse.[42] They concluded that the major risk factors prior to the murder were previous violence to the victim (especially choking), estrangement, forced sex, threats to kill, and threats with a gun. Relevant risk factors at the point of the murder itself, the "incident level," included the victim leaving the perpetrator and/or having another partner, the perpetrator's use of alcohol or drugs, and the use of a gun.[43]

Alcohol and Drugs

In the U.S. 11-state-wide study of intimate murder, Campbell and colleagues found that 80% of male perpetrators had been drinking at the time of the murder and two-thirds were described as intoxicated while one-quarter had consumed both alcohol and drugs.[44] Thomas, Dichter, and Matejkowski's comparison of 71 intimate partner murderers (IPMurderers) and 291 other types of murder in Indiana, found a high prevalence of "alcohol use" prior to the murder in both groups (81% IPM, 74% Other).[45] Australian research based on a national database revealed a much lower prevalence, with only one-third of the IPMurderers defined as intoxicated at the time of the murder.[46] In our own previously published comparison of IPMurderers and nonlethal abusers, we found that a reasonable proportion of both types had a history of alcohol abuse but this was significantly more likely among the abusers than the murderers (53% vs. 38%), and that at the time of the violent event, abusers were more likely to be intoxicated than murderers (47% vs. 20%).[47] In most studies, drug abuse was found to be less prevalent than alcohol abuse. Analysis of two large datasets from Chicago and North Carolina, found significantly less drug abuse in cases of IPH than in cases of other types of homicides, and the Indiana study cited above found little difference in drug use of IPMurderers and other types of murderers (58% vs. 62%).[48] Common problems about evidence concerning the use and effects of alcohol and/or drugs include the general lack of specificity about the nature of "use" and/or "abuse" and the role of legal and illegal substances in the life of the offender and in the violent event itself. These and other issues will be examined in the following chapters.

While previous violence to the woman partner, possessiveness, and alcohol abuse occur in many intimate relationships, they rarely lead to murder. Across the world, relationships of all types break up as boyfriends and girlfriends, cohabitants, and married couples separate and divorce, and this often involves intense emotions but rarely leads to violence or murder. In short, problems and conflicts are relatively common in intimate relationships, but murder is rare.[49] However, the extreme negative consequences of murder both for the individuals concerned and to the wider society in which they occur, lend them a level of importance far beyond the numbers involved and assign to them a significance that stretches to the very fabric of how the affairs of daily life are conducted and how the conflicts between individuals are resolved. As such, the lifecourse of perpetrators, from childhood to adulthood, and the situations and circumstances of their lives at the time of the murder are of relevance in the wider exploration of IPM. Who are these men? How do they live? What do they think?

Lifecourse of Men Who Murder an Intimate Partner

CHILDHOOD AND ADULTHOOD BACKGROUNDS

There exists a fair amount of research on the backgrounds and orientations of men who abuse women partners but very little about the backgrounds of those who murder a woman partner.[50] For most homicides, basic sociodemographic information about the perpetrator includes age, ethnicity, education, and employment, which are commonly reported. As discussed in chapter 1, the central focus of developmental criminology is the background of perpetrators, particularly their childhood, but the research usually concentrates on those who have committed offenses that do not involve violence or murder. Examinations of the lifecourse of men who murder an intimate are rather rare, but those that do exist have shown that such men are usually young, poor, undereducated, unemployed and, in the United States, members of ethnic minority groups.[51] However, little else is known about the backgrounds of IPMurderers. In earlier publications from the Murder Study, we examined the child and adult backgrounds of men who commit murder in several ways: in terms of the "onset of offending," that is, the age when men began offending; a comparison of those who appeared to come "out of the blue," when they murdered a woman but had no known history of offending in their background either as a child or as an adult; a comparison of the backgrounds of men who abused and those who murdered an intimate partner (lethal nonlethal); and a comparison of the backgrounds of male-male murderers (MMmurderers) and IPMurderers.[52] These comparisons yielded some important similarities and differences, particularly between MMmurderers and IPMurderers that will be developed more fully in the next two chapters. Of particular importance is the finding that some of the IPMurderers had fewer problems in childhood or adulthood than men who murdered other men and were therefore described as "more conventional."[53]

Other studies have also found that the backgrounds of men who murder an intimate partner appear to be less problematic than those of men who murder others. A Finnish study of all homicides over a period of several years compared male and female IPH offenders to offenders who killed others and found that the two groups differed in terms of background and personality characteristics. The male IPM perpetrators were less likely than men convicted of other types of homicides to have a history of property offenses and less likely to be antisocial and to suffer from an antisocial personality disorder or psychopathy. The researchers concluded these men were more likely to resemble men in the wider population.[54] In his U.S.-based qualitative study comparing 31 cases of men convicted of murdering their partners with 20 cases involving the victims of attempted homicide and 19 cases of abuse, Adams found that the majority of the IPMurderers had more conventional backgrounds than the other two groups.[55] Although one-third of the murderers had at least one previous conviction, only 16% could be described as "career criminals," with 48% having completed high school, 87% in blue-collar jobs, and 13% in white-collar occupations. Around a third were unemployed at the time of the murder, although Adams points out that "some of the unemployed men quit their jobs in order to monitor their partner's activities," and other men had been fired because they were absent from work in order to conduct surveillance of their partner.[56] Adams, cofounder of EMERGE—a foundational program for the treatment of abusers—has spent many years working with men to end their violence against intimate partners, concludes that IPMurderers, like abusers, do not always fit the stereotype of the persistent alcoholic, the criminal, or the mentally ill. Research from Spain revealed that men who murdered their intimate partners were less likely to exhibit personality disorders and mental illness than men convicted of assaulting their partner and that the incidence of mental health problems in both groups was only slightly higher than that in the general Spanish population. In addition, men who murdered an intimate partner were less likely than abusers to have a criminal conviction (12% vs. 48%).[57] The researchers concluded that the "murderers were adjusted to everyday life" prior to the homicide and most were "relatively normal" men without a previous prison sentence. Despite this, they found that the men in both groups were likely to hold distorted thoughts about women.

In the United States, an extensive comparison of the backgrounds of IPHs and of other types of homicide found significant differences in the backgrounds of the men in the two types. Fewer men in the intimate partner group experienced problems such as a caregiver with a criminal history, being raised by a single biological parent, school expulsion, and juvenile offenses, and more of these men obtained a high school education or higher. Important issues where there was no difference in the childhoods of the two groups included alcohol abuse of a parent or caregiver, and physical or sexual abuse of the child. As adults, men who killed an intimate partner were significantly more likely to be married and employed but were also more likely to be defined as having suffered severe mental illness. Similarities across both groups included alcohol abuse, drug abuse, at least one prior arrest, and one arrest for assault/battery. The use of a firearm was significantly more likely in other types of homicide, while IPHs were more likely to occur in a shared residence where the victim was strangled, and the perpetrator was defined as in a "rage." Overall, the authors conclude that men who murdered an intimate partner appeared to have "a higher stake in conformity" and to be more "socially bonded."[58]

Collateral Murder of Others Related to Intimate Partner Conflict

MURDER OF CHILDREN, PROTECTORS, ALLIES, AND NEW PARTNERS

The majority of IPHs involve the death of one person, usually the woman, but some involve the death of more than one person and some involve the killing of a person other than the woman partner, such as a child, relative, or new partner. We describe these as "intimate partner collateral murders," which may also include some homicide-suicides, familicides, and, in rare cases, mass murders. In this context, the term "collateral murder" refers to the killing of another person but is intrinsically linked to the man's conflict with his woman partner, for example, the killing of a child in order to inflict pain and punishment on the woman partner (i.e., mother of the child), or the killing of the woman's new partner as an act of revenge motivated by jealousy. Others, such as the woman's parents, friends, or neighbors, may be murdered in the context of trying to protect the woman from the man's violence or abuse or to give her accommodation after separating from her male partner.

There is very little research on "collateral murders" related to intimate partner conflict, as they are often difficult to identify in police or other official records and reports. In 1998, Langford, Isaac, and Kabat investigated homicides related to intimate partner violence in Massachusetts over a 5-year period and found that 30% of the 175 cases involved the killing of a person who was not the intimate partner.[59] A brief, online report from Florida suggested that nearly half of victims killed in "domestic violence disputes" in 2007 were not intimate partners but were coworkers, roommates, relatives, or bystanders.[60] Using findings from the Murder Study about the murder of children who had been abused, Cavanagh and colleagues found that in three-quarters of the cases the birth-mother had also been the victim of violence.[61] A 2009 report from Virginia found that the killing of coworkers, police officers, and friends represented 40% of all intimate partner–"associated" homicides.[62] In 2012, we reported the findings of 62 collateral murders related to conflict/violence between intimate partners, which will be developed further in the next chapter.[63] This accumulating body of evidence, and the further delineation of such cases in the next chapter, suggests the need to examine the relevance of the conflict between intimate partners in cases where someone other than the woman partner is murdered.

Intimate Partner Homicide-Suicides and Familicides

Although the Murder Study does not include cases involving homicide-suicide because the sample is based on convicted murderers, it is important to consider the existing research on this topic because the killing of a woman partner followed by the suicide of the perpetrator constitutes yet another type of homicide that has yet to be fully explored in terms of the overall category of IPM. Existing research provides evidence about the contextual and situational factors associated with such cases and the gender dynamics involved.

HOMICIDE-SUICIDES

Most cases involving more than one death within the family are homicide-suicides, and these cases may not always be entered in the national datasets because no one is arrested, charged, and/or convicted. However, in the United States, these data are increasingly derived from coroner's reports rather than from criminal justice sources. In 2012, the highest rate of homicide-suicide per 100,000 was reported in South Africa (.89), with a lower rate in the United States (.27–38) and still lower rates in European countries ranging from the highest in Finland (.20) to the lowest in England/Wales (.05), Scotland (.05), and the Netherlands (.05).[64] In the United States, the fullest and most informative accounts of homicide-suicides at a national level, are produced by the Centers for Disease Control (CDC). These are defined as a murder followed by the suicide of the perpetrator within 24 hours that is motivationally linked to the homicide. Using unique data from the National Violent Death Reporting System, Logan and colleagues at the CDC compared 408 homicide-suicides, 20,188 suicides, and 5,932 homicides from 17 U.S. states.[65] The data were collected over a 3-year period from several official sources, including death certificates, coroner reports, and police records. Although compiled by various agencies, the information was gathered from friends, family members, neighbors, and acquaintances who had knowledge of the circumstances of the homicide-suicide, including conflicts and violence within intimate relationships. Current or former spouses, cohabitants, and girlfriend/boyfriend relationships constituted 75% of the homicide-suicides. In 92% of these cases, the perpetrator was a male, and in 54% there was a history of conflict and/or violence against the woman victim. A history of intimate partner conflict/violence also existed in 36% of the murders of a child (filicide) followed by a suicide, and in 36% of extrafamilial-related homicide-suicides.[66]

In the CDC study, a history of mental health problems such as depression was *not* common among the perpetrators of homicide-suicide, the majority did *not* appear to have alcohol or drug abuse problems, and only one in five was suspected of being intoxicated at the time. Firearms were used in 88% of the cases, regardless of whether the victim was an intimate partner or a child. Only 1 case in 20 was "believed to have been the result of a mercy killing." Overall, the perpetrators of homicide-suicides were mostly white males in their middle to late adulthood. The women victims were current, separated, or divorced partners, and the couple was often in the process of separating or divorcing. At the time of the incidents, some of the perpetrators had restraining orders against them and/or were involved in court cases (possibly involving divorce and/or child custody). Research from several states in the United States reflects similar findings: Between 66% and 84% of all homicide-suicides involve intimate partners, most perpetrators are men, most have a history of domestic violence against the victim, the acts are usually premeditated, and the use of a firearm is common. When firearms are not used, the main method of killing is strangulation and/or stabbing.[67]

As early as 1965, a British study by West suggested that most homicide-suicides were "domestic," and that they were usually perpetrated by men who murdered a woman partner.[68] These patterns continue, and findings of a recent European-wide study of homicide-suicides in seven countries revealed that nearly three-quarters of these cases involved intimate partner homicide-suicide, and about one-third of all cases classified as homicide-suicides were actually parasuicide (attempted suicide).[69] Most cases involved male perpetrators who used a firearm to murder their woman partner or ex-partner often in an attempt to maintain or regain control of her, and most had a history of physical abuse against the victim.[70] The men were usually older than those who killed a partner but did not commit suicide, and they were more likely to be middle class, employed, from the ethnically dominant group, and to have a mental health problem. They were likely to be narcissistic and to have a strong emotional bond with the victim that included a dependence on her and a belief that her identity and/or existence were inseparable from his own. This included a limited recognition of her autonomy, of her right and/or ability to live apart from him, and/or her right to live with a new partner, with some blaming the victim and others blaming themselves "for the problems which they intend to solve violently."[71]

The same general patterns were found in a study of one South African city with a high incidence of homicide-suicides in which the vast majority of perpetrators were men from the majority ethnic group (95%), most of the victims were women intimate partners (75%), and a firearm was used in 87% of the cases.[72] The use of a firearm is particularly important in countries with high rates of access to guns such as South Africa and the United States. A comparison of "domestic homicide-suicides" with "other domestic homicides" in the Netherlands, Switzerland, and the United States found that the perpetrators were almost always men (90%) and that the use of firearms differed significantly between Switzerland (82%) and the United States (84%), where access to firearms is common, and the Netherlands (37%), where it is not.[73] The researchers conclude that the presence of a firearm might lower the threshold for the use of violence and, when used, is more likely to result in a death.[74] It is important to note that in European countries firearms are rarely used when a man murders only his woman partner but are frequently used when he kills both his partner and himself.

FAMILICIDES

Familicides usually involve the killing of at least two members of a family and may involve the killing of the entire family. The victims usually include the woman intimate partner and at least one child,[75] and the murders are almost always perpetrated by men (95% in United States), who sometimes, although not always, end the violence by killing themselves. Women rarely commit homicide-suicides and almost never commit familicides, but when they do, the victims are usually the woman's child/children and herself and rarely her male intimate partner. Women who kill their children and themselves often do so in the context of depression.[76] Familicide is extremely rare, with as few as 23 cases per year in the United States between 2000–2009, that involved the murder of an intimate partner and children.[77] Obviously these cases attract a great deal of attention in the media, where details of the context of the murders and intentions of the perpetrator are exhaustively examined. Although very rare, such killings appear to be more likely to occur in the United States than in Canada, Britain, or Australia.[78] From a small sample, Wilson and Daly identified two types of familicides: the "angry and accusatory" (with various grievances involving his jealousy and her attempt/s to end the relationship) and "despondent" men with underlying depression and/or mental illness with thwarted ambitions who often see suicide as the only way out for themselves and believe that the victims are unable to live without them.[79] One type may be viewed as acting out of anger while the other may be seen as acting out of a false sense of "mercy or rescue," but the male perpetrator in both types has a proprietary sense of possession about those he kills and "feel[s] entitled to decide his victims' fates."[80] Websdale has categorized the murderous familicidal acts of such men as those based on anger or fury in his "Livid Coercive Hearts," or out of a sense of rescue or mercy in his, "Civil Reputable Hearts," with both types defined in terms of "emotional styles" of men acting on a sense of "humiliated fury." The two types are characterized as working-class men who are "abusers, angry, jealous and vengeful," and middle-class men who are socially conforming, nonabusers who are despondent, depressed, and more likely to follow the murder with their own suicide.[81]

The conclusions that emerge from research in several countries is that homicides followed by suicides are predominately those of men using a firearm to kill a current or former woman intimate partner and sometimes the children in the relationship. Although the prevalence of homicide-suicides is low and familicides is even lower, the majority of these types of murder should, nonetheless, be considered as a part of the overall complex of IPMs. In contrast to perpetrators of IPH, these offenders are more likely to be from the dominant ethnic group, middle class or living in a middle-class area, and employed, with conflicting evidence concerning mental health problems. The usual contexts and situations in which these murders occur frequently involve possessiveness, separation, and acts of revenge that closely parallel those of IPMs that do not involve the killing of another family member.

SUMMARY

The evidence reveals strong and consistent patterns associated with the murder of women, and particularly the murder of women intimate partners. Worldwide, women victims constitute around 20%–40% of all homicides, and intimate partners constitute at least 50% of these. Women are much more at risk of being killed by an intimate partner than are men—a historical and global pattern—and this strong asymmetry exists in intimate partner homicide-suicides, where the evidence shows that most involve a man killing his woman intimate partner followed by his own suicide.

The research findings further suggest that the type of intimate relationship is linked to the risk of the murder of a woman. Cohabiting and boyfriend/girlfriend relationships seem most at risk of murder, although there is continuing speculation about why this pattern exists and some researchers report these differential risks no longer prevail. That is, whether women are married, cohabiting, or in a boyfriend/girlfriend relationship, they are equally at risk of lethal violence. Subsequent chapters will explore these possible differences and consider how certain types of intimate relationships may place women at a greater risk of being murdered by their male partner and of a being subjected to a sexual attack within the murder.

When considering the dynamic contextual and circumstantial aspects of IPM, there are some clear patterns. Jealousy, possessiveness, and a woman's attempts to leave a relationship, particularly one plagued by the man's violence, are significant features of IPM. The few large studies of known cases of IPM using primarily quantitative evidence appear to show that men's proprietary thinking and separation are important correlates of IPM. While we think these results are compelling, the evidence presented in the next two chapters provides fulsome qualitative narratives that demonstrate the dynamic context and circumstances of the murders of intimate partners and also provides an important addition to the quantitative results of earlier studies. It is the qualitative evidence that can demonstrate how thinking about possessiveness and separation may coalesce to generate murderous intent that was previously limited to coercive and/or violent efforts to control and dominate.

Another possible contextual correlate in IPM is the consumption of legal and/or illegal substances. Here there is conflicting evidence, with some research showing that men who murdered an intimate partner were more likely than those who killed others to have consumed "substances," especially alcohol, while other research suggests the opposite. Thus, it is unclear whether IPMurderers were drinking more, less, or the same amount as those who kill others. In addition, it is not possible to assess what effect the consumption of alcohol might have had on perceptions and judgments that may have played a part in the murder. Qualitative evidence may assist in considering the role of alcohol. Is it simply drinking that elevates the risk of lethality? Is it the level of intoxication? Is it the life-style associated with persistent consumption? Or, is it some combination of these factors? The qualitative accounts presented in the following chapter provide evidence about the role of substances, particularly alcohol, in the events that end in murder.

In the next two chapters, we will use the evidence from the Murder Study to extend the existing knowledge about IPM. Both qualitative and quantitative evidence will be used from the casefiles and interviews with men convicted of murder. The first of the two chapters will focus on the murder event, including the relation between the perpetrator and the victim and the situations and circumstances at the time. Both qualitative and quantitative evidence are used to explore and illustrate the context and immediate circumstances associated with these murders. Considerable attention is given to the murder itself in order better to understand the context of the events, actions within them, and men's thinking and emotions at the time. These are central to an understanding of these murders. This will be followed by a chapter that focuses on the lifecourse of the men who murder an intimate partner.

To date, there is limited evidence about the backgrounds of men who murder an intimate partner. Wider evidence on the backgrounds of men who kill indicates that many can be characterized as disadvantaged, poorly educated men who find it difficult to obtain and maintain employment. A considerable proportion of the male murderers considered in the following chapters fit this description, but some do not. We present evidence about the men who seemed to come from more conventional backgrounds but are similar in other respects, such as their orientations to women, their denial of responsibility for the murder, and their lack of empathy, which appear to be very similar to men with difficult backgrounds. We complete Part I by considering how intimate partner murderers adjust to the prison regime and their willingness to engage in the process of personal change and reform by participating in prison programs focused on issues such as taking responsibility for the murder and for behaviors and attitudes associated with it. Successful completion of these programs is necessary before an offender can be considered for parole and released into the community.

Intimate Partner Murder
—The Murder Event
Relationships, Contexts, and Circumstances

What happens when men murder their intimate partners? In this chapter, the murder of intimate partners is explored using evidence from the Murder Study. We begin with the nature of the relationships between the perpetrators and their victims, before considering the sources of conflict and the situations and circumstances in which the murders occur. The examination of the murder itself includes the nature of the physical attack and injuries, whether there was a sexual attack within the murder, and the treatment of the body after death. The section "What the men say" includes their accounts of the murder and their denials, rationales, and justifications. We also examine the collateral murders of others, including children, allies/protectors, and new partners, who are killed by men in the context of conflicts with their woman intimate partner. Finally, comparisons will be made between male-male murders (MMs) and intimate partner murders (IPMs) in order to delineate differences and similarities between men who murder an intimate partner and those who murder other men. Both quantitative and qualitative data are used to explore the main patterns and to illustrate them in some detail with the aim of providing more knowledge and a fuller understanding of the nature, complexities, and dynamics of this type of murder.

As stated earlier, the quantitative and qualitative data are drawn from two sources: from the casefiles, which include accounts, observations, and statements from a wide variety of professionals, and from our own interviews with men in prison (for details see chapter 1 and Appendix I). The main patterns are based on the quantitative data extracted from the casefiles and presented graphically in the figure shown at the end of this chapter and numerically in the corresponding table in Appendix III. The qualitative accounts from the casefiles and interviews are used to illustrate the wide range of behaviors and orientations and are labeled conceptually from those that occur most frequently to those that occur less frequently, that is, from the more usual to the more unusual and from the more "ordinary" to the more "extreme." Each quotation is followed by an identifier such as *222cf1.1.1, or *444cf1.4.2, or *666cf1.2.6, with the first three digits indicating the number of the case and the researcher who gathered the data, followed by the source of the data as

cf (for Casefile) or iv (for Interview), and the type of murder: For example, 1.1.1 signifies the murder of a woman intimate partner by a male partner, 1.4.2 signifies the
sexual murder of a woman by a male acquaintance, and 1.4.6 signifies the murder of
an older woman by a male.

RELATIONSHIP BETWEEN THE PERPETRATOR
AND THE VICTIM

The nature of the relationships between the perpetrators and victims among the
105 IPMs is shown graphically at the beginning of Appendix III, and includes those
who were married (43%, n = 45), cohabiting (32%, n = 34), or in a serious boyfriend/
girlfriend relationship (25%, n = 26). A few of these relationships were of a short
duration, while others had lasted for many years. The nature of the relationship
between the man and the woman he murders may be one that signifies more or less
permanence and commitment. It may be underpinned by the social practices and
legal obligations associated with the institution of marriage or without them but
within a relationship of cohabitation that may otherwise resemble the orientations,
conventions, and practices associated with marriage. Those in serious dating relationships do not reside together but may nonetheless be in a relationship that they
associate with varying degrees of commitment, obligations, and "permanence."
While notions of obligations, commitment, and permanence may vary with the
type of the relationship, they may also vary with the length of the relationship and
the length of time the couple have been together. Such notions may also vary for the
man and for the woman as each negotiates the varying aspects of daily life together
and, for some, as they negotiate the ending of a relationship. In short, the type of the
relationship, the length of the relationship, and whether the person concerned is the
man or the woman are all relevant in the conduct of daily life.

Questions have been raised about whether it is differences in the type of intimate
relationship (married, cohabitating, or boyfriend/girlfriend) or differences in the
types of individuals within each that might be associated with the risk of violence
and/or murder. We considered this question by comparing the three types of intimate relationships. The average age of the men varied across the different types of
relationship: married = 35 yrs, cohabitants = 37 yrs, serious dating = 30 yrs; and
the range of ages was quite wide: married = 20–51 yrs, cohabitants = 24–50 yrs,
serious dating = 17–54 yrs. For women victims, the average age by type of relationship was married = 33 yrs, cohabitants = 33 yrs, and serious dating = 27 yrs, and
ranged widely from married = 17–56 yrs, to cohabitants = 16–51yrs, and serious
dating = 16–47 yrs. Although the ages of both perpetrators and victims ranged in
age across much of the lifespan, most couples were similar in age to one another,
with the youngest couples among the boyfriend/girlfriend relationships.

Other comparisons of the men in the different types of intimate relationships
indicated few differences between them in childhood, but as adults the men in
boyfriend/girlfriend relationships were more likely than married men to be unemployed, to have at least one previous conviction, to have had two or more previous
intimate relationships, and to have a problem with alcohol. The men in marital or
cohabiting relationships were more likely than boyfriends to have previously used
violence against the woman they kill, but this may simply reflect the fact that some

of the boyfriend/girlfriend relationships were of a relatively short duration and thus had not had time to develop a history of previous incidents of violence prior to the murder. In addition, boyfriends were significantly more likely than husbands or cohabitants to commit some form of sexual violence as a part of the murder. Overall, the differences in demographic factors and personal characteristics across the different types of intimate partner relationships lend some support to existing findings about the relative importance of the type of relationship itself (marriage, cohabitation, and dating) and those about the differences between the individuals who are more likely to be in each type, with men who are younger, unemployed, and so forth, less likely to be among those who are married. Although the type of intimate relationship and the characteristics of individuals within each type differ in some respects, it is unclear what, if anything, this might have to do with the risk of murder. As shown in the following examples, these and other issues are complex and do not lead to straightforward conclusions about the relative risks of a lethal outcome within different types of intimate partner relationships.[1]

DYNAMICS OF INTIMATE PARTNER MURDER

Evidence from the Murder Study suggests that while the nature of the relationship may be relevant to some aspects of the daily lives of intimate partners, other dynamic factors may be of even greater importance in those relationships that end in murder. Of particular importance are conflicts that are highly charged, such as those relating to possessiveness, jealousy, and infidelity, whether real or imagined, and conflicts relating to separation and/or attempts to leave the relationship. These and other conflicts are often entwined and may also include other issues, such as the woman's attempts to leave and the man's refusal to accept the end of a relationship and/or to prevent her from leaving. Men may try to punish women for leaving, for beginning a new life away from him, and/or for beginning a relationship with a new partner apart from him. These are acts in which men attempt to possess women and "keep" them and may be followed by acts of revenge when possession, control, and authority are lost. These may be very dangerous moments for a woman, particularly if the man decides to "change the project" from attempting to keep her within the relationship to destroying her for leaving it.

   This section begins with an overview of the situations, circumstances, and conflicts at the time of the murder as shown in the quantitative data, and this is followed by examples from the qualitative data that illustrate the unfolding of events that begin with various conflicts and end in the murder of an intimate woman partner or the collateral murder of a child, protector, or new partner as an act of revenge against her. The textual materials are organized conceptually around themes such as "possessiveness" or "separation" and are used to illustrate the complexity and interwoven nature of these dynamic events as they "progress" from differing sources of conflict to the act of murder. However, it is important to stress that it is not possible to recount these events in a rigidly linear fashion from beginning to end. The "beginning" may be viewed at various points: just before the murder, the weeks or months before the murder, or across a much longer period within the relationship. The "end" may be viewed as the murder itself, the treatment of the body after murder, or the subsequent reflections by the perpetrator about the murder itself or about the woman he killed, which are part of the process of reform and which of necessity take the men back to the "beginning" as they reflect on how they might have acted differently. With this in mind, we have attempted as much as possible to present the complex and interwoven elements of the murder event in a relatively progressive fashion although, as will be seen, some issues become relevant at differing points in the progression of events before and after the murder.

Circumstances at the Time of the Murder

The quantitative evidence in Figure 3.1 and Appendix III, Table 3.1, focuses on the circumstances at the time of the murder that provide the backdrop to the murder. These include the ages and relationships of perpetrators and victims; circumstances at the time of the murder, including the use of alcohol and drugs; ongoing disputes; previous violence by either person; and a confrontation prior to the murder. Evidence about the murder event includes the location, number of injuries, and the method of killing. The involvement of various professions at the time of the murder includes information about contacts with police, probation, social services, and health carers. The comparisons of IPMs and MMs shown in Figure 3.1 and Appendix III, Table 3.1 will be discussed at the end of this chapter, but we begin by focusing only on the evidence about the IPMs.

At the time of the murder, just under half of the men were employed (49%), the average age of the men was 34 years, and the average of the women victims was 31 years. Of the couples, 43% were married, 32% were cohabiting, and 25% were boyfriend/girlfriend relationships. Among the offenders, 41% were drinking and 21% were drunk, while 25% of victims were drinking and 11% were drunk. Of the men who were drinking, 17% had been drinking all day and 37% had been drinking for 3 to 6 hours on the day of the murder. In 71% of the cases, there was an ongoing dispute between the offender and the victim, 59% of the men had previously used violence against the woman, and there was a confrontation immediately before the murder in 74% of the cases. Two-thirds of the men were defined as angry or in a rage at the time of the murder, and many had been angry for a long time prior to the murder. Few professionals were involved at the time, including police (13%), social work (9%), or others.

The key to understanding many of the cases lies in the history of previous violence to the victim, the nature of ongoing disputes, and the confrontation immediately preceding the murder. Here, we shift to the narrative accounts in order to more fully explore the nature of these conflicts as they progress to a lethal outcome. Some of the most typical areas of conflict involve "possessiveness and jealousy" and the various stages of "separation," from initial efforts to leave to establishing a new life apart from the man, often with children and sometimes with a new partner, who, as will be shown, may themselves become the target of revenge and be killed instead of the woman in an effort to inflict a terrible form of punishment on her. The narrative accounts are presented at length in order to illustrate the interwoven nature of the circumstances before, during, and after the murder as they progress from the "beginning" to the murder and beyond. Some issues, such as "separation," are examined at different points in the process from the initial suggestion of separation to the killing of the woman or the collateral killing of a child or new partner after separation. Similarly, the issues of "possessiveness" and "jealousy" are presented in the discussion of several topics including "Sources of Conflict," "Previous Violence Against the Woman," and in the section titled "He Says," which includes accounts of the men about themselves, their woman partner, and the murder.

Possessiveness and Jealousy

Extreme possessiveness and/or jealousy existed in relationships that were intact at the time of the murder, and often continued even after separation and divorce. Jealousy involved issues that were imagined as well as those that were real. Jealous men imagined that their woman partner was seeing another man or being unfaithful every time she left the house, whether she was going shopping or visiting other women, including mothers, sisters, women neighbors or friends. They were suspicious even in circumstances where contact with another man was extremely unlikely. The reality of the woman's actions, movements, and contacts may have little effect on the man's imaginations about them. On the other hand, romantic contact with another man may be real. In some cases, this may involve an illicit affair, but in others it may more closely resemble circumstances in which the woman is in the process of leaving the relationship with the perpetrator and beginning a new relationship with another person. For the woman, this may represent an end of one relationship and the beginning of another. But for the man who fails to accept that his partner has left him, her behavior may be defined as an infidelity against him and the relationship between them, which he continues to view as ongoing. The "other man" might be a new partner in a new relationship or he might be a friendly protector of a woman who is in the process of separating from an abusive male partner, or, it might be a complete figment of his imagination. Despite the reality of the "other man," issues of possessiveness, jealousy, and imagined and real infidelities may become sources of conflict and confrontations that are complex and interwoven with other issues, as seen below.

The following case of a man who murdered his wife on her birthday is presented at length in order to explore several of the themes in this chapter, which focuses on the murder event. These include the situations and circumstances at the time of the murder, previous violence to the victim, ongoing disputes, the confrontation immediately preceding the murder, drinking and drunkenness, and the nature of the attack and injuries inflicted in the murder event. In addition, this account also touches on some of the themes that will be examined in the next chapter, which focuses on the men who commit these murders, particularly their life-styles, previous offending, and orientations to the murder itself, including remorse and empathy. In this case, the man was described as someone who "insisted on having his own way" particularly at home; who was extremely jealous of his faithful wife throughout their married life even to the extent of having the children take DNA tests in order to establish paternity; who was entitled to behave as he wished; and who would not be challenged by his wife even when he returned home late at night and drunk on her birthday.

Possessive, jealous, and controlling husband
who murders his wife on her birthday

It was the victim's birthday. They [perpetrator age 51, victim age 49] spent the morning and lunchtime with another couple in normal recreational pursuits. After lunch, the women went shopping and the men went drinking. The drinking continued over many hours, but the defendant was normally a heavy weekend drinker and he was not significantly intoxicated. She was surprised not to see the defendant again in the late afternoon and early evening and made enquiries as to his possible whereabouts, including at the local Police Station. By about 11 pm, she went to bed. The son was in his bedroom. Soon afterward, the defendant returned. She came down and asked, "Where the bloody hell have you been?" The defendant attacked her in a vicious way in and outside the house. He used two kitchen knives. The pathologist found at least five stab wounds, one of which severed the main artery in her neck. He also stamped on her and kicked her about the head when she was on the ground outside, having previously inflicted the fatal stab wound. The 26 year old son witnessed the continuing attack and also received a superficial stab wound to his own back in the course of his attempt to intervene. It was stated at the time that the 31year marriage had **not** been violent [NB. he later admitted to one incident of violence], but he was a jealous and obsessive man. In the early years, he unjustifiably accused his wife of having affairs. Even in recent years, he caused two of his adult children to undergo DNA testing to prove that he is not their father. In fact, the tests proved that he is their father (*938cf1.1.1).

The account describes an extremely possessive, jealous and controlling husband with a strong sense of entitlement to behave as he wished and who responded with fury to a criticism of his behavior which he viewed as an unacceptable challenge to his authority.

Separation—Women Attempt to End a Relationship

Separation is an important source of conflict associated with the murder of an intimate partner; it may include not only the act of separation itself but also the process of terminating the relationship and threats to leave. In another publication, we examined "separation" and the nature of the relationship (married, cohabiting, or serious dating), and found no significant differences between the type of the relationship and a lethal outcome related to separation.[2] At the time of the murder, 37% of the couples were either separated or the woman was attempting to leave the relationship. This is a dangerous time for women and for those who might assist them. When separation occurs, issues of possessiveness and jealousy are elevated, as are conflicts about the separation itself.

Possessiveness, sexual demands, and serious threats
if she attempts to end the relationship

[Letter from the perpetrator to the victim]
Take these instructions to be very serious. Fuck me about, or refuse to do anything I ask and you will be tied up and gagged. I will not repeat myself! You will

not get a second chance! If I have to use violence to get what I want, I will. It will make no difference to me. I am going to get what I want either way. The choice is yours. Be good and willing to me and you will come to no harm. I will be gentle. You must get completely undressed then stand with hands on your hips and legs wide. Look into my eyes and say, use every part of my body for your pleasure.

[The murder that followed this letter]
She, a professional woman, age 44, was a divorced mother of three children. As the relationship developed, she confided in friends that he (age 47) was becoming more possessive and she was thinking of terminating the relationship. The relationship became tense. She made various attempts to break it off, with the most recent just days before the murder. She told friends of strange and silent phone calls she was receiving and was convinced it was him, and two days before the murder, he had been seen hanging around her house. [The Judge]: "You forced your way into her home, terrorized her into submitting to your sexual demands and then held her down in a bath of water with your hand across her mouth so that she died from a combination of drowning and suffocation." Her body was found by her 15 year old daughter rolled up in a carpet in the loft of their house. Police found his semen at the scene—DNA match—also his fingerprints were near her dead body (*1132cf1.1.1).

This account reflects the notion that the man viewed it as essential that the woman behave as he expected; that it was unacceptable to separate from him even in the context of his own abusive behavior toward her. He felt entitled to make extreme sexual demands and expected compliance with his wishes that were backed by strong and explicit threats of retribution should she fail to comply. He was focused and clear. In the words of the prosecution, "He had made up his mind what he was going to do with the woman who no longer wanted his attention—she was going to die." This man clearly "changed the project" from one of attempting to *keep* the woman and demanding specific behavior from her to one of *destroying* her for ending the relationship in order to escape his demands.

Failure to accept the end of a relationship was common. Men simply would not "allow" it to end and might go to great lengths to ensure that it continued, including persistent phoning, uninvited visits to her home, stalking, and threats of violence, murder, and suicide. The following accounts are of men who would not let go. The first is about a brief relationship, the man's anger at the woman's refusal to continue with him, his threats with a knife, and, finally, the act of killing her after failing to force her to remain in a relationship with him. A chilling note indicates that he had previously killed another wife in another country that only became known in the investigation following the second murder.

Refusal to accept the end a brief relationship
He (age 44) was employed as a bus driver, and on a trip formed a relationship with the deceased (age 32). The relationship became very intense on the defendant's part and continued after the trip. When the deceased wanted to end the relationship, he became depressed and wouldn't accept it. He drank in various pubs until he was sure she was at home and her mother had gone to bed. Knowing where the key was kept, he let himself into her house at 1:00am. She kept saying she did not

love him, and he felt frustrated and angry because he was unable to convince her otherwise. He felt the only way he could persuade her would be through threat, and so he went into the kitchen and obtained a knife. She put her arm around him and said, "If you don't go I'll call the police", and shepherded him towards the door. He said he felt "blank—distant," pushed her off, went to hit her and "realized I'd stabbed her." The knife penetrated six inches and severed the aorta. He was described as a binge drinker, but the evidence suggested he had not drunk a great deal prior to the killing [NB: prior to this murder, he had killed a wife in another country, for which he served 7 years in prison] (*838cf1.1.1).

Excessive possessiveness, jealousy, and violence frequently occur as men attempt to isolate women and prevent them from having a wider social life with friends. As illustrated in the following accounts, attempts to separate from such men are fraught with coercion, threats of physical violence, threats of sexual violence, and threats of murder. In some cases, men even threaten to kill themselves in an effort to ensure compliance with their wishes and to "keep" the woman in a relationship with them.

Separation, jealousy, and previous violence to the woman

He (age 40) killed his ex-partner (age 28) because she had left him. He strangled her then burnt the top half of her body to conceal identification. Prior to the murder, the perpetrator phoned the victim's father and complained that she had left him. The father described how he considered the perpetrator to be obsessed with the deceased and her daughter. During the course of the investigation, others expressed their opinion of the jealous nature of the perpetrator. Eighteen months before the murder, a work colleague said that the deceased had called round at her home with two black eyes and a swollen face. She states that the deceased told her that the perpetrator had assaulted her because she was going out at night to visit her friend (*1050cf1.1.1).

Separation and a court order to keep the man away

He (age 47) met the victim (age 43) through a personal column in the newspaper. They became engaged, and then she broke it off and asked him to leave. He was incensed and over the following weeks he threatened, assaulted and attempted to rape her. She obtained a Court Order to force him to leave the house and keep away. He and the victim were moving his furniture out of the house when he stabbed her in the garden shed. There was no confrontation, he simply collected a knife from the kitchen and stabbed her in the chest. He then phoned his employer to arrange for the money owed him to be sent to his son, and handed himself into the police (*651cf1.1.1).

Separation and the decision to kill the woman and commit suicide

First of all tell me about your life, at the time? Well my girlfriend and I split up. I could not cope with it. I didn't want her to leave me so I decided I was going to kill her and kill myself. I killed her but failed in killing myself. *So, you broke-up and she left you. How long had you been separated?* Two weeks. *And had you been thinking about this before she left or was it more of a reaction?* No, no it was brought on when she left and I was convinced that she was not coming back. *You were also thinking about suicide? And seriously?* Yes. *So had you a specific plan?* Pretty much, yes. I was going to bring her back to the flat where we lived and I was going to kill her and then take a load of tablets that I had there and die of an overdose. I suppose really, if I killed her I was going to be in very serious trouble anyway, so I think it was how depressed I was at the time. I just felt, I'm going to die, but if I'm going to die she's going to come with me 'cos I couldn't leave her being happy and thinking I'm dead, so I think that's pretty much what was happening. *Then did it go to plan?* Pretty much so until I took the tablets, I passed out and I woke up being sick [vomiting], and so obviously I lost the momentum then to kill myself, but she ended up dying later on in the hospital. *You came around after taking the overdose, then what happened?* Then I realized obviously I wasn't going to die, she wasn't dead yet, I rang the ambulance to try and get some help, and I made up a story that her and I had a suicide pact and we were going to die together so this was to try and get myself out of trouble. I'm in serious trouble, I'm alive and I don't want to go to prison for that long (*1194iv1.1.1).

For some men, the act of separation is never allowed. Even after the formal act of divorce, after moving house, and after establishing a new relationship, the woman is still deemed to be "his" and her new life viewed as unacceptable to him and punishable by her death and possibly that of others.

He won't let go—Kills his ex-wife and attacks her new male partner

This perpetrator (age 38) went to his ex-wife's house where she (age 31) lived with her new partner. They argued and he wanted to know if she was having sex with the new partner. Then, he stabbed her twice with a kitchen knife on the right side of her abdomen severing her liver and causing almost immediate death. Her new partner heard screams and came into the living room and struggled with the perpetrator who slashed his hands. He needed emergency surgery for the wounds. The perpetrator had previous convictions for assaulting his wife. [Trial judge] There was also an element of jealousy concerning her relationships with other men. I do not consider that the defendant will be a danger to other persons except in so far as he might be placed in the same domestic position again (*582cf1.1.1).

The accounts of the previous cases illustrate the dangerousness of separation whether from a long and well-established relationship or from one that is just beginning or, in some cases, one that has not even begun in the eyes of the woman, although the man may view it differently. It can be seen that the men had a sense of "ownership" of the women that they saw as unbreakable and that they were willing to go to extreme lengths first to "keep" the woman and, failing that, to go to even more extreme lengths to punish a woman who defied his sense of ownership and possession.

Other Sources of Conflict—Children, Money, and Others

Other sources of dispute involve conflicts over a wide range of issues including the expenditure of money, debts, alcohol, custody of children, and even the failure to produce a male child. While these and other sources of conflict may differ widely, a common thread can be seen running across them as men blame women for the problem whatever it might be, expect her to fix it, and make her pay if she does not. The first account involves custody of the children; the second involves a man who beats his wife for years because she is an alcoholic, calmly murders her, and tries to make it look like an accident; and the third account involves a woman who is first starved and abused and then murdered for *her* failure to produce a male child. This murder was described by the judge as one of the worst he had ever seen and will be described in the later section on the nature of the attack and injuries involved in the murder events.

Child custody, marital breakdown, and a new relationship
Two days before the hearing regarding custody of the children after the marital break-up, he (age 34) rented a car and travelled to his ex-wife's (age 33) house. There was a brief argument on the doorstep, and he stabbed her in full view of her new partner and the children. He drove off and was stopped by the traffic police. [Note: During the hearing process about custody, her whereabouts was inadvertently revealed to him in correspondence from the court, which allowed him to trace and kill her] (*719cf1.1.1).

Husband kills alcoholic wife after many years of beating her
His wife (age 42) was an alcoholic and he (age 41) had a long history of beating her dating back to the death of their baby years earlier, and recent arguments about him having an affair. After the murder, he phoned his boss and informed him of his wife's death stating that he had found her at the bottom of the stairs, but what stuck in the boss's mind was the fact that he sounded very calm considering the circumstances (the police operator makes the same comment). Blood was found everywhere and the autopsy revealed 63 separate injuries. The main injuries were: bruising to both eyes, a lacerated right eye brow, bruising and cuts to the inner lips, bruising to the neck, arms, elbows, ribs and abdomen. There was internal bruising to the stomach, intestines, pelvis and bladder. The numerous injuries were compatible with being kicked and punched. Also noticeable were fifteen old fractures and four recent ones. The pathologist regarded these as the worst kicking injuries he had ever seen. After considerable questioning the perpetrator confessed and admitted he had been assaulting his wife for over five years (*910cf1.1.1). [Note: it might be asked whether the man beat his wife because she was an alcoholic or whether she was an alcoholic because he beat her]

Wife failed to produce a male child—recent hospitalization for malnutrition and physical violence—vicious attack by husband—and family help in attempt to cover up
It was reported by the Domestic Violence Unit that he (age 22) had said she (age 22) had utterly failed by producing a girl child and that his parents treated her with contempt [this was an arranged marriage]. He called his family to come over to the house when he realized he had killed his wife, and there is some evidence that they colluded in altering the circumstances in which her body was found (cleaning it and removing evidence of the violent assault) (*1026cf1.1.1).

These and other cases involved intense disputes and conflicts about a wide variety of issues, but the core theme that runs through them is the sense that the men were entitled to have whatever they wanted and were willing to use threats and violence to get it. They insisted on compliance with their wishes, would tolerate no deviations from their expectations, and were willing to use threats and violence to obtain what they wanted, no matter how unfair or unjust.

Previous Violence to the Victim

As previously stated, 59% of the men had previously used physical violence against the woman partner that they eventually murder. This violence was often repeated and severe. In many cases, it had been reported to the police or social services prior to the murder, but in others, previous violence may only have been revealed after the murder in the police interviews with relatives, friends, neighbors, and work colleagues. About one-third of the men had a previous conviction for assault of some type, not necessarily against the victim of the murder, but in over half of these convictions for assault the usual victim was a woman. These men specialized in using violence against women. However, even when the violence was known to others, the men made claims that minimized the violence: that it rarely occurred, that it was not severe, and/or that it was her fault. It should also be stressed that while over half of the men had previously used violence against the women they subsequently murdered, only 6% of the women had used any form of violence against these men. The following are some of the typical statements that reflect the level of denial and minimization of previous violence committed against the women.

> ### No previous convictions and no formal charge of violence, but previous violence did occur
> He has no previous convictions and no reported violence. He admits that there were occasional arguments in the marriage but denies there was any violence before the incident, however comments in the police reports suggest that he had assaulted his wife on previous occasions (*1086cf1.1.1).

> ### Another man claims only one previous incident
> *How did you usually get on with her, did you have a lot of arguments or fights?* No, no. *Had you ever hit her before?* Only once, like once. I'm not a wife beater. I came home and she said something about the male next door. I hit her and slapped her face, right (*840iv1.1.1).

> ### Previous physical violence but no official intervention
> It was a stormy relationship. There were a number of occasions when the applicant was violent toward the deceased (*1008cf1.1.1).

Statements from others about previous incidents of violence against the women provide very different accounts about the frequency and severity of the violence that go well beyond the men's claims of single incidents and/or few injuries. The first of these is a "victim statement" made by the woman about a previous violent attack against her by the man who would later murder her. Other accounts include those from a sister, from a witness, and from arrest records.

Victim statement by the woman about previous incidents of violence against her
[Wife's "victim statement" after a previous incident] We [argued], and these would be quite aggressive verbally. This was quite frightening because the look on his face just said it all. He has thumped me in the past and has grabbed me by the throat and threatened to "spoil my face." He has also banged my head against the wall but this has not been in front of the children. It got to the stage where it would wear me down mentally. He would never let it rest if I disagreed with him, but if I didn't say anything, then he would go on at me for not talking to him. You just couldn't win no matter what you did (*1024cf1.1.1).

Previous violence as reported by the victim's sister
Previous physical and sexual violence to the victim, report from victim's sister
[Police interview]: My sister [the victim] then started telling me that he used to beat her when they were short of money, and also that he used to insist on sex all the time and if she refused he beat her. Several times my sister told me she was going to leave him (*810cf1.1.1).

Previous violence as reported by a male witness
Another witness describes injuries to the deceased approximately two years prior to her death, including bruising to her face and eye. He describes the aggressive nature of the defendant and recalls that he told him that if he ever found the deceased in bed with another man he would "kill them both stone dead" (*1050cf1.1.1).

The following reports of convictions for various offenses involving women partners include assault, destruction of property such as her clothes and personal possessions, and setting a house on fire.

Previous conviction/s for violence against the victim
Even during the first year of the marriage, the defendant used violence towards his wife. He assaulted her whilst he was drunk which resulted in her sustaining bruising to her arms and legs. This was reported to the police and he appeared in court where he agreed to be bound over to keep the peace. Following this incident she moved back to her parents address and obtained an injunction preventing him from visiting their home (*934cf1.1.1).

Previous convictions for assaults against his partner and prison for arson
He has several convictions for previous assaults on his partner. One conviction resulted in a three year prison sentence for setting fire to his brother's house and stealing a shotgun because he thought his partner and brother were having an affair (*582cf1.1.1).

Previous charge for Actual Bodily Harm, and attempted suicide

He told me that on one occasion, he came home and he knew from the general appearance of the house that "someone had been there" [another man]. This was apparently confirmed to him by "the way she couldn't look at me" and was "evasive" on the telephone. The following day, he went over to discuss the relationship, but she wasn't there so he decided to cut up her clothes, destroy her soft toys and, "smash everything I gave her." When she returned, he grabbed her necklace and watch, and the injuries she sustained led to the charge of "Actual Bodily Harm." After this he returned to his caravan, took an overdose of drugs and "expected to die" (*1062cf1.1.1)

These accounts illustrate how dangerous and vindictive some men become when women leave. For some men, this is the turning point as he shifts his efforts away from retaining possession of her to those focused on killing her. They say it, they mean it, and they do it without delay.

When Men Change the Project—The Decision to Destroy

As stated, men who murder an intimate partner may begin by trying to prevent her from leaving him or trying to get her back but end by "destroying her" once he realizes that she is truly lost to him.[3] "If I can't have her, no one can" seems to characterize this change from "keeping" to "destroying" once he believes that she has, in fact, left and cannot be "retrieved." The transformation from the use of nonlethal violence in order to continue to possess and control the woman to the use of lethal violence in order to punish and destroy her is intentional with respect to the outcome. This view of intent contrasts with those who suggest that the murder is an "accident," an inadvertent and unintended outcome associated with a bungled attempt to continue to possess and control the woman by using violence against her.[4]

He abused his wife for years, and tracked her down and murdered her after she left.

She wrote this letter to him when she left:

Hello [his name], I am sorry I have to leave like this but this is the way it has to be done. The way you treat me is no way for a husband to treat a wife. For in every step of the way you make me unhappy and for six years of it I just can't stick it any longer. You cause me to be afraid of you and each night I go to bed I remember what you have done to me, the different things, and I always forgive you but I can't forget what you did to me in May [letter written in July same year] because I am still suffering with my back. So goodbye dear, and if we don't meet again we will meet in heaven for I still love you as my husband. But I can't live in fear any longer, so I will pack up my job and take a holiday, so please don't run around looking for me for I won't come back to you.
Signed
Your loving wife
XXXX
Best wishes and all good luck

After she (age 45) left him (age 46), he made every effort to trace his wife but was unable to do so until a man who had tried without success to have sex with her, took his revenge by giving her new address to the perpetrator. He visited his wife on numerous occasions to attempt to persuade her to return. In his statement, he claims she told him that she would not return to him, that she preferred to be dead, and she wanted a divorce. He states that from then on he lost control of himself. On the morning of the murder, he went to her street and waited until she left home to go to work. He was carrying a kitchen knife in his coat pocket. He approached his wife and asked her to return to him, but she would have nothing to do with him. He followed her for a short distance and stated that he caught hold of her in order to talk to her but she ignored him and said she would be late for work. He then said that he lost his temper and took the knife from his pocket. His wife asked him why he had the knife and he replied "I want you back." She then shouted "murder" and at this, he stabbed her. She fell to the ground and he stabbed her again while she kept saying "I'm coming back." He states that his reply was, "it's too late, too late." Immediately after the offense, he made his way to the police station, saying "I have committed a crime. I have just stabbed my wife." He then placed the kitchen knife on the counter. He had the above letter in his pocket, and when the police officer asked about the ill treatment he said, "it is only domestic, between man and wife" (*810cf1.1.1).

From separation and no hope of reconciliation to setting her on fire
Police Report: He (age 36) says he visited his ex-girlfriend (age 31) in the hope of reconciliation. He forced entry into the house and assaulted the victim. There was a struggle and he cut her on the body and then threw a can full of petrol on her and on a door. When she tried to leave he used a lighter to ignite his girlfriend's clothes and she burned to death (*280cf1.1.1).

Separation, new partner, and she would not return
He (age 33) says they argued regarding her (age 41) *"affair"* [after separation] and her being reluctant to return to him, and he flew into a temper. He punched her in the face and strangled her with a nylon rope. In his account to me he maintained that he did not know whether he killed her or she killed herself. He said that her behavior was "too much for a sick husband to put up with" (*252cf1.1.1).

Separation—woman leaves and begins relationship
with new partner, but he won't let go
Once she left and got her own house, he "often called at her new house wanting to sort things out." He used to drive by her house on a number of occasions and said, "one day you're gonna push me too far and I'm gonna fucking kill you." They broke up because of his infidelities and violence. She explained how she had told him on a number of occasions that she was through with him—apparently he wouldn't listen and kept trying to win her back. On one occasion, he forced the new boyfriend to leave and the boyfriend phoned the police who attended. The police recorded an incident but no action was taken because the victim did not want any and the accused agreed to leave. She later told a friend that the accused had called her a slag, chased her upstairs, thrown her on to a bed and hit her. Her friend saw her injuries [not apparent when police arrived] consisting of a bruise on her inner thigh, bruising around her ankles and swelling to her left hand. She

was obviously frightened of him. On another occasion, the accused tried to strangle her whilst she was in the bath and had hurt her throat (*922cf1.1.1).

THE MURDER EVENT

Physical Attack and Injuries

As shown in the preceding examples, most of the murders involved several forms of violence in the attack and were characterized by punching, kicking, stabbing, choking, and beating with fists, feet, and blunt instruments. Those involving some kind of instrument/weapon/tool (75%) included knives and screwdrivers, blunt instruments such as bricks and bats, and ligatures such as cords, scarves, and ties. Just over one-third (36%) included strangling, choking, or smothering. Guns were used in only four cases. Most (64%) involved five or more injuries (Figure 3.1 and; Appx.III-Table 3.1), and although not shown in the figure/table, 44% of the cases involved 10 or more injuries. The duration of the attacks ranged from under 10 minutes to more than 1 hour, with most lasting less than half an hour. Attacks and deaths almost always occurred in the same location, overwhelmingly in the home of the couple or the woman (89%), and the women usually died alone and without assistance from other individuals or the emergency services. In 92% of cases, the murder was committed by only one perpetrator. The following examples illustrate the nature of attack and injuries.

The murder—punching, kicking, and stabbing
His son (age 26) saw his father (age 51) punching and kicking his mother (age 49), and she was clutching the side of her neck where she had been stabbed. The father then pushed her down the stairs and outside, and the son saw him stepping off the driveway in a deliberate act, stepping directly onto his wife's face. The son pushed and punched his father to force him off and away from his mother. The son began cradling his mother's head in his hands and kissing her. At this point, the son was positioned so that his back was towards the front door. He recalls feeling a "sharp implement" striking him in the back between his shoulders and then "a bit of a thud as if a hand had hit me afterwards." The perpetrator began to drag his wife's body to the road, walked toward her and kicked her in the face again. The son states that at this point he launched an attack on his father punching him to the ground and kicking him in the body. When the police arrived, the perpetrator was clutching a knife and officers disarmed him with a blow to the stomach. The victim was taken to the hospital and declared "life extinct" at 1:00 am. [Postmortem] There were eight incised wounds, seven to the lower part of the face, neck and left shoulder. The fatal wound was directed into the neck and severed the carotid artery. There were an additional 25 injuries caused by kicking and stamping (*938cf1.1.1).

The murder—stabbing and cutting her throat
The deceased (age 28) had lived together with the accused (age 34) for approximately two years. The relationship ended four months before the killing, and was described by witnesses as "turbulent" with clear indications of violence

being inflicted on the deceased by the accused. The deceased had recently been associated with a new boyfriend. The perpetrator spied on his ex-partner and her new partner, then left, changed his clothing and returned with a knife, wearing a pair of washing-up gloves and intending to kill them both. He broke into the house around 1:00am and attacked the boyfriend with a knife, stabbing him a number of times resulting in extensive wounds to his upper body and right arm. The boyfriend attempted to escape and ran upstairs to the bathroom, and was followed by the accused who continued to attack. The deceased rang the police at 1:05am from the house. She ran from the house dressed in a bathrobe and was pursued by the accused to a grassed area adjacent to the house. The accused attacked her at this location, stabbing and slashing her throat with a knife. A number of witnesses saw the victim viciously and savagely attacked by a male who took hold of her on the road and placed her down on her back on the grassed area where he was seen to sit astride her, pinning her arms down with his knees whilst stabbing and slashing her throat with a knife. Another witness said: The woman was pleading with him to stop and was screaming. He recalls the male took hold of the deceased, held her back to him holding her hair with his left hand, gripping her left shoulder with his elbow as he moved her to the grassed area. Her attacker brought the knife to her throat which she took hold of with her right hand causing her to scream loud and hysterically. There were numerous injuries to her throat and head—also classic "defence injuries." When the allegation of murder was put to him, he said, "It wasn't me" (*944cf1.1.1).

The following murder was described by the judge as one of the worst he had ever seen. This is a continuation of an account begun in the earlier section "Other Sources of Conflict" and is about a woman who was murdered because she did not produce a male child.

The murder—prolonged attack and massive injuries

The defendant called police and they found her body in the bedroom. The bedding, her clothing and the house itself were all found to be absolutely and suspiciously clean. She had died from massive injuries, namely a severe compression injury of the chest which broke ribs at the front and the back, caused bleeding into the lungs and two tears in the substance of the heart. The pathologists indicated that these injuries would have been caused by extremely forceful stamping or even jumping upon her. She also had 95 separate areas of bruising, areas of laceration and five separate blunt force injuries to the head resulting in subdural and subarachnoid hemorrhages. A neighbor had heard prolonged thumping and screaming from the house at about 4:30 am and again at about 6:30am. The evidence was that she had been severely beaten with about 89% of her body area covered in bruising mainly to the head, arms and legs. Social Services and Domestic Violence Units have records of two hospitalizations of the victim in the year of her death for malnutrition and physical abuse. [Judge]: "You have inflicted a prolonged and vicious attack on your wife—one of the worst cases of violence without a weapon in all my experience in court. You carried out a callous, brutal, prolonged and pitiless assault upon your wife, resulting in injuries of such severity as I have rarely seen in all my forensic experience to have been inflicted by one person upon another without the use of a weapon." The jury was unanimous and returned their verdict after twenty minutes (*1026cf1.1.1).

Sexual Attack Within the Murder

Of the 105 cases of IPM, 17 cases (16%) also included a sexual attack along with the physical attack, with boyfriends accounting for the majority of them (59%, n = 10/17), followed by cohabitants (29%, n = 5/17), and least among men who were married to the victim (12%, n = 2/17). Of the murders that involved a sexual attack or a sexual element of some type, 39% of the men had previously used sexual violence against the woman. It should also be noted that of the IPM cases that *did not* involve sex in the murder itself, 9% of the men had previously used some form of sexual violence against the woman. It is also notable that 4 of the 17 men who used sex in the murder of an intimate partner had also committed sexual violence against another woman outside the intimate relationship in which the murder occurred.

The murders of intimate partners that involved sex ranged across circumstances that usually involved jealousy but extended to one that involved an elaborate sexual fantasy. The most extreme of the physical acts involved a "frenzied" attack with over 100 stab wounds, and acts of sex before, during, and after the murder. A few involved mutilation of the sexual parts of the body. These sexual acts need to be considered as something apart from the injury that resulted in death. Although it is possible to murder solely using the act of rape or the brutal attack on the vagina, this was rarely what was happening in these cases. The women were killed by stabbing, strangling, or bludgeoning and not by sexual penetration. As such, the sexual part of the murder needs to be viewed in its own right and somewhat differently than the physical acts used to kill. The act of sex within the murder might be seen as a form of humiliation, of possession, of conquering, or of subduing the victim. It might also be viewed by the man as a form of pleasure or fun or the fulfillment of a fantasy. It could be an angry response to his inability to perform sexually accompanied by blaming the woman for his inadequacy and punishing her for his sexual failure.

As illustrated below, the sexual element of the murder varied from rape to some form of attack on various parts of the body. When sex was involved in the murder, the physical attack that resulted in death was much more likely to involve strangulation, a pattern that will be seen again in the chapter on sexual murder. Although boyfriends were more likely than cohabitants or husbands to commit a sexual act in the context of murdering their intimate partner, the following accounts include examples from each type of relationship, which is identified at the end of each account.

Frenzied stabbing attack and sex immediately before or during the murder (by boyfriend)
The perpetrator (age 30) killed his girlfriend (age 25). Death occurred as a result of numerous stab wounds principally to the neck and there was evidence of strangulation. [Forensic evidence] suggests that she had not moved after the sexual intercourse, which was therefore contemporaneous with or immediately prior to the killing. She died of approximately 113 stab wounds. Some of the wounds around the breast were caused after death. In short, it was a frenzied attack. The top half

of the body was completely covered in knife wounds. When sentenced for murder he shouted abuse at the police officers and the jury. He had nine previous convictions including numerous fines, (ABH) Actual Bodily Harm carrying an offensive weapon, and one assault conviction for slapping a girlfriend across the face twice and punching her in the mouth knocking out a tooth (*980cf1.1.1). [Sex—boyfriend]

Savage attack including rape with instruments after years of physical abuse (by cohabitant)

The perpetrator (age 28) savagely sexually assaults and then kills his long-term co-habitee (age 22) after years of physical violence against her. An ambulance arrived at the scene very shortly after the emergency services received a 999 call. They entered the premises through the open front door and subsequently discovered the battered body of the deceased lying face up on the kitchen floor partly clothed. The defendant, when questioned by the ambulance crew, stated that he had been upstairs and came down to find that she had collapsed on the kitchen floor. The ambulance crew was not satisfied with this explanation and the police were called. Whilst the ambulance crew was attending to the body, the defendant disappeared and could not be traced. [Post mortem] the deceased had numerous broken ribs and severe bruising over her entire body. Her knees had been smashed, and her anus and vagina had been forcibly penetrated by unknown instruments causing horrendous injuries. She had numerous marks over her body which was consistent with a horrific beating. The cause of death has been established as drowning which is consistent with her body having been found near the bathroom which adjoined the kitchen and the bath was almost full of murky brown water and bloodstained. He was found and arrested at a friend's house (*1008cf1.1.1) [Sex—cohabitant].

Raped and murdered third wife when separated [also murdered his second wife]

The perpetrator (age 50) killed his third wife (age 49) when she left him a few days before the murder. This was described as a "turbulent" relationship and his aggressive and violent behavior led to the victim obtaining an injunction to keep him away from her. However, about one month later the victim allowed him back when she became ill. The relationship deteriorated still further and she started to treat him as a lodger. They had separate bedrooms and she made it clear she wished him to leave. He moved out [to a nearby location], and on the day of the murder he asked her to bring him his remaining possessions and cutlery to equip him in his bedsit and it was when she was complying with this request that she was murdered. [Post mortem—Three stab wounds in chest, throat, and eye. The perpetrator plunged the knife into her with great power almost passing through her body. A large blood stained knife with a five inch blade and black plastic handle was recovered next to her body. The blade was repeatedly plunged up and down amongst her internal organs causing massive injury to her heart, liver and lungs. Death was due to multiple (13) stab wounds and compression of her neck. The killing was not frenzied but concentrated on the neck and heart area of the deceased. It seems the perpetrator had attempted to cut out her right eye after death. No remorse or signs of distress were shown throughout [the police interview].

About Sex—The perpetrator asserts that there had been no sexual relations between the two for a long time. Forensic evidence revealed recent intercourse. This would indicate rape and that the deceased had been detained by the perpetrator in the premises against her will. It may have been an effort to stop their separation initially but when it became clear no reconciliation would follow, the perpetrator raped and killed the victim. (*921cf1.1.1). [sex—husband]

Sexual fantasies, sadism, and previous physical and sexual violence

When he was 14, he attempted to strangle a female friend of his mother. He said that he had strange dreams in which a woman with long black hair and glasses is seen [a famous singer]. He had fantasies regarding intercourse and then strangling her and ejaculated at the thought of this fantasy and other related violent fantasies. The victim, his 22 year old girlfriend, had arranged to meet him on a Saturday afternoon. He (age 23) described how he took her home to the bungalow where he lived with his parents who were away on holiday at the time. For no reason, he hit the young women over the head with a sledgehammer then carried her to his parent's bedroom placing her on the bed where he stabbed her in the throat, slit her vagina and slashed her breast. He left the country and went to another country but later confessed to a priest who contacted the authorities and the police collected him and escorted him back to this country.

[NOTE]: There were numerous previous sexual offences against others before the murder but they were not discovered until after the murder. After conviction and imprisonment for this murder, he was charged with 25 sexual offenses that occurred before the murder. He was found guilty of 14 charges of indecent assaults on males, 4 charges of taking indecent photographs of children, 7 charges of buggery and indecency with a child, gross indecency, and conspiracy to indecently assault two children for which he got 16 years imprisonment. He is now subject to child protection measures and categorized as a "schedule one sex offender" which is the most serious category (*209cf1.1.1). [sex—boyfriend]

The Body After Death and Attempts to Avoid Detection

After the murder, most men immediately left the scene (70%), but a few engaged in further acts against the body after death. Most of these involved attempts to cover up the murder and avoid detection such as removing the body from the scene of the murder (15%), burning the body (8%), or dismembering the body (3%), and a few (2%) involved a sexual act after death. The following accounts illustrate the nature of some of the further acts against the body after death.

The body after death—hammer attack, dismember body and place in deep freeze

In the evening, the defendant attacked his wife, hitting her 20 times with a hammer. He then cut her body into pieces and placed the severed parts in a deep freeze. He first pretended to his step-daughter, neighbors and the police that she had gone missing. However, two days later, blood was seen near a drain outside the house, the body was discovered and he then pretended he had found his wife in the bath with her throat cut and that she had committed suicide. He said that to avoid shame to the family, he decided to dispose of the body. Initially he claimed to have tried to smash his wife's head with a hammer to help him dispose of the body down the lavatory. Only when the pathologist's report showed the cut to his wife's throat had occurred after she was dead and the hammer blows to the head occurred before she was dead, did he then suggest that he was provoked (*940cf1.1.1).

The body after death—strangle, dismember and dispose of body parts across the countryside
The defendant (age 26) met another woman and started an affair with her. He tried to persuade his wife (age 23) to let the other woman live with them as a threesome. She point blank refused. It seems the other woman told him she was ending the affair, and he determined to kill his wife. His wife was eight months pregnant with their third child and was sleeping downstairs. He murdered her by strangulation and then set about disposing of the body. He took it to the house where he was carrying on the affair, and dismembered the body with an axe and a hack saw. He reported his wife missing and then drove around the neighboring countryside dumping parts of the body on grass verges and setting fire to the verge in the hope of destroying the evidence. The fire brigade were called to each of the fires and made the grisly discovery of the parts of the body. Witnesses had seen the defendant's distinctive taxi at the various sites, and he was arrested. [Trail judge] aggravating features—he not only killed his wife when she was eight months pregnant but, secondly, was the horrific and callous way in which he disposed of the body (*1086cf1.1).

The body after death—destroy evidence, move and bury. Discovered by foxes after five months
The accused (age 30) and the victim (age 29) became acquainted about six weeks before her death. They began a relationship, moving from place to place living on social security. Probably as a result of a quarrel, he punched her in the face, breaking her nose, and then strangled her manually. He and his stepmother later took the body in the boot of a car and buried it in a ditch. It was discovered five months later when foxes disturbed the site. In the meantime, he took steps to remove any signs of blood, etc., from the flat. He also left town and arranged for the car to be crushed. When arrested, he declined to answer questions, claiming she had left him long before the murder. While on remand, he confessed to two fellow prisoners who reported it to the police. He eventually gave two separate accounts. In those accounts he suggested— for different reasons in each case—that he had been provoked (*1038cf1.1.1).

The final account does not follow the pattern of further acts against the body undertaken in an attempt to disguise the murder, and is particularly unusual and bazaar.

The body after death—murder to cover financial deception and sex after death to "say goodbye"
He (age 25) killed his common-law partner of eight months (age 25). He saw the murder as a solution to his problems [financial debts]. She (victim) was about to

find out about his financial deception of her. He hit her on the head with a heavy claw hammer. She awoke. He lost control and kept hitting her on the head with the hammer, fracturing her skull in several places. Sometime after he killed her, he "made love to her" [his words] after she was dead, saying he had sex with her as "a way of saying goodbye" (*1048cf1.1.1).

Although a few men went to extreme lengths to avoid detection, most did not. Overall, 18% were apprehended at the scene, 20% reported themselves to the police, 20% told someone else who reported them to the police, and 23% were apprehended after a straightforward police investigation. Only 9% required an extensive investigation by the police. Most men were apprehended fairly quickly, some within a few minutes or hours and most with a few days.

Detection after the murder—turned himself in to police
He beat her up and strangled her. Two hours later, he walked into the Police Station and said to the officer on duty, "I think I've murdered my girlfriend" (*1040cf1.1.1).

Detection after the murder—police alerted by her work colleagues—he immediately confessed
The police went to the address on suspicions raised by her work colleagues. Once in the house he said, "I strangled her on Monday morning. I have killed her. She is in the room on the left." He said he strangled her, but several fractures of the skull were also inflicted with a blunt instrument possibly a round headed hammer (*1048cf1.1.1).

He Says—What Were They Thinking? Perpetrators Accounts of the Murder

Detection usually occurred very soon after the murder. At this point, some men stated that they were innocent, while most admitted that they had committed the murder but, at the same time, offered a range of rationales, justifications, and excuses for their actions that they saw as exculpatory. They minimized the violence and deflected responsibility for their own actions in a variety of ways. They blamed alcohol, claimed it was an accident, and/or blamed the victim in particular or women in general. Some claimed that the assault was minimal and/or that they only intended to frighten or punish the woman but not to kill her. In a variety of ways, the men removed themselves from responsibility for their own behavior, and many viewed the events as "just happening" and not as a result of their own actions. The following are typical accounts of what the men had to say. They include declarations of innocence, efforts to minimize the violence, statements meant to remove themselves from responsibility, and those meant to declare a lack of intention to do harm.

He says—he is innocent
He is unwilling to discuss the alleged offense except to protest his innocence. He says that he had been out drinking and when he arrived home he was informed by the Police that his wife had been murdered (*1078cf1.1.4).

He says—he killed to avoid being disappointed by a woman

He says he killed his common-law partner of eight months in order to avoid being let down by a woman. His rationalization for killing her "was that he had been let down before and he wanted to prevent a repeat of those experiences" (*1048cf1.1.1).

He says—minimization of the weapon, the attack, and the injury

You used two knives? Yeah, the other one was a knife I used to use for fishing, for filleting. But really it wasn't like a real knife. It was a kitchen utensil more than anything else. *At that point did you realize how seriously she was hurt?* I mean she'd just been nicked more than anything else. Because I didn't actually feel the knife go in and then when I lay [her] down there was just a tiny little nick, it was only about half an inch long and it didn't look deep and it wasn't bleeding so I assumed that it was just a scratch more than anything else. *Why did you bother calling the ambulance then if it was just a wee nick?* You tell me, I don't know. She was hurt, it was a knife wound. To be on the safe side, get an ambulance there. *Was she fainting or anything like that?* No, she was still stood up when I looked up and she was looking down at this, I thought it was small wound, two inches above the waistband of her jeans. It wasn't a place that you'd associate with being a real injury, you know what I mean, and I thought, well—She started to look a bit wobbly which I thought might have been a bit of shock coming from getting hurt. So I lay her down and went to phone an ambulance to be on the safe side. There's no way I thought it was going to be a fatal wound (*646iv1.1.1).

When cautioned by police, he said—it was a good marriage and no intent to murder

The Murder: "I didn't believe she was hurt too bad by the first knife. Apart from the blood, like you know, I thought I'd caught her in the shoulders."

The Marriage: "I have been with my wife thirty odd years. A marriage which had no love in it couldn't have lasted so long. There was much love in it. We both had everything to live for. I cannot believe this thing has happened at all. I never meant any serious harm which has robbed us both of good lives" (*938cf1.1.1). [NB: Extremely jealous and authoritarian]

Intimate Partner Collateral Murders

In some cases, the conflict within the intimate relationship resulted in the murder of someone other than the woman partner, including children, allies/protectors, and new partners. In addition to the 105 cases of IPM, another 62 cases involved the killing of a person other than the woman partner but where the source of the conflict leading to the murder was between the male perpetrator and his woman partner. Using evidence from the Casefiles, three types of intimate partner collateral murders were identified: the murder of children (n = 19), allies/protectors (n = 19), and new partners (n = 24).[5]

The 19 children who were murdered were aged between 3 weeks and 4 years, were almost evenly divided by gender with 10 boys and 9 girls, all were the children of the women partners but only one-third were the biological children of the men who murdered them. The men who murdered children were often jealous of the attention given to the child, resented the time their partner spent with the child, or were angry because the child was fathered by another man. Thus, the murder of the child could be viewed as an act of punishment or revenge against the woman partner. The 24 new partners included 22 men and 2 women. In most cases involving a new partner, the women were separated from the perpetrator (sometimes for months or years) but the men resented the new arrangements and often considered themselves to be the "victims" and, accordingly, viewed themselves as justified in punishing the woman and/or her new partner. Men who murdered new partners, were often angry, jealous, and resentful because the woman was no longer his and neither she nor another man, nor another woman, had a right to take her away from him. The 19 allies were mostly relatives and friends of the women partners and included 7 men and 12 women, 5 of whom were also raped. Frequently, allies were attempting to harbor or protect a woman and her children from an abusive partner, and the men murdered them because he objected to their interference in "his affairs" and was angry with them for providing his partner with protection, assistance, or refuge. Most of the collateral murders occurred in the context of previous violence against the woman partner. Most of the children who were murdered had also been the victims of previous acts of violence by the perpetrator. Previous acts of violence against allies or new partners were uncommon, but various forms of harassment frequently occurred.

It is important to note that 14 of the 28 adult women who were NOT classi-fied within our three types of murder (because they were not an intimate partner, there was no sex in the murder, or they were not over 65 years of age) were, in fact, the victims of intimate partner collateral murders (see Appx.II-Figure II.2). Of these women, 2 were new partners and 12 were female relatives or friends who were attempting to offer assistance to the woman partner of the male perpetra-tor in her efforts to separate from him and/or to escape from his violence. While investigating and understanding intimate partner collateral murders is important in its own right, a clearer understanding of the context and circumstances of these cases extends the range of murders that should be included in the domain of those related to conflicts between intimate partners and, more widely, gender-based violence.

The following accounts illustrate some of the contexts and conflicts associated with the murder of intimate partner collaterals. The majority are characterized by previous violence against the woman partner and intense conflicts about a number of core issues relating to the relationship. Again, possessiveness, jealousy, separa-tion, and revenge are recurring issues.

Collateral murder of their child—revenge—after woman leaves and begins a new relationship

The victim (age 2 years and 9 months) was the youngest by four years of two sons of the perpetrator (age 42) and his partner. They lived together for 18 years in a volatile relationship and eventually married three years before the murder. One major source of difficulty throughout the relationship was his obsession that his wife was or might be unfaithful. This almost certainly reflected his own pattern of infidelity during two earlier marriages. His wife decided that they must separate because of his erratic and violent behavior towards her, and the court ruled that she should have custody and he should have contact with the children at the matrimonial home. He sent messages to her that varied from affectionate to threatening. He spoke more than once of killing himself and wrote to her [saying], "all I can think of is, that if I can't have you and the children at home I know I will do something very stupid."

On the day in question, he had a visit with the sons, and neighbors spoke of them enjoying football and cricket with him in the garden. The precise sequence of events is not entirely clear because at some stage, and possibly several times during the evening, he took a potentially fatal dose of Demerol which was ingested with alcohol. He decided to kill his youngest son and himself, and he probably also intended to kill his other son. While his mind was perfectly clear, he went to the garage and found four cable ties, returned to the victim's room where the child was fast asleep, fixed the cable around the child's neck, and then pulled it tight until the child was dead.

He wrote a number of revealing messages on furniture and mirrors to his wife and family. The content was mixed but the following examples are self explanatory. To the older [surviving] son: "I love you too, sorry. Hope your mum can explain this to you. She has all of my money, the thief. I love you all." "I am sorry, but you are alive. It's all Mum's fault, please blame her." His message to his wife: "Now what the fuck are you going to do with the bastard [new partner]" and, "What are you going to do now? I've passed my test, have you? It just did not work out as you planned, did it? Never mind. Take a photo of this then, ha." On the following morning, the eldest son found his brother dead in bed and his father unconscious on the sofa downstairs. He found help from a neighbor and the emergency services were called.

[Trial judge] My own judgment is that he was motivated by a desire to hurt and punish his wife and to assert his rights over the affection for the [victim/ son]. He knew perfectly well she would suffer intensely as a result of the victim's death. [Prison report] "All outgoing letters *must* be monitored by the censors as this inmate is constantly bombarding his ex-wife with death threats" [three years after sentencing] (*961cf1.1.2).

Collateral murder of intimate partner and woman friend
[rare example of use of a firearm]

The two victims (age 18 and 19) worked together as part time barmaids and resided with their parents. The two girls made frequent visits to a local club and at some point several months earlier had met and befriended the accused (age 21) at these premises. All three kept in touch but he became attached to one of the girls, and they had a sexual relationship. The accused appears to have looked upon their association as both permanent and serious. It was suggested that she was not of the same mind and within a couple of months broke off the affair. This situation clearly upset the accused and he made it clear that he did not fully accept the separation. He also resented any other likely suitors and disliked the close relationship between the two women. He became even more distressed when he saw the two girls during the late evening in the company of a local man. On the morning of the following day, the accused armed himself with a twelve-bore-single-barreled shotgun and a quantity of ammunition which belonged to his father and was kept at the family home. He visited the girls, and a short time later the neighbors heard screams and two shotgun blasts. These noises were followed by the sound of two persons running from the bungalow, and a very short while later, by the sound of a third shotgun blast from the road. Several neighbors went outside and saw the body of one of the victims lying on the pavement. She had severe shotgun injuries to the back/top of her head and was dead. Two uniform [unarmed] officers arrived within minutes. They faced the accused who was still holding the shotgun, and after a lengthy conversation persuaded him to hand over the weapon. It was then found to be loaded with a fourth live cartridge. The other victim had also been shot in the back of the head and was dead. He admitted being responsible for the two killings, and to some previous planning (*1062cf1.1.1).

Collateral—allies/protectors—murders wife's mother and father, another of the few killings involving a firearm

After a quarrel in which he (age 27) struck his wife, she took the baby, cleared out her own and the baby's clothes, and returned to her parents. He said that "basically, I knew that she was gone for good." He phoned his father-in-law (age 47) who told him he was fed-up with him always knocking his daughter about. The perpetrator subsequently visited the farm and had a violent argument with his in-laws resulting in him bruising his mother-in-law (age 44). The morning of the offense, he went to the house, left the car at the bottom of the drive, walked up loading the shotgun, and walked into the house where he shot his father-in-law. He then reloaded the gun and shot his mother-in-law (*1178cf1.1.2).

Collateral—new male partner

In evidence the defendant said that he caused the injuries [of the deceased] by jumping and stamping on him. He admitted that his girlfriend had broken the relationship off weeks ago and that she had taken up with another man. When confronted, he admitted to slapping her, but said "she asked for it, she made me do it." She regularly went to Refuges [for abused women]. He said he doesn't like to be told what to do by a woman, and clearly he has misogynistic ideas and attitudes. He blames the killing on his partner, "if she didn't do what she did [leave him] the geezer would be alive today" (*270cf1.1.2).

Collateral—two murders—a contract to kill ex-intimate partner and her new male partner

The couple had been happily married for 20 years and had one adult child. Two years before the murders, she (age 38) left the marital home after long standing domestic difficulties [including violence against her]. Divorce had been applied for but had not yet been granted. The split was a nasty and vindictive affair with the accused (age 44) never coming to terms with the breakdown of the marriage and her new relationship, and made numerous attempts at reconciliation. He was consumed with jealousy and revenge and had already made threats of violence. He refused to accept that his wife was no longer his and would not come to terms with the fact that she was living as man-and-wife with another man. He hired a contract killer to search out and kill his wife but in the end he and the contract killer carried out the murders. The bodies were found lying next to each other in a pool of blood. She had received stab wounds to the head and body and her throat had been cut. Cause of death: severing of the spinal cord due to stab injury to the neck. Her partner suffered from [and died of] a number of stab wounds to the head and upper body (*1180cf1.1.1, ex-wife and collateral – new male partner).

COMPARISONS OF INTIMATE PARTNER
MURDERS AND MALE-MALE MURDERS

As indicated in chapter 1, the vast majority of murders involve men who kill other men, and this type dominates both the statistics and the explanations of homicide. Thus, it is necessary to examine the murder of women separately if we are to develop a fuller and more adequate understanding of homicides in which women are the victims. As shown graphically in Figure 3.1 and numerically in Appendix III, Table 3.1, the quantitative data are used to make direct comparisons between MMs and IPMs. When read together, the comparisons highlight both the similarities and the statistically significant differences between these two types of murder. When read separately, the figures provide an overall characterization of each type in terms of the prevalence of the various factors examined. For all comparisons, the percentages are shown as MM vs. IPM. The average ages of perpetrators and victims are based on individuals age 16 and older and excludes all children and infants. The differences suggest very different dynamics when MMs and IPMs are compared.

The average age of men who murdered other men was younger than the average age of men who murdered an intimate partner (MM = 27 years vs. IPM = 34 years). By contrast, the average age of the victims was MM = 40 years vs. IPM = 31 years. In addition, the age span between the male perpetrators and their victims varied considerably, with a span of 13 years in MMs and only 3 years in IPMs. On average, the intimate partners were both in their early to mid-30s with only 3 years' age difference between them. By contrast, MMmurderers were in their late twenties (age 27) and murdered men much older than themselves (age 40). The figures contradict two very popular images: that of the much older man who kills a woman partner who is much younger than himself and the image of young men who murder other young men in some form of encounter between them. Instead, the more appropriate characterizations are of relatively young men murdering men who are much older than themselves and of men in their 30s murdering women partners just slightly younger than themselves. While the imagery of young men murdering other young men may be a fairly accurate characterization in countries with very high rates of homicide as discussed in chapter 1, it may be less likely in countries with much lower rates of homicide.

At the time of the murder, nearly one-half of MMmurderers were single while all IPMurderers were obviously in some type of intimate relationship, although many were separated at the time. Nearly one-third of MMmurderers and one-half of IPMurderers were employed, a statistically significant difference. Few of the perpetrators were involved with social and/or criminal justice agencies at the time of the murder. Prior to the murder, ongoing disputes between the perpetrator and the victim were significantly more likely among intimate partners than MMs (MM = 30% vs. IPM = 71%), although the majority of the murders of both types were usually preceded by a confrontation (MM = 61% vs. IPM = 74%). The nature of the disputes between males often involved money, legal and illegal business, and the like, while those between intimate partners usually involved possessiveness, jealousy, and separation. While confrontations between males may sometimes involve disputes in which two men enter into some kind of "notional agreement" to engage in "combat," those between a man and woman clearly do not follow this pattern. Previous violence by the victim toward the perpetrator was unusual in both types of murder (MM = 11% vs. IPM = 6%).Previous violence by the offender to the victim was also unusual when men murdered other men but very common when men murdered women partners (MM = 11% vs. IPM = 59%). Again, the contrast is notable and suggests a context of previous beatings, violence, and attacks against women partners who are subsequently murdered that, for the most part, are not a part of the context in which men murder other men.

Drinking and drunkenness at the time of the murder were both more likely in murders between men, and for all comparisons the differences were statistically significant. The perpetrators were more likely to be drinking (MM = 68% vs. IPM = 41%) or defined as drunk (MM = 49% vs. IPM = 21%). Similarly, the victims of MMs were more likely to have been drinking (MM = 47% vs. IPM = 25%) and defined as drunk (MM = 33% vs. IPM = 11%). Of those who were drinking at the time of the murder, about one-fifth of both groups were drinking together. At the time of the murder, the use of drugs by the perpetrator was much less prevalent in both groups, but significantly more likely among murders involving males than those involving intimate partners (MM = 19% vs. IPM = 8%).

The involvement of two or more perpetrators was fairly common in murders between men but unusual in the killing of a woman partner (MM = 43% vs. IPM = 6%). For both types, the scene of the murder was often in or near the home of the victim, but this was much more likely when women partners were murdered (MM = 50% vs. IPM = 89%). The use of an instrument was common in both types (MM = 88% vs. IPM = 73%), as was the infliction of five or more injuries (MM = 71% vs. IPM = 64%). Women victims were significantly more likely than men to be strangled or choked (MM = 7% vs. IPM = 36%).

SUMMARY

In summary, intimate partners were usually murdered in the context of ongoing disputes, and previous violence by the perpetrator against the victim was common, although some did appear to come "out of the blue," with no known history of previous violence. The nature of the relationships included those who were married, those cohabiting, and those in serious boyfriend-girlfriend relationships, with the latter more likely to be younger and unemployed. At the time of the murder, nearly half of the men had been drinking and one-fifth were drunk. Most murders involved an argument or confrontation, and possessiveness, separation, and/or threats to leave were common sources of conflict. The man's sense of authority, entitlement, and control were usually apparent. Many of the women saw separation as the ending of an intimate relationship while the men did not. Instead, these men viewed separation as inappropriate and unacceptable and as a challenge to their ongoing possession of, and authority over, their woman partner. When women ended their relationship with the perpetrator and established a new relationship with another person, many of the men viewed this as an "infidelity" to them and the relationship they defined as ongoing. Threats of separation and the act of separation itself often led to a shift from trying to retain the woman within the relationship to the act of destroying her for leaving it.

Most of the murders occurred in or near the home of the couple or the home of the woman if they were separated. The attacks usually involved beating, kicking, and hitting with blunt instruments such as clubs, hammers, and bricks, as well as choking and stabbing. Choking/strangling was the most common cause of death, and firearms were rarely used. Injuries were numerous; five or more were common, and a few of the murders involved more than 100 injuries. After death, most of the men inflicted no further injuries and simply left the scene or remained where they were, although some committed further acts of physical violence and a few committed acts of sexual violence against the body after death. After the murder, a few men tried to avoid detection by burning, dismembering, and/or moving the body, but most did not. The claims of perpetrators included total denial, self-defense, and a lack of intention to do harm.

Of the 105 cases, 16% contained a sexual element within the murder, and the proportions that did so varied dramatically with the type of relationship. Sex within the murder was least likely among those who were married and most likely among the more tenuous relationships between boyfriends/girlfriends. In this respect, the boyfriend/girlfriend relationships bear some resemblance to the sexual murders between acquaintances that will be examined in the section on sexual murders and the men who perpetrate them (chapters 6–7). In some of these cases, the distinction is blurred, as some of the boyfriends appear to more closely resemble men who murder women for sex than men who commit a sexual act within the context of murdering a woman partner. This will be explored again in the chapters on sexual murder.

In some of the cases, the conflict between the intimate partners resulted in the murder of someone other than the woman partner. Although the victims of intimate partner collateral murders included children, allies, and/or new partners, the conflicts and circumstances associated with these murders usually paralleled those when the victim was the woman partner. In these cases, the men killed someone other than the woman partner but for reasons that related to the intimate relationship and conflicts within it. Women partners were punished for separating by inflicting the pain of killing her/their child. Relatives and friends were killed for providing the woman partner with support or protection from perpetrators who were harming them and/or from whom they wished to separate. Finally, men murdered other men, and sometimes women, who were selected by the women as a new partner.

In the next chapter, we will focus on the lives of the men who committed these murders, from early childhood to adulthood, and from the circumstances at the time of the murder to later reflections up it.

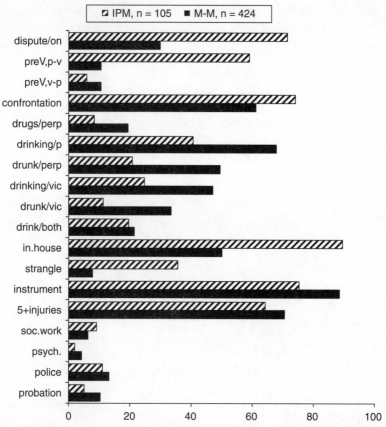

Figure 3.1 IPM—Circumstances at Murder. Male-Male Murder and Intimate Partner Murder.
* Statistically significant difference.

4

Intimate Partner Murder
—Perpetrators

Lifecourse, Orientations, and Cognitions

Who are the men who murder their intimate partners? The analysis in the last chapter focused on the contexts and situations in which intimate partner murders (IPMs) occur and the murder event itself. Here we focus on the men who perpetrated these murders. The examination of the lifecourse of men who murder an intimate partner includes several stages: childhood, adulthood, and imprisonment after conviction. The focus on childhood includes early family life, caretaking, violence in the home, physical and sexual violence against the child, progression and problems at school, early abuse of alcohol and/or drugs, and onset of offending. The focus on adulthood includes employment, alcohol abuse, and relationships with and violence toward women, including previous intimate partners. The time after the murder when the men are in prison includes: behavior and adjustment to the routines of prison; relations with prison officers, including women officers; responses to prison programs focused on offending behavior and issues related to change, including remorse for the murder, empathy with the victim, and dangerousness as well as notions of personal responsibility and the prospect of change.

First, the various experiences across the lifecourse are presented at length using qualitative examples in order to illustrate their nature and diversity. Then, the quantitative data are used to show the overall patterns and to compare men who murder an intimate partner with the men who murder other men.

LIFECOURSE—CHILDHOOD

Initial questions about the men who murder an intimate partner relate to those about the early experiences of the boy at home and at school followed by those about the man as an adult How did he begin, and how, if at all, might this relate to the progress of his life, his orientations, his behaviors and, ultimately, to the act of murdering his intimate partner? Beginning with early childhood and the family of orientation provides knowledge about early life circumstances and experiences that might be relevant in shaping later thinking and behavior. Children live their lives within three main domains: in and around the home with their family of orientation/caretakers and others; at school with teachers and peers; and outside in places of recreation in the community, the street, the park, the town center, shopping mall, open spaces, fields, and abandoned buildings. The amount of time they spend in each of the three domains varies with age.

As infants, the vast majority of time is spent in the home with caretakers, siblings, relatives, and near neighbors. Here, their world is primarily shaped by the actions, orientations, and caretaking of those within this relatively contained domain. When they reach school age, the child is no longer located almost exclusively within the domain of the home but also spends many hours of each day at school in the company of teachers and numerous other children, some who may become friends and playmates while others may become enemies or bullies. Home and school are both domains that, in theory, involve care and nurturing, learning and development, control and rules. In short, these domains involve numerous developmental tasks within the context of adult care, control, and restraint. Within the domains of home and school, various limits, controls, and rules constrain the actions of the child, and freedoms are limited and managed in a variety of ways by adults, siblings, and other children. The third domain of parks, streets, and the like is one of recreation, association with other children and adults, a world of relative freedom from the constraints of the other two domains more explicitly shaped by adult rules, oversight, and control. Although the world of recreation is also shaped by rules and constraints, it is usually less restrictive than the domains of the home or school. Given the choice, it is to this third domain that children may be most drawn and in which they may spend most of their time, but the dictates of home and school place limits on access to this domain, and some form of balance is usually struck between them in shaping the overall world of most children. Today this is also shaped by the electronic world of computers, the Internet, social media, and mobile phones, although these were unlikely to have been a part of the childhood of the men in the Murder Study, as widespread usage mostly occurred after their childhood years. Beginning with the qualitative evidence, we focus on childhood within the family and the school.

Family of Origin and Caretakers

Early childhood experiences within the family and with other caretakers provide an important environment for the learning of a variety of attitudes, orientations, and behaviors through observation of the behavior of others, particularly parents and adult caretakers, and interaction with others, including parents and siblings, within that environment. Interactions between fathers and mothers (and other carers) as well as their treatment of the child may range from positive nurturing and support to indifference and neglect, and may extend to physical and/or sexual abuse of the child. Some families had very few problems, while others were replete with problems of almost every type. The accounts begin with illustrations of families that were more conventional, happy, and unproblematic before progressing to those with more problems and more serious problems ranging from carers who were strict and uncaring to those who were absent or abusers.

Conventional, unproblematic, and happy
He is an only child and there is nothing exceptional about his family background: well-educated and loved by his parents (*288cf1.1.1).

No family problems. He went to a good school but left with no qualifications (*280cf1.1.1).

He reports a very happy close knit family and that he was very happy in childhood (*146cf.1.1.1).

He grew up in a family of six children, no unusual problems in his upbringing. He describes his childhood as "happy," although he mentions he was a reserved child (*1040cf1.1.1.

Strong parental discipline—but not viewed as a problem
When you were growing up what sort of things would you get into trouble about, say with your mum and dad? We didn't really have any trouble as regards discipline. It was a case of, if my mum said "no," it was "no," it was as easy as that. You just didn't go against mum or dad. You knew better. It was just the way we were brought up. We didn't really have any hassle. *If you did get in trouble, what sort of things would they do?* Oh, you'd end up getting your rear battered. And if my dad put his hand on my rear, brother you knew about it because he had hands like cast iron shovels. With working down the foundry and the pit, his hands were like lumps of rock. If he clipped you, you'd know about it. *Did you ever hit your mum or dad?* Oh, you're joking! No way! (*646iv1.1.1).

Childhood—strict father and soft mother, both died early of illness
He is the fourth child of a family of five. His father was in the merchant navy and was away from home due to his job for long periods. He recalls an uneasy relationship with his father who he describes as very strict, and he was chastised. He describes his mother as a soft and gentle person. Both parents died in their fifties due to heart attacks. He is not aware of any family history of criminality. There are no reports of learning difficulties and he left school at the age of fifteen with no qualifications and worked as an apprentice tiller. His work record has always been disrupted by periods in custody (*1120cf1.1.2).

Stability in caretaking but problematic and unhappy with an uncaring mother
How would you describe your relationship with your mother as you grew up? It was not good, it was quite poor. Not really a loving mother-son relationship or family as such, as I said it was almost like her and I lived in the same place because she had to look after me because I was sort of still young obviously but that was about it [his father left when he was two]. *You don't think she cared much for you?* Well no. I wonder if she actually did ever love me really, and wanted me as a child, I'm not really sure but I don't think that would be too strong. *Did she mistreat you?* Yes, from about seven, she did physically hurt me excessively too. You know, tell a child off, maybe smack him to excess. I suppose it was verbally, mentally and physically. *And did you respond to her, did you respond aggressively to her—finally?* Yes, I did start fighting back and sometimes I think now I would be happy to kill her, you know, that much anger and hatred toward her. I would have killed her

quite happily. *So, you started getting into trouble, thieving and that sort of thing?* Yeah, and I went into two Assessment Centers and then I ended up in long-term children's home. I actually quite enjoyed it. I had a big family with all the other kids. *And did you continue to act out?* No, I didn't get into any more trouble until I actually left the children's home (*1194iv1.1.1).

For the child, there were issues relating to the number carers and quality of caretaking including various forms of discipline that might extend from physical chastisement to physical abuse. In addition to the treatment of the child by adult carers, some children also grew up in families characterized by violence between their parents or other adult carers. For the most part, this involved violence against their mother by their father, stepfather, or other father figure.

Violence by Father Against Mother

He tells me he witnessed the violence of his father to his mother (*209cf1.1.1).

Was there any violence between your parents? I think there have been a couple of occasions, two or three occasions of violence. Not in front of us kids or anything, but during their marriage there have been a couple of times (*811iv1.1.2).

You say your father and mother argued? Was there any violence? Yeah. *Was this your father to your mother; your mother to father, or both?* I can remember them being as bad as each other but as I got older it was mostly from my father's side. *Do you know what this was about?* Very often money and later on, when I was a teenager, my mother found a photograph of another woman in my dad's pocket, so that started a lot of arguments (*1114iv1.1.1).

Physical and/or Sexual Abuse of the Child at Home, School, or Elsewhere

As children, one-fifth of the boys (20%) were physically abused (usually by fathers/"stepfathers"), and a small proportion (5%) were sexually abused. Such abuse usually occurred within the context of the family, but a small minority occurred at school, in other organizations, and elsewhere, as shown at the end of this chapter in Figure 4.1 and in Appendix III, Table 4.1.

Physically and sexually abused in children's home
I was about six when I was first put into Care and I think I was about nine or ten when I was in foster care. *Why did you go into Care?* I was beaten. *By your mum and dad?* Mother and father. *So how would you describe the relationship with the people who brought you up: foster parents, residential care workers?* I didn't like none of it. I was being physically abused in the children's homes, with washing up liquid, bars of soap, shoe polish, and [hot] mustard down my throat. *Sexually abused as well?* No, not until I got to my foster home. *And who did this to you?* My foster father. *Did it go on for a long time?* All the way until I left, from age nine to about

sixteen. *And how did your stepfather and mother get on?* He would beat her. *Did you see this?* You could hear it every night and he was always drunk. *And your mother, did she have a drink problem?* No, not as far as I know (*1108iv1.1.2).

Did you ever have any bad sexual experiences as a child? When I was 14. *Can you say a bit about it?* It wasn't a normal sexual thing, there was a couple of them and they had me down on the floor and they raped me. The only other person baring (except) you who knows, is my solicitor. It is not something I am proud of. I didn't report it. *Did it happen more than once?* Twice, when I was in the "army cadets," a cadet service not really attached to the army, like the Territorial Army [National Guard]. We went out on exercises and they taught us the basic training which held me in good stead for going into the Army. *Were these two other cadets?* Yes, about the same age as me (*1011iv1.1.1).

The preceding accounts of family and childhood illustrate the diverse land-scape of circumstances and experiences from the more ordinary and unproblem-atic to the more extreme examples of various problems and abuses, but it should be stressed that these are illustrative of different types of experiences and should not be read as indicators of the prevalence of such experiences, which are shown in the quantitative data presented in the tables and figures. Here, it can be seen that the general patterns of childhood caretaking and experiences were often not problematic nor obviously the cause for concern. At the time of their birth, 92% of the men's parents were married. The majority (71%) grew up in families that were intact with both a mother and father, and they were mainly cared for by their parents. When, during the interview, men were asked who was the most important person in their childhood, the vast majority spontaneously replied that it was their mother or their grandparents. Intact families are not always caring, nurturing, or unproblematic: 11% had a father with an alcohol problem; 11% had a father who was violent to their mother; and 5% had a father with convictions, although these were often of a minor nature. The parents of 29% of the men divorced, and 17% of the men had three or more caretakers apart from their birth parents that included relatives and foster carers. Overall, 13% spent some time in care or in various types of institutions. A minority (20%) grew up in a family that had contact with social services, and 17% of the families had contact with mental health services for a variety of reasons (Figure 4.1; Appx.III-Table 4.1).

School

At school, over half of the boys had few, if any, problems, and the majority were not disruptive. About half left school before age sixteen, and slightly fewer obtained some form of qualifications before leaving school (Figure 4.1; Appx.III-Tables 4.1 and 4.2). They experienced varying levels of success and achievement.

School—stable and happy with varied levels of educational achievement
He is an only child who left school at sixteen with good grades in English, mathe-matics and science at GSE Level. He has worked at various jobs, such as a plumber

and meat packer, and on the whole has been regularly at work, and was employed at the time of the offense (*1136cf1.1.1).

He is the eldest of three brothers and had "numerous friends at school." His aunts and uncles were in professional occupations, he left school at the age of 16 with four successful examinations in maths, physics, chemistry and English. He describes his early family life as happy, though his mother divorced from his father because of his affairs and she then had a nervous breakdown (*938cf1.1.1).

School—mixed experiences

You lived with your grandparents and really got on with them then? Oh, yes, they are more like a mother and father figure to me than my own parents were. *Would you say you were happy at school?* The last twelve months I was. I decided at age fourteen to join the army, and I was trying my hardest to improve myself in order to go to Army College. So, for me, education sort of took off from the last twelve months. I sat down and really studied. I got primed up to take the army exam and they offered me a full apprenticeship so it paid off (*1011iv1.1.1).

Would you say you were happy in school? Fifty/fifty, yes and no. There were some particular classes I didn't like. Certain teachers, I certainly didn't like. Apart from that, at school I was happy enough. Overall, it weren't too bad. *Did you have many friends?* Oh yeah, I had plenty. *Were you ever bullied?* No probably the reverse, probably I did a bit of bullying when I look back. *Did you get into any trouble while at school?* No, not really, never (*811iv1.1.1).

Failure at school included failure to learn, failure to integrate with other children, and failure to attend. When school is not a place of achievement, happiness, or success, it becomes a site of failure and discontent that may include disruptive behavior, truancy, or a complete failure to attend. Overall, 41% of the boys had problems at school and 30% were defined as disruptive, while 10% attended a Special School for those with learning difficulties and 4% were placed in schools for behavioral problems/disruptive behavior (Figure 4.1; Appx.III-Table 4.1).

Special schools—for learning difficulties

He is the third youngest of nine children and a surviving twin. At school he was a slow learner, had difficulties learning to read and write and attended a Special School. According to his mother he suffered ill health all of his life and has a poor work record (*1061cf1.1.1).

He had terrible problems at school with literacy and was sent to various residential establishments which he hated and described as "more like prison." All of his siblings are successful, have completed university and now are in professional jobs (*246cf1.1.1).

Special schools—for problem behavior

His behavioral problems had been identified by the time he was 12 years old and he was seen to have problems with his temper (*891cf1.1.1).

He's always been a problem to his family and all forms of authority. In his early years, he was slow to learn and cocky, violent, aggressive and an inveterate liar. He had no close friends and a tendency to be a loner, finished his education at a Special Unit for maladjusted children (*719cf1.1.1).

So at age 13 you went into a Special School? No; a Children's Home. *Why was that?* My mum said I was uncontrollable at home and she couldn't cope with me. *And how did you get on at school?* Rotten I suppose or maybe reasonable. I was average at school work, I wasn't exceptional, I wasn't thick, I suppose just reasonable. *Were you happy at school?* I'm not really sure I was happy. I went to school, but I wouldn't describe it as happy. *Were you ever bullied?* Not at school, no. *Did you get in trouble; did you ever truant?* Towards the end of my school time, coming up to about 13 was when I started to get into trouble, but before that no (*1194iv1.1.1).

Expelled from school, disruptive, and violent

How old were you when you left school? I was expelled at 15. *What was that for?* It was bad behavior. *What did that involve?* Well, eventually I *had* to hit my teacher because she called me a bastard and I hated that name. I think it's because it brings into question your parents, that's what I don't like. *You said earlier on that you were in quite a bit of trouble at school?* Yeah, smoking, drinking. *Did you get into fights?* It's funny that I very rarely had any fights at school (*217iv1.1.1).

Early onset of very disruptive behavior, care homes, and nonattendance at school

What about your schooling and education? Didn't have any! I got expelled the second year. This is a little infant school, apparently I went "do-lally" [crazy] with a chair in the classroom and they threw us out. *This is at primary school?* Yes, this is infant school, apparently. I went absolutely potty. I was having none of it. They threw us out and refused to have us back. So I then went to another Primary School and survived about two weeks before I was expelled from there. I was there a lot longer but I never went. And then I went to a school for maladjusted children. I only went there for about two or three months, I very rarely attended and that was the end of my schooling when I was about thirteen. Three schools altogether, and in that time, I suppose, total time between the three schools I must have had a maximum of "in attendance" of about three months. *So what was all that about, what was going on?* I'm not too sure. I was in care [homes] a lot, in and out of care when I was younger quite a lot. I did have a couple of tutors at different times when I was in children's homes, but that didn't last very long neither. Like, I was very disruptive as a child apparently. *What sorts of things did you do?* Oh, I was extremely disruptive. I'd smash anything to pieces. Why I was like that I don't have a clue, it was just the way I was, and that was it really, and then my schooling finished. I then went to like into a community home which—I was there for about a year before that fell to pieces and then I was left to my own devices really, I was just getting on with it (*718iv1.1.2).

Problems of the Child—Alcohol, Drugs, and Early Offending

Although obtaining educational credentials and the basic knowledge represented by such credentials is relevant to future prospects as an adult, other social and personal achievements and failures at school age are also relevant and include many of the daily activities and routines of the child. For some, the daily activities involved alcohol abuse (20%), drug abuse (14%) before age 16, and early onset of offending before age 13 (13%). Offenses were often petty but led to early contacts with the police and the justice system, including a few that resulted in five or more convictions before the age of 16 (12%). Fewer (9%) had been convicted for a violent offense before they were 16, even fewer (3%) had committed a sexual offense by that age, and still fewer 1% were defined as having a sexual problem by that age. Violence to animals was extremely rare. By the age of 16, a minority (13%) had been incarcerated in a criminal justice institution for juveniles such as an Approved School (Figure 4.1; Appx.III-Table 4.1).

Childhood—alcohol problems and fighting
Before the age of 16 did you have any issues of alcohol or drugs? Oh yeah, alcohol, probably fourteen or so, drinking cider. *So was this an issue?* Well, I'm a chronic alcoholic, but it didn't become a problem until I was in my late twenties. *So you started drinking when you were about fourteen? What age were you when it became a problem?* It's always been a problem. I never could handle alcohol properly. *What happened when you drank in excess?* Well, when I was younger that's when the fights would start. It definitely marked changes on the mental side. It just wasn't me, I used to lose control. I wasn't in control when I drank, simple as that. *When you were drinking, were you usually at the pub?* Since I were sixteen I could go in because I used to look eighteen. I only ever got in trouble when I drank, are you with me? I never got into any trouble at all unless I was drinking. It always seemed to be when there was alcohol about, that was the one for me (*811iv1.1.2).

Childhood—offending
Before the offense that brought you in here, what sort of things were you convicted of? Well, basically it was more burglary as a young child, a bit of deception and the odd drunk and disorderly. But I mean that was just stupidity, and was basically only for a short period of time. *Did you ever attend a special school, anything like that [because of offending]?* Approved School they used to call them, yeah. *What age were you?* Fourteen I think. *How long were you in the Approved School?* About eighteen months all told. Well, I just got into trouble with the courts - behavior and generally being a nuisance. *So, was it like a sentence?* Yeah, it was a sentence from the Magistrates Court. *What was it like?* It's not the picture that a lot of people had of it. I wouldn't say there was any brutality or anything like that. It was a place where—you are here and you should make the best of it. At the end of the day I wouldn't say it was hard and I got my qualification there. It was being away from home that was the hard bit. I suppose it's the same as being in boarding schools. No it wasn't a hard regime, no (*832iv1.1.2).

LIFECOURSE—ADULTHOOD

As adults, over half of the men were usually unemployed or sporadically employed, and the other half held jobs that were mostly unskilled. One-third of the men abused alcohol (38%), and a few abused drugs (15%). Some (28%) had a mental health problem that had resulted in contact with a mental health professional, and some were identified as having sexual problems (23%) (Figure 4.2; Appx.III-Table 4.2). Overall, the majority of the intimate partner murderers (IPMurderers) experienced various forms of adversity as adults, although a minority of them did not have negative experiences with respect to education, employment, and offending. This minority did not reflect the general profile of either the male-male murderers (MMmurderers) or of the majority of IPMurderers and will be discussed separately.

Adult Life-style, Employment, and Convictions

The accounts begin with characterizations of men who had few problems with employment, alcohol, or previous offending, and progress to accounts of men with an increasing number of problems and/or problems that are more serious or debilitating. Men were often defined as being of "good character" if they were employed and had no previous convictions. Problems with alcohol abuse were often cited as putting an end to the steady employment and were associated with conflicts with their women partners.

A man of good character—employed and no previous convictions before murder
Trial judge: "He was a man of good character and well regarded" (*810cf1.1.1).

A man of good character—murdered his wife who left him for another man
The defendant was a man of good character although of limited intellectual capacity who was attempting to do his best for his wife and children. The deceased wife was intelligent and left her husband (perpetrator) for a man of superior social status (*252cf1.1.1).

A man of good character—employed and seen as "not dangerous"—but kicked his wife to death
Trial judge: He is a man of good character with high local reputation employed in a steady [blue-collar] occupation and membership of local charities. Not dangerous and unlikely to re-offend. Prior to [the murder] he was a hard working member of the community. He owned his house and seemed to enjoy the rewards of hard work and conformity. [NB: The pathologist regarded these as the worst kicking injuries he had ever seen] (*910cf1.1.1).

Fully employed as a young adult
He lived with his mother while growing up and attended a local grammar and secondary modern school. He left school at age 16 and worked as a delivery boy for a local butcher but left after five weeks. He then worked as an apprentice for a ship building firm while living with his mother whom he paid for room and board (*955cf1.1.1).

Employed in various jobs, no previous convictions
He had no previous convictions. No family history of suicide, psychological problems, alcohol or drug abuse. His father is a retired Army officer. He apparently enjoyed a happy childhood and had a satisfactory relationship with his parents. He had various jobs: police officer, car salesman, security officer. He says he drinks 2-3 pints a couple of times a week, is a keen amateur photographer and enjoys hill-walking and gardening (*940cf1.1.1).

From employed to unemployed but with no previous convictions
He is the youngest of three children and was bullied and teased at school. After school, he did well in work and by the age of 21 was managing a vegetable section in a supermarket and at one point owned his own business and married at age 26. While in full employment, he volunteered as a youth leader and counsellor. Ten years before the murder, he had a serious road traffic accident and never worked again, although he did complete university (*1118cf1.1.1).

Various jobs, problems at work, and numerous previous convictions but not for assault
What sort of jobs did you have? Bricklayer, and that sort of thing, but I always got the sack for being late. I was always about ten minutes late, and they got the hump with me like and said any more of this and you're out. I can't get up in the morning, that's my problem (*892iv1.1.1). [four previous convictions, none for assault]

Employed and with previous convictions for assault
He's an articulate, convincing and self-confident man. He's been a loner most of his life and travelled round the country, working in hard, hostile, male-dominated environments [e.g., bouncer in nightclubs] (*646cf1.1.1). [three previous convictions, two for assault]

Alcohol and/or Drug Abuse

Over one-third of the IPMurderers had serious problems with alcohol. For some, it was the center of their daily life and a great deal of time and financial resources were spent obtaining and consuming alcohol. Issues relating both to consumption and to finances were often the source of conflict between partners. In some cases, alcohol was also related to criminal acts such as burglary to finance drinking and sometimes violence toward friends and/or intimates. Most did not view alcohol as a problem regardless of the amount they consumed or the problems that appeared to be associated with their drinking. Although drugs also figured in the lives of some of the men (15%), for the most part, the problem was alcohol not drugs (Figure 4.2; Appx.III-Table 4.2).

Began drinking as a child and an undeclared alcoholic at the time of the murder
You started drinking when you were twelve? About twelve, yeah. *And then what? Did it just kind of escalate or -?* I just carried on, non-stop. I never had any problems

with drinking. *You never had any problems?—[and you drank] as much as was available?* None at all. Actually, to be honest, I must have been on about four liters of vodka a day by the end. And I had probably slightly more than that a day. *So from twelve years on, your alcohol intake just steadily took off?* Yes, it just grew and grew and grew. I loved being drunk. *Straight vodka?! How could you stand up?!* I think I've got a high tolerance system. But I never considered myself an alcoholic whereas a lot of people turned round and said "Oh yes you are." *And were you taking any drugs?* No, not into drugs at all (*718iv1.1.2).

Excessive drinking at the time of the murder
Were you drinking at that time? Well, yeah. *Were you drinking a lot?* That's a debatable fact that, I mean some people have got a very high tolerance for alcohol. Others haven't, and I used to spend an awful lot of time in the pub. People said, I don't know where you put it but, you know, I was fine. In some peoples' eyes, yes you do [have a problem], but I've never been an alcoholic or anything like that. I never had an alcohol problem. *Were you doing drugs at the time?* No, I never did drugs. *Overall how would you describe your life at the time?* Wild! (*832iv1.1.2).

Various jobs, sacked for drinking
Since you left school how many jobs have you had? About seven. My first one was a gardener for the Parks and Recreation Department, my second one was a barman, the other was a builder and laborer, grill chef, hotel porter, and then I was a self-employed roofer and my last job was a security guard. *And why did you move from job to job?* Well, at the time, some jobs you'd have to leave. I lost a couple through my own fault, really, through my drinking. *What happened with the drinking and work, was it you turning up drunk or something?* It was my first job in the Parks, and I got drunk the Christmas week and got sent home. Next thing I got sacked from the security guard one. It was just boredom, really, sitting on building sites drinking (*217iv1.1.1).

Alcohol abuse and ongoing conflict with his wife
Do you think looking back now, that drink was part of the problems? Yes. The arguments [with my wife] were more and more frequent because when I had been drinking I was in a more argumentative mood. I said things that I wouldn't of said normally. You let your feelings come out. I used to let my feelings come out (*1011iv1.1.1).

Although the drug of choice was usually alcohol, some men also used other drugs. In some cases, the use of alcohol and/or drugs was related to offending and convictions either for the use of the substances per se, or because of other types of offending such as theft and violence.

Regular user of cannabis and crack cocaine at the time of the murder
There is no history of self harm or psychiatric illness, and no use of medication. He drinks only occasionally although he uses cannabis and regularly uses crack cocaine (*980cf1.1.1).

Using and selling speed and cannabis at the time of the murder
[Probation report]: at the time of the murder he was working as a taxi driver and
selling and using drugs (speed and cannabis) daily (this was his main source of
income and funded his own habit). He says he was using drugs partly to try to
control his emotions and temper including towards taxi customers. He is a very
aggressive person (*613cf1.1.1).

Previous Criminal Behavior and Convictions

Many of the men (76%) had at least one previous conviction for various types of
offenses including theft, public order, or violence. A considerable proportion (45%),
had five or more previous convictions, and 60% could be defined as persistent
offenders. Some had convictions for physical violence involving a minor assault
(32%) and/or a serious assault (14%), and over half of those with a previous conviction for physical assault, the usual victim a woman. Convictions for sexual assault
were rare (3%) (Figure 4.2; Appx.III-Table 4.2). In the following examination of
previous offending and convictions, we begin with men whose previous offences did
not involve an intimate partner.

Previous conviction—numerous convictions for petty offenses
So you've had convictions but never prison? How many convictions? Thirty-two all
together—fines, community service, probation, deferred sentences, attendance
centers, all the sort of smaller [things] (*1194iv1.1.1).

Previous conviction—fraud, theft, and fire raising
How many convictions have you got as an adult? About five. *And what were they
for?* Fraud, deception, theft and willful fire raising. *And the most serious?* The
fire raising. I worked in a hotel up at Scotland and they wouldn't pay me my
wages so I burned down one of the chalets. I got twelve month imprisonment
(*217iv1.1.1).

Frequent offender—a villain
*How would you describe yourself in terms of your offending behavior before
coming in here?* I was a villain, really. I did things that villains do, I suppose
(*718iv1.1.2).

Previous Sexual Violence Against Women
and Previous Convictions

Even though convictions for serious sexual assault were rare, 9% of the men had
committed sexual violence outside the domestic sphere, 13% had committed sexual
abuse against an intimate partner, and 23% were identified as having various sexual
problems or issues as adults although they may not have led to any form of official
attention or intervention (Figure 4.2; Appx.III-Table 4.2). Many of the men with

previous offending behavior that involved sex were the same men who committed a sexual act within the context of murdering their intimate partner.

Probation for indecent assault on a girl and previous convictions for nonviolent offense

At age seventeen, he received a two year probation order for an indecent assault on a sixteen year old girl. As a condition of probation he attended as an out-patient at a local psychiatric clinic. He was also convicted of willful damage of property, breaking and entering, and taking and driving away motor vehicles (*955cf1.1).

Previous rape of women acquaintances

Have you ever committed a sexual offense? Em—well, I've raped a couple of women, so I suppose it's got to be "yes." *Were they strangers, friends, or acquaintances?* I did actually know the victims, yeah (*718iv1.1.2).

Previous convictions and prison for rape, Grievous Bodily Harm (GBH), and attempted murder

At the age of 19, he was convicted of ABH [actual bodily harm] and threatening behavior. After release from prison, he was sentenced to eleven years imprisonment for rape, false imprisonment, GBH [grievous bodily harm] and unlawful wounding. The rape involved "binding and gagging your victim in order to carry-out the offense and causing serious injuries to her face and head. Also, you carried out an attempted murder about one month after serving the sentence for rape and assault. And when the attempted murder took place, you had only been released from prison for about one month from a total sentence of twelve years imprisonment imposed for rape and associated offenses" (*1132cf1.1.1).

Previous conviction and prison for sexual violence but views himself as innocent

He has numerous previous convictions and custodial sentences including four years in borstals, and 10–12 years in prison. His offenses include: 24 for theft; 2 robberies; 1 indecent assault; 1 rape and assault; and various other minor convictions for drugs and breach of the peace.

[Probation Report]. I also discussed with him three other previous convictions for offenses against females, the first being for robbery with violence and indecent assault. He said "I may have touched her somewhere I shouldn't have but that wasn't intentional." He does now realize however that she would have been terrified by the attack and how she might have interpreted his actions. The second [some years later] for theft, buggery, rape and indecent assault, he totally denies. He states he was having a sexual relationship with the victim's mother. When this affair cooled he started a sexual relationship with her daughter [the victim]. He was threatened by the girl's father and told to leave, but he refused. He also told me that the victim came across at the trial as young and innocent, "butter wouldn't melt in her mouth," and this is what swayed the jury in her favour. I told him that this account was hard to believe, at which point he became annoyed and refused to discuss it further apart from saying he didn't care what I thought, he knows he is "totally innocent of this crime" (*835cf1.1.1).

No Previous Convictions Before the Murder—Men Who Come "Out of the Blue"

Although three-quarters of the men who murdered a woman partner had a previous conviction for some type of offense prior to the murder, the remaining 24% had no record of previous offending for any kind of behavior (Figure 4.2; Appx.III-Table 4.2). Why not? What might this mean? Who are these men? The differences between the men with a history of previous convictions before the murder (76%) and those with no previous convictions (24%) have been examined in other publications and were reviewed in chapter 2.[1] Men appear to "come out of the blue" because they commit a murder but have no prior history of convictions. They do not "fit" the profile of an abuser who kills the woman he has previously abused, nor do they "fit" the profile of the majority of perpetrators of homicide, who usually have a history of previous offending and convictions. In an effort to better understand what, on the face of it, appears to be an anomaly, we compared the IPMurderers with previous convictions for any type of offense with those who murdered an intimate partner but had no record of previous offending.

These comparisons reveal differences in their backgrounds as children and as adults, but they also reveal similarities particularly in their orientations to and relationships with women. The men with no previous convictions for any kind of offense at any time before they kill their intimate partner were less likely to experience a whole host of problems across the lifecourse from childhood to adulthood and, in that sense, lived lives that were more "conventional" in nature. As children, they were *less likely* to have a father who was an alcoholic or had convictions, and they were less likely to have problems at school, to be disruptive, or to abuse alcohol before age 16. As adults, they were *less likely* to abuse alcohol, to have a breakdown of an intimate relationship, or to have used violence in a previous relationship. They were *more likely* to have educational qualifications, to be regularly employed, and to be married to the woman they murdered. By contrast, the men with previous convictions before they murdered their intimate partner were *more likely* to be undereducated and underemployed, to have problems with alcohol, and to have numerous convictions for a variety of offenses.[2]

Despite these and other differences in the backgrounds of men with and those without previous convictions, there were many similarities in the characteristics that were more dynamic and contextual in nature, and particularly those concerning their relationships with women in general and with their woman partner in particular. It is these issues that are most relevant to the understanding of some of the fundamental factors associated with the murder of an intimate partner. Although not shown in the figures and tables, the proportion of men with and those without previous convictions were almost identical with respect to the existence of a long-term dispute within the relationship at the time of the murder (71% and 72% respectively) and whether there was a confrontation at the time of the murder

(72% and 79% respectively). The fact that the disputes were long-standing within the relationship rather than something that had newly arisen immediately prior to the murder provides evidence that refutes the notion that the man somehow just "snapped" and committed a murder within the context of a relationship that had previously been without conflict.

For men with no history of previous convictions and whose lives were more "conventional" in terms of demographic factors such as education or employment, the murder may initially seem to come from "nowhere," but a closer look may tell another story. Despite appearances to the contrary, 46% of the men with no previous conviction had actually been violent to the woman at some time prior to killing her, although, for a variety of reasons, this had gone completely undetected or, if known, had never resulted in a conviction. In some cases, the lack of a previous conviction may be related to the fact that the man was gainfully employed and/or was deemed to be a person in good standing in the community such as the man of "good character" as described earlier in this chapter. Despite the differences in the background characteristics of men with and without a record of previous convictions, most of the men were very similar in terms of their orientations to women and particularly to women partners.

PREVIOUS VIOLENCE TO WOMEN PARTNERS

Broken relationships were more likely among the men with previous convictions compared with those with no convictions (84% vs. 52%). However, across all of the 105 men who murdered an intimate partner, the majority (75%) were considered to have had problems in their relationships with women, and 77% had a previous divorce or broken intimate relationship (see Figure 4.2; Appx. III-Table 4.2).[3] The casefiles were filled with men's expressions of negative notions about women and especially about women partners who were either explicitly or implicitly deemed to be subordinate to them, expected to provide them with domestic services, and required to remain in residence with them and faithful to them as long as the men so desired. These notions are most clearly and strongly articulated in the context of conflicts within relationships and men's use of violence as a means of asserting their authority and ensuring compliance with their wishes and demands.

Orientations to women—all women exploit men
He has three areas which cause great concern: his sexuality, his violence and his antipathy to women, and of these the latter is the most important. He makes a clear distinction between a professional relationship with a woman [e.g., his current probation officer] and any sort of relationship that involves an emotional attachment. If the latter occurs, he seems to regard it as a deliberate method of the woman to find and exploit any vulnerability he might have. He does not restrict this view to himself only, but regards this as the base for any ongoing male/female relationship. It seems that he rationalizes all such relationships back to his parents who obviously had a very bad relationship. He talks of his mother exploiting his father and having numerous affairs, and regards this behavior as the feminine norm (*835cf1.1.1).

Orientations to women—all women betray men and must be controlled

[murdered four collaterals] There would appear to be a common thread running through all of the defendant's descriptions of his relationships. He has tended to become involved with younger women, in some cases significantly younger. In all of his relationships, the woman is described as "betraying" him sexually and bearing a child which is not fathered by him. He describes in his two marriages, the need to teach his wives how to behave, cook, clean and house-keep. Failure to conform to his high standards on the part of his wives resulted in friction, arguments and the defendant taking his temper out on doors and walls. The overall picture that emerges is that of a man who feels a great need to control his partners, and very possibly his children. He denies the chronic abuse of alcohol and the habitual use of domestic violence in order to impose his will upon his family (*1090cf1.1.2).

Orientations to women—all women are either "sluts" or "princesses" and to be controlled by instilling fear

Earlier reports suggest his actions may relate to an attempt to exert emotional pressure on the women involved. He denies using violence within his relationships but acknowledges that he has sought to gain control by instilling fear. He reports identifying women as "sluts" and "princesses" and has stated that he prefers relationships with women who are less intellectually able than himself (*1036cf1.1.2).

Violence to Previous Intimate Partners—Specialists in Violence Against Women

As previously stated, the majority of the men (70%) had been violent in a previous relationship, and 57% of the men with a previous conviction for assault had attacked a woman, often an intimate partner (Figures 4.2 and 4.3; Appx.III-Tables 4.2 and 4.3). This and other evidence suggests that these men tend to specialize in violence against women and especially women partners, whether past or present. Their violence toward a previous woman partner was usually persistent, serious, and similar to their behavior in the relationship in which they committed the murder. Some also committed "collateral" violence against others in the context of conflict with their intimate partner. It should be noted that knowledge about violence against a previous partner may have only come to light in the subsequent investigation after the murder and thus would not have appeared in any records of previous offending or resulted in any form of intervention or action. However, the following cases illustrate past histories of violence to previous partners that were reported and recorded, and ended in criminal justice sanctions including convictions and incarceration.

Violence to a previous intimate partner—five years in prison

He previously received a five year sentence for wounding his common-law wife. He says he did this because she had their children removed from his care (after their separation) and put into Social Services [foster] care (*655cf1.1.1).

Violence to two previous intimate partners—used a knife and threatened to rape

The summary of convictions indicates that he has used violence against two previous partners and their families, and in one incident he used a knife. [In one relationship], when she broke off their engagement and asked him to leave, he became incensed; assaulted, threatened and attempted to rape her over the several weeks. She obtained a Court Order and forced him to leave the house and keep away (*651cf1.1.1).

Violence to a previous intimate partner—facial injuries and fractured both wrists

This is not the first occasion that he has attacked a woman with whom he has had a relationship. He was responsible for a prolonged attack on another girlfriend which caused serious injuries. [Police report] Following a domestic dispute he grabbed her round the neck with both hands and squeezed tightly. She ended up kneeling on the floor, he then punched her in the face with his clenched fist, knocking her backwards where she hit her head on the fireplace, cutting her head. She received fractures to both wrists, a broken nose, bruises and swelling to her face (*1136cf1.1.1).

Violence to two previous intimate partners—isolates, assaults, and tortures

[Police report] He claimed that she caused him mental grief like she did to her first husband. His two previous partners traced by the police revealed their physical abuse by him. He gains the confidence of his victims, then isolates them, assaults and tortures them for his own gratification. He violates them until they have lost all their pride and are not able to fight back. We have the past and the recent [pattern] showing him as a cold calculating man who under the banner of his religious "truths" has influenced and controlled his victims. This perpetrator is a psychopathic killer from whom women need protection (*256cf1.1.1).

Violence to Several Previous Intimate Partners—and Threats to Kill

All his partners have left him and the last two relationships have ended due to him physically abusing them. [During the murder investigation] Efforts have been made to obtain evidence detailing these complaints but the respective former partners do not wish to get involved and fear for their safety if and when he is released. He made statements to witnesses and his ex-cohabitee that he intended to kill either her, her new partner, or both (*944cf1.1.1).

Violence to a previous partner for 19 years—three times in prison

He systematically physically abused his first wife over the 19 years of their marriage. He was convicted on several occasions of assaults and was imprisoned for these assaults three times. His pattern of violence to his first wife and the victim of this murder were known to be escalating. Indeed, on one occasion he was charged with attempted murder of his first wife (*106cf1.1.1).

As illustrated above, most of the men who murdered an intimate partner had previously committed violence against the woman they killed and many had also committed violence against previous partners. For the most part, these men focused their violence on women and particularly those with whom they had an intimate relationship, and some also attacked/murdered others in the context of conflicts with their intimate partner. Their orientations to women and to relationships between men and women provide insight into their rationales for their use of violence and suggest the level of difficulty faced by those professionals who work with these men in an effort to effect changes in their orientations and future behavior once they are in prison.

GUILTY AND IN PRISON—TWO CHALLENGES

Upon being found guilty of murder, the men receive a "life sentence" with a specific tariff set by the trial judge. The "life sentence" means that they will be under supervision for the rest of their life whether inside or outside prison. The tariff specifies the minimum number of years that must be spent in prison before parole can be considered. In prison, they face two major challenges. First, they must adjust to the prison regime and cooperate within it. Not only is this necessary in order to live life within the prison but also the record of behavior and discipline is taken into consideration when prisoners are subsequently considered for release. Second, those found guilty of murder must address their offense and relevant offending behavior before they can be considered for parole. This is usually done by participating in programs designed to address various issues that relate to the possibility of reoffending should the man be released back into the community. We will first consider discipline and adjustment within the prison regime and then examine the process of addressing aspects of the offending behavior with prison programs.

Adjustment to the Prison Regime

The men found guilty of IPM received an average tariff of 14 years imprisonment that ranged from 5 to 30 years, with one man receiving a "full life" sentence, meaning that he would never be released. Upon entering prison, the challenge of adapting to the prison regime begins. It is noteworthy that as we conducted the research in several prisons, we were repeatedly told by prison staff that men who murdered an intimate partner were often defined as "model prisoners." They caused little or no trouble, adapted to the regime, and were generally not a cause for concern for prison staff in the conduct of daily affairs. As shown in Figure 4.3 and Appendix III, Table 4.3, one-third of the men were defined as model prisoners, although one-third were unwilling to participate in the prison programs.

It is very common to receive at least one discipline report while serving a prison sentence. This might involve infractions of a very minor nature as well as those that are quite serious. Two-thirds of the IPMurderers received at least one discipline report during their sentence, and about one-quarter received 10 or more such reports. When the men with and without previous convictions were compared, those with previous convictions were more likely than those without to be placed on a discipline report (66% vs. 40%) and significantly more likely to receive 10 or more discipline reports (46% vs. 13%). Overall, the men with no previous convictions before imprisonment were more likely to adjust to the prison regime, have fewer discipline reports, and therefore to be viewed as "model prisoners" as shown in the following accounts.

Model prisoner

He has never been placed on report. He presents as genuinely willing to conform, and mixes freely with staff and inmates alike. He attends evening classes and is a regular church goer (*910cf1.1.1).

He is no problem to staff. He is polite and respectful at all times. He has quite a few friends and, on the whole, gets on with most individuals on the wing (*1078cf1.1.1).

Unless seen and accounted for you would not know he was on the landing at all (*914cf1.1.1).

How have you been getting on in prison? Fine, with [having been in] the Army, the Army is a lot harder than this. The Army is good training [for prison] (*1011iv1.1.1).

Model prisoner—but important risk factors remain to be addressed

Their relationship appears to have been turbulent from the outset as a consequence of his insecurities about her faithfulness, and it would seem that this often resulted in his use of physical violence against her. Individuals with this risk factor often present as model prisoners who throw themselves enthusiastically into educational and work activities. However, this should not detract from the offense focused work which is necessary. Prison reports indicate continual problems with anger and aggression, yet he is supposedly not suitable for [the prison program on] anger management because his violence is instrumental and he is in poor health. He only gets one-to-one help from the Probation Officer (*934cf1.1.1).

Addressing Offending Behavior—From Denial to Responsibility

The second challenge is dealing with the offense and the offending behavior. The process first involves admitting that he murdered his intimate partner, then taking responsibility for the murder, and then being willing to undertake the process of personal change. This involves an emotional process related to the murder, including denial, responsibility, guilt, and remorse, and related to the victim, including empathy. The process begins with overcoming denial. Denial of the murder often begins at the outset of the legal process, with declarations of innocence to the police followed by those to a lawyer and continued with a plea of "not guilty" in court, and may be continued even after conviction and imprisonment. Denial may be wholesale or partial and sometimes continues for years before the man begins to admit to the murder.

Admissions may simultaneously contain rejections of specific aspects of the act, particularly sexual elements, and may contain varying levels of minimization of the act or responsibility for it. Complete denial may be steadfastly maintained. It may be variously modified at different stages in the criminal process or after interventions within prison. Others, particularly the victim, may be blamed, and responsibility may be placed elsewhere. Many of the following statements reflect comments made by the men after conviction and once in prison. They were made to a variety of professionals including probation officers, psychologists, and others, and some are from our own interviews with the men in prison. Beginning with examples of total denial of the murder, we progress through varying stages of acceptance of responsibility for the murder, and to varying levels of empathy with the victim. Although the entire process is shown, it should be noted that some men never begin this journey while others begin but do not complete the journey to personal change. Even after conviction and imprisonment, 17% of the men maintained that they did not commit the murder while many others were in varying levels of denial.

Total denial of the murder
[Two years after sentencing]. He is appealing and strongly denies any connection with the offense (*1050cf1.1.1).

He is unwilling to discuss the alleged offense except to protest his innocence (*1078cf1.1.1).

Total denial of the murder and efforts to appeal against the conviction
He continues to vehemently deny committing the Index Offenses and is pursuing his appeal through the services of another legal adviser (he sacked his solicitor). Until his attitude changes, little progress will be observed, no programs will be scheduled and specific intervention work ignored (*1090cf1.1.2).

His conversation revolves around himself and the case; he repeatedly and constantly states his innocence and becomes very emotional. He continues to strongly deny his guilt for the offense and as such presents a high level of denial (*093cf1.1.1).

Implicit denial of the murder by deflecting responsibility—blamed her family for her death by agreeing with doctors to turn off the life-support machine
How did you feel at the time of the trial, your court appearance? I just wasn't bothered about it. *And when they told you that her life-support machine had been switched off, did you have any feelings about that?* Yeah, I blamed her family. *Did you feel angry or upset?* [At the remand hearing], I remember them shouting, "hang him," and I remember turning to her family and saying, "You should be charging them" and shouting "You killed your own sister on her birthday. How could you do that to your own sister? Didn't give her much of a chance did you? Turned the machine off!" (*280iv1.1.1).

Murder without an actor—externalizing—denial through abstraction, depersonalization, and distance from the murder
So looking back why do you think the whole thing happened the way it did? I think I've had about ten years to reflect on that one, and I still haven't come up with an

answer. Not a real answer. I think it's a culmination of a lot of small things. If she hadn't been so deceitful, if she'd been straight-up front with me, it wouldn't have happened. If my own pride hadn't got in the way, it wouldn't have happened. If that particular evening's events hadn't actually taken that particular turn, it wouldn't have happened. A lot of small, insignificant factors made it into what it was, that particular evening when that **particular event** took place. A lot of things I could have done that could have avoided the whole scene. A lot of things she could have done that could have avoided it. It was just a whole group of circumstances rolled into one which *culminated in, unfortunately, somebody dying. But it sounds to me as though you're not a stranger to violence, and you can control your level of violence [worked as a bouncer].* But things got out of hand, like smashing the mirror up *and the knife coming out* [his actions], a catalogue of errors [NB: he broke into her house in the possession of two large knives and attacked the victim and her male friend] (*646iv1.1.1).

End of denial and beginning to accept responsibility
At what point did you actually say that you had actually done it as opposed to carrying on saying you hadn't? It was a couple of years really. It has only been recently I actually started trying to express, you know, what took place and why. I think I spent a lot of time trying to run away from it and not accept it. I think I finally realized there was just no point. I am here and that's the end of it. Unless I accept it and try and figure out what really led to that event taking place, I am never going to learn from it (*1114iv1.1.1).

Acknowledge Murder but Deny Responsibility by Rationalizing and Blaming Others

The complete denial of the murder may be followed by varying levels of minimization of the violence and injuries. These include claims that the murder was not as violent as described in the police and forensic report, or that it did not contain certain elements within the attack or specific injuries. Men may accept that they committed the murder but suggest that they do not remember anything about what actually happened within it. They may also suggest that it was "deserved" because of the woman's behavior, or should be "excused" because of his circumstances at the time or because of some real or perceived grievances in his past. Blaming the victim and/or factors external to his own actions or intentions, particularly alcohol, are evident in many of the accounts.

He had no insight
He had little insight into his offending, shrugging it off as "just something that happened" and that will not happen again (*1132cf1.1.1).

He was not responsible
Can you tell me about it? I wasn't responsible for my actions, 99% of all murders are one-offs, and 99% of all the victims are perpetrators of the act in the first place. For me to be an offender—I've been married, divorced, have kids from her, gone through a custody battle—there's no way I can be an offender. The Probation

Officer said that to reduce the risk of re-offending you must do this, this, and this. Rubbish! For me to re-offend, I would have to get married and I'm not going to do that (*719iv1.1.1).

He claimed the official report was incorrect
Whilst he acknowledged he was wrong, he suggested that the matter had been exaggerated and showed little insight into the seriousness of the offense (*1136cf1.1.1).

He accepts that he committed the murder but blames the victim
[Probation report] While accepting full responsibility for the murder and expressing shame and remorse, in my opinion, he has no real insight into the circumstances leading up to the offense. He said that the women he killed "made me feel inadequate," and that his first wife, whom he also killed, "was a very bossy woman you know" [NB: he murdered two wives] (*838cf1.1.1).

He claims to accept responsibility but blames the victim
"I fully accept responsibility for my actions. On the day of the offense, I was provoked by my wife's rages which made me lose control of myself and use violence. I never knew that my actions would result in my wife's death. I thought she was in a deep sleep. I only knew of her death after being told by the paramedics which put me into a shock." [Probation Report] He continues to describe the assault as "restraining" her and, as such, distorts his perception of his behavior. He informed me that when she went quiet he thought that she needed a rest and did not at the time think he'd injured her. His account continually minimizes the amount of violence used in the attack resulting in the "the traumatic rupture of his wife's heart" [a vicious attack involving stomping and jumping on the victim] (*1026cf1.1.1).

He blames the victim and claims he just snapped
[Probation officer] He insists his behaviour stemmed out of severe provocation from his wife's actions. He is keen to describe himself as a "henpecked husband" and states his wife was "loud and boisterous" and regularly used to ridicule, taunt and belittle him. He says he panicked and cannot remember a thing after the event, however, police information states that great care had been taken to avoid blood being present on the carpets and walls [he dismembered the body and hid it in the loft]. None of this behavior could be described as acts taking place out of panic. He is keen to express his remorse at his actions concerning the murder of his wife, but firmly believes he was a victim also. He states he was provoked on a number of occasions by his wife and, on this occasion, "finally snapped" (*9401.1.1).

A Few Professionals Also Blame the Victim

While the vast majority of comments and assessments by various professionals were detailed, measured, and insightful, a few might be described as reflecting notions that, in various ways, also blamed the victim.

[Consultant Psychologists] I saw the defendant for a brief assessment and found him to display almost typically, the consequences of the rage of a continuously castrated man. You are probably aware of some of the details of his history but essentially he lived a most anguished marriage with a woman who he finally killed who was the "archetypal witch." This marriage was certainly an extreme case of a sado-masochistic relationship with him playing the role of masochist and she of sadist. She obviously, by all accounts, took the role of a sadistic witch, who was going to torment, aggress and finally destroy him. I have a strong suspicion that he chose this woman as his psychological opposite as it were, he being the angel and she being the dark witch. These relationships are notorious for a sort of path-ological mutual dependency, a mutual need for the other to act out the other half of each other. I suspect that he has very deeply repressed rage, probably deriving from childhood, and I would not be surprised if the early history revealed a pic-ture of him being the "parental child" [that is] looking after mummy and having to deal with a very negative destructive male figure in the father (*940cf1.1.1).

[Judge]—He is not an inherently violent man, though he had thumped her once or twice in the past (which she asked for to a certain degree). He is highly unlikely to do anything remotely like this again [Casefile information indicates that he was an extremely possessive and violent man—long-term abuse against his part-ner] (*914cf1.1.1).

Responsible for Murder, but No Remorse and No Empathy with the Victim

No progress can be made toward reformation unless and until the offender moves beyond denial of the murder, which implies that there is nothing to be done and no reform is required. Remorse for the murder may follow, but even this is complex. The perpetrator may be sorry that the murder occurred because he is in prison and not because someone else is dead. Such self-pity does not translate into remorse for the murder. Among IPMurderers, 36% expressed no remorse for the murder and 49% had no empathy with the victim (Figure 4.3; Appx.III-Table 4.3). These orien-tations may wax and wane as men shift from one position to another in the process of personal change. Remorse for the murder and empathy with the victim may be expressed, withdrawn, and then reexpressed.

No remorse for the murder
I feel sorry for what I've done to my kids. I feel sorry for what I've done to my wife. I feel sorry for losing my head but I don't feel sorry for her death. I cannot feel for her. She perpetrated the crime and obviously deserved it [after divorce she obtained legal custody of the children, he "kidnapped" them and received a criminal conviction. He views her "crime" as obtaining custody of the children] (*719iv1.1.1).

[Woman Psychologist] He appeared cold and emotionless when describing his wife's death and was unable to describe his emotions and thoughts at the time.

No remorse was evident and he continued to minimise his involvement and transfer blame on to his wife. His behavior towards me during the interview [was threatening and] gives cause for concern given that his offense consisted of violence towards a female (*914cf1.1.1).

No remorse for the murder but pity for himself
After several years in prison he states that [she deserved it because] she had been unfaithful and told him lies [and that] there was no need for that woman to die. It appears his regret is fully due to his own grief [about himself], and he doesn't have any victim empathy. He has always blamed several other factors for his own behaviour, and he blames alcohol for the present crime (*836cf1.1.1).

[Probation officer] I could find no evidence of spontaneous empathy or appropriate remorse apart from the effect on himself. He accepts responsibility for the offense but tends to minimise some aspects of his actions. He illustrates a lack of consequential thinking (*944cf.1.1.1).

He showed very little emotion while recounting the details of his offense and there was little to indicate any remorse. On balance, he is more eloquent about the consequences of his victim's death for himself than the consequences for others (*1062cf1.1.1).

Denial, self-pity, and failure to recognize the position of others (survivors)
[After 5 years in prison] With a fatalistic air, he compares his circumstances with those of renowned political prisoners and casts himself in the role of one of life's victims. He explains his wife's death as a suicide. The logic of that enables him to see himself as a victim twice over: through the loss of his wife and the conviction for killing her. The poor relationship with his in-laws, their belief in his guilt, and the absorbing nature of his own sense of victimisation may explain the apparent failure to accept that his late wife's parents have suffered the loss of their daughter, and to accept [understand] their denial of his access to their grandchildren. He cannot understand how the grandparents do not allow him to see his children (*878cf1.1.1).

Lack of Empathy for the Victim or Others

The lack of remorse for the murder was frequently accompanied by a lack of any form of empathy either for the victim or for others affected by her murder. As shown in the accounts below, some men either could not or would not accept or try to understand the position of the person they attacked and killed or the subsequent effect on others. They had no recognition of the position of the other person or compassion for them either before, during, or after the murder. While some men acknowledged that they had actually killed another person, they focused on minimizing their own actions and expressed sorrow for themselves. Overall, there was a general lack of understanding of the views of the woman they killed as well as those of her relatives and friends. In short, a general minimization of the murder itself and of the consequences for all concerned.

No empathy with the victim

He is unable to understand the predicament and circumstances of the victim—his wife (*806cf1.1.1).

[Probation Report] I am concerned that he is able to intellectualise and distance himself from the murder to a great extent and shows little if any spontaneous empathy for the victim. His attitude and perceptions are distorted (*940cf1.1.1).

Particular attention should be drawn to his lack of empathy and a preparedness to take advantage of others. He displays a callous lack of empathy and egocentricity in relationships (*1036cf1.1.1).

There was no spontaneous remorse expressed for the offense, and when asked directly about how he felt about the murder his responses were rather egocentric saying, "both of us have upset families and friends. I miss her myself, who wants to see me stuck in here and who wants to see her having died in that horrific way?" He had little empathy for the victim, his previous partner and their sick child. Rather, he tells me "my offense is down to my being on drugs and how I felt when on drugs." While now admitting the Index Offense, he distances himself from it and describes previous convictions as "being trivial." He denies sex was involved but the post mortem noted: sex immediately before death and a "circle of stab wounds around one of the victim's breasts" (*980cf1.1.1).

Limited responsibility, remorse, empathy for victim or her family

One year after sentencing, he shows some remorse at the death and the effects on her family. However, he seems to have limited understating of the long term effects on her family. He continues to minimize the offense and told me, "she may have hit her head on the fireplace when she fell," and also that she had a scar on her head from an earlier injury so "that spot would have been weaker." He states a willingness to undertake group work and wishes to use his time constructively (*1040cf1.1.1).

Concerns of Professionals About "Dangerousness" and the Risk of Reoffending

For the professionals who work with and assess the men once they are in prison, concerns about the issues of remorse, empathy, and responsibility relate to questions of possible dangerousness and the risk of reoffending should the offender be released from prison. These are salient at the time of sentencing, continue to be relevant during the period of imprisonment, and are especially important in the reviews of progress when considering the prospect of release. At the time of the research, prison professionals judged 41% of the men as a "risk to public safety" and 42% as "dangerous" (Figure 4.3; Appx.III-Table 4.3).

Danger to a future partner, but not a risk to others
[Trial Judge] The questions of dangerousness and re-offending concern me. I consider that there is a real and continuing risk in any future domestic situation, but not outside. The risk may diminish but that is for others to judge at the appropriate time. The three [adult] children must be devastated. The youngest certainly is. I saw him in the witness box (*938cf1.1.1).

No remorse, manipulative, and a danger to women
[Trial Judge] He is without remorse. He is plausible and highly manipulative. Before his release is considered any evidence which may suggest he no longer represents a danger to the public (and in particular to women with whom he might make contact) will need to be examined with care. The defendant is a dangerous sexual pervert who killed his wife for his sexual gratification and his dangerous inclinations are likely to continue for the foreseeable future. (*1114cf1.1.1).

Dangerousness—no emotion, controlling personality, and history of violence
[Probation Report] He always presents as extremely cool and laid back and speaks very methodically and rarely, if at all, have I seen any sign of feelings. He is a very cool customer who is in control. Risk factors: he has a history of relationships that have failed, quite probably as a direct result of his personality characteristics which have manifested themselves through jealousy, sexual jealousy, wanting control, suspicion of outsiders, intolerance and violence. Moreover, he has been relatively successful in forming relationships in the past and I think, therefore, that he has the potential to form new relationships in the future (*1102cf1.1.2).

Egotistical, arrogant man who says he would do it again
He is resigned to events being beyond his control and sees himself very much as the "victim." He tended to minimise the extent of his involvement and the nature of the injuries inflicted upon the victim. He said, "I am such a jealous man, jealous and possessive." And later, he said, "I know if I am ever in the same situation again, I would do exactly the same" (*1060cf1.1.1).

Even in the controlled environment of the prison, some men treat women staff in ways that indicate a lack of change in their attitudes and behavior that, in turn, reflects a continued danger to women.

Problems with women staff in prison
For several years he was generally regarded as a model prisoner but after a few years it was alleged that he assaulted a female teacher. He says they were having a relationship and he stopped it and she got upset. He denies the allegation of assault. Continuing reports of his very excellent behavior in prison then another incident with a female member of staff that he had been pestering and said he was going "to have her." His sexual fantasies and drives are noted as giving cause for concern but he is still described as articulate, intelligent, plausible, and likeable [10 years into his sentence]. Considerable concern has

been expressed regarding his attitude to women who he claimed had always manipulated him. He is regarded as very dangerous despite his cooperativeness because of his extreme mood swings which give occasional glimpses when he lets the control barriers down. He is said to have very black and white views of the world (*230cf1.1.1).

REFORM IN PRISON—RESISTANCE AND PERSONAL CHANGE

During his sentence, a man convicted of murder will likely have spent time in prisons ranging from the highest security to the lowest security. He must work his way through prisons with different levels of security by "proving" that he has made sufficient progress to move to the next level. Finally, he may be sent to an open prison with the lowest level of security, where he might be allowed to make home visits and/or work in the community. In order to do this, he must participate in prison programs and achieve a level of self-awareness and commitment to personal change. Obviously, this requires going well beyond denying the murder and blaming others to taking responsibility for his previous actions and for subsequent behavior should he be released. He can only be considered for release if he has actively engaged in efforts to eliminate his risk to others should he be returned to the community. This stage in the lifecourse is very challenging. It is neither easy nor straightforward, and no matter how it eventually ends, the process frequently begins with varying levels of resistance and failure as shown below.

Resistance—Not interested in participating
He has no interest in addressing his offending behavior. Therefore, no targets have been established. He is an extremely dangerous sexual aggressor with previous convictions for GBH [Grievous Bodily Harm] and rape (*1132cf1.1.1).

Willing to work on other offenses but not the murder
He refuses to undertake work on the Index Offense, but will undertake work relating to previous violent offenses against females (*1136cf1.1.1).

Rigid thinking and unwilling to see the views of others
[Thinking Skills course] He does not listen to others' viewpoints. He is impulsive and rigid in his thinking. He finds it difficult to see things from another person's perspective, and so presents as being inflexible in his thinking (*1050cf1.1.1).

Failing to understand program content
He stated he could not remember the specific courses that he had completed nor could he explain to me what he had gained from attending them. This implies that he has not yet successfully confronted or addressed his offense related behavioral problems, and has therefore not developed insight in those areas (*914cf1.1.1).

Not able to apply lessons to real life

The "Thinking Course" tutors were concerned that he was not able to apply skills to real life situations and believe he needs to demonstrate them in his day to day life in prison (*980cf1.1.1).

Rejects professionals and prison programs, does not want to change

Have you been involved in any of the programs, Thinking and such? Not really. I've sort of been evaluated, but she's [psychologist] saying I've no compassion, no remorse, stuff like this, and I totally disagree with every word she says. She was telling blatant lies saying there's no change in me, and [being] in jail for as long as I have, how could she come to that sort of conclusion? She never even spoke to me really. I agreed to be assessed, but there's no way that would ever happen again. I've learned from that. I know that inside me, I don't need anybody else to tell me [what I'm thinking]. Half of these things these people [say], I mean listen to her, supposedly a psychologist, supposedly a professional. I don't know what she's basing her premises on, but they are not right, do you know what I mean? (*840iv1.1.1).

Beginning the Process of Change

Reflection and self-awareness are essential parts of the process of taking responsibility for the murder and other behaviors related to it. The professionals involved in this work must assist the man in coming to recognize how his own views of himself and others have contributed to the situations and circumstances in which he chose to act violently and commit murder.

Taking responsibility—blamed others before taking responsibility

Can you remember any of the feelings that you had when the whole thing [the murder] was happening? I remember feeling mixed up. My feelings were all totally confused, my emotions were mixed up. I mean one minute I hated her and then next minute I hated myself, and the next minute I hated her mother because it was her mother that kind of put her against me and told her to split up with me. *So she went back to her mother. So all these emotions were running through your head?* Yeah, but what I always said was that I hated myself the most. I was at fault, totally, but I was looking for something, I don't know. They've [other offenders] got excuses, they're looking for people to wind them up or somebody to let it blow with [to be violent], but at the end of the day you've got to live with yourself, and it's me who's got to live with it (*280iv1.1.1).

Taking responsibility—and not blaming a negative childhood

Any negative thoughts about your childhood and how come you've ended up here? No not really, at the end of the day you end up here because of yourself. That's it, I'm not one of these people who blame the circumstances, you know. Other people, they have worse lives than I had and ended up having perfectly normal lives, so I'm not prepared to blame my childhood on the way I ended up. It's not there. I might have had a bad childhood by some people's standards but, to me, it seemed reasonable (*718iv1.1.2).

In prison—wants to change from life of no concern
or empathy to a better person

Do you see yourself as someone who has actually changed since you have been in prison? Yeah, I think I have. Having thought a lot about my past, the way I was brought up, my whole life and married life, I have got to realize that, at the end of the day, it has been me. I have gone through life without any direction. I have just wandered through life without caring about anything and just screwed up all the time, made a mess of everything. I am trying not to do that now. Even if I don't get out of prison, I want to lead a better life in here (*1114iv1.1.1).

Taking responsibility—after a life of blaming alcohol and others

Totally wrong, these things [mistreating his partner and children]. I've gotta carry'em with me through my life. So I have a lot to live with because I know that it's all my fault. I can't blame anybody else, whereas I've always been able to blame other people before. Whether I've been drunk or not, I've always been able to blame other people. Today, I can't. I have to take responsibility for everything. That's what it is. That's what will haunt me actually, the first couple of years of coming into jail, I could have these thoughts, this-that-this, was their fault. No, it's not. It was me. I was the problem.

[more from the same man]:
Alcohol abuse—how do you start to change

You've got to be sick and tired of "being sick and tired," before you're ready to stop drinking or you'll carry on. But they also talk about a rock bottom, don't they? I've hit that a couple of times, but you soon bounce back up. It's a very strange, very, very powerful drug. Its cunning, powerful and valuable is alcohol. It were like [I was] pressing a self destruct button at the end. It's unbelievable, you know, I used to drink and drink. I couldn't even buy myself a pair of socks [even though] I'd have hundreds of pounds in my pocket. It was a mental thing, you know, so it's a physical, emotional, spiritually sick illness. With Alcoholics Anonymous, physically you can get well quite quick, if you are not damaged like me—I had some liver damage [in hospital several times for alcohol related conditions]. Emotionally, it can take a couple of years. The spiritual side of the program is ongoing for the rest of your life, but today I haven't any desire to drink (*811iv1.1.2).

Positive assessment of prison programs/courses and group work

So, what do you think of the courses? I have enjoyed all the courses. *Why is that?* Well, the Alcohol Awareness made me realize that I had a problem. I didn't think I had a problem until it was shown that I did have a problem [binge drinking]. It did give me a good insight into the facts about alcohol. I wasn't used to talking in groups of people. I am more of an individual. "Inmate Development" helped me to discuss things in a group. I think group work did us all a lot of good, although when I started I was a bit shy at first. I did open up. It made a good impression on me, [made me] quite forthcoming. Basically, it did me good. If I had known these basic skills years ago—to define a problem, to stop and think about it—what is easier than that? If we had been taught it in school, it would have saved a lot of problems. It was a very intense course, about twenty weeks, but at the end of the day when it all came together, I thought it was so easy. And I thanked the tutor afterwards (*1011iv1.1.1).

After prison, the future and a new life? [intimate partner collateral murder]

Last thing, when you leave what sort of things do you want to do? What do I want to do with the rest of my life? Well, I've a lot of amends to make to people, to them who I can. My children, I owe them a lot, you know, but like I say, things have gone on. Then, I was forty. It's gone hasn't it? It's gone. You never know what happens in the future and, what can I say, I just want to live another life. Maybe take up painting and decorating, I've done my level 2 [qualifications] and I want to do level 3. I've been able to apply myself and get the education that I didn't get when I were younger. I did alright at English, I'm good at things like that, anything like that, you know, words, writing and everything like that. I did well, and that was the first certificate. I'd never had it in my life, I never had a medal. That was the first one, you know, I kept picking it up looking at it—the first City & Guilds. I thought, you could have done all this. *But you still can?* Yeah, but I could have done all these things, I don't know with some guidance or something I could have done these things outside. Been wasting all my life, just wasted my bloody life. I'll be at least in my fifties [when I get out], and to try and get a job today in your fifties, you've not much chance (*811iv1.1.2).

COMPARISONS OF INTIMATE PARTNER MURDERERS AND MALE-MALE MURDERERS

Comparisons of IPMurderers and MMmurderers across the lifecourse from childhood to adulthood and after imprisonment are shown in the figures at the end of this chapter and in the tables presented in Appendix III. They reveal the prevalence of each of the many factors examined and also illustrate the differences and similarities between the two groups. Together, the findings provide an overall characterization of each type of murder and comparisons between them. In order to investigate the specific ways in which IPMurderers might differ from MMmurderers, the quantitative data are used to compare the child and adult backgrounds of the two types on a number of factors. Childhood experiences are divided into general areas relating to parents, caretakers, problems of the child, and the involvement of professionals with the family of orientation. Not all of the comparisons are shown in Figure 4.1, but all are presented in Appendix III, Table 4.1.

Childhood

There were statistically significant differences between IPMurderers and MMmurderers in all comparisons except physical abuse, sexual abuse, mental health problems, and five or more convictions before the age of 16. With respect to problems of parents during the childhoods of the offenders, the IPMurderers were significantly less likely than the MMmurderers to have grown up in families in which their parents' relationship had broken down or their father had abused alcohol and had a criminal record. One difference that was unexpected was that violence used by their father against their mother was more prevalent among MMmurderers (23%) than IPMurderers (11%). Social services and criminal justice agencies were much more likely to have been involved with the families of MMmurderers, which suggests that these families could be characterized as having multiple problems. Stability of and type of care differed, with MMmurderers significantly more likely to have experienced three or more changes in caretakers and to have been taken into institutional care before the age of 16. They were also much more likely to have experienced problems at school and to have been assessed as generally disruptive. Before the age of 16, substance abuse, not mere "experimentation," particularly of alcohol, was a problem for a fair proportion of both groups but was much more likely for the MMmurderers. Compared with the general population, early-onset of offending before the age of 13 was relatively high in both groups but highest among the MMmurderers, as was frequent offending and incarceration in a criminal justice institution before the age of 16. Overall, although a reasonable proportion of the men in both groups experienced a number of problems during childhood, a greater proportion of the men who murdered other men had problematic lives as children.

Adulthood

As adults (16 years and older), the two groups were compared in terms of a number of static and dynamic factors, including education and employment, personal problems, intimate relationships including violence, criminal behavior, and involvement with professionals. As shown in Figure 4.2 and Appendix III, Table 4.2, most of the comparisons revealed statistically significant differences between men who kill other men and those who kill an intimate partner, with a greater prevalence of problems among the former than the latter. The IPM group was significantly more likely than the MM group to have achieved the equivalent of a high school education and to be regularly employed. One-quarter of MM and one-half of IPM group were usually employed, mostly in unskilled or skilled blue-collar jobs. Chronic alcohol abuse, although a problem in both groups, was more likely in the MM than the IPM group (57% vs. 38%), as was drug abuse (35% vs. 15%). About one-quarter of both groups reported some form of mental health problem as adults. Around three quarters of the men in both groups had at least one conviction for any type of offense, and the groups were about equally likely to have a conviction for minor and/or serious assault. Persistent criminal behavior was common to both groups but more likely among MM than IPM (81% vs. 60%), and previous imprisonment was not uncommon (46% vs. 32%).

Overall, these results suggest that, when the group is considered as a whole, men who murder an intimate partner appear to be less likely to display typical criminogenic characteristics including various personal problems and criminal behavior and, as such, this group might be characterized as more "conventional" than the MMmurderers. However, it should be noted that this overall characterization of IPMurderers fragments when the men with previous convictions and those without previous convictions are examined separately. Despite this, the comparisons presented here treat the IPMurderers as a whole for the purposes of comparing them with MMmurderers. These comparisons reveal that the men who murdered other men were less likely than those who murdered an intimate partner to have experienced a broken relationship (61% vs. 77%) or to have used violence against a previous intimate partner (31% vs. 70%), and that those who had a previous conviction for an assault were far less likely to have assaulted a woman (11% vs. 57%) (Figure 4.2; Appx.III-Table 4.2). By comparison, IPMurderers were more likely to have problems with intimate relationships and to specialize in using violence against women rather than against other men. The absence of a criminal record of any type of offending among about one-quarter of all of the IPMurderers who may have limited the use of violence to an intimate partner may be a reflection of a period in time when such behavior was much less likely to be reported to police or, if reported, to result in any form of official processing that would lead to an arrest and conviction resulting in a criminal record. In that sense, the lack of a criminal record may reflect the historical reluctance to arrest and prosecute this type of violence rather than the lack of such behavior by the man against his partner.

In Prison

Once in prison, the men need to learn to live within the context of prison life and regimes, which requires working, living with other prisoners, staying out of trouble, and getting on with prison officers. They must also begin to deal with their offense and their offending behavior, which requires them to participate in programs designed and delivered by various professionals to assist them to address various issues associated with problem behavior and develop orientations and skills deemed necessary for their reentry into society should they be released from prison.

The comparisons shown in Figure 4.3 and in Appendix III, Table 4.3 characterize the two groups and reflect similarities and differences between them with respect to some of the tasks associated with getting on in prison (model prisoner, cooperative, and discipline reports) and those more closely aligned with reform and prospects for release, which include risk to the public, dangerousness, remorse, empathy, and problems with women, which is of particular importance for men who murder a woman. Overall, IPMurderers were more likely than MMmurderers to get on in prison and to be defined as a "model prisoners."

Although both groups were fairly similar in terms of issues of risk, dangerousness, and empathy, IPMurderers were far more likely to be defined by professionals as having various and ongoing problems with women. Well, they would say that, wouldn't they? After all, the man murdered a woman, so it stands to reason that he would be defined as having problems with women. It should be stressed, however, that apart from the assessment of these professionals, numerous reports of problematic relations with women are contained in the casefiles. These include police interviews with ex-partners, relatives, and friends as well as medical records, social work reports, and the like. Concerning the men's relationships with women and orientations to them, the comparison between MMmurderers and IPMurderers are stark and extreme, and stand in contrast to the cooperative, model prisoner who is not a discipline problem in the controlled and relatively male environment of the prison regime, where domestic relations with women are not tested and attitudes toward relations with them may continue unaltered.

The examination of the murder of women partners began with an exploration of existing research on this topic before a detailed examination of the murder event followed by an examination of the lifecourse of the men who commit this type of murder and, finally, a comparison of these men with those who murder other men—how they are alike, and how they differ. Across the numerous comparisons and within the detailed accounts of the murder event and the lifecourse of the men who perpetrated the murder, issues of gender and gender relations stand out as of relevance both in the factors related to the murder itself and many of the factors that characterize the lifecourse of the men who commit murder. Male authority and control over women, and particularly women partners, provides a foundation for extreme forms of possessiveness that are related to a variety of behaviors from extreme forms of control to physical and sometimes sexual violence used against women partners.

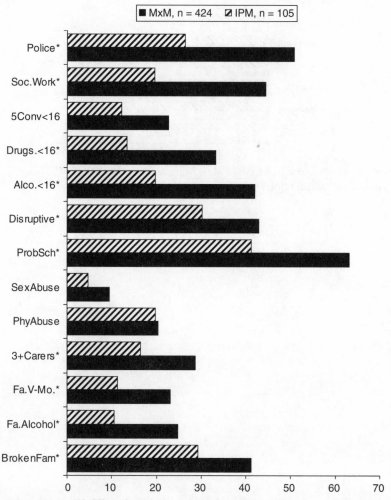

Figure 4.1 IPM—Childhood: Male-Male Murder and Intimate Partner Murder. * Statistically significant difference.

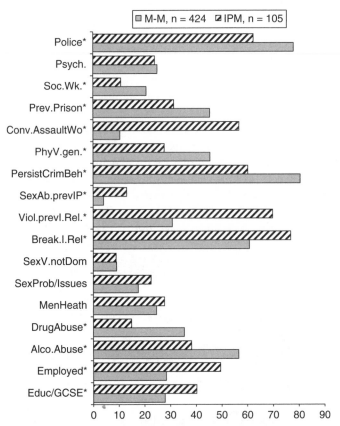

Figure 4.2 IPM—Adulthood: Male-Male Murder and Intimate Partner Murder.
* Statistically significant difference.

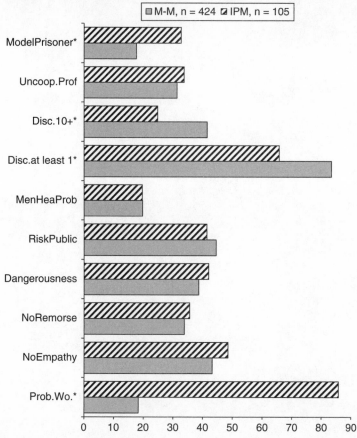

Figure 4.3 IPM—Assessments in Prison: Male-Male Murder and Intimate Partner Murder.
* statistically significant difference.

PART II

Sexual Murder

5

The Knowledge—Sexual Murder

FOCUS ON SERIAL KILLERS

Serial sexual killers have been a focus of public interest, concern, and fascination for at least two centuries. Public fascination has been amplified and consolidated by the representation of serial killers in novels, films, numerous television programs, and even museum exhibitions. The focus, however, is not sexual murders but serial killers, who are generally depicted as sex murderers. The beginning of a serious research tradition focused on serial killers appears to have begun in the 1970s, when the Behavioral Science Unit of the U.S. Federal Bureau of Investigation (FBI) began an investigation of unsolved and seemingly "motiveless killings" that initially focused on "crime scene patterns" that might assist agents in profiling offenders. The FBI agents found a "sexual component" in the majority of these "motiveless killings," and attempted to enhance the existing evidence and understanding by conducting interviews with sexual killers and gathering data from the official records in several U.S. prisons for the years 1979–1983.[1] They found that the majority of victims were females over the age of 13 and, perhaps quite startling, that 25 of the 36 sexual murderers were, in fact, serial killers who had committed three or more murders.[2] Based on this work, they proposed two types of serial killers, "organized" and "disorganized," and suggested that they were isolates who were driven by violent sadistic fantasies associated with a disturbed and disrupted childhood that resulted in negative personality traits.[3]

Even at this early stage of research, and in contrast to media representations, there were very few serial killers in the United States. In the 1990s, the FBI estimated that there were about 35 serial killers across all of the United States.[4] In 2005, Proulx, Cusson, and Beauregard noted that although the numbers of serial murderers were small, accounting for about 2% of all *sexual murders* in the United States and about 3% of those in Canada,[5] it is "hardly surprising that of all sexual murderers, it is the serial killer who predominates in literature—both professional [academic] and fictional."[6] The fascination with serial killers is not new, as exemplified by the case of "Jack the Ripper" that occurred in 19th-century England yet still resonates today and continues to be the subject of popular books and films.[7] In a similar fashion, the FBI study of "motiveless killings" with the discovery of serial sexual murders fascinated both the public and academics. The influence of the original FBI study and subsequent work based on it cannot be overestimated.

In an overview of the early literature based primarily on the 36 cases initially investigated by the FBI, Myers and colleagues describe various definitions and typologies based on the analysis of crime scenes and the resulting speculations about the backgrounds and sexual orientations of offenders.[8] In this literature, the stereotypical image of the sexual serial killer is of a man who not only sexually assaults and kills several women but also mutilates and dismembers their bodies, retains trophies from the murders, and has sexual fantasies that fuse sex and sadistic violence. Such descriptions emphasize the "otherworldliness" and "weirdness" of these men, and generally place them outside the realm of humankind with labels such as "lust killings/murders, compulsive, sadistic lust murders, and mutilation murders."[9] Some early explanations were bizarre and included notions of "disorganized sexual impulses evolving out of the pre-oedipal matrix of individuals," with mutilations of the body viewed as expressions of "the wish to re-enter and to explore the interior of the mother's body."[10] Others emphasized internal states or ways of thinking and orientations, suggesting that serial murder was caused by "a breakthrough of underlying sexual conflicts or where the killing itself is sexually gratifying."[11] Still others emphasized the fusion of thinking with contextual and motivational factors with "power, control and sexuality" viewed as leading to aggressive brutality.[12] Serial/sexual killers were characterized as sadistic, which leads to extreme violence and mutilation of the body of victims. They were deemed to have attachment problems, to be withdrawn loners. Beginning in childhood, they set themselves apart from and were indifferent to others. Difficult, conflicted relationships with mothers were stressed. Paraphilia, particularly transvestism, was not unusual, and violent sexual fantasies were viewed as an integral part of the daily lives of these men, beginning with compulsive daydreaming in childhood.[13] The themes of fantasies involved "dominance, revenge, violence, rape, molestation, power, control, torture, mutilation, infliction of pain on self and others and death."[14] Various types have been proposed, including psychopathic sexual sadists, crime spree killers, organized crime members, custodial "poisoners," and, "supposed psychotics," with offenders classified by location as, "geographically stable" or "geographically transient."

The Lifecourse of Serial Killers

Based on the 36 cases initially identified by the FBI, an explanatory framework of the developmental backgrounds of sexual/serial killers was developed.[15] They were described as starting life with "certain advantages." They were relatively intelligent, white males who apparently grew up in stable, economically comfortable two-parent households, but problems emerged. In 47% of the cases, their father left home before they were 12, 68% experienced instability in family residence and two-fourths resided outside the family home (in the care of grandparent, foster parents, and/or a state institution) before the age of 18. The majority failed to finish high school, and about two-thirds performed poorly at school. According to self-reports, many were physically or sexually abused and nearly three-quarters experienced some type of psychiatric assessment suggesting that most serial sex murderers experienced "trauma" and considerable disruption and disadvantage in childhood. As children, the majority engaged in chronic daydreaming, masturbation, lying, rebelliousness, destruction of property, and cruelty to children and animals, and this problem behavior continued into adolescence. As adults, aggressive and violent behavior was a common problem for 86% of the offenders. Daydreaming and fantasy played a central role in their lives and their orientations, ways of thinking, were fundamental to their violence: "These men are motivated to murder by their way of thinking," particularly when they feel that they have been thwarted "slighted, rejected or betrayed."[16] They react to others in an inappropriate and antisocial manner and are, in turn, not much affected by the reactions of others with egotism, grandiosity, and a sense of entitlement prevailing. Established ways of thinking and inappropriate responses to others lead to increased isolation, where aggressive fantasies become a "substitute for human encounter(s)."[17] An inability to relate to and empathize with others leads to escalating isolation and anger with a preoccupation with "thoughts of dominance over others," and eventually they are only able to deal with conflicts by using aggression and violence.[18]

One of the most commonly used classifications, or typologies, is the FBI's "organized/disorganized" killer.[19] For the "organized serial killer," the murders are deliberate, methodical, and committed against strangers. Such killers are driven by fantasy, take pride in their "expertise," stage their murders, and "commit sexual acts with live victims." By contrast, the acts of "disorganized" serial killers are "spontaneous," and the killers are more likely to position/stage the body of the victim and commit sexual acts after the victim is dead. Accordingly, it was speculated that the "organized" serial killer was an intelligent, socially competent man with a high birth order who used alcohol, while the "disorganized" serial killer had the opposite characteristics. While evidence from crime scenes and resulting speculations about the characteristics of the unknown murderer may help identify a serial killer who remains at large, such notions should not be viewed as a substitute for understanding the perpetrator if and when he is apprehended. Even more importantly, it cannot be assumed that notions about serial killers, however derived, can simply be transferred in a wholesale manner to men who commit sexual murder.[20]

In brief, the early work of the FBI on "motiveless killings" made important contributions to the knowledge about these crimes, particularly the facts that most of the victims were women, that many of the murders involved a sexual element, and that some of the men had committed more than one murder and were, in fact, serial murderers. Unfortunately, but probably not surprisingly, the unintended consequences of the focus on serial murderers had the effect that the resulting findings and speculations about serial murder and serial murderers were frequently conflated with those of sexual murderers who had not committed multiple murders. Although there a very few cases of serial murder and many more of sexual murder, the imagery of the one was and still is superimposed over the other to such an extent that it became difficult, if not impossible, to disentangle them and to examine sexual murder in its own right.

REFOCUSING ON SEXUAL MURDER AND SEXUAL MURDERERS

Over the last few decades, the study of sexual murder and sexual murderers has emerged from the early shadow of attention given to serial murders and the frequent blending of the two. With the sharpening of focus on sexual murder as such came an expansion of the definition of what counted as "sexual" that not only included rape and penetrative sex but also extended to other behaviors of a sexual nature. To the question of what counts as a sexual element, the answer has varied with differing definitions and the resulting evidence. By the late 1980s, the FBI researchers proposed broader definitions of acts contained within a murder that might be defined as sexual in nature, such as the removal of clothing, positioning of clothing, sexual posing of the body, and "substitute sexual activity" such as masturbation over or near the body.[21] Definitions of what counts as a sexual murder continue to vary from those that are quite narrow to those that are fairly broad, and most current research includes some or all of the broader elements across these definitions.[22]

Using varying definitions, national estimates of the proportion of homicides that might be labeled as "sexual" vary from 1% to 16%. In Canada, from 1974 to 1986, 4% of homicides could be classified as sexual murders, while a later estimate for 1991–2001 indicated that the proportion was 2.7%.[23] From the United States, national estimates repeatedly suggest that no more than 1% of *all* homicides are sexual murders, while a large Chicago database compiled over 45 years indicated that 1.6% of *all* homicides could be classified as sexual and that 8.6% of all homicides *perpetrated against females* involved a sexual assault.[24] Research on homicide in Jamaica suggests that about 5% of homicides of females also included rape.[25] An estimate from the United Kingdom, for the years 1985 to 1994 indicated that 3.7% of all homicides in England/Wales occurred in "sexual circumstances," and a subsequent estimate for 1995–2000 suggested a reduction to 2.5%.[26] Estimates for South Africa appear to be the highest—in 1999, 16% of all homicides of women (age 13 and over) were "suspected" rape/sexual murders.[27] The estimates for South Africa differ because they are based only on the proportion *of women* killed rather than on the proportion of *all* homicides. These estimates are likely to be more reliable than other estimates because the information is obtained from several sources, including 25 medicolegal laboratories across the country, mortuary files, autopsy reports, police files, and interviews with police officers, rather than solely on police reports.

Although prison-based studies of incarcerated murderers generally report higher proportions of sexual murders than those based on crime statistics, one British estimate found only 6% of imprisoned murderers had committed a sexual attack within the murder.[28] By contrast, a study based on Michigan's prison population estimated that 42% (2,476) of all incarcerated homicide offenders were sexual murderers.[29] In two Canadian prisons, 30% (n = 28/125) of men incarcerated for homicide had committed a sexual murder.[30] The Canadian researchers note that "sexual homicides may be more common than previously estimated" and that their results are probably "something closer to the true prevalence of the phenomenon" because of their access to more fulsome crime reports and information gathered from the perpetrators.[31]

The variation in the estimates of sexual murder in the research literature may relate to several factors. Police officers, pathologists, and others involved in the investigation of a homicide may not be trained to identify signs/indicators of sexual behavior against the victim at the scene of the murder or during the autopsy. The prosecution may pursue only the most serious charge against the offender and, as such, the charge of murder or manslaughter is pursued rather than any sexual charges. This may be done in deference to the memory of the victim and survivors. On the basis of our own investigation carried out in English and Scottish prisons we think the above estimate of the numbers and proportions of sexual murderers in English prisons is much too low. It is unclear, but these estimates may be based on the national Homicide Index classifications, which includes "sexual circumstances," but, to our knowledge, there is no national prison register of the category "sexual murderers." In order to calculate such an estimate, it would be necessary to access the files of all, or a sample, of those convicted of homicide and to extract information regarding any sexual element that occurred during the murders. The English estimates might have been based on a conviction for a sexual offense, for example, rape or sexual assault, that was also committed during the murder. This is, of course, a very imperfect way of assessing the prevalence of a sexual attack among those imprisoned for homicide, because for various reasons, as our review of 866 casefiles suggests, cases involving a sexual attack/element (including rape) do not usually result in an additional charge, let alone a conviction, for the sexual offense.

Another example of the problems associated with estimating the prevalence of sexual homicides comes from a Centers for Disease Control and Prevention (CDC) study of sexual murder. Using the CDC National Violent Death Reporting System for 17 *states* and a broad definition of sexual homicide, the researchers identified 193 cases over a period of 5 years.[32] By contrast, over a comparable 4-year period the FBI's Uniform Crime Report for homicide recorded only 169 victims of sexual homicides *nationwide*. Clearly, this points to a huge discrepancy that might be explained by a difference in definition, broad versus the FBI's reliance on the identification of rape. But the CDC researchers point out that the main source of divergent estimates arises from the FBI's reliance on a single data source, police reports, whereas the CDC estimates were derived from a range of sources including police reports but most importantly those of coroners and medical examiners of murders. Contrasting research results such as these point to the limitations of relying on only one source of data and suggest that the higher estimates reported above may more closely reflect the actual levels of homicides that should be defined as sexual in nature.

Despite growing recognition of the need for additional research aimed at identifying and investigating sexual murder, few studies go beyond the estimates of prevalence and straightforward sociodemographic characteristics of victims and offenders. The research is hampered by definitional diversity and various methodological limitations, and an overview in 2009 identified as few as 32 published papers on research focusing on sexual murder with some reporting on the same piece of research.[33] As discussed above, there are numerous problems in the definition, conceptualization, and characterization of sexual murders, especially, but not exclusively, those associated with the conflation/collapsing of all sexual murders into a single category based on the early FBI cases of serial killers in the United States.[34] Much of the existing research is based on very small samples, some with as few as 10 cases. Importantly, comparisons have been made between sexual murderers and men convicted of rape or other types of homicide, but even the most basic information, such as age and gender of offenders and victims, is often missing. Some studies include children and adult victims of both genders in a single unit of analysis, which makes it impossible to differentiate between them or to make basic comparisons. In their comprehensive review of publications on sexual murderers, some which also included serial killers, Chan and Heide found only 6 of the 32 studies clearly specified the gender and age of the victim(s).[35]

Carter and Hollin reviewed 10 studies that included sexual murders of women and girls age 14 or over. Most had small samples that ranged from 13 to 58 cases, although one Canadian study contained 305 cases (which only reported the sociodemographic aspects of the murders) and another from Germany contained 166 cases.[36] In identifying these 10 studies, Carter and Hollin used a broader definition that included sexual assaults before, during, and after the murder as well as other sexually related behavior, such as the arrangement of the victim's body and/or clothing.[37] Data in these studies were obtained from diverse sources, including semistructured interviews and paper-pencil questionnaires completed by perpetrators, casefiles, and clinical records. In the effort to ascertain the differences between men who committed sexual assaults and those who committed a sexual murder, most of the studies included a comparison group, usually men convicted of rape and/or sexual assault, but the use of diverse definitions made it difficult, if not impossible, to draw conclusions across the studies.[38]

Motivations, often intuited, form an important part of many definitions and typologies of sexual murder. Many intrapsychic factors, often similar to those linked to serial killers, have been posited about motivations including "sexual perversion," "a breakthrough of sexual conflicts where the killing is sexually gratifying," "sexual gratification through subjugation, rape and suffering," "symbolic sexual assault through insertion of objects into the woman's orifices," "brutally and sadistically killing the woman to achieve sexual satisfaction," and others.[39] One Argentinean study focusing on the motivations of 16 sex murders that involved "sexual intercourse" classified 10 of the offenders as organized and 5 as disorganized. However, determining motivations was difficult and included many factors such as "displaced anger, hidden sexual fantasies, cultural patterns, mental handicap, or toxic abuse."[40] Many of the conceptualizations of sexual murders, including this one, mimic those made about serial murderers by fusing sexual fantasy, lust, brutality, and sadism and defining the violence as driven by motivations, conflict, or problems inferred from the analysis of the crime scene. Occasionally, motives have been conceptualized solely or primarily based on power, control, and subjugation, which are driven by anger and directed at an individual woman because of her actions toward the offender or directed at "any" woman as an expression of anger at all women.[41]

LIFECOURSE OF SEXUAL MURDERERS

Childhood

An important focus of much of the research on sexual/serial killers has been the lifecourse, particularly the childhood of these murderers. When the lifecourse of sexual murderers and sexual aggressors are compared, the evidence is contradictory, with some findings indicating that childhood trauma and adversity are more prevalent among sexual murderers and others indicating that they characterize both groups. Some evidence suggests that sexual murderers were more likely than rapists to have grown up in a household with "controlling mothers" and violent fathers, and to have been physically and/or sexually abused as children.[42] In their comparative study of 40 sexual murderers and 101 sexual aggressors in Quebec (hereafter the Quebec studies), Nicole and Proulx reported that half of the offenders in both groups grew up in households characterized by alcohol abuse and that the same proportions witnessed physical violence.[43] Two-thirds of murderers and two-fifths of sexual aggressors reported physical abuse, which was significantly more likely among the sex murderers; they were also significantly more likely to report having been the victims of incest (21% vs. 6%). Despite these levels of childhood victimization, there was no significant difference in the average scores of the two groups on a Victimization Scale that encompassed the frequency and duration of victimization (49.80 vs. 37.86).[44] Although most studies point to significant differences in the experience of childhood victimization between sex murderers and sexual aggressors, this is not always the case and unremitting adversity has not been reported across all studies.

In his intensive interview study of 21 sex murderers and 121 rapists incarcerated in English prisons, Grubin used a range of measures of childhood adversity and found that "the killers and non-killers did not differ over a range of characteristics such as the incidence of conduct disorder, possible neurotic traits, or self reports of childhood victimization including sexual abuse."[45] He also reported greater stability in the families of murderers than rapists, and that the murderers were significantly *less* likely than the sexual aggressors to have experienced a change in their primary carer (45% vs. 66%) and/or to have experienced three or more changes in carers during childhood (10% vs. 36%), with 91% of the murderers and only 76% of sexual aggressors living with their parents for the first 10 years of their lives. Comparisons of the attributes of fathers and mothers, including criminality, unemployment, alcoholism, and chronic ill health, revealed that sexual murderers were consistently rated as more "stable" than sexual aggressors.[46] Langevin's comparative findings were similar, although the numbers in this study were quite small, with only 13 cases in each group.[47] These results suggest that the prevalence of traumatic experiences in the childhoods of sexual murderers and sexual aggressors is quite high but that adversity in childhood may not differentiate the two groups.

Similar findings were reported in a British study of incarcerated sexual murderers (n = 58) and rapists (n = 112) waiting to participate in sex offender treatment programs.[48] Using a multimethod approach including interviews, questionnaires, and casefile materials, the two types of offenders were compared on a number of scales, including the Shipley Institute Living Scale, Memories of Childhood, Multiphasic Sex Inventory, and the Antisocial Personality Questionnaire. The two groups did not differ significantly on a number of assessments, with over half of the men in both groups reporting being sexually abused as children (52% of rapists vs. 65% of sexual murderers), and about one-third reporting penetrative sex. While most men reported being sexually abused by a known male, just over one-third in both groups indicated that they were abused by a "female perpetrator acting alone."[49] This level of reported female abusers is much higher than that reported in most other studies of child sexual abuse.[50] In addition, the vast majority in both groups (82% of rapists vs. 68% of sexual murderers) reported being physically abused in childhood with, for example, a belt, although there may be a tendency to automatically equate physical chastisement with physical violence. This is not meant to excuse or condone such practices, but rather to note that the interpretation of such acts by the men that experienced them may vary in terms of whether they are defined as violence, abuse, or "legitimate" chastisement.

In the Quebec studies, Nicole and Proulx compared the childhoods of sexual aggressors and sexual murderers and found little difference in the parental and family backgrounds of these men but considerable differences in various assessments of their adolescent years.[51] About half of both groups was judged to have a learning disability, but sex murderers were significantly more likely to have discipline problems at school and to have achieved much lower educational levels. Although the patterns of consumption of alcohol and illicit drugs did not differ significantly, sex murderers were more likely to have started drinking regularly and to have consumed and abused illicit drugs at an earlier age than sex aggressors. As well as early onset of alcohol and drug use, sex murderers were significantly more likely to have engaged in other inappropriate and problematic behavior in childhood and adolescence including persistent daydreaming, habitual lying, reckless behavior, and running away from home. Social isolation and low self-esteem were also more prevalent in the childhood and adolescence of sex murders. Deviant sexual fantasies were evident in the backgrounds of a reasonable proportion of both groups, but significantly more likely among sex murderers (39.5% vs. 22.7%). The occurrence of "atypical sexual behaviors," such as compulsive masturbation was very low in both groups. Nonetheless, a summary measure of "inappropriate behavior" in childhood revealed that the average combined scores of sexual murderers were significantly higher on 16 distinct types of such behavior.[52]

Although the body of research about the childhoods of sexual murderers is small, several studies suggest considerable commonality between sexual murderers and sexual aggressors. While some of these men grew up in stable two-parent families, adversity and untoward experiences were common, including broken homes, instability, multiple changes in carers, physical abuse, and, to a lesser extent, sexual abuse as children. For many, especially sexual murderers, their own behavior as young children and adolescents was problematic and often marked by the early onset of disruptive behavior and the abuse of alcohol and/or drugs. Several reports on the backgrounds of sexual murders stress the importance of an increasing sense of separation, isolation, and loneliness, but missing from these reports is a more developed account of how this was manifested in their adolescent and adult lives. Here, the context of schooling might be important, but existing research usually reveals little except the age of leaving school, lack of academic qualifications, and existence of disruptive behavior. It would be useful to know the sorts of early behaviors that were defined as disruptive, problematic, violent, or sexual as well as the types of crime they engaged in as boys and how these and other factors might have affected their progression to adulthood with different sets of challenges.

Adulthood

The adult lives of the majority of sexual murderers are beset with increasing isolation, antisocial behavior; difficulty in relationships with others; criminal behavior, often violent; and periods of incarceration. In his comparison of sexual murderers and sexual assaulters, Grubin noted that the social isolation that characterized the childhood of sexual murderers persisted and may have intensified during adulthood with a significantly greater proportion of the sexual murderers than sexual aggressors likely to be socially isolated (86% vs. 45%). Although the prevalence of general types of offending was similar, with about half of both groups having previous convictions for violent offenses, over 40% of the murderers were diagnosed as "alcohol dependent" and two-fifths had previous contact with psychiatric services (the prevalence in the aggressor group was not reported). Significantly, sexual murderers were much more likely than sex aggressors to have a previous conviction for rape (29% vs. 7%).[53]

Comparing a range of factors in the adult lives of both groups, the Quebec data yielded only a few significant differences between the sexual aggressors and sexual murderers. Minimal evidence was presented about previous employment or intimate relationships, but a "high proportion" of both groups were reported to have alcohol and drug problems. Most had previous criminal convictions (81% of sexual aggressors vs. 72% of sexual murderers). The sexual aggressors scored significantly higher on a measure of "global severity" for convictions of crimes against property (112.7 vs. 49.5) and much higher on a scale of severity of sexual crimes (17.42 vs. 7.6), though this difference was not significant. By contrast, the sexual murderers' mean score on a severity of crimes against the person measure was almost twice as high as the sexual aggressors' (64.7% vs. 33.5%). They were, however, similar in age at the time of their first conviction for any type of crime (24 years for both groups) and at the age when they were first convicted for a crime that involved sex (31 years for sexual aggressors vs. 29 years for sexual murderers).[54] Oliver and colleagues compared rapists and sex murderers in England and found no differences in the type and amount of self-reported juvenile sexual offending between them. Sexual murderers were slightly more likely than sexual aggressors to have committed a previous sexual offense (49% vs. 34%), but the difference was not statistically significant, and rapists were significantly more likely than sexual murderers to have committed a violent offence. Overall, they concluded there were few differences in the backgrounds of sexual murderers and rapists.[55]

In summary, the existing body of evidence that compares a range of factors in the adult lives of sexual aggressors and sexual murderers is rather small and contains diverse definitions of sexual offending and different methods of measurement. Despite this, the evidence to date suggests few significant differences in the adulthoods of sexual aggressors and sexual murders.

Personality and Psychological Problems

Research on the mental health of sexual murderers is sparse and/or equivocal. In 1994, Grubin compared his own results about sexual murderers with the earlier findings of Brittain on sadistic murderers. In 1970, Brittain published one of the earliest and most influential pieces of research on serial killers, in which he emphasized fantasy and sadism.[56] Grubin found an almost total absence of nearly all the features ascribed to serial killers by Brittain, including sadistic fantasies and a preoccupation with sadism, which were rare among sexual murderers and rapists alike. He concluded, "If relevant, these features are more likely to relate to sexual offending in general rather than to sexual murder in particular."[57] For Grubin, isolation and anger, rather than fantasies and sadism, distinguished sexual murderers from sexual aggressors. However, a number of researchers have reported personality disorders and psychopathic attributes among sexual murderers. Early research, based primarily on psychiatric clinical assessments, biographies, and newspaper accounts of serial/sexual murderers, reported that almost all suffered from some type of mental disorder such as psychosis, paranoia, and schizophrenia.[58] These judgments were not based on systematic investigations and often used techniques such as the highly impressionistic Rorschach test, which has now been discredited.

Contemporary psychological assessments usually investigate the presence of some type of personality disorder, such as psychopathy, antisocial behavior disorder, narcissistic personality disorder, and borderline personality disorder. In Canada, Britain, and the United States, many studies and therapeutic interventions now use the Hare psychopathy checklist and label offenders who score above a certain level as "psychopaths."[59] The scales created to determine these "disorders" focus on a number of personality traits such as narcissism, grandiosity, emotional detachment, lack of empathy, and little or no sense of responsibility, guilt, or remorse. One of the major factors is "disturbed interpersonal functioning" and "impairment in their capacity for relationships with others."[60]

A number of reports suggest that a considerable proportion of sexual murderers might be classified as "psychopathic." Porter and colleagues found that nearly one-half of a sample of 38 sexual murderers could be classified as "psychopaths."[61] The results from the Quebec studies suggest that while a reasonable proportion of sexual murderers can be diagnosed as suffering from some sort of personality disorder, the prevalence levels emerging from their tests are much lower than those in other studies and, in the main, suggest little difference between murderers and the sexual aggressors. While about one-third of sexual murderers and one-quarter of sexual aggressors were assessed as "antisocial" and suffering from a "borderline disorder," the differences were not significant. However, sexual murderers were significantly more likely to be assessed as narcissistic (25% vs. 10%). The Quebec-based researchers found that mental disorders such as anxiety and psychosis were rare among both groups but that personality disorders such as psychopathy and borderline personality disorders were relatively common among both groups.[62]

Context, Situations, and Circumstances of Sexual Murders

The focus on the situations and circumstances at the time of the murder includes factors about the perpetrators and the victims at the time of the murder as well those that relate more generally to the murder itself. These include, for example, the characteristics of the perpetrator, such as age, employment history, offending, and substance abuse; the nature of the relationship between the perpetrator and the victim; interactions between them that serve as a backdrop to the murder; and the event itself as it progresses and unfolds. Also of importance is the nature of the sexual attack within the murder as well as behavior immediately following the murder and subsequent reflections, including denial of the act and/or rationalizations that minimize responsibility. Not all of these topics have been the subject of existing research, but findings will be presented for those that have been the subject of study to date.

Characteristics of Perpetrators and Victims at the Time of the Murder

AGE OF PERPETRATOR AND VICTIM

The ages of perpetrators and victims are not always presented; those that are indicate that most perpetrators are in their 20s and 30s and that they are fairly similar in age to their victims, although some are older. Although the evidence is somewhat varied, this age range is generally reported in research in Britain, Canada, the United States, and South Africa. While the ages of sexual murderers and their victims are usually fairly similar, there are two main variations from this pattern, particularly the sexual assault and murder of children and those of older women.

Some comparisons of the ages of sexual aggressors and sexual murders include the following:

- In their review, Carter and Hollin found that most sexual offenders were in their 20s and 30s.[63]
- Using the Quebec data, Cusson reported the average age of sexual murderers and sexual aggressors at the time of incarceration was 32 years.[64]
- In England, Oliver and colleagues found that the sexual murderers were younger than the rapists (24 years vs. 30 years).[65]
- Grubin found the opposite—sexual murderers were older than the sexual aggressors (30 years vs. 26 years).[66]
- In Canada, Roberts and Grossman reported that half of the offenders were aged 16–25.[67]
- South African research found that both sexual murderers and other homicide perpetrators were usually in their mid-20s or early 30s, although sexual murderers were generally about 7 years older than their victims while there was only 1 year's age difference in other types of murders.[68]

Grubin's evidence points to a potentially significant age disparity between victims and offenders. He found that the average age of victims of sexual murder was 38 while victims of sexual assault were much younger (age 28). He notes that in contrast to sexual aggressors, sexual murderers were much more likely to have killed a woman who was at least 10 years older than himself. Grubin seems to have uncovered the possibility that sexual murderers, in contrast to sexual aggressors, target older women.[69] This parallels findings from South Africa and England, with the latter indicating that 16% of sexual murderers killed a woman over the age of 65 while only 6% of rapists attacked a woman in this age group.[70]

A note of caution about figures in homicide research: When both children and adults are included in the calculations of the average age of victims of murder or sexual assault, the results are often both misleading and unhelpful in trying to understand how the different ages of perpetrators and victims might be related to events that end in murder. For example, Oliver and colleagues reported the age of victims of rape as ranging from 3 to 88 years and victims of murder ranging from 7 to 86 years.[71] While the stated range of ages is no doubt correct and may be useful for some purposes, it is easy to see how a figure based on the midpoint (the median) between them (i.e., 42.5 years and 39.5 years) would be misleading, as would a calculation based on the average age of each group. The resulting impression that victims of sexual murder and victims of rape are all about 40 years old would be erroneous and would lead to a wholesale misrepresentation of the actual age of the respective victims and of what, if anything, age might have to do with the dynamics of the events being examined. This is not meant to imply that these researchers used the figures in this way but, rather, to illustrate how the use of even an apparently straightforward calculation such as an average age might be useful for one purpose but may be misleading for another.

The overall findings about the age of perpetrators and victims indicate that sexual murderers are generally in their 20s and 30s and that they are usually fairly similar in age to their victims although often a few years older. Cases that involve a wide difference in the ages of perpetrators and victims are apparently more likely among those that end in a murder rather than a rape or sexual assault. To be clear, this means that in the minority of sexual murders in which there is a wide disparity between the age of the perpetrator and the age of the victim, this usually involves a younger man murdering an older woman and in some reports a much older woman.[72] The cases involving the murder of an older woman that involve a sexual attack/element are not considered in this section, but will be presented in Part III, which focuses on the murder of older women.

Situations, Circumstances, and Decisions Relating to Sexual Murderers

In their comparative study of sexual murderers and rapists in England, Oliver and colleagues found that at the time of the offense, 12% of rapists and 38% of sexual murderers were *not* in an intimate relationship.[73] Grubin found that the vast majority of sexual murderers were living on their own at the time of the murder, most were not in an intimate relationship and only a few had meaningful social contacts. He concluded that one of the most robust findings from his study related to social isolation that began in childhood and extended into adulthood. The men also reported being angry, either continuously or just before or during the murder and particularly when the victim resisted.

Grubin also found that one-third of the sexual murderers gained access to their victim by breaking into her home and another third stalked the woman. Strangulation was the main form of violence in 67% of the sexual murders, and knives were present in 38% of the murders, although only 10% of the attacks involved stabbing. Only one murder involved the use of a firearm, and it was used to shoot the victim's male companion before using the barrel of the gun to beat her to death. With only one exception, Grubin found that the violence used in the sexual murders was "extreme," and that some offenders reported a sexual dysfunction, such as premature ejaculation or an inability to ejaculate, during the murder, which they described as provoking their anger and leading to violence. Of the 21 sexual murderers, 7 had sexual intercourse with the woman when she was either unconscious or already dead, and most of them had consumed alcohol just before the murder, although only 2 were assessed as alcohol dependent. Although other comparisons were made of the men who committed a sexual act against a woman before her death and those who committed such an act after she had died, the numbers are so small it is difficult to draw conclusions about the possible differences in these two groups of men.[74]

Using data from the Quebec studies, Chene and Cusson conducted a "scene-by-scene" analysis of events that resulted in death compared with those that did not in order to determine the differences between them. Using a "rational choice" model, they note that while "sexual murder may appear irrational, it is not."[75] Although violent acts are usually purposeful and often involve a fixed intention to do harm, it is difficult to conduct a "scene-by-scene" analysis of murder. Usually, there is no witness, which means that such an analysis is likely to be based on police reports and/or the accounts of the men who commit the murder. Police reports, although useful in many respects, usually contain overall summaries of events and may not include the level of minute-by-minute detail required for a "scene-by-scene" analysis. While perpetrators sometimes offer full and detailed accounts of their violence and the circumstances preceding it, their accounts are often partial and they may be selective in revealing only those details that reflect more favorably on their actions. What perpetrators can provide are their own views, perspectives, and orientations about their behavior and interpretations and their own explanations and justifications that may, in turn, be used to extend knowledge about how they see their own violence and the rationales they provide for it. However, considerable caution must be used in the wholesale use of such information as though it is an unproblematic account of a "scene-by-scene" progression of events.

In the "scene-by-scene" analysis, Chene and Cusson construct a "decision tree" composed of *three pathways*: two that lead to a sexual assault and one that leads to a sexual murder.[76] In the two pathways leading to a nonlethal sexual assault, the perpetrator is not angry and the victim is not a family member or an intimate partner. However, the two nonlethal pathways differ in whether or not the victim resist. By contrast, the pathway to a sexual murder includes premurder anger of the offender, a victim who is not a family member or an intimate partner (i.e., a stranger or acquaintance), the use of a weapon, and a victim who resists either "verbally or physically." Alcohol consumption appears to be implicated in the sexual murders, although the importance of "consumption" in contrast to inebriation is not discussed.

Of all the potentially important situational factors, Chene and Cusson stress, "the attack is most likely to end in a sexual murder when the victim resists."[77] The researchers are very aware of the potential for victim blaming in this finding and offer a nuanced interpretation of the results. They note that resistance may be "the victim's adaptation to an extremely violent attack" that may be driven, at least in part, by anger and therefore be more brutal. As such, resistance to an attack that is particularly brutal should not be interpreted as implying that it is the act of the resistance that results in a lethal outcome but, rather, that the ferocity of the attack is such that murder as well as forced sex were intended from the outset. These brutal attacks were also much more likely to involve the use of a weapon, which also increases the likelihood of death.

The researchers do not fully consider the potential importance of the relationship between the murderer and the victim in the step-by-step sequence leading to a sexual murder. The men who murder are more likely to attack a stranger or an acquaintance, possibly of very short duration, which means that the perpetrator will, of necessity, have taken their victim by surprise and with an attack that is sufficiently fierce to quickly overwhelm her. Being "taken by surprise" may result in a defensive response in which the woman is fighting not to be raped and may also be fighting for her life, which may increase the likelihood of a heightened response from the man. This means that while it is important to understand the physical nature of the attack it is also important to fully understand the relationship between the victim and offender as a potentially important aspect of the murder.

Although the use of the decision tree is interesting, the number of cases included in the murder pathway is very small—only 9 murders out of 34 valid cases include all of the four relevant factors judged to be associated with sexual murder. The researchers stress that situational and circumstantial factors are important and conclude that few of the murders are premeditated and "intentional" and that sexual murders "may be the result of "accidents" or "escalation" or "simple assaults gone wrong."[78] While agreeing that the original intention may have focused on forcing sex and not on committing a murder in doing so, these conclusions are surprising for researchers who begin by endorsing a rational choice model of (purposeful) violent behavior. Whether the murderers intended to kill is, of course, important, but we must also ask whether the perpetrators were prepared to inflict severe, even fatal, violence on the victim in order to obtain sex from her. And, if they encountered resistance, did they decide to "change the project" by increasing the level of violence in order to obtain sex and also to "punish" the woman for resisting. Overall, the men appear to be reckless to the consequences of their acts. Additionally, descriptions that point to "accidents" may be solely based on the account of the perpetrator, who might very well suggest the victim resisted or "fought back" as a way of rationalizing his violence, indeed, he might suggest the murder occurred in "self defense."

SUMMARY

Much of the literature about sexual murder has been highly skewed by the characterization of the 36 serial killers initially developed by the FBI in the 1980s. The FBI profile was intended to assist investigations of unexplained murders through an examination of information gathered at the scene of the crime. Subsequent research and interpretations of sexual murders were much influenced by the explanations and classifications produced by the FBI researchers. It also seems that media and academic discourses merged and intermingled, resulting in possible misrepresentation of serial killers that portrayed them all as fantasizing, sadistic, and crazed killers who commit murder in order to achieve sexual gratification. There may be a few such individuals, but they do not represent the vast majority of sexual murderers or even serial killers. For some time, and still today, commentators and researchers have conflated serial and sexual killers usually without producing evidence that might demonstrate similarities. Gradually researchers are overcoming the fascination with serial killers and moving beyond a simple equation that transfers the assumptions and conceptualizations associated with serial killers to those associated with the sexual murder of only one woman.

Efforts to move beyond the lumping together of serial murders and sexual murders have not been directed at a straightforward disentangling of the two but have instead refocused attention on sexual murder and sexual murderers by comparing them with men convicted of rape. Although it is sexual murders, and not serial sexual murders, that constitute the vast majority of murders involving a sexual element, perhaps somewhat surprisingly there has not been a great deal of research on such murder. Those studies that do exist have presented numerous challenges and problems, making it difficult to disentangle and interpret results. Similarities or differences in results may not arise because of evidence but because the definitions, conceptualizations, and methodologies of research efforts make it difficult to compare research results. This means it is also difficult to arrive at generalizations about sexual murder or to draw comparisons with other offenses such as rape and sexual assault that do not have a lethal outcome or to compare them with other types of murder that do not involve a sexual element.

Problems with research on sexual murder include, for example, definitions that vary from the very narrow that only include rape to broader definitions that include the positioning of the body; sexual attacks on the woman's body before, during, and after the murder; and behavior such as masturbation on or near the body. Importantly, broad definitions are now more common in research efforts, yet this is not always standard. Other problems include the use of very small samples, samples that do not differentiate the victims by gender or age, and results that do not present the most basic information about the perpetrator and/or victim. Conceptualizations and the specification of relevant variables have sometimes been weak, so that it is difficult to ascertain what characteristics and behaviors are being studied. In short, researchers have faced numerous problems and challenges in attempts to examine sexual murder in a fashion that is more meaningful than procedures that automatically conflate serial and sexual murders. As such, upon completing their systematic review of 32 reports of research on sexual murder, Chan and Heide concluded, "Studies of sexual homicides are still in their preliminary stages" and research procedures do not generally lead to "reliable" results.[79] Carter and Hollin drew similar conclusions from their comprehensive review of 10 studies of sexual murder.

Despite these problems, it is possible to draw some general conclusions. It seems clear that what is known about serial murders and serial murderers cannot and should not be used uncritically as a basis of knowledge about sexual murders and sexual murderers. For the most part, with some exceptions, many of the characteristics of serial killers are not apparent in sexual murders. For example, while claims about persistent sexual fantasies involving sadistic orientations and violent actions associated with them may be common among serial killers, they are very rare among sexual murderers. While sexual murders do not constitute a large proportion of all homicides, the emerging evidence points to the possibility that a significant proportion of the murders of women are sexual in nature. The problem with most current estimates is that they generally rely on only one source of data, usually the police. Although police reports of murders are usually very informative, many police officers and other criminal justice professionals may not be trained to search for indicators of a sexual component within the context of a murder. Additionally, as discussed above and in earlier chapters, most national datasets that rely solely or primarily on criminal justice reports of homicide suffer from problems that threaten their reliability. As shown in the reports from South Africa and the CDC in the United States, using more than one source of information, especially from autopsies and coroner's reports, produces higher prevalence levels and estimates that are more reliable. The CDC database is clearly an example of a more meaningful approach to obtaining estimates of sexual murders, and developments in other countries suggest that new procedures may produce more valid and reliable estimates.

Research focusing on the perpetrators of sexual murders that compares them to rapists/sexual aggressors presents mixed results, although there are some clear patterns. Problems in childhood, such as difficulties in the family of orientation, disruptive behavior at school, sexual and/or physical abuse or victimization, and substance abuse, appear to be relatively prevalent in the backgrounds of sexual aggressors and sexual murderers. However, some research suggests that physical and sexual abuse is more likely among sexual murderers, while other comparisons show that sexual murderers were much more likely than sexual aggressors to have grown up in a relatively conventional family and were less likely to be abused. Importantly, the levels of problematic families and problematic behavior in the childhood and adolescent backgrounds of both types are much higher than would be expected in the general population. One of the persistent patterns that distinguish the two types of sexual aggressors is the emergence in the childhoods of sexual murderers of loneliness, isolation, and difficulty in relationships with others.

While much of the lifecourse evidence only relates to developmental aspects of childhood, a few researchers have investigated the adult lives of sexual murderers and found that the isolation that begins in childhood persists and probably increases as they move into adulthood. For example, the evidence suggests that in contrast to sexual aggressors, sexual murders were less likely at the time of the murder to be in an intimate relationship and more likely to never have been in such a relationship. As adults, many of the men were not able to form meaningful intimate relationships, and many had problems relating to others, which might, in turn, reflect problems of loneliness, isolation, anger, and a lack of empathy. Loneliness was also apparent in the backgrounds of the initial group of serial killers investigated by the FBI, and this attribute constituted a significant aspect of the explanation of the serial killers.

Another oft-repeated finding is evidence of anger—primarily in sexual murderers. Some reports suggest this is chronic and persistent, while others suggest it is situational and related to the context and circumstances of the murder. The initial research of the FBI noted that styles of thinking were a crucial aspect of the pathways to serial killing, and subsequent research has found similar patterns in the men who commit a sexual murder. Since the majority of research in this arena is conducted by psychologists, ways of thinking—orientations to self and others—are often subsumed under the concepts associated with personality disorders. Deconstructing the attributes associated with this term and the tests used to determine its existence, the research suggests that sexual murderers are likely to be egotistical and antisocial and to have a strong sense of entitlement. We would add that the sense of entitlement extends to sexual access to women when the perpetrator considers it appropriate.

In the next two chapters, we focus on sexual murder and consider various aspects of the murder event and the lifecourse of sexual murderers. In so doing, we seek to extend the existing research and to add to the present level of knowledge, understanding, and explanation of sexual murders and of the men who commit them. There are very few studies of situational and circumstantial factors at the time of the murder, and the intensive evidence gathered from case-files and interviews extends the existing knowledge about the sexual nature of such murders. Once again, these results suggest the importance of gender in the understanding of the contexts in which men murder women. Again gender and gender relationships constitute a core component of the explanation of sexual murders.

6

Sexual Murder—The Murder Event

Relationships, Contexts, and Circumstances

What happens when men murder women for sex? The evidence reviewed in the knowledge chapter provides the background for this chapter and the next. An important aspect of the research on sexual murders is the wide variation in definitions used to study this type of violence. In the Murder Study, a broad definition was used. In most cases, the sexual nature of the murder was very clear, as the casefiles included forensic evidence of sexual assault and/or rape before, during, or after the murder. There was also evidence of acts such as mutilation of the sexual areas of the victim's body, masturbation over the body, and the absence of clothing or the arrangement of clothing that indicated a sexual element in the murder.

In this chapter, the narrative materials are used to illustrate the diversity of the contexts and immediate circumstances of 98 sexual murders. The presentation is first organized around the nature of the relationship between offenders and victims, from strangers to close acquaintances, friends, and relatives. The sexual murder of intimate partners was examined in chapter 3 and, as such, is not included here. Using both the qualitative and quantitative evidence from the Murder Study, the contexts and circumstances of the murders are presented in considerable detail in order to increase knowledge and understanding of the reality of this type of murder and, in turn, to contribute to the ongoing development of definitions and conceptualizations of sexual murder. The murder event is examined from the initial contact of the perpetrator with his victim to the act of murder, including the various forms of attack and injuries as well as further acts against the body after death. The perpetrators' accounts of the murder include their reflections, rationales, and justifications for the murder as well as their views about the victim. In the second of the two data chapters focusing on sexual murders, we will examine the lifecourse of the perpetrators from childhood to conviction and imprisonment.

RELATIONSHIP BETWEEN THE PERPETRATOR AND THE VICTIM

As previously stated, much of the research on homicide focuses on the nature of the relationship between the perpetrator and the victim that assumes an altercation between two men that escalates to violence and homicide in which the combat is mutual. There is an implicit agreement to engage in violence with an uncertain outcome about who will become the perpetrator and who will become the victim. With respect to sexual attacks by men against women, nothing could be farther from the reality. The individuals are neither "evenly matched" nor do they "agree" to a violent encounter. The type of relationship between perpetrators and victims is highly relevant, but in a very different way. The nature of the relationship between the perpetrator and the victim varies in terms of the man's *access* to the woman and her vulnerability to attack. It is not a question of two equal combatants squaring off with one another and considerable uncertainty as to who will prevail and who will be defeated. Instead, the dynamics are very different.

The nature and level of social access a man might have to a woman by virtue of their relationship ranges from almost no access for strangers to considerable "agreed" social access for friends and relatives. Also, there is the issue of how guarded a woman might be with a man known to her compared with a stranger. The man's level of access to the woman and the woman's level of caution about the man are filtered through the prism of their relationship to one another.

These relationships are examined at length in order to isolate and highlight the dynamics of sexual murders. These include how the perpetrator made contact with the victim. Were they total strangers or somehow known to one another? If acquainted, what was the nature and duration of the acquaintance or relationship between them? Were they old friends, long-term neighbors, or only known to one another for as little as an evening, a day, or a week? The level of acquaintance may be related to any fears or concerns the woman might have had about getting into the man's car, walking home accompanied by him, or inviting him into her home. Some degree of acquaintance may obviate against precautions that might be brought to bear about a total stranger or suggest a degree of safety that is not present.

The analysis begins with strangers, the most distant relationship, in which the perpetrator has little or no legitimate social access to the woman and the woman is most likely to be on guard against any form of contact with the man. It ends with relatives, the closest relationship, in which the man has the greatest access and the woman is least likely to be on guard. Sex workers are reported separately and in two categories, as strangers and as acquaintances of the perpetrator. By virtue of their occupation, all sex workers are relatively vulnerable to violence and sexual attacks from "customers," but the nature of the relationship with the perpetrator (e.g., as stranger or neighbor) may be related to the murder in different ways. The diverse nature of all of the relationships between perpetrators and victims in the 98 sexual murders is shown graphically at the beginning of Appendix IV. They include total strangers (37%); various types of acquaintance, ranging from those known as little as 1 day (10%) to 2 or more days, with the majority over 1 month (24%), neighbors (6%) who might have known one another for years; friends (15%); and relatives (8%) but not intimate partners. Given the small size of some of the categories, the different types of relationship are combined into two categories for the purpose of quantitative analysis: strangers (37%) and all other acquaintances (63%). The diversity of these relationships has, however, been retained in the qualitative material in order to provide a more nuanced view of sexual murders from the most distant relationship to the closest. The examples are both numerous and lengthy in order to capture as much as possible the diversity and complexity of the different kinds of relationships. The illustrations also include information relating to the immediate context of the murder and subsequent acts such as the treatment of the body, which are provided in order to capture the reality of the whole event rather than a single aspect of it.

Strangers—No Legitimate Access to the Victim

The popular imagery of sexual murder is that of a total stranger attacking a woman late at night on a city street, country road, lonely path, deserted lot, or field. The woman may be walking home from work, from visiting a friend, or from a social night out with friends. A man attacks, rapes and kills her, and then disappears as she is left already dead or dying and unlikely to be discovered for many hours or even several days. Such cases often attract considerable news coverage, a high level of police action, and heightened public attention and alarm. Wide-scale manhunts may follow along with speculations about the possibility of a serial killer undetected in our midst. The level of public alarm, concern, action, and outrage is sometimes tempered or elevated in relation to who the victim was, her age and marital status, what she did for a living, and her general standing in the community. In addition to the known details about the victim, and those that may or may not become known about the perpetrator, are also those about how the strangers came together in what becomes a sexual murder. Was it a random attack on the only woman to walk down the lonely path, the next blonde woman to walk down the same path, or someone who was followed only on the one night of the murder or who has unknowingly been stalked or followed down the same path for several days or even weeks?

The following cases involve the sexual attack and murder of women who were complete strangers to the perpetrators. Without some form of legitimate access, the perpetrator must either take the woman completely by surprise or somehow overcome any reservations she might have about having contact with him such as accepting a lift in his car. In this respect, some sexual murders of strangers occurred at night and outdoors or in secluded or deserted locations rather than in the home of the victim or the perpetrator or some other more public place.

Strangers—followed and attacked in isolated location
About midnight (after attending a wedding reception), the victim (age 48) was walking home along a main road and passed the defendant (age 34) who had spent the evening in a pub. He turned and followed her. After she turned into a side road, he forced her into an adjacent orchard and raped her. When she resisted, he lost his temper and attacked her violently, strangling her sufficiently to cause loss of consciousness but not death. He began punching her face causing fractures and the inhalation of blood from which she died (*1035cf1.4.3).

Strangers—attacked in isolated location, numerous injuries
A 21 year old man sexually assaulted and strangled an 18 year old girl, who was a complete stranger. The victim was walking home about 3 am on the outskirts of the town. The defendant saw her pass and somehow got her into some wasteland and raped, buggered, and beat her up. There were 72 separate injuries, including three broken ribs and a dislocated jaw. She was strangled with her own skirt (*659cf1.4.3).

Strangers—attacked in isolated location, numerous injuries in a symbolic shape

A 27 year old man raped and killed a 16 year old girl who was a total stranger. He offered a lift to the victim who was walking along a road. In the car, they chatted and she became suspicious, and asked him to let her out. She was frightened. He hit her, took her to a woody area, raped and partially strangled her, hit her head and threw her into a ditch. Her body was found six weeks later. The cause of death was head injuries and drowning in the ditch. When the body was found, there were knife wounds on her buttocks and thigh in a grid shape (*713cf1.4.3).

Strangers—attacked in isolated location, disposed of body and evidence

On a late afternoon in early winter, the accused (age 32) forced the victim (age 16) into his car on a lonely country lane. He indecently assaulted her and when she tried to fight him off, he strangled her. After the killing, he displayed a cool cunning in the way he had the car repaired and disposed of the girl's body and belongings. He admitted to the police that he wanted to rape his victim because she was a young girl and a virgin. He also admits to *fantasizing* about "touching up" his niece (age 6) while he was having sex with his girlfriend (*1130cf1.4.3).

Some sexual attacks by a stranger took place not in an isolated location but, instead, in the victim's home. Initially they might involve a property crime that turned into a rape and murder as the next account demonstrates, or they might involve a break-in for the purpose of committing a rape but not a murder, and a few began with the firm intention of committing both a rape and a murder.

Strangers—property crime turned into a rape and murder

The perpetrator (age 29) was in the process of stealing aluminum from an elevator-shaft in the block of flats where the victim lived, and was disturbed by the victim (age 28). He attacked her, forced her to the ground, and kicked her several times in the head and face until she was unconscious. When she began to recover consciousness, he began to strangle her but then started to stab her in a sadistic way—placing the handle of the knife against his own chest and the blade against hers and several times slowly pressing the blade into her chest. Then he cut off her jeans and underclothes and raped her when she was dead or dying before pushing her body into the elevator shaft. He stole some of her property which he shared out among his relatives (*636cf1.4.3).

The following case was very unusual. It involved a woman who was a stranger to the perpetrator but visited his home in her capacity as a public official. Although they were strangers, the nature of her contact with him meant that he did not have to follow her, seek her out, or take her by surprise in order to have access to her. While the following account demonstrates some aspects of the vicious and sadistic nature of this man, other details not reported here illustrate the extraordinary depravity of this perpetrator, who had a history of imprisonment for a number of sexual crimes.

Strangers—access through official visit, hostage taking, and sadistic violence

Upon release from prison [for a sexual offense], he (age 33) was re-housed in a location heavily populated with local criminals and more than its fair share of problem families. The [relevant social service department] arranged for him to be interviewed at his flat in order to assess the validity of his various claims. Because of the department's practice of destroying claimants' files after they had lain dormant for 18 months, the victim was not aware of the perpetrator's background and his previous record of violence. The victim (age 27) was last seen alive on her way to his flat. Her car was recognized outside his flat. When the police forced entry they found her body on a single bed underneath a blanket. There was a plastic bag over her head and a length of plastic string was tied tightly around her neck together with a blue belt. All her clothes were blood-stained as were the bedclothes, carpets and curtains in the room. A blood-stained dish-cloth was lying on the floor and there was a saucepan nearby with blood-staining on its base. There was pornographic literature on the bedside table and the [victim's] official papers were on a chair. She had been held hostage for sometime, repeatedly raped, sodomized, tortured, and brutally murdered (*1054cf1.4.3).

"Legitimate" Access to Women Who Are Sex Workers

Women working as prostitutes are frequently subjected to physical and sexual violence from customers, pimps, and others while working or in their everyday lives. Survey research from Britain and the United States has shown that almost all women working as prostitutes on the streets have been victimized and most have been raped and assaulted on numerous occasions.[1] These attacks occur during negotiations regarding the sexual transaction and during and after the sexual act. Women attempt to assess the relative risk of customers, although this is not always successful especially if the man is a stranger. Evidence collected in the Murder Study indicates that sex workers are attacked and killed both by men who are total strangers to them and by those with whom they have some form of acquaintance. Of the total sample of 98 sex murders, 18 women victims (18%) were sex workers. Of the sex workers, nine were killed by strangers while they were working and the other nine were killed by an acquaintance when they were not working. Here, sex workers are included both in the category of "strangers" and in the category of "other acquaintances" in order to reflect the different dynamics of these relationships as they relate to the murders. For strangers, the nature of the man's access to the woman differed by virtue of the commercial relationship between them. With respect to sex workers, men who are total strangers have relative access to the woman, and she does not automatically put up protective barriers to a male stranger and, subject to her negotiated agreement, a sexual act may occur. That is, they are strangers but with an implicit or explicit agreement to a sexual act. However, the opposite may occur with respect to the relationships of sex workers and men with whom they are socially acquainted, such as male neighbors or friends. For a woman working as a prostitute, contact with a male stranger when at work may imply an acceptance of his sexual advances, while contact with a male neighbor when they are at home does not imply such access. Hence, sex workers' contacts with strangers and those with other acquaintances differ with respect to these issues and are therefore treated separately in this discussion.

Although they are strangers, the man has a degree of access to the woman sex worker so that he does not need to conceal his presence from her, take her by surprise, jump her from behind, or drag her into the bushes. There is no need to surprise her or to use violence against her in order to have sex with her, but many of the men did use physical and sexual violence, and often with great brutality. So, what might this be about? If sex could be obtained from a total stranger without the need to resort to a surprise attack or to force compliance in order to have sex, what else might be involved in such encounters? The following cases highlight issues relating to the man's failure to perform sexually, the use of rough or violent sex, and the interweaving of the sexual act and actions related to killing such as choking, kicking, or bludgeoning. Others involved disputes over what sexual acts were expected or deemed to have been agreed and/or disputes about payment, and a few began with the clear intention to kill.

Strangers—unable to perform sexually and serial attacks on young sex workers

The perpetrator (age 28) killed a 17 year old prostitute and had recently been charged with offenses, including rape, against other young prostitutes. All of the offenses were committed at a multi-storey car park. He had a predilection for sex with young prostitutes. The murder victim came from a good home. She agreed to have sex with the perpetrator for a sum of money. Immediately before, he had had intercourse with another prostitute but had been unable to ejaculate. He could not ejaculate with the victim either. He became frustrated and angry and took hold of her hair at both sides of her head and repeatedly struck her head on the floor. He then placed one hand on her throat and put all his weight on it (*1069cf1.4.3).

Strangers—argument with wife and clear intention to kill a woman

The perpetrator (age 38) and his wife had an argument, and his wife put two suitcases of his clothes out the front door and locked it. He collected the suitcases, put them in his car and picked up the victim. The defendant drove the girl, a sex worker (age 18) to an industrial estate used by local prostitutes. Her body was found less than two hours later. She had been strangled by an arm held tightly across her neck stopping the flow of blood to the brain. Death could have followed in 15 seconds but before she died, she had lost control of her bowels. A used condom was found near the body. The DNA of the semen matched the DNA in a plucked hair root of the perpetrator (*1009cf1.4.3).

Stranger—sex worker dispute over money

[Casefile note—DANGER—not to be interviewed by a woman] Once back with her he noticed that his wallet was on top of his jacket on the chest of drawers and concluded that the woman had stolen his money. He wanted to check his wallet, but she asked him whether she could be trusted, to which he answered, "yes." She agreed to allow him to attempt intercourse with her again, but insisted that he would need "to hurry up" as she had to go back to [another City]. He told me that when he lay on top of the woman he put his hands around her neck and asked for the return of his money. She pushed him to the floor where they continued to struggle, and she threatened him with a knife which she was carrying in her handbag. He managed to disarm her and threw the knife across the bed. He claimed that she started pulling his pubic hair. The account became confusing

at this point, in that he described her going for him with another knife and stabbing him twice in the abdomen. He got hold of his tie, put it around her neck and
pulled hard until she lost consciousness. It seems that he must have known that
the victim had died as he said that he attempted to kill himself initially by suffo-
cating himself with a pillow, then trying to stab himself with a knife, and later by
setting his hair on fire (*949Cf1.4.3).

Stranger—sex worker said to have ridiculed him
Male (31) beats female prostitute (40) to death with a car jack because she ridiculed him when he was unable to have intercourse with her (*291cf1.4.3).

The above examples illustrate recurring patterns regarding the murder of women
working as prostitutes: Some men who were strangers were angry at a specific
woman or all women, some experienced sexual dysfunction and vented their "frustration" and anger on the victim; and for others who seemed intent on murdering
a woman, sex workers were most readily accessible and thus an "available" target.

Strangers—Serial Sexual Attacks and Serial Murders

As stated, serial killing makes up an extremely small proportion of sexual murders
and an even smaller proportion of all murders. However, they dominate much of
the popular media for public consumption as well as academic literature, which has
often led to the misconception that most sexual murderers are serial killers. Among
the 98 sexual murders, two of the men had committed more than one sexual murder and another two were identified as likely to become serial killers. Despite these
small numbers, but in light of the overwhelming interest in this area, all four cases
are presented below. In the first case, the police identified a perpetrator who was
apprehended for the murder of one woman and defined as a potential serial killer.

Strangers—sexual murderer and potential serial killer
The victim (age 42), never married but had a long term co-habiting relationship of
25 years, had three children and worked as a prostitute. The perpetrator (age 37),
a single, skilled, white-collar worker, was caught red handed by police plain
clothes just after he had killed the victim in his own car in a location frequented
by prostitutes and their clients. He tried to bluff his way out of the situation but
they insisted on seeing his "girlfriend" in the car and discovered her body. The
deceased's blouse was open exposing the neck and top part of the chest and a
map was covering her stomach and upper thighs. The defibrillating equipment
showed that life was extinct. Her face and neck were heavily bloodstained, her
eyes were barely open and her mouth was open. Her skirt was pulled up to the
waistline. Two metal skewers approximately six inches long, both bent over forming a 'U', were found on either side of the front door sills. The one on the driver's
side was heavily bloodstained. A briefcase was found on the back seat containing
a black knitted ski mask, a chair leg, a claw hammer, four further metal skewers,
a pair of sun glasses, four new black plastic bin liners, a plastic flashlight, and two
playing cards both depicting the ace of Spades. After a close examination of the
car and its contents and with the body inside, the investigating officer contends

that before death there was one almighty struggle in the vehicle between the deceased and the accused. The cause of death was manual strangulation, and before death occurred, one of the puncture wounds situated below the left breast had in fact penetrated the chest cavity and entered the lung and the heart. [Police Comment] There is significant evidence in this matter to show that this was to be the first of a series of similar killings (*970cf1.4 3).

The following case involved a man who raped and killed a young woman, and 1 month later attempted to do the same again. It appears that he intended to commit a series of rape/murders.

He (age 34) followed a 20 year old woman who was on her motor bike. He was in his van and stopped her pretending to be lost. He then attacked her, bound her hands, forced her into his van, and drove to a secluded spot where he raped her and strangled her. There was a big police hunt, and he was questioned but police were satisfied with his answers. One month later, while driving his van, he knocked a 26 year old woman off her pedal bike and forced her into the van at knife point, bound her hands, raped her, stabbed her in both sides of her throat, cut her throat from ear to ear and dumped her in a field. He returned a few minutes later to check that she was dead. She feigned death and he left. Although she was bound and unable to call out because her larynx was cut, she managed to get help and gave a description which led to his capture (*580cf1.4.3).

The following two cases are of serial killings, one within a short period of time and the other over a much longer period.

Strangers—serial rape/sexual assault and murder of three victims
[All three victims were described as being of good character] The first and second murders occurred on two consecutive days. The first victim was never found [although he later confessed to the murder and to dismembering and burning her body]. The second victim was a barmaid who left work at about 2:15 am. She was found partially buried and covered with cardboard. Her clothes had been torn open to reveal the upper part of her body, and her slacks and underclothes had been almost entirely removed to leave her virtually naked. A blood stained brick was found next to the body. Death was due to head injuries and strangulation by a ligature, namely a pair of tights. There were lacerations and extensive bruises to the head, and the front part of the skull, the facial bones and jaws were fragmented, and part of the left nipple had been removed, possibly by biting, and there was a lacerated wound of 1.5 inches length and bruising near the upper part of the vulva, which could have been caused by kicking or a blow from a blunt object.

The third victim attended a promotion party at a hotel, and left at about 10:30 pm with several colleagues to catch a train. She had had about five drinks of port and lemon, and on arrival in the city she walked with a fellow male colleague to an all-night bus stop. A girl of her description was seen by a bus crew and a police officer to get off a bus about 1:00 am and walk toward a housing area. At about 1:10 am, a woman living in the area heard several screams coming from the direction of the canal which would have been her route home. At 8 am the next day, a man walking to work saw the third victim's naked body lying face upwards in the canal with a ligature tied around her neck. [Three days before this murder], he attacked a 20 year old woman in a pub. He followed her into the toilets put his arms tightly around her and placed his hand between her legs for a few seconds until she managed to push him away. He also put his hand around her neck and squeezed so hard that she bit through her tongue (*1082cf1.4.3).

Strangers—serial sexual assault/rape and murder of two victims within 2 months, body mutilation

The perpetrator (age 24) lived with his parents, was engaged to be married, and employed as a skilled manual laborer. It is almost certainly the case that he did not know any of his victims prior to the murders. The first victim (age 36) had been married for 16 years and lived with her husband in the home of her mother-in-law. She and her husband were self employed taxi drivers. The second victim (age 48) had been married for 22 years, lived with her husband and two daughters, and worked as a nurse in a hospital. In the early hours of the morning, the body of the first victim was found in the luggage compartment of her taxicab. A sum of money had been taken. Police questioned a number of witnesses who had testified that the taxi had been parked in the street and there appeared to have been a struggle between the driver and the passenger. A man was seen leaving the taxi about 20 minutes after it had stopped. The cause of death was stab wounds to the chest. Two months later a second murder occurred in the same town which was bizarre and ritualistic and from the outset motiveless. The body of the second female victim was found at 10:30 am on a railway embankment in the same town. The murder had taken place about 11 pm the previous night when the victim had been walking home from the station following an evening out with a friend. Her family became anxious when she did not return home and reported her missing. She had been stripped and strangled with a chord from an anorak. A second ligature had been loosely wrapped round her neck (*109cf1.4 3).

As stated, a man who is a stranger to the woman has no easy or "legitimate" access to social contact with her and certainly no sexual access. Thus, he needs to take her by surprise and to use immediate and sufficient physical force to overwhelm any resistance to his sexual attack, or he needs to somehow "trick" her into a sense of safety that allows him to remove her to a place where he can attack her. Surprise attacks usually occurred in isolated places outdoors where the man could act without being detected, but some also took place in the home of the victim that the man had entered for the purpose of a robbery, a rape, or both. There was often evidence of a ferocious struggle as women attempted to protect themselves once an attack began. When the approach was from a total stranger, the woman was more likely to view the situation as dangerous and to become alarmed and defensive, although this was not the case when women were killed while working as prostitutes. In these cases the men did not need to launch an attack but could simply approach the woman in order to buy sex. Although a few of the men who murdered prostitutes did carry out an immediate attack, most did not. It was not necessary to overcome the woman if she judged the offender to be "safe" and agreed to engage in a sex act. In many of these cases, the perpetrator and the woman then moved to another location, often the car of the murderer, and drove to an isolated location, where the murder occurred.

Acquaintances

The context of the murder and the immediate circumstance were usually quite different when a man murdered an acquaintance such as an established friend, neighbor, or work colleague. Yet the "relational distance" of those who were acquainted varied, and some of the murders involved short-term acquaintances. The murder of acquaintances of short duration, when the man had ceased to be a total stranger but was not a long-standing acquaintance, raises different issues about the murderer's ease of access to the woman and her sense of caution, alarm, or danger concerning various forms of social contact with him.

The perpetrator and victim may have been acquainted for as little as a few hours or for as long as many years. They may have just met at a dance or in a club and spent a few minutes or a few hours together, or been neighbors for years or even decades. We begin with short-term acquaintances of a few hours or days. For the most part, the initial contact between the perpetrator and the victim did not involve forced contact, coercion, or violence but, instead, was based on some implicit or explicit agreement to a limited degree of social contact such as a conversation or sharing a drink or a dance. This might extend to the woman accepting a lift in the man's car but with no expectation on her part of any form of sexual contact. In turn, some limited form of intimate contact such as kissing may occur but with no expectation or intention on the part of the woman of engaging in sexual intercourse. For some men, such forms of contact may become the source of differential expectations, disagreement, or dispute about whether sexual activity is implied or agreed. For other men, the woman's intentions are completely irrelevant, and her efforts to rebuff his advances are of no concern to him. Any resistance from the woman is simply to be overcome by force. For others, such resistance is viewed as an affront to his pride or prowess that is to be punished, sometimes with great ferocity. The following cases begin with brief acquaintances that are similar to those involving strangers, and then proceeds to those of a more established or long-standing nature.

Brief acquaintance—limited access and no agreement to sex
The perpetrator was a 30 year old barman who had met the victim (age 24) through his job the night before the murder. The evidence was that at no time that night had the victim given the perpetrator any encouragement at all, nor been flirtatious in any way. She had consumed very little alcohol and was quiet but sociable in the assembled company. She accepted a lift back to her flat with the perpetrator. He did not drive her back to the flat but, instead, drove out to a secluded area. She obviously had no sexual interest in him and refused sex with him. He then subjected her to a savage attack using the heavy boots that he was wearing to virtually kick her head in. There was extensive fracturing of the bones around the eyes and the cheek bones and brain hemorrhage. After he had attacked her, he left her unconscious or barely conscious and naked below the waist. She was found in that state the next morning by a jogger and died in hospital one day later (*1071cf.1.4.3).

Brief acquaintance at house party, agreed to a lift home but not sex
The perpetrator, a martial arts expert (age 25) was exceedingly drunk having begun drinking at 11 am that day, and had smoked a number of joints of cannabis

before he met the victim (age 16) at a party. He took her home after the party and attempted sexual intercourse [he said it was consensual]. He failed to penetrate and ejaculated prematurely, then fell asleep and woke up with the victim hitting him on the left knee with a rolling pin. [He says he is unaware why she might have done this except that she was disappointed with the sexual encounter]. He says he reacted instinctively and applied a hold to her neck. His intention was to render her unconscious, however, the strangulation hold led to her death. The forensic report suggested that death was caused by a strangulation hold being maintained for 3-10 seconds crushing the larynx. Her knickers and ski pants had been pulled half-way down her thighs and there was blood on her knickers which he was unable to explain (*1021cf1.4.2).

Of the 23 cases involving an acquaintance of more than 1 day, the majority (59%) had known one another for 1 or more months. They were not strangers nor so newly acquainted that the man was likely to be viewed with a high level of caution or suspicion by a woman who might accept a lift in his car or invite him in for a coffee or drink or other such activities engaged in by acquaintances. This would seem to constitute a "middle zone" that involved varying degrees of social access by the man and differing levels of caution by the woman depending on the context and the type of activity in which they were engaged.

Acquaintance at office party, woman agreed to a lift home
He (age 31) stabbed a woman colleague (age 51) after an office party. They both worked in the county court offices and attended a party at work. They left at 7:30 pm and had a drink in a local pub before he drove her home as arranged, and he went into her house. He was attracted to the victim and hoped to have a relationship with her. He was encouraged when she started kissing him, but became disgusted when she vomited because of the alcohol. He tried to help clean her up, but she pushed him away. He got a bayonet and stabbed her, left the room and returned when he could no longer hear her gasping (*701cf1.4.2).

Acquaintance at house party, woman agreed to walk home
He (age 21) strangled and sexually assaulted a female acquaintance (age 22) while walking her home at night. They'd known each other from contact in pubs and doing karaoke for about two years, but as acquaintances rather than friends. On the night of the murder, they spent the evening together and witnesses said she was affectionate toward him. He walked her home which he had previously done. When he made sexual advances, she screamed, he hit her about the head, strangled and sexually assaulted her (there was some evidence that he assaulted her vagina and anus). It is not certain that penetration was after death but, according to police and forensic reports, this seems likely (*621cf1.4.2).

Acquaintance at house party, woman agreed to be walked home
The perpetrator was married (age 22) and wanted to have sex with a single woman (age 17). She refused and he assaulted and killed her, and was about to rape her when he was disturbed. The victim knew the perpetrator who offered to walk her home as a friend and others saw him do so. At about 11:40 pm on Friday, a number of resident's near the river walk heard a woman's screams but took no action. At about midnight,

three teenagers were walking along the path when they heard a low moaning noise and the sound of someone moving in the bushes. The path was unlit, misty and damp, and this frightened the teenagers who quickly made their way home. Early Saturday morning, a man was walking along the riverbank when he saw a woman's half naked body. He went to a nearby house and called the police who arrived within twenty minutes. There was a puncture wound to the left breast, head injuries, scratch marks, bruising and abrasions. The coat and blouse were undone and pulled off the shoulders revealing the bra and the left breast. The skirt was pulled around the waist and the tights were pulled down to the top of the thighs (*850cf1.4.2).

Acquaintance and/or Neighbor?—A Sex Worker Can Never be Just a Neighbor

As indicated, women who work as prostitutes are vulnerable in several ways to men who intend to physically attack or kill a woman. By virtue of their occupation, they are generally "available" to men who approach them seeking sex. They may refuse men who appear to be dangerous, but men who are strangers and seeking sex are not a general cause for alarm. These are issues relating to when the woman is at work, but what about when she is not? What about her relationships with men who are friends or neighbors? For the woman, such relationships might be outside the boundaries of her work and expected to remain as such. The man who is the friend or neighbor of a woman who is a sex worker might, however, presume he is entitled to sexual access to his neighbor by virtue of her occupation.

The man may view the woman, as a sex worker, as having no right to reject his sexual advances. On the other hand, as a friend or neighbor, he might view her as having no right to seek payment should sex occur. In other words, he sees her as a prostitute, and not as a friend or neighbor, and therefore views her as available to his sexual advances without the right to refuse him. The following cases illustrate relationships of neighbors or acquaintances where the woman is targeted because the man is aware that she is a sex worker.

Acquaintance—sex worker murdered for refusal of sex
The perpetrator (age 25) raped and killed a woman (age 37) he knew quite well. Her naked body was found in a churchyard close to the defendant's address. She had been sexually assaulted and strangled. He had stolen her watch and revealed details of the murder to his friends, but denied any involvement. The victim worked as a prostitute, had something of a drink problem, and had drunk an enormous quantity of alcohol that night. The perpetrator lived at a variety of addresses, normally wherever someone would allow him to sleep. He took her back to his flat and started heavy petting. She said "no," and started screaming when he tried to force her. He then strangled her with some sort of ligature and subjected her to forceful sexual interference before death (*984cf1.4.2).

Acquaintances—sex worker offered accommodation and murdered for refusal of sex
This 42 year old man killed a woman (age 21) working as a prostitute to whom he had offered a bed in his flat so she could bring back clients. On the night of the

incident, the evidence suggests that the perpetrator made advances towards the victim and when she rejected him he battered her about the body and strangled her. It should be noted that he has previous convictions for sexual violence to women, including a previous murder with a similar pattern [for which he served time in prison]. Both of the women he murdered were prostitutes known to him but not in a relationship with him, and he became violent when they rejected his advances (*207cf1.4.2).

Acquaintance Through Occupational or Commercial Contact

For a very few of the women, contact with the perpetrator was based on her occupation such as a social worker or real estate agent, and for a few others, contact was based on the occupation of the perpetrator such as a car salesman, barman, handyman, and the like. Either way, it is the occupation that provided the opportunity for the man to have access to the woman.

Acquaintance through commercial contact—used car salesman

The perpetrator (age 24) was a serious sexual aggressor although never convicted of any offenses. He was working at a car dealership which sold her (age 33) a car and he then came around under various real and contrived circumstances to "help" her with the car. It is clear that he flattened her tires and did various other things to the car so he could come to her house to help her repair them. He attempted to form a relationship with her and although she remained friendly it is clear that she did not want a sexual relationship. This was not acceptable to the perpetrator, who considered that ALL women should want to have sex with him. He drove to the victim's flat [late at night] where police speculate he was let in because she knew him, and he then made advances. She rebuffed him and he killed her. The police went to many of his ex-female clients finding that he tried to initiate intimate contact with them and/or had tampered with their cars. [Police Report stated] He is a pathological liar, almost incapable of telling the truth in even the simplest of conversations (*1142cf1.4.2).

Friends and Neighbors

Male friends and neighbors are rarely viewed with suspicion or treated with caution by women unless there is some clear reason to do so. They are known to the women, and these familiarities usually render them "safe" and not a source of apprehension or fear. There are exceptions as some male neighbors are viewed with suspicion, suspected of leering, voyeurism, or following the woman next door. Others may simply make the woman uneasy for reasons that are vague or unarticulated, and are kept at bay by a woman neighbor who is cautious or on alert.

Friend/previous professional relationship—murdered
after perpetrator's release from prison

Previously, when age 31, the defendant (age 40) committed a violent rape on a middle-aged woman, binding and gagging her for which he received a 13 year prison sentence. While in prison for this rape, he met a woman prison therapist and she befriended him. She saw him many times and corresponded with him extensively while he was in prison (there is no suggestion of an unprofessional or inappropriate relationship). He was last in touch with her when he was released from prison. Upon leaving prison, he moved in with a female partner but three years later and six weeks before the murder, she asked him to leave. After separating from his partner, the defendant called unexpectedly on the victim. They appeared to have talked before he assaulted her. He states that during the talk they had a disagreement about something he said about his woman partner and he went berserk. He assaulted her, tore off all her clothing, bound her hands with tape, gagged her and raped her with great force, causing extensive injury to her private parts and his own penis. He tried to smother her with a pillow then strangled her with considerable violence using her own bra. He left and remained at large for some days before confessing to his partner (*1023cf1.4.2).

Neighbor—assumed intimate relationship when none existed
The perpetrator (age 52) killed a 47 year old woman who was his neighbor but not his girlfriend. For some time, he had been attempting to force himself onto the victim who had recently divorced [he was a friend of her ex-husband]. It seems she continually refused and there was never an actual relationship, although he thought otherwise and was very sexually possessive toward the victim, even threatening other potential suitors. Eventually he went to her flat, and raped and killed her in a vicious attack. He had a history of physical and sexual violence against women (*836cf1.4.2).

Neighbor—perpetrator previously imprisoned for raping
the woman he eventually murdered
The woman (age 42) had previously been the victim of offenses committed by the perpetrator (age 25) [a neighbor]. Previously, he broke into her home, savagely attacked and raped her and stole a television set from the premises. He was convicted of rape and whilst in prison he told his probation officer (PO) that he wished to contact the victim in order to express his remorse to her. In the event, the PO was unable to contact the victim. Upon release, he agreed with his PO that he would not visit the housing estate where his victim lived. [The deceased actually met with the murderer's PO and told her she was frightened because he was out on parole.] However, he immediately broke this agreement. He was at liberty for ten months when he attacked, raped and killed the same woman he had previously raped [for which he had spent four and one-half years in prison]. The victim was employed for the same firm for 23 years, was unmarried, unattached and very much a loner. She was a quiet woman who liked children and had few close friends. She was loved and respected by everyone. The offense happened on a massive housing estate where about 8,000 people live, many who have employment and social problems (*1002cf 1.4.2).

Female friend of his intimate partner, murdered for sex and money
The perpetrator (age 22) murdered a woman friend (age 22) of his co-habitant, apparently for money but a rape [either before or after death] was also involved. He had been living with the deceased's friend for several years and had a good relationship

with the deceased and her mother. When the police found her, she had severe head injuries with blood and brain matter adjacent to her head and heavy blood staining around the room. Her body was clothed in socks, her T-shirt was pulled up exposing her breasts and her bra had been ripped. The post mortem revealed the cause of death was cerebral contusions and lacerations which resulted from fractures of the skull and secondary impact injuries to the head (*1088cf1.4.2).

Relatives

For the most part, men who are related to the victim have the greatest and most unchallenged access to the women and girls in their family. Fathers, uncles, brothers, cousins, and in-laws are generally able to visit a woman/girl in her home, take her for a drive, and have easy social access to her, as illustrated below. Although there are exceptions, women do not generally expect sexual advances from male relatives or to be on the receiving end of violent or sexual attacks from them. Evidence about incest and domestic violence clearly indicate that while such behavior does occur, it is generally assumed, at times erroneously, that men in the family are "safe" with respect to their female relatives. It is likely that most women begin with this premise unless the behavior of the male relative proves otherwise.

Relatives—giving a lift to his wife's cousin
At the time of the offense, he (age 31) was a married man living with his wife and eighteen month old daughter. He offered a lift to his wife's cousin (age 45). When she was in the car, he drove her to a secluded spot where he savagely punched her face, breaking several bones and rendering her unconscious. He then sexually assaulted her and ran over her with his car, causing fatal injuries to her chest and head. He had no previous convictions on record, but he was charged with an offense of raping an elderly lady. However, she [the elderly woman] did not wish to go through with a court appearance and the matter was dismissed (*1112cf1.4.2).

Relatives—perpetrator's sister
The victim (age 20) was the perpetrator's sister, and she had agreed to babysit for the child of another brother who was married and lived nearby. The perpetrator (age 21), who lived at home with his sister (the victim) and their mother, had spent the early evening drinking and at about 10 pm volunteered to go and see how his sister was getting-on with the babysitting. A few minutes later, he went to a neighbor's house and told them that his sister was dying. He said that she was lying naked on the bed and that she had been strangled. He showed no sign of emotion. There were no signs of forced entry, and a knife was found to be missing from the house. Suspicion fell on him and he agreed to a medical examination which revealed a bite mark on his arm. The victim had been in an upstairs bedroom of the house when he appeared at the door with a knife. He claimed that when she saw him, she asked him what he was doing there and began shouting at him. He went towards her with the knife and she fell on the bed. He then stabbed her, stripped her from the waist down, and strangled her with her tights. A sexual act had taken place [sodomy] and doctors concluded that the girl was already dead before this occurred (*118cf1.4.1).

Murdered stepdaughter and male friend (sexually abused his partner and her two daughters)

The perpetrator (age 41) imprisoned his partner and her two daughters, and frequently beat, raped and buggered them. He forced his partner and her daughter [first victim, age 16] to indulge in lesbian activities with each other. At one point, he heated a blade and forced the victim to bend over a sofa, put a handkerchief in her mouth to prevent her from screaming, and placed the blade on her vagina. After murdering the first victim (16 year old step-daughter), he forced the other step-daughter (age 13) to stay with her body for 24 hours. He made the second murder victim (a male friend, age 27) bury the body in the cellar of his house. For several months, he continued to keep the victim's mother and the 13 year old prisoner, and subjected them to continuous physical and sexual violence. During this time, he argued with the male victim, beat him with a poker and rolling pin, and then strangled him. The survivors/witnesses (mother and surviving daughter) were obviously terrified of him, and only started to speak of his violence when they knew he was in custody (*601cf1.4.2).

Relationships Between Perpetrators and Victims—Comparing Strangers and Others

The different types of relationships provide various pathways to a sexual attack that ends in a murder. The numerous examples from the qualitative evidence presented above illustrate the wide range and complexity of the varied routes to sexual access as shaped by the relationship between the man and the woman who becomes his victim. Strangers, with the exception of men who killed women working as prostitutes, had no "legitimate" access to the victim and usually carried out a sudden physical assault intended to overwhelm the victim in order to commit a sexual attack. When men were acquainted with the victim, the circumstances were usually quite different. The men already had considerable social access to the victim because she was an acquaintance, neighbor, friend, or relative. In the cases of friends or relatives, access was generally available to the perpetrator. In cases of attacks on neighbors, this was not always the case, and the man's access sometimes did not involve mutuality and thus was more like those involving strangers. In the murders of friends and relatives, men did have access and it was a matter of engaging in a social contact that facilitated the sexual attack and murder. In a few cases, the perpetrator held his relatives hostage and committed persistent sexual and physical violence against them before committing a sexual murder. Such cases were unusual, but what was more usual was a history of persistent physical and sexual abuse of a relative such as a niece, stepdaughter, or sister.

Although the lifecourse of the perpetrators of the 98 sexual murderers will be examined in detail in the next chapter, here we compare some of the elements of the backgrounds of those who murdered a stranger and those who murdered an acquaintance. Evidence about the childhood and adulthood backgrounds revealed almost no differences between the two categories. At the time of the murder, both the men who were strangers and those who were variously acquainted were likely to be unemployed, living on their own, not in a relationship, to abuse alcohol, and to have extensive criminal backgrounds. Men who killed strangers were more likely than those who murdered acquaintances to be single (47% vs. 37%), or separated/divorced

(28% vs. 17%), and to be living on their own, although the majority of both types lived on their own. Men who murdered strangers were significantly more likely (75%) than those who murdered acquaintances (59%) to have five or more previous convictions and were significantly more likely to have a history of at least one previous conviction for a serious sexual assault or rape (36% vs. 13%). Both categories had histories of crime and contact with the justice system including police, prisons, and probation, although this was more likely among those who murdered a stranger.

The ongoing circumstances at the time of the murder, the location of the murder, and the number of injuries revealed only a few significant differences between the two types. There were no ongoing circumstances when the perpetrator and victim were strangers (0%), but 26% of the acquaintances had some type of previous physical and/or sexual violence against the victim. The murder was less likely to occur in the home of a victim who was a stranger than of a woman who was an acquaintance (33% vs. 72%). Men who murdered an acquaintance were more likely to stab their victim (25% vs. 6%), although the two types were almost equally likely to strangle their victim (54% vs. 69%). The proportion of the two types that inflicted five or more injuries was almost identical (71% vs. 69%). Many other comparisons also revealed similarities, including drunkenness of the perpetrator; previous violence to the victim; the time of the attack; the use of a weapon; the treatment of the body after death including mutilating, hiding, and moving the body in order to avoid detection; and others. As shown in the qualitative materials, the type of relationship between perpetrators and victims is of particular relevance concerning how the perpetrator obtained access to the woman before the attack and the speed and duration of the attack itself, but appears to be less relevant to other aspects of the context of the murder, the murder itself, subsequent treatment of the body, and efforts to avoid detection. Accordingly, the following examination will no longer separate the men according to the relationship between the perpetrator and victim but will, instead, focus on the entire group as a whole.

CONTEXT AND CIRCUMSTANCES AT THE TIME OF THE MURDER

The circumstances of the men at the time of the murder are shown in Figure 6.1 at the end of this chapter and in Appendix IV, Table 6.1. The average age of the sexual murderers was 29 years, and the average age of victims was 31 years. It should be noted these averages exclude the 21 women victims aged 65 or over, who are discussed separately in the section on the murder of older women). Most of the 98 men were single (41%) or separated/divorced (21%), and others were married (17%), cohabiting (15%), or in a serious dating relationship (4%). Many had a history of failed intimate relationships, a minority were employed at the time of the murder (45%), many had a history of serious abuse of alcohol (60%), and most had a criminal history, including sexual offending. At the time of the murder, 10% were involved with the police (e.g., arrested for another offense but not in custody), and 14% were on probation and under supervision, and many had previously been in prison (see Appx.IV-Table 6.1). In brief, at the time of the murder, the daily lives of the men were characterized by unemployment, excessive alcohol consumption, problematic or failed relationships, criminality, and periods of incarceration.

Alcohol

The context of the sexual murders often involved alcohol and drunkenness of the perpetrator and sometimes of the victim as well. For the most part, the issue is one of alcohol and drunkenness rather than drugs, although the latter did figure in some cases, with 17% of offenders using illegal substances at the time of the murder. However, alcohol consumption and drunkenness were far more likely. Across the entire sample of sexual murders, 74% of the offenders and 45% of the victims had consumed alcohol at the time of the murder, and many had consumed a considerable amount. For example, of the entire sample, 51% of the perpetrators and 30% of the victims were defined as drunk. Of perpetrators who were drinking, 39% had been drinking from 3 to 6 hours before the murder while another 14% had been drinking all day. Importantly, the perpetrator and victim had been drinking together prior to the murder in 33% of the cases (see Figure 6.1 and Appx.IV-Table 6.1). For the perpetrator, some of the issues relating to the altered state of thinking and behavior associated with inebriation include being overly sensitive to personal insults or slights and elevated levels of physical and/or sexual aggression. Insults may be seen where none was intended or occurred. Sexual situations may be invented or misread, intentions and putative agreements may be misunderstood, and refusals of sexual advances may be completely ignored or disregarded. Victims who are inebriated may be unable to assess danger and may be less able to defend themselves if attacked. The following account illustrates these patterns.

> ### Drinking, perceived insult by a woman and taking revenge
> The perpetrator had a considerable history of violence, especially against women. He seems to have had built up a strong animosity toward women and on the night in question he was involved in heavy drinking. [He claimed that] some women insulted him and he took his revenge by brutally killing, and then raping one of them. A police patrol attended at the location described and found the almost naked body of the victim lying on the ground in an alleyway. She was already dead. Later that day a post mortem was carried out on the body of the victim. It was established that she had been penetrated both vaginally and anally and her body and head had been subjected to a brutal battering. The cause of death was established as asphyxia caused by strangulation and head injuries. The defendant was subsequently interviewed and initially declined to answer questions. However, he did admit attempting to have sexual intercourse with the deceased at the location where she was found, but stated it was with her consent. He denied committing the murder. He stated he had never seen the girl prior to this occasion (*1076cf11.4.3).

Disputes, Previous Violence, and Confrontations

Whereas homicides are sometimes preceded by long-term disputes, as was evident for example in IPMs, only 4% of sexual murders involved an ongoing dispute between the victim and perpetrator, and this was usually associated with acquaintances, friends, and relatives. Previous violence against the victim was unusual (4%), but when it did occur it was usually near the time of the murder, although in a few cases this occurred sometime before the lethal attack. Confrontations at the time of the murder (40% of the cases) usually involved those who were acquainted, not strangers, as women with closer relationships experienced a threat or violence and responded in a defensive manner. Confrontations usually involved issues relating to various forms of social and/or physical contact of any type as well as those relating to sex, which included disagreements about consent to have sex as well as those relating to the content of the sexual act and what was acceptable to each party. Prior to the murder, a few of the men were angry at women in general or at a particular woman, such as their intimate partner. During the attack, about one-third of the men were defined as angry. This was usually associated with being rebuffed or in some way rejected by the woman; in some cases it was a response to the woman's attempts to defend herself against the physical/sexual attack.

What Were They Thinking? Advanced Planning and Fantasies

Prior to the murder, very few of the men had elaborate, specific, well-worked-out plans to rape and kill. For some, the murder was relatively spontaneous and more of an immediate act, while for others a greater element of advanced thinking and/or planning was involved. Many had a previous history of sexual and/or physical violence to the women in their lives; some included the woman who was to become the victim of murder. As noted above, a few of the men were angry and resentful of women in general, of a particular type of woman, or of a specific woman. Irrespective of these notions and of any form of advanced planning to rape and/or murder, most had strong notions that they wished to have sex either with any woman or with a specific woman on the day in question. When these plans or fantasies did not work out or were thwarted, as by the woman resisting their sexual advances, the men *changed the project* from one of seeking sex to one of using brutal force to obtain sex and/or of making the woman pay for refusing it, in these cases paying with her life. In some cases, the men intended to use violence and brutal force against the woman even if they anticipated compliance. A few imagined that the woman would not only consent to sex with him but would fall in love with him. Others imagined a brutal and vicious attack, both sexual and physical, on a specific woman or on any woman. A few had a complete script involving sex that included various forms of physical violence or even torture. While the latter is unusual, it is important and relevant to delineate it in order to illustrate what some of the men were thinking and the nature of such fantasies.

Fantasy—kidnapping for "love" and collateral murder of two men in another European country

The perpetrator (age 33) was a non-commissioned officer in the Army who was very responsible and had no previous convictions or violent offenses. He became obsessed with a woman officer, planned and then executed an elaborate abduction in which he fantasized her coming to love and have sex with him. He stated that the woman he kidnapped had appeared to him to be the personification of the perfect woman, "my ideal" about whom he had fantasized over a period of time. He saw the victim about the military camp, was sexually attracted and planned to have sexual intercourse with her. In abducting her he had hoped to talk to her about his difficulties in relating to women and to engender her pity and sympathy. It was his ultimate wish that her pity would lead her to voluntarily becoming his first complete sexual partner. He added that had she not reciprocated he "would like to think" that he would have caused her no harm and would have eventually returned her home. Such thoughts and plans had reached obsessional proportions. He photographed his victim and ultimately admitted that these were to be used as masturbatory material and as such he must have found the act of taking them arousing. In the fantasy, he would masturbate to the intended sex act and so it became a more powerful fantasy reinforced by masturbation. As such, it was typical of fantasy driven behavior found in sex offenses. He saw an opportunity to contact her when he learned that she had a car that she wished to sell. He abducted her using a gun and handcuffs and took her to a forest where the fantasy was to unfold. In the event, two foresters came upon the scene before he had entered into his proposed lengthy catharsis with her. When the foresters arrived she was handcuffed. The two foresters actually rescued her but he then shot them in cold blood. He stated: "these two people were taking her away from me; she was everything I ever wanted" (*974cf1.4.3).

A script of brutal sexual acts against his wife
but acted out against another woman
He (age 45) murdered his son's ex-girlfriend (age 28) who was mentally disabled. *The script:* I was plotting to kill my wife and I would have followed a script. I used to buy [pornographic] magazines, and there were photos of a woman putting cucumbers and carrots into her vagina. [In the fantasy] I thought I'd surprise my wife with the sex aids she wanted, but I didn't think she wanted me to use the needles [to stab her breasts]. [The reality—Trial judge] He is a sexual pervert who had actually written a script for murder. In the murder, he appears to have followed the script fairly closely [tying her to the bed, shaving her pubic hair, inserting objects such as vegetables, candles, a brush handle and a bottle into her anus and vagina, and stabbing her breasts with needles] save that he killed the girl earlier in the proceedings rather than at climax. There was no motive other than sexual gratification and perhaps even the thrill of killing itself (*645cf1.4.2).

Sexual fantasy involving torture, rape, and murder
The perpetrator went on to describe his masturbatory fantasies which involve him going into a wooded area or graveyard with a knife, where he waits until a woman appears. He puts the blade of the knife to her throat, telling her to strip and gets her to lie on the ground and proceeds to have sexual intercourse with her. He added that the focus of the fantasies can be any woman, real or imaginary, but not a blonde haired woman—he added that his sister has blonde hair. On occasions he also fantasies about hurting females. When asked whether he had ever fanta-sized about killing prior to the alleged offense, he told me that he has had fantasies where he takes a woman into a house, tortures her by burning her with cigarettes, whipping her and generally humiliating her before finally killing her by cutting her throat and burying her in the back garden. He denied any fantasies regarding necrophilia. He said that these fantasies had become more intense since the kill-ing but admitted that they did pre-date the killing. He has also incorporated the victim into his fantasies since the killing. He told me that he derives great pleasure

from these fantasies whilst they are in progress, but occasionally feels bad afterwards. He told me he had acted out or "rehearsed" his fantasies prior to the offense. This involved hiding in woods with a knife with a balaclava over his face. He added that he has attempted to rape women in graveyards in the past (*1005Cf1.4.2).

Men fantasize. They fantasize about who they are, about their relationships with women, about sex and, in some cases, about violence against women, sexual violence, and even murder. A very few of the sexual murderers had explicit and vivid fantasies that included entire scenarios of violent, sadistic sex and murder that they repeatedly visited. While only a few of the murderers followed an elaborate advance plan based on a clear script containing sex and murder, it must be stressed that all of them did include an orientation toward having sex with a woman and doing so in spite of her wishes even if she said "no" and put up a struggle as he continued. For the men, all of the sexual attacks were purposeful and without regard to the consequences of their efforts to obtain sex even to the point of killing the woman in the process of doing so.

THE MURDER EVENT

Time and Place

Of the 98 cases, most of the sexual attacks and murders occurred in the evening or late at night, with 68% between 10 pm and 4 am. Indoor locations included the familiar surroundings in or near the home of the victim (58%). Those occurring within the residence of the victim included not only women known to the perpetrator but also those who were strangers to a man who entered their home in order to rape, rob, and/or kill them. Outdoor locations included urban streets, alleyways, wasteland, public parks, and car parks (29%) and the more remote locations of woodland and countryside (13%). A few of the women were moved to a second location by the perpetrator or managed to make their own way to another spot in an effort to escape and seek assistance. Most of the women (92%) died within 1 hour of the attack. The time from attack to death ranged from 1 to 10 minutes (30%), 11 to 30 minutes (42%), 30 to 60 minutes (20%), to more than 1 hour (8%). The vast majority of the attacks were perpetrated by one man (92%), and nearly all of the women (93%) died at the location of the sexual attack, with 3% dying alone in a second location and 4% dying in the care of medical staff, ambulance, or the police who attended the scene of the attack.

Physical Attack and Injuries

Most murders, including sexual murders, involve many forms of violence, and it is rare for an assault that results in death to involve only one type of violence. The most common forms of attack included the use of some type of instrument (73%), and strangulation or smothering (53%) (Figure 6.1; Appx.IV-Table 6.1). Of the instruments or weapons used, most (33%) were ligatures, followed by knives and sharp instruments (20%) and by blunt objects such as bricks, stones, and clubs (11%). Other forms of attack included punching, kicking, and stomping, as well as drowning. The woman's clothing was often used as a ligature. Guns were used in only 4% of the cases.

These attacks involved numerous injuries in addition to the one that caused death. The face was often crushed, and sexual areas of the body were often attacked before, during, and after the murder, which included cutting, burning, and mutilating the breasts and genital areas. Five or more injuries were inflicted by 70% of the men, and a substantial proportion (43%) inflicted 10 or more injuries, with the maximum number of injuries reaching 229 stab wounds (Figure 6.1; Appx.IV-Table 6.1).

The murder—stabbing, burning, and smoke inhalation

The victim suffered a horrendous death. She had a large carving knife thrust into her chest cavity. This knife, was subsequently removed *in situ* in her chest, it missed her heart but punctured her left lung. Her hands were tethered behind her back by her dressing gown cord, and whilst still alive, her prostrate body was doused with an accelerant, probably petrol, before being set alight. The likely cause of death is considered to be shock, brought about by the inhalation of hot fumes.

A witness heard screaming at various points but did nothing. When interviewed by police, the perpetrator had several injuries including a cut to his face and a cut to his lower lip. These were defense wounds caused by the victim. Blood from the victim was on his tie and jacket, fibers from his jacket were found at the scene of the crime, and fibers from her carpet were found on his trousers and on an empty petrol can found in his car (*1142cf1.4.2).

[Post mortem]—40 bruises, scratches and abrasions on various parts of her body. There was blood staining on her face and her hair was matted with blood. The bedclothes were bloodstained and blood splashes were found on the bedroom door. The cause of death was compression of the neck probably by the use of a pillow with some severe force used. She had also suffered a violent assault to her face. Both the defendant and the deceased had consumed alcohol, although the deceased was likely to have been more affected. He punched her at least seven times to the face, causing serious injuries including a fractured cheekbone. He then smothered and strangled her. At or soon after death he forced an aerosol container into her vagina (*1070cf1.4.2).

The Body after Death—Further Physical or Sexual Attack, Mutilation, and Moving the Body

After the attack, 47% of the perpetrators immediately left the woman who was already dead or dying. Others engaged in further acts of a physical and/or sexual violence against the woman's body. Further acts against the body included sex, mutilation, destruction of various sexual parts of the body, and cutting symbols into the body. Other acts against the body in an effort to avoid detection included moving, burning, or burying the body as well as attempts to avoid identification of the victim by dismemberment or destroying her face or fingers.

The body—sex after death

The police surgeon, with over 20 years experience of examining victims of sexual offenses, indicated that the state of the body suggested that the victim was either unconscious or dead when intercourse occurred (*1021cf1.4.2).

The body—five hours with the body, further sexual assault, and set fire to house

The murder was committed while he was on parole for rape. He abused the dead body by dressing it in her under clothes (knickers, stockings and suspender belt) and inserting a rolling pin in her vagina, then "nodded off." He spent at least five hours in her house after killing her. Before he left, he set fire to cushions placed around her body aware that her eleven year old son was asleep upstairs (*617cf1.4.2).

The body—undressed and mutilated

Her body had been stripped, and she had severe lacerations to her wrists and body. Her bra had been stuffed into her mouth and a tree branch had been broken and pushed into her vagina. Her clothes were strewn about her body, and some of her clothes had been tied in a neat knot (*109cf1.4 3).

The body—mutilation of breast, returning to the body and stealing jewelry from it

He kept going back to the body, stealing bits off of it—including a watch and ring, Post mortem—Death was due to strangulation by a ligature, namely a pair of tights. There were numerous abrasions, bruises and scratches on the body, with a stab wound of four inches in length below the left breast. The left nipple was missing with ragged edges to the wound which suggested that it could have been removed by biting, and additional scratch marks of up to four inches in length in roughly parallel groups were observed on the left breast and on the skin below the breast which could have been produced by scratching with the tip of a nail file (*1082cf1.4.3).

The body—mutilation of breast

Police information to prison: the body was found bound by wrists, gagged and strangled with a ligature around the neck. She was raped vaginally and possibly anally, although this was not pursued in court. He caused injury after death using an unknown instrument to cut a thin line along her breast bone and underneath one breast. He was arrested after his DNA was taken for a different offense of "going equipped" [for burglary] (*664cf1.4.3).

The body—kept at home for weeks

He put her body in a black plastic bag and left it in his flat. The body was discovered when he committed a very serious assault on another prostitute five weeks later. During this attack, he fell asleep, and she escaped and got police help. When the police went to his flat and arrested him, they noticed an odor, and later returned to investigate the odor and search the flat. They discovered the body hidden in a large black bin bag and concealed under cushions, an anorak and curtains (*628cf1.4.3).

A very few cases involved even more extreme examples of the carrying-out of fantasies from infamous films, religious imagery, and a bizarre attempt to use the body to invoke "empathy."

The body—remove eyes—influenced by Silence of the Lambs
He removed the victim's eyes and fantasized about violence having read "Silence of the Lambs" a number of times (*081cf1.4.3).

The body—tied to crucifix and photographed
After death, he tied her body in various positions to a crucifix and photographed her. During the investigation, the police found the photos (*645cf1.4.2).

Request to see the body in order to "feel" something about the murder
On the way back from the Magistrate's court, he asked to see her body because, although he knew he'd done a dreadful thing, he couldn't feel anything about it. He thought seeing her might alter this. Request denied (*611cf1.4.2).

Detection by Police and Efforts to Avoid Detection

Very few offenders (7%) were caught by the police at the scene or apprehended in pursuit. Most of the men (46%) were caught after straightforward police enquiries, and 20% were caught after extensive police investigations. Ten percent made no effort to avoid detection, and went to the police, reported the murder, and identified themselves as the perpetrator. About one-quarter confessed to the police upon apprehension. Other means of identifying the offender (16%) included reports by known others, apprehension for another offense, or the perpetrator contacting the police in an attempt to place the blame elsewhere or to try to collect a reward. Efforts to avoid detection included moving and hiding the body (15%), hiding the body at the scene (9%), burning the body and/or setting fire to the house (6%), and burying the body and other acts (16%).

The body—no attempt to avoid detection
The investigation into the killing began on a Friday afternoon when the defendant walked into the Police Station and stated he had killed someone. He then spoke to the Inspector and told him that he had murdered a prostitute by strangling and smothering her but, on advice of his Solicitor, made no further comment to questions put to him (*1070cf1.4.2).

The body after death—simulating sex and moving the body to avoid detection
When dead, he stripped her body, took off his own clothes, lay on top of her body, touched her breasts and genitals, and simulated intercourse but no penetration as no erection. He put her body in a plastic bag, and the next morning put it in his car and pushed the bag down a river bank. He drove home, cleaned the car, and washed the bayonet, his clothes, and the house. Three days later, the police were called because she hadn't turned up at work. They searched his house and discovered the bloodstained items. After further interviews, he made a full confession to the police (*701cf1.4.2).

The body after death—mutilate body and move it to avoid detection
A young unemployed man killed a young woman neighbor in order to steal her property and cover up the offense. He planned in advance of the robbery to kill her and to dispose of her body by cutting it up and dispersing it about the city in garbage bags. He also planned to give the property to his girlfriend/cohabitant in order to retain their relationship. While burgling her flat in the same block as his own, he was disturbed by the victim. He grabbed her, hit her around the head with a blunt instrument and cut her throat with a bread knife. He removed the nipples and made two 7 inch cuts to the abdomen and "V" shaped cuts toward the pubic region. Afterwards, during a one week period, he returned to her flat twice and attempted to dismember the body using an electric carving knife, and cut off her nipples but failed to remove her limbs [note: information in police report but not revealed in interview]. He then wrapped the body in a bed sheet and hid it in the attic of the house. [NB: In the research interview, he spoke with apparent pride about his ability to move the heavy body alone and lift it into the loft, and said the police believed he must have had a co-defendant as it would be difficult for one person to carry such a heavy weight. He was a slim 5'10".] (*1089cf1.4.2).

The body—set fire to avoid detection with potential
for collateral murders of children
He said that he stood back from her and saw that she was neither moving nor breathing. He lit a fire on the chair on which she had been sitting and left the room. The two small girls (ages 5 and 6) were asleep upstairs. He then lit a fire at the bottom of the stairs. He said that he lit the fires to hide the fact that he had killed the deceased. He then walked away from the house and gave himself up at a motorway service station some hours later, saying he had tried to kill someone that night. He was not able to explain what he had done. There had been no animosity between him and his victim save for the gentle rebuff to his sexual advances (*917.2cf1.4.2).

He Says—What Were They Thinking? Perpetrators Accounts of the Murder

After apprehension, the men gave accounts of the sexual attack and murder that often included denials, rationales, excuses, and justifications. According to many, the sex act did not occur or was consensual, the physical assault was minimal, and the murder was an accident that somehow just happened. The accounts usually contained an admission of involvement in something, but, for the most part, the event was not defined by the men as a sexual assault or a rape. Rather, they were initially defined as a consensual sexual encounter that somehow went wrong and resulted in an outcome for which he was not responsible. While some men went out with a plan to rape and kill, others did not, although their actions reflected those of someone focused on their own desires and with little awareness or regard for the intentions or preferences of the other. In both the casefiles and our interviews, some of the men's accounts reflect a sense of achievement, sexual prowess, or conquest and bravado. A few of the accounts were pornographic in nature, and during the interviews a few of the men appeared to be obtaining sexual pleasure when recounting the event. The most extreme of these are not reported here.

He says—a game gone wrong
The perpetrator raped and stabbed with a broken milk bottle a young woman he met the week previously at a club. He described the offense to the psychiatrist as "as game that had gone wrong" (*234cf1.4.2).

He says—she led him on, agreed to sex and enjoyed it—victim imprisoned
She completed her official business, and he claims that at the end of the interview "lust built up inside" him and he grabbed her, placing his hand over her mouth causing her to black out. He carried her to the bed where she came round and was ordered to strip. He claimed that he then had sex with her six or seven times in various postures and reluctantly admitted buggery and biting her on her neck and breasts. He indicated that when he first sexually assaulted the victim she was in a dazed condition but claimed that after a while she agreed to have sex and began to enjoy his treatment of her. He suggested that she may have led him on, but said that the victim had pleaded to be released and had on one occasion attempted to escape when she believed he had fallen asleep (*1054 cf1.4.3).

He says—consensual sex with a stranger
He maintains that he did not commit the offense. He told me that he had consensual sexual intercourse with the victim who he knew by sight. He was unable to explain how or where he had first met the victim and said it was a casual affair. He was slow to answer questions about the offense and the events leading up to it (*1094cf1.4.2).

He says—self-defense
He says he was annoyed that she was a prostitute and asking for money. He claims he refused to pay and she "flew at him with her nails" attacking him. He retaliated and noticed that she was going for a knife which he saw on the bedside table. He therefore grabbed the victim by the throat and throttled her to death. The victim's facial appearance was that of somebody who had been very severely battered. He was extremely boastful (*1070cf1.4.2).

He says—he intended to have sex and to hurt her, but not to kill her
He said he did it to hurt her but not to kill her and said that his first thought was to have sexual intercourse with her. He thought that she was unconscious and took her from the chair and placed her on the floor. He undressed her until she was naked and said the purpose of undressing her was so that he could rape her. He denied raping her and indecently assaulting her although the medical evidence showed a recent tear injury to the vagina which he was unable to explain (*917.2cf1.4.2).

He says—response to sexual refusal
He said that he was taking her home through the woods when she started taking the "mickey" [making fun of him] because of his wife and baby, and he grabbed her and strangled her. He said he had kissed her a few times but she said no

to sex. All she kept saying was that it was wrong and I wouldn't get anything because I was married. At this point I became angry and grabbed her around the neck. I do not understand why in my mind I did this but once I started strangling her I couldn't seem to stop. I got her onto the ground and kept strangling her all the time and hitting her. After a while she fell limp into sub-consciousness and I started ripping her clothes off. I covered her mouth with my hand because she seemed to be coming round again and someone was coming through the woods. Once these people passed, I once again started to strangle her and it was at this point I took my penknife and started to stab her. I did not know why I was stabbing her, nor the reason why I was doing it. I then started ripping her clothes again and biting and punching her. After this, I stopped and looked at her and became scared so I took my matches and set light to her dress or blouse (*850cf1.4.2).

The above narratives demonstrate a number of recurring exculpatory accounts offered by sexual murderers. They include denial of intent to harm; existence of an ongoing sexual relationship with the victim, even when she is a stranger; a claim of consensual sex; the violence was proportionate because it was in self-defense; and, explanations that invoke an excusatory claim linked to the victim's sexual refusal, which is one of the most common explanations, suggesting a sense of entitlement that accepts no refusal or resistance to sexual desires. These are some of the immediate responses and explanations that were offered near the time of the murder—possibly in an attempt to avoid prosecution or a charge of murder. Yet, as shown in the next chapter, some men maintain these exculpatory accounts even after years in prison.

COMPARISONS OF SEX MURDERS AND MALE-MALE MURDERS

The comparisons of male-male murders (MMs) and sexual murders (SexMs) are shown in Figure 6.1 at the end of the chapter and in Appendix IV, Table 6.1. At the time of the murder, the male perpetrators in both groups were of a similar age (MM = 27 yrs vs. SexM = 29 yrs), but the average age of the male victims of male-male murder (40 yrs) was nearly 13 years older than the perpetrators, while the average age of women victims of sexual murder (31 yrs) was only 2 years older than the age of the perpetrators. For both groups, few of the men were employed (MM = 32% vs. SexM = 45%) and most were either single (48% vs. 41%) or separated/divorced (18% vs. 21%). As shown in Appendix IV, Table 6.1, the type of relationship between the perpetrator and the victim in both groups was very similar: One-third were strangers (31% vs. 37%), and two-thirds were acquainted in some way. Despite these similarities, the context of the murders differed in several ways, with male-male murders generally occurring during a theft, street robbery, or burglary (often a younger man robbing and killing an older man) or in a confrontation between two males who were both young and similar in age. Only 7% of the 424 male-male murders included a sexual attack/element.

Prior to the murder, ongoing disputes between offenders and the victims were significantly more likely among male-male murders than sexual murders

(30% vs. 4%). There were also significant differences in presence of a confrontation immediately preceding the murder (61% vs. 40%), previous violence by the offender to the victim (11% vs. 4%), and previous violence by the victim to the offender (11% vs. 1%). Although the nature of these disputes, confrontations, and previous violence are not considered in detail for male-male murders, the evidence indicates that they differed in content, with issues of sex and gender relations primarily characterizing the one but not the other. For the most part, the offenders in both groups were drinking at the time of the murder (68% vs. 74%), and about one-half of both groups were defined as drunk (49% vs. 51%), For the victims, nearly half were drinking at the time of the murder (47.0% vs. 45%) and about one-third were defined as drunk (33% vs. 30%). Offenders and victims were drinking together in a substantial minority of the cases (21% vs. 33%).

For both groups, most murders were committed in or near the home of the victim (50% vs. 58%). The use of instruments as weapons such as a ligature, a screwdriver, or blunt object used as a bludgeon was common (88% vs. 73%), as was the infliction of five or more injuries (71% vs. 70%), but strangulation was significantly more likely in sexual murders (7% vs. 53%). Although not shown in Appendix IV, Table 6.1, the vast majority of the murders lasted less than 30 minutes (80% vs. 72%). There was usually only one perpetrator in sexual murders (93%), while 43% of male-male murders involved two or more perpetrators. Both the attack and death usually occurred in the same location, although some male victims died in a second location including an ambulance, hospital, or other medical care (22% vs. 3%), which suggests they were more likely to have received some form of assistance before death and less likely to die alone. Almost all of the women victims died alone and without assistance.

SUMMARY

For the most part, sex murderers were in their late 20s, unemployed, single, and had problems with crime and alcohol. The victims of sexual murder were about the same age and came from all walks of life (women aged 65 and over are not included here but are examined in the next section). These included stay-at-home mothers, shop assistants, hair dressers, professional women, and sex workers. The men had different types of access to the victims based on the nature of their relationship, which ranged from strangers with no legitimate social access to long-term acquaintances, friends, and neighbors with varying opportunities for contact. Access to the women provided diverse opportunities for the men to seek sex from them and to commit violence against them, including murder.

For strangers, the usual pattern of murder involved the element of surprise or deception in order to gain access to the woman, the immediate use of violence in order to overwhelm the woman and/or overcome any resistance, retreat to a place away from observation in order to commit a sexual attack which, in these cases, also involved killing the woman. Some examples of these circumstances include a man on foot who stakes out an isolated place where he is unlikely to be observed and attacks a woman who comes into that space, which could be a darkened city street, alleyway, park, playing field, or countryside; a man who persuades a woman to get into his car by some means such as offering her a lift, pretending to be a taxi driver, and then drives to an isolated location and sexually attacks the woman; a man who attacks a woman on the street and drags her into his car or van; a man who approaches a woman sex worker and takes her to an isolated place for the agreed purpose of sex and then violently attacks her; or a man who attacks a woman after breaking into her house.

For short-term acquaintances, the usual pattern of murder involved those who recently met in various social settings such as a dance, pub, or club and spent a few hours together, which might have included talking, dancing, and drinking together, and may also have involved some form of intimacy such as casual kissing and embracing in a public setting. They leave the location together either for the purpose of going elsewhere or in order to return to her home, where he attempts to have sexual intercourse. A confrontation occurs when she resists his sexual advances, he insists on sex, she begins to fight him off, and he "changes the project" and escalates the physical violence in an effort to obtain sex, which often involves strangulation and/or other violence in order to subdue and overwhelm her resistance. In addition, he may be angered by her resistance and use violence as a means of "punishing" her for resisting. While the man may not have set out with the intention of sexually assaulting, raping, or murdering a woman, his fixed intention is to have sex, and he is willing to use force in order to overcome any resistance even to the point of killing the woman.

For longer term acquaintances, friends, neighbors, and relatives, the usual pattern of murder did not require an element of surprise or deception in order for the man to obtain social access to the woman—it was granted by virtue of their relationship. However, some form of deception was used in order to shift the "activity" from one that is strictly social to one that involves sex. While no force or deception is required to obtain access to the woman or her home, it is used when he attempts to have sex with her. Prior to the attack, the woman has been selected as someone with whom the man wishes to have sex. Unlike with some of the strangers, the woman has not been randomly selected but, instead, is a targeted choice for sex. At the point when the man begins the sexual attack, the woman resists his sexual advances, he persists, and there is a confrontation. He physically assaults the woman in order to have sex with her, and kills her either as a part of the sex act and/or as a "punishment" for her resistance. These attacks usually occur in the home of the victim.

For the woman who is an acquaintance or neighbor but is also known to be a sex worker, the usual pattern of murder differs in several ways. Although sex is not the basis of their relationship (as it might be if she were at work), the male neighbor may assume sexual access to the woman by virtue of her occupation, while, on the basis of their relationship as neighbors or acquaintances, she may assume otherwise. The male neighbor may believe he is entitled to sex in exchange for some real or imagined material assistance he has provided, whereas the woman neighbor accepts no such assumption. He may think that he can have sex with her because she is a sex worker, but that it should be free because she is a neighbor or a friend. For a variety of reasons the woman may not wish to have sex with him, but if she chooses to have sex with him she may expect to be paid. These and other cross-cutting expectations result in conflict and confrontations in which he is willing to use force and violence to obtain sex and/or to "punish" her for failing to meet his expectations either through resistance to sex or because she expects payment for it.

Before these murders, all the men wanted sex but they had differing orientations about what they were willing to do in order to get it. The orientations included the following: Men who wanted sex and did not have violence in mind in advance but used it in the act; Men who wanted to have sex and were willing to use violence to get it; Men who wanted to use violence against women and to use sex as a part of the violence; Men who wanted to live out a pornographic fantasy which usually involved a script containing violence and sometimes, but rarely, one that focused on romance; and, finally, Men who wanted to rape and kill a woman. After the murder, most of the men simply left the scene and continued their usual activities. A few inflicted further injury on the body after death, often in ways that "sustained" the sexual attack including sexual intercourse, inserting objects into various parts of the body, cutting the body in sexual areas such as the breast, nipples, vagina, and anus, which might have been symbolic and/or ritualistic. Others attempted to obscure the victim's identity by destroying the face, hands, or the entire body through burning or dismembering. Fundamentally, the men began with a sexual intent and a willingness to use violence in order to obtain it. Some focused on a specific woman known to them, while others did not. Men who murdered strangers did not generally select a specific woman for attack but, instead, set some kind of trap and randomly attacked the woman who fell into it. Some men targeted women working in prostitution because they were "easy" to locate, approachable, and were likely to accompany them to an isolated location where they could carry out an attack.

In brief, sexual murders were first examined in terms of the different relationships between perpetrators and victims, and then all of the sexual murders were considered as a whole in terms of the context and circumstances at the time of the murder and the nature of the murder itself including the forms of attack, nature and number of injuries, treatment of the body after death, and various claims made by perpetrators. For the most part, there were no prior disputes between the man and woman, or a history of his violence toward her. Many of the men had been drinking at the time and were drunk. Prior to the murder, many of the men had thoughts about sex and some had detailed fantasies about sex, some including violence, and a few were sadistic and included murder. Some included the specific woman who was to become the victim, while others were more general in nature. A few had well-developed scripts of the event, and some were obsessional. The usual cause of death was strangulation, and common forms of attack included kicking, stomping, and beating with blunt instruments, often to the face and sexual parts of the body. Attacks often occurred in the home of the victim, while others occurred in isolated locations away from public view, where the murder was committed in a relatively short period of time and without witnesses. After death, most perpetrators left the scene and resumed their normal activities, although some continued a sexual or physical assault on the body after death and a few involved mutilations. A small minority attempted to avoid detection by burning, dismembering, and/or moving the body. The claims of perpetrators included total denial of the murder and/or of the sexual attack, a lack of intention to do harm, that the sex was consensual, and that the attack was in self-defense.

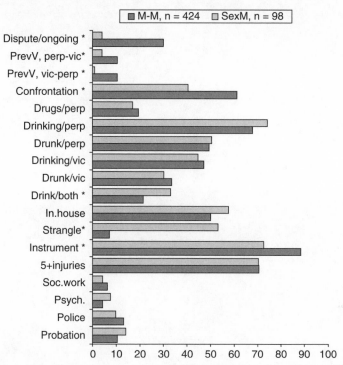

Figure 6.1 SexM—Circumstances at Murder: Male-Male Murder and Sexual Murder.
* Statistically significant difference.

7

Sexual Murder—Perpetrators

Lifecourse, Orientations, and Cognitions

Who are the men who murder women for sex? The preceding analysis of the nature of sexual murders and the contexts and situations in which they occur illustrates the complexities of these murders and provides insight into possible explanations. Here we examine the attributes and thinking of men who perpetrate sexual murders. The men's circumstances in childhood and adulthood are examined, especially relationships with and violence toward women, as well as their sense of remorse for the murder and empathy with the victim. Their behavior and adjustment in prison, especially toward women prison officers, is also considered, as it is an important aspect of the lifecourse and because it allows for additional knowledge regarding the relevant orientations of these men.

Questions that might immediately come to mind relate to those about sex, including early experiences of sex, orientations to sex, problem behavior, and early sexual offending. As shown in the relevant knowledge chapter, some of the usual questions investigated about the childhoods of sexual murderers include whether they grow-up in a stable, intact family; whether there was violence between their parents; whether their family had frequent contact with the criminal justice system and social services; whether they were physically and/or sexually abused; whether they had friends; how they got on in school; whether they abused alcohol or drugs; and whether they were in trouble with the police and courts when they were children. Questions about the adult lifecourse of murderers are not always considered in the research on sexual murderers, but we explore the adult lives of these men, especially their relationships with women, in some detail. In order to consider the possible uniqueness of sexual murderers we round off the chapter with a comparison of the characteristics of sex murderers (SexM, n = 98) with those of men who murder other men (MM, n = 424). Overall, the qualitative accounts characterize the breadth of the lived experience as children and as adults and ranges across the spectrum of extremes in order to provide depth and detail about the experiences and circumstances that may be of relevance in shaping the person who eventually commits murder.

LIFECOURSE—CHILDHOOD

For men who commit a sexual murder, questions generally arise about their sexual development and experiences as children and adults, usually with a considerable focus on childhood. There now exists a vast literature in developmental criminology on childhood, usually with a significant focus on the early onset of offending, which suggests that individuals who begin to engage in antisocial and/or offending behavior at an early age, usually prior to their teens, are at greatest risk of becoming persistent, chronic offenders who commit the vast majority of crimes.[1] Using population-based cohorts and longitudinal methods, research in several countries has revealed important relationships among developmental problems in childhood, antisocial behavior, and criminality.[2] Correlates of childhood offending appear to be associated with several constellations of factors: family formation/structure; parental relationships and the characteristics of parents; relationships between parents and the child; personality and intellectual and behavioral characteristics of the child. An important limitation of this work is a rather narrow focus on individual factors, although more recent research has moved beyond individual factors to consider the wider context of individual development and action as well as situational and environmental factors.

Missing from this literature is a focus on homicide offenders such as those considered here. Homicide, albeit the most serious form of violence, is a rare event, and, as such, those who commit such violence do not generally appear in the population-based longitudinal studies associated with developmental criminology. An intensive investigation of murder, such as the Murder Study, is generally the only type of research that can focus on and gather a considerable amount of information regarding the backgrounds of those who commit homicides.

In this chapter we explore the child and adult backgrounds of sexual murderers. While the data do not include all the factors that might be associated with persistent offending and violent behavior, it does include a wealth of information regarding the backgrounds of these offenders. We begin with a consideration of childhood. As stated in chapter 4, children live their lives in three domains: the home, the school, and the wider community. Here we focus on the domains of the home, including patterns of parenting and care; the school; experiences of abuse; and the behavior of the men when children with a particular focus on early onset and patterns of offending, substance abuse, and contact with the criminal justice system.

As they move into adulthood at age 16, these men encounter the wider world of employment and intimate relationships for which many are ill-prepared. The period of transition from childhood and adolescence into adulthood is particularly important, and many of the sexual murderers failed to make this transition and continued or started a lifecourse of problematic behavior, difficult relationships with women, substance abuse, and crime. Yet this is not an unrelenting story, some sexual murderers, similar to some of the men who killed an intimate partner, did not have difficult childhoods and appeared to be reasonably successful adults, and these are also reported. We start with examples of the more conventional childhood of some of the perpetrators.

Family of Origin and Carers

Conventional, unproblematic, and happy
In our extensive discussions concerning his background, he recalls a happy childhood spent in a closely knit community in which his family played a prominent role (*1142cf1.4.2).

He was the third of five children. His father was a regular solider, a Sergeant in the Army. He was described as a "good father, very stern," and he had good contact with his mother. No history of crime, alcohol or mental health problems in the family. He describes his childhood home as "very happy" and himself as an average scholar and good at sport. No truancy or discipline problems, and he left school at age fifteen with no educational qualifications (*1076cf11.4.3).

His family was close knit. His father worked for the railroad, and is now retired. He left school with 5 qualifications and completed a full indentured apprenticeship. His childhood and adolescence appear to have been quite unexceptional, pursued throughout in a working class environment but his parents always owned their home. His recollections of his earlier life were of a happy existence within a stable and supportive family environment. The parents have always enjoyed a happy and cohesive marriage, free from domestic violence or acrimony. To the age of sixteen he was a regular Sunday school attendee and a member of the Boys Brigade. He generally reflected upon a happy and uneventful upbringing with annual family holidays being the high point of the year (*974cf1.4.2).

The above examples reflect childhood patterns of a few of the men; what was more likely was a childhood replete with problematic care; numerous changes in carers, for some this meant being in the care of the state; and the onset of difficult, sometimes aggressive and violent behavior. The casefiles of sexual murderers were filled with relevant examples, but only a few representative cases are presented here.

Problems within the family and of the child
Background—very disturbed. Large family, each parent had at least one child to a previous relationship, with eight children together. Material conditions were always very poor with lots of kids and dogs in the house, and lots of social work intervention. Both parents were violent to him and his siblings, and the mother was prosecuted for willful neglect of the children. At five years of age, all kids were taken into care and he and two brothers were placed in an ESN boarding school [England—Independent School for the Emotionally Disturbed] where he was very unhappy. But his family relationships remained very strong despite verbal abuse towards each other, and they closed ranks against outsiders. As a child, he never socialized, had no friends, absconded frequently, and was often in trouble for fighting. He had numerous blackouts and dizzy spells, was of low-average intelligence, and wet the bed until the age of fifteen (*636cf1.4.3).

Violence in the family, disturbed, violent, and early onset of offending
He was the second oldest of three brothers. His father worked for the railroad as a guard, and was an authoritarian figure and a heavy drinker who apparently became very violent towards his wife and children when drunk. His mother was thought to be overprotective and to spoil him. At school "he was regarded as outstandingly disturbed and violent." At age thirteen, he was committed to the care of the local authority, and thereafter he served numerous sentences in residential schools, remand homes, approved schools where he absconded at least fourteen times, detention centers, borstals and prison (*1082cf1.4.3).

Violence by Father Against Mother

Domestic violence, particularly that committed by their father—there were very few reports of mothers committing violence against their father—occurred in the families of some of these men. In our interviews men often described this violence in considerable detail and reflected on how it affected them and in some cases appeared to constitute an overriding memory of their childhoods.

My parents split up, when I was age six. It was violent. My last memories are of them fighting each other, just violence. My father was violent towards my mum. Punching my mum, kicking my mum, and hitting her with his hands, at her throat, stuff like that. [She had] black eyes and bruises. *Was your mother violent towards your father?* No. *Did you get involved in that?* I was too young really. I don't know. *Were the police ever involved?* No. *Did you see very much of this when you were a kid?* I can say that, yes, that's my last memories of them being together. *How did this affect you?* I resented my father for a long while (*917iv1.4.1).

When did it happen? It [father beating mother] was when he went out to the pub and come back. *That was weekly?* Well, he would just come home from the pub and just start beating on her. It wasn't rows or nothing. He would just come in drunk and, boom, away he goes—just slap her about. And he used to punch her. As far as I can recall she never went to hospital. *Only when he was drunk?* Yeah. He was as kind as anything when he was sober. I was always up in the bedroom, like cowering underneath the beds—the fear of him taking it out on us, [but] he never did. No, he just beat my mum up (*984iv1.4.1).

Violence by father against him and his mother
as well as sex abuse of other children
His mother tells me that his father was violent throughout the marriage and was violent to their son from his being very young. She can recall incidents when the offender was three months old, twelve months, two and three years, when the injuries were sufficient for her to seek help from Social Services. There was no violence against him when at school but there was a lot of violence toward his mother. She left his father on numerous occasions but returned because she had no money and no alternative home. He can remember his father hitting him once only. He can remember incidents of violence between his parents and being required to fetch his grandparents in order to seek help for his mother against his father's attacks. His father had been convicted of the sexual abuse of a six year old girl and subsequently of indecent assault of a girl aged four. His father also abused his cousin and one of his daughters over a period of ten years (*1192cf1.4.2).

While these accounts of family and childhood demonstrate the backgrounds of some of the men, the quantitative data on the entire group helps determine the general patterns. The vast majority (93%) were born into families with mothers and fathers who were married. This reflects the era into which they were born, when marriage was the norm and divorce was rather difficult to obtain. Nearly two-thirds (60%) spent most of their childhood in an intact family in which their parents remained their main carers. Intact families are not always free of problems, and about one-fifth of these men had fathers who had problems with alcohol, were violent to their mother, and had a conviction for at least one criminal offense (see Figure 7.1; Appx.IV-Table 7.1). One-third of these relationships (33%) ended in divorce or permanent separation. Although it is impossible to say for sure, this may have been the point when these boys entered into a childhood characterized by a series of different types of caregiving.

The experiences of care beyond birth parents involved a number of arrangements, such as the presence of a male carer who was not their biological father and/or residence with other relatives, particularly grandmothers. At some point in their lives, one-fifth of the men were in the care of the state, including care in a foster home and institutional care. A considerable amount of research suggests that although caretaking outside of the nuclear family may be linked to a problematic childhood, the most significant factor in childhood development is the stability of care. A considerable proportion of these men experienced a least one to three changes in caretaking. In the current context of family arrangements, one change in carers may not be remarkable, but one-quarter of these men (25%) experienced three or more changes in carers. Clearly, adversity in early childhood was apparent in the backgrounds of some of these men, but for most, serious behavioral problems were associated with school attendance. One of the frequent findings in the research literature on sexual murderers is the presence of isolation and loneliness in childhood. The reports of professionals and the materials collected during the interviews sometimes reflect the beginning of isolation at school, mostly linked to the absence of friends.

School

The school often played a minimal role in the daily lives of many of these boys. The majority had problems at school; some had learning difficulties, many were disruptive, and some simply did not attend school. There were Special Schools for those with learning difficulties and for others who were seriously difficult and disruptive. For a variety of reasons, school did not work for them; they were either unwilling or unable to participate in the project of learning or in the activity of socializing with their peers. For many, adhering to rules was problematic, disruption was persistent, and absconding was common, although for some men school was not problematic and they appeared to be reasonably successful. While a few of the men did reasonably well in school, the following examples illustrate in graphic detail a pattern of serious problems.

Poor academics but no problems in school
He was a dull pupil who had to remain after school for extra work to improve his academic skills. He enjoyed sports, complied well with school discipline, a quiet reserved pupil with female friends (*949cf1.4.3).

Educational achievement
He had a happy childhood, no physical or sexual abuse, no emotional or behavioral problems but a brief period of bed wetting. School—lots of friends, five GCSE passes (maths, English, geography, cookery and local studies), left school at fourteen and trained to be a miner [GCSE passes while training in the mines] (*959cf.1.4.2).

While the above reports illustrate reasonable success, this was not the norm. The following demonstrate the usual pattern. Learning difficulties were not uncommon and these men were described, often from an early age, as disturbed, angry, disruptive, aggressive, and sometimes violent toward other students and/or members of their own family. Many were expelled, and a few spent time in Special Schools for children with problem behavior.

Special schools—for learning difficulties

He lived with his mother and her common law husband in a council house [social housing], and also lived with grandparents. First, he was sent to a school for learning difficulties, but because of his unruly behavior he was sent to a Special School but no crime when under sixteen. He was bullied at boarding school for children with behavioral problems. He developed a pattern of disturbed behavior during his childhood and teenage years. His mother has, on a number of occasions, expressed her fears about her son's destructive and violent behavior. This included outbursts of temper within the family, and a fascination with lighted matches. He has himself assaulted his mother, and describes a number of occasions when family arguments have led to him becoming violent (*1096cf1.4.2).

Special schools for learning difficulties and for problem behavior

At age five, it was realized he was somewhat backward. He was regarded as being generally educationally subnormal with the result that at the age of nine he went to a Special School. At the age of twelve, he returned to normal schooling. He attended local primary schools where his behavior was said to be problematic. When he was twelve, he was expelled from secondary school for stealing £100 from the school. His mother then sent him to live with an aunt and uncle. He was placed in another school but truanted and because of misbehavior was expelled again after one year. He described himself as having no friends at school, being a misfit and often being bullied. He admitted resorting to physical violence and theft whilst at school (*1002cf1.4.2).

Special schools—for problem behavior

He was abandoned by his mother when he was a child when she could not cope with his father, an alcoholic who was violent to her and to him. He absconded from school trying to rejoin his mother with whom he got on well. And he spent much of his childhood in a special school or community care. He was in Care from age nine to fourteen, in Borstals [institution for young offenders] and in a hostel, and with his mother for a short time. He spoke at length and with pride about all of the dangerous and risky pranks he engaged in at the numerous schools from which he was expelled (e.g., climbing onto roof tops, falling over tall walls). He spent time as a rent boy for which he has no regrets except for one incident when he was raped by a club owner and several bouncers. He has spent the majority of his life in penal establishments. (*1005cf1.4.2).

Special school—disruptive and violent

He was seen by a psychiatrist at the age of ten for violent outbursts, and at the age of fourteen went to a Special School. At school, he had poor concentration and was disruptive. His mother describes his adolescence as being very difficult and she recalls that she was always aware of her son's presence by the noise he made (*956cf1.4.2).

Violent, aggressive toward other pupils and his sister

He was in Care when a teenager, and described as beyond control. He was well known to the various authorities during these years as a difficult teenager, unhappy at ordinary school and at home. At secondary school, there were several incidents of him being seriously violent towards other pupils. There are also incidents of him being violent to his younger sister. He is recorded as being quick to anger and, at one point, to having seen victims as "deserving it" (*930cf1.4.2).

What is very apparent in the childhood and adolescence of these men is a failure at school, sometimes related to educational demands but also related to the social dimensions of schooling such as staying in their seat, cooperating with the teachers, relating to peers, and refraining from violence. While aggressive and problematic behaviors were usually reported, other issues such as separateness, sometimes described as shyness, or an inability to integrate and engage with other children, may have been overlooked. All of this often led to absconding and expulsion. In some cases, the boys just stayed away from school and spent their time in other pursuits, which often involved loitering, petty crime, and substance abuse and offending. The following examples illustrate these patterns.

Aggressive, violent, and expelled from school

He has never known his father and mother, and is no longer in touch with his brother. He was a troublesome and somewhat aggressive person in childhood who was excluded from school and taken into care, into special facilities—a child guidance clinic—and appeared in juvenile court. When sixteen, he attacked his brother with a hammer and threatened a farmer with a sheath knife (*998cf1.4.2).

No school—absconder—never went to school

So tell me about your time at school, how old were you when you left school? Well I left school when I was sixteen, officially. *What about unofficially?* I never actually went in all my life. *Really for all of your life?* My dad used to let me stay at home. I lived with my dad, my mum and dad split up when I was four. I lived with my dad, a chronic alcoholic, and my little brother and I used to do all the cooking, the cleaning, and everything like that, never used to bother going to school, you know, he needed me at home, and then, they must have took me into foster care. I went into foster care and then went back to my dad's, and then to foster parents so I've got little bits of schooling. *Why did you not like school?* I always got bottom—on one test he [his teacher] give me 2% for getting my name right. He shamed me in front of the class, I didn't like that, the other kids may be brighter but they are all children, and I was very mature. I just couldn't see the sense in it, so I thought well "knock it on the head, school" [leave school] all together (*630iv1.4.2).

No school—What to do all day?

Whew!—Well, things started to get—things weren't too good family-wise. And being the eldest of the family I had a lot of worry put on my shoulders. I did from the age of nine, so—I was sort of made to grow up quicker than I should have done. *Did you have many friends at school?* No, I never, I had hardly any friends. *Was that because of what was happening at home?* It was just through choice. *Can I ask why you chose not to have friends?* I don't know—I just sort of was a loner. And I just preferred my own company. *Then you went to high school.* I didn't like it. I couldn't fit in with the other kids there. They led totally different lives to what I had led and I couldn't bring myself into their way of thinking and their kind of lifestyle. *Was this because you had actually lived in a residential school or?* I had always been martyred since I was a child, I understand that now. I have gone through things with a psychiatrist, and I have always been that way, always had problems since I was a young child, like dealing with people and situations. And school was just too harsh an environment to get involved in. The class sizes were huge and I just couldn't fit in to their social calendar of events and things like that. I just couldn't deal with them. *So did you actually play truant from school quite a bit?* Yeah, a lot. *So what did you do when you were truanting?* I would go and get drunk with the lads drinking cider (*642iv1.4.2).

In childhood, these offenders experienced considerable adversity beginning with caretaking and followed by the challenges of school. At school, they failed to learn, to integrate with other children and some even failed to attend. For most, the traditional school was not a place of achievement, happiness, or success but one of failure and discontent. As shown in Figure 7.1 at the end of the chapter and Appendix IV, Table 7.1, the vast majority had problems in school (69%); many had discipline problems at school and in the family and were disruptive (44%). A small minority spent time in a Special School (9%) for learning difficulties, and 4% resided for some time in an institution for disruptive children. Some spent time in both. Many grew up in families that had contact, often considerable, with the social services (42%) and around one-third of these families (32%) came to the attention of the mental health services.

Days without school left a great deal of "free" time, which was sometimes spent at home but often spent in the street or neighborhood with others who were not in school. Stealing and drunkenness were common to many, along with police contact, arrest, and conviction, and a considerable proportion were already experiencing problems with alcohol abuse (34%) and/or drug abuse (20%) before the age of 16 (Figure 7.1; Appx.IV-Table 7.1). The shift of focus and action away from the context of the school was problematic not only in the failure to obtain learning and educational credentials that might be used as an adult but also in the daily activities that were problematic both as a child and later as an adult. In addition, the daily activities of crime, often petty but frequent, led to childhood contacts with the justice system and set a pattern for later behavior.

Problems of the Child—Alcohol, Drugs, and Early Offending

As well as difficulties at school and home, a considerable proportion of the men began offending at an early age, and a few had been convicted of a number of offenses before the age of 16. One-fifth could be classified as early-onset offenders with at least one conviction before the age of 13, with just over one-half having at least one conviction before the age of 16. One-fifth (21%) had five or more convictions before the age of 16, a similar proportion (23%) had been convicted of a violent offense before the age of 16, and 7% had committed a sexual offense by that age. Only two (2%), had been violent to an animal. As boys, many (19%) experienced institutional foster care, and a reasonable proportion (25%) were incarcerated before the age of 16 in a criminal justice institution for juveniles, such as an Approved School or Borstal. The following three narratives illustrate the early onset of problem behavior and offending and the subsequent patterns of incarceration for young offenders.

Speech impediment, truanting, disturbed behavior, and offending
He made slow progress in primary school mainly due to a speech impediment and partial deafness. He frequently truanted and was taken into local authority care as a result of disturbed behavior and persistent stealing. At the age of ten, and following offenses of shop-breaking and larceny, he was committed to an Approved School where he remained for five years. After a short time at home on his release at the age of fifteen, he served another two years in a Borstal [reform school] for further offenses of shop-breaking and larceny. Since completing full time education at age fifteen, he has rarely been in employment. His life between prison sentences has increasingly revolved around "heavy drinking, Hells Angels, and rock and roll" (*1054cf1.4.3).

Frequent truancy, very early onset of offending, and incarceration
From the age of eight he began truanting from school and stealing and as a result was placed in an Approved School. When allowed home, he quickly returned to breaking and entering and spent further years in an Approved School and subsequently graduated to Borstal [reform school]. At the age of eighteen, he was home for a short period from Borstal when he committed rape. The circumstances of that offense were that he was asked for directions by a twenty-one year old woman; he then waylaid her on route and raped her. He was sentenced to five years in a YOI [Young Offenders Institution] and was released two months prior to the murder (*118cf1.4.1).

Pattern of serious offending from an early age becoming
a persistent offender by age 16
At school he was regarded as outstandingly disturbed and violent. His first offense was at the age of eight. At age thirteen, he was committed to the care of the local authority and thereafter he served numerous sentences [for larceny, housebreaking, and robbery with violence] in residential schools, remand homes and Approved School (absconded at least 14 times), Detention Center and prison (over 30 offenses before age 16) (1082cf1.4.3).

Physical and/or Sexual Abuse of the Child
at Home, School, or Elsewhere

Either within the context of the home, the school, or the wider community, a small proportion of the boys were physically and/or sexually abused. As children, 28% were physically abused, mostly by their birth father (75%) and some by their birth mother (11%). In addition, 13% were sexually abused. Sexual abuse was mostly committed by birth fathers (50%), stepfathers, or other male relatives (13%), although 37% was committed by an unrelated male. Only one of the men reported being sexually abused by a woman (Figure 7.1; Appx.IV-Table 7.1). The experiences of physical and/or sexual abuse as a child may work to damage the child in a variety of ways and also to shape their subsequent orientations to the act of sex itself.

By mother's male partner

Did that stop him [when you told your mother about the abuse]? He [mother's male partner] left. He packed up and went. I was relieved. But I mean things didn't get back to normal. I just went off the rails. I did, no one else [his siblings] did, just me. Burglaries, I just got into trouble. Because of the rape, I know it was because of that. *So you were raped when you were nine, and did you go off the rails immediately?* Well, no. It was when I was about eleven or twelve. Because I didn't understand what happened until I started getting older. See, I couldn't ask for someone's advice because I was a loner. I felt confused, frustrated, angry, and very angry. I still do. When I think about it, [I feel] unclean and all that, do you know what I mean? I still do. I still, like even when I get in the shower, if I want to clean my back passage and all that, I just get the shakes all over me and just start crying. *And you say you have actually talked to people since you have been in [prison]?* Yes (*984iv1.4.1).

By a male neighbor

Did you ever have any bad sexual experiences when you were a child? Yeah, when I was younger I used to go to this bloke's down the road. And I went and he used to give me comics and that and then, after a bit, he started to play with me down below and he used to give me money and say, like, if I said something that I would get locked up and he would as well—we'd both get into trouble. So I never used to say anything. And I used to come back with money and I didn't get much money myself [at home], so I used to go back. I don't know why. I just went back and he kept doing it. He would give me more money, and he used to play with me. And once, I come home and I told my stepdad that something is happening down there and what was happening. And he said who was doing that to you. He knew anyway, he went down and brought the police and that, but [nothing] happened because he said that he hadn't done it (*960iv1.4.1).

By a male teacher

From age eleven, he was abused by a teacher two or three times per week, and he became involved in sex perversions with another teacher and fellow students. Very disturbed childhood, all family had grossly sociopath attitudes (*636cf1.4.3).

Sexual Issues and Sexual Offending as a Child

As children, a few of the men began engaging in various sexual behaviors (12%) and/or sexual offending (7%) with or against other children. Some of this behavior might be characterized as that of early childhood curiosity, exploration, and experimentation like that seen in activities such as "playing doctor" when children engage with friends and siblings in looking at and touching bodies of the same or opposite sex. However, the evidence suggests that much of it involved an early introduction to sexual behavior some of which included sexual offending involving physical force or violence. This behavior sometimes led to the intervention of various adults ranging from parents and caretakers to official agencies particularly social services and/ or police, courts, and probation.

Problems of the Child Related to Sex

And why did you go into Care at this time? I got caught with my sister, lying on top of my sister, when I was younger—when I was fourteen. She is a few years younger than me and my dad walked in and I had my trousers down and I was laid on top of my sister. But I had been messed about with, well before—before all this. My mum went and saw the social worker, and I said that I wanted to go into Care. I didn't want to stay at home because of what had happened. My mum had had different boyfriends and I was stressed and I went into Care because, I told them I didn't want to [stay at home] (*960iv1.4.1).

His father a sales representative—he was second of three children. As a child, family relationships appear to have been close with him helping his father's business interests or harvesting with local farmers. He stated that his sister got him seduced into mutual cross dressing and sexual activities which involved her lying naked and him putting his fingers into her vagina and touching her breasts. This went on for about three years starting when he was only eight years old. At the age of fourteen, he was on two separate occasions seduced by older men to participate in masturbatory activities, with more involvement by masturbating him or getting him to pose for nude photos. At the age of thirteen, he started masturbating using pornographic pictures and his sister's underwear as stimulus material. At the age of fourteen, he started to have sexual intercourse with calves on the farm. He says he got the idea from watching artificial insemination and it helped him to relieve his sexual frustration. He continued to do this over the next four years and again when he was working on a prison farm. He tried to have normal intercourse from the age of fifteen but not successfully. Although he denied any sexual interest in minors he admitted to interfering with a six year old niece by touching her vagina and then licking his fingers (*1130cf1.4.3).

He was cautioned at the age of twelve for indecent assault. At the age of fourteen he approached a young girl, grabbed hold of her, put his hand up her skirt, knocked her to the ground and touched her thigh. He was given a twelve month conditional discharge. At age fifteen, he was convicted of another indecent assault. On the school grounds after hours he attempted to kiss her and pushed her to the ground. He lowered his trousers and underpants, sat astride the girl and attempted to remove her knickers. He was disturbed by a passer-by. At age seventeen, he assaulted an eight year old victim. He approached the girl and pointed a knife at her neck. He then picked her up and carried her into a nearby house. He is said to have put her down on the bed and touched her indecently. He unfastened his trousers and told the girl to open her mouth but she refused. He then lay on top of the girl but was disturbed and ran off. Another offense: He enticed the boy into the backyard, fondled and sucked the boy's penis and then asked the boy to kiss his own penis (*1088cf1.4.2).

LIFECOURSE—ADULTHOOD

Both the narratives and the statistical data indicate that a sizable proportion of the sexual murderers experienced problems in childhood and most were ill-equipped for the transition to adulthood. For the many with little or no success in school, the shift to the world of paid employment was difficult if not practically impossible. The skills obtained in school that are necessary to obtain and retain employment, such as reliable attendance, time-keeping, completion of tasks, adherence to authority, and the like, were weak or nonexistent as they moved from one world into another. The shift from the childhood family of orientation and/or caretaking by relatives or the state to adult relationships represents another set of challenges that may be made more difficult or problematic for those who had disrupted child-caring or were institutionalized as children, and/or for those who were sexually or physically abused as children. The tasks of developing personal or intimate relationships in adulthood were made more difficult or impossible by the lack of an opportunity or failure to develop in childhood the social and personal skills necessary for this transition. Men who commit sexual murders come to adulthood woefully deficient in the skills and orientations necessary for a successful adult life; especially, it seems, the ability to relate to others. As a group, they are undereducated and underemployed (Figure 7.2; Appx.IV-Table 7.2). For the most part, they leave school early before the age of 16 (53%), and only one-quarter (27%) obtain any formal qualifications. For most of their adult life, the majority are either chronically unemployed (about 60%) or employed sporadically and in unskilled jobs. A sizable minority abused drugs (26%), a majority had problems of alcohol abuse (60%), and even more had sexual problems of various types (73%). About one-third (38%) experienced mental health problems and had contact with mental health professions such as psychologists and/or psychiatrists.

Adult Circumstances and Employment

The qualitative materials are used to examine the lifestyles including employment, the abuse of alcohol and/or drugs, and criminal careers of the men. Most were usually unemployed or only held jobs infrequently or sporadically, although a few were in reasonably steady employment.

Employed

He had various jobs, mostly unskilled and of a short duration, and is currently employed wiring new buildings. He was well thought of by his employers and fellow employees, enjoyed his work, had no recognizable qualifications but was competent at his job (*1017cf.4.2).

Employed and then homeless

He worked for two years in the pits [coal mines], and in a bookshop for five years, part-time in a cinema and then as a barman for one year, and five years working for a company in France, then casual work fruit picking. He said he left home "in order to be homeless"—he researched the "best places" in which to be homeless (by which he meant areas or towns offered the best facilities to homeless people). He said he had no close friends (*959cf.1.4.2).

Employed and a loner

[At the time of the murder] He lived in the family home where his mother had died several years earlier. He had been in the same job for about fifteen years, had few social outlets, led a very quiet life, was "cloistered" and spent much of his free time watching TV and using the computer or photographic equipment (*701cf1.4.2).

What little money he received from temporary employment, he appeared to squander on gambling in pubs and alcohol. He is best described by persons who knew him (at work and former school colleagues) as a "loner" (*937cf1.4.2).

He was in the Army for twelve years, and dismissed for misconduct, mostly assault. His Commanding officer describes him as "a complete and utter loner, a man of few words, who has no friends" and "very short tempered" and "highly volatile, hard to get on with and a bully." According to his mother, he has had only one girlfriend during his lifetime. He does not smoke, drink, and according to his mother does not leave the house, although this point will be refuted by the police (*1130cf1.4.3).

Alcohol and/or Drug Abuse

Nearly two-thirds of the sexual murderers had serious problems with alcohol (Figure 7.2 Appx.IV-Table 7.2), and it was often the center of their daily life. The case-files and interviews provide descriptions of what this meant on a daily basis and how it was related to criminal acts including robbery and violence. Drug abuse figured in the lives of 26% of the men, but for most the problem was alcohol and not drugs.

And again when you were drinking, how much did you usually drink? A lot, I became near an alcoholic. *What does a lot mean?* I couldn't walk past a pub without walking into it (*984iv1.4.1).

He began drinking at age eleven with friends of his own age. This continued to increase over time and has resulted in a number of rows [arguments] with his parents about his excessive drinking. He says he could drink up to seven pints [of beer] per hour. His aggressive behavior followed heavy drinking, which includes two incidents of criminal damage to his parent's home when he was told to leave eight years ago. His heavy drinking occurs now mostly on weekends so as not to affect his [full-time] employment. He would spend £40–£50 [approximately $65–$85] on drink per night at a pub and would routinely consume three pints of cider or home brew before leaving his home. He describes drinking as his main pastime. He infrequently used cannabis, magic mushrooms or LSD on a recreational basis—there was not a regular or sustained drug use (*1017cf.4.2).

At age 17, he returned from Local Authority Care [foster parents] to his mother but left to live with his father after a few weeks. At 20, he got his own local authority flat. He started a cohabiting relationship with a woman, but due to his excessive cannabis use and violent outbursts, she left after one year (he chopped up bedroom furniture and threatened physical violence to her). Not much employment—couple of work schemes, unemployed for three years and unemployed at time of murder. Successful drug treatment but he became over-dependent on support and formed emotional attachment to a female key worker (*509cf1.4.3).

ORIENTATIONS TO WOMEN AND WOMEN PARTNERS

Orientations to Women

Of considerable importance are the orientations these men have toward women. Some demonstrate extremely negative attitudes, while most hold views that place women in subordinate positions and illustrate a predatory approach to sexual relations. Their backgrounds provide evidence of a link between these attitudes and violence against women, including murder. The casefiles were replete with perpetrators' comments about women that reflected the notion of them either as good or bad (Madonna—Whore) or as purely bad in the sense that they cheated, mistreated, and generally behaved badly in their relationships with these men. Comments of this nature in both the interviews and the casefiles were often lengthy, and filled with detail and emotion.

Simplistic and distorted views of women
In talking with him about the offense and his feelings towards the victim, it is very clear that he has a considerably distorted view of both women and sex. His view of sexual morality, particularly as it relates to women, appears to be extremely rigid. He describes women in simplistic terms as either, "pure and innocent" or, in his words, "tarts." He had viewed the victim in the former category, but when she is said to have initiated intercourse, immediately relegated her to the second category. At this point he seems to have totally lost the ability to see her as an individual, or to respond to her as the friend she was supposed to be. When he talks about sex he talks in very negative terms, using words such as "dirty" and "disgusting," which he relates to others' sexual activity as well as his own. Despite this he displays a clear interest in young women, leading to considerable confusion as to what he expects from relationships and how he interprets women's behavior (*1096cf1.4.2).

Difficult and angry relationships with women
He stated in interview that his offending was not sexually motivated but more related to anger and frustration he has/had towards women. He claims females "made me feel like shit" and he wanted to "degrade them" and chose to take it out on total strangers. He acknowledges he has had difficulty dealing with relationships, especially at "being rejected and laughed at." His low self-esteem,

poor self-confidence, along with emotional insecurity is a factor in his offending
(*1132cf1.4.3).

He says—anger at women precipitated the murder
His previous experience with women, had, he felt, been a factor in his loss of temper which precipitated the murder. He had been badly let down by his two ex-
girlfriends (*984cf1.4.2).

Distorted views of women and hatred of prostitutes
In [mental] hospital he said, "I don't go around messing with them [women]. I have
no doubt that girls in the hospital would like to go out with me. I can tell when
women like me, they ask me to do favors for them, like going to the shops. I have
no strong feelings against women, but against prostitutes, not them personally
but what they do, living on immoral earnings, I just think it's wrong. They make
money so easily, and there are people out of work who can't do that" [in hospital for
slashing and attempting to strangle a woman working as a prostitute]. After dis-
cussing the offense he said, "anyway it was only a three inch knife" (*998cf1.4.2).

Previous Physical and/or Sexual Violence Against Women

Many of the men appeared to specialize in using violence against women that may
or may not have included a sexual component. About two-fifths (43%) committed
physical violence against a person other than an intimate partner, including both
males and females, but women victims were prominent (Figure 7.2; Appx.IV-
Table 7.2). Some of the victims were unknown to them, but most were not. Of these,
intimate partners figured most frequently as the victims of both their physical and
sexual violence, but a few of these men appeared to be indiscriminate in their choice
of a woman victim and assaulted strangers. The three examples illustrate the apparently indiscriminate violence of men committed against a woman.

> While on bail, he had an argument with his sister and her sister-in-law during the
> course of which he attacked the latter, knocking her to the ground and kicking her
> face and body [public setting]. When arrested, he assaulted the arresting officer
> who was forced to draw his truncheon (*1054cf1.4.3).

This man is two months into a forty year life sentence for murder. This occurred
only days after being released from a ten year sentence for attacking another
female. In fact, he has been attacking any member of the opposing gender since
the age of fifteen for no other reason than them being female. When he was only
sixteen, he came up behind a girl who was a schoolmate and hit her on the head
repeatedly with a hammer (sentenced to three years supervision with a condition
of residence). On various occasions over an eight month period when he was aged
eighteen, he targeted lone females, entered their homes by force or on pretence
and then savagely attacked them, punching and kicking them about the head and
groin (sentenced to five years in Youth Custody). Within three days of release he
attacked a woman and a girl who were walking together on a riverside path. The
girl he punched, the woman he stabbed four times in the body and neck, besides

slashing her face. Though charged with intent to rob there is no doubt that his motivation was sexual as well as the desire to inflict serious injury (sentenced to eight years in prison). He was released on parole nine weeks before this killing. [*Trial Judge*] "Anyone who takes it upon himself to release this man before senescence has totally debilitated him and his desires will have to answer for the consequences—and the answer will not be easy to find" (*911cf1.4.3).

Physical and Sexual Violence to Intimate Partner/s

The sexual murderers stand in contrast to the popular notion of men who are either complete loners or those with little or no contact with women as intimate partners. Three-quarters of the sex murderers (75%) had at least one intimate relationship (either marriage or cohabitation) that lasted for 1 year or more, while a quarter (25%), had no such relationship. Just over one-half (55%) had two or more intimate relationships, and a few had more. The break-up of intimate relationships was a common occurrence for these men (64%), and it is not surprising that almost all of them (87%) were described as having problems with women, primarily associated with intimate relationships (Figures 7.2, 7.3; Appx.IV-Tables 7.2, 7.3). Physical violence, often chronic, was a significant aspect of their previous (44%) and current (25%) relationships and for some sexual violence was not uncommon (13%). These men were usually extremely controlling and abusive within intimate relationships and sexual proprietariness was common. Casefiles were filled with examples, and physical and sexual violence often resulted in the failure of their relationships.

Intimate partner—violence and sexual pleasure
His wife divorced him during his first sentence for rape—she reports his violence in pursuit of sexual pleasure (*580cf1.4.3).

Intimate partner—physical and sexual violence
He was released after a few months for sexual assault. One month after release, he was arrested following a complaint by his wife that he had assaulted and buggered her on a number of occasions. She claimed that he had also attempted to force his complete hand into her vagina. When arrested, he was found to be in possession of a bread knife with a razor sharp blade tucked into the waist-band at the back of his trousers. Asked why he was carrying the knife, he said that he was aware that his wife was intending to make a complaint against him and that if he could have found her first he would have "put her into the grave." Whilst in custody [awaiting trial] his wife visited him. At the end of the visit he grabbed her by the throat and dragged her into his cell. A violent struggle ensued during which several police officers had to restrain him. Three months later, he was convicted of two offenses of assault and possession of an offensive weapon and was sentenced to a total of four years imprisonment. After this conviction his wife obtained a divorce (*1054cf1.4.3).

Intimate partner—pornography and violent perverted sex
[Police Report] His ex-wife describes the relationship as "horrific." She was frightened of him due to his sexual harassment. Initially their relationship was normal until he began to read certain magazines and wanting to experiment.

She describes numerous sexual deviations which he forced her to take part in. When she refused he would assault her. He'd put bananas, bottles, vibrators and cigarettes "inside her" and take photos. At one stage, he put a mask over her face indicating that it would prevent her being recognized in the photos. He kept a diary describing various sex exploits and described his first sexual relationship at twenty-one with a fourteen year old girl (later fined for unlawful sexual intercourse with a minor). Throughout his adult life, he had a tendency to become aggressive in arguments and, at a certain point, to become physically aggressive. There had been a lot of rows [violence] at home and he had separated from his wife on two occasions. His ex-wife claims he sexually assaulted his daughter when she was very young [which he denies] (*645cf1.4.2).

PREVIOUS CONVICTIONS AND SEXUAL VIOLENCE

A vast majority of the men (77%) had histories of persistent criminal behavior of various types that involved numerous contacts with the police, but 23% had no previous convictions for any type of offense. In addition, many (64%) had five or more convictions as adults (Figure 7.2; Appx.IV-Table 7.2). Convictions for physical violence included minor assault (38%) and serious assault (19%). The usual victim of those men convicted of a physical assault was a woman (56%). Convictions for sexual assaults against women, including rape, were apparent in the background of 21%. There were probably many more, as a great deal of sexual offending does not result in detection, arrest, or conviction. Here, we focus both on those with a previous history of sexual offending that may have gone undetected and on those with convictions for sexual offending (not including offenses such as voyeurism and flashing).

Previous conviction for rape
Previous offenses—a list as long as your arm. He went into the Army at age nineteen, and had been in court 25 times, mostly for burglary and driving offenses. From age 21 onwards, he spent a great deal of time in prison. No drugs problem but a heavy drinker and drinking increased when having relationship problems with his woman partner—6–7 pints most days. He had one previous prison sentence for rape [similar type of attack to that of the murder] (*1023cf1.4.2).

Previous conviction for burglary and intent to rape
Age 24, after a row with his wife he followed a young woman in his van as she walked on the pavement [sidewalk] in the evening. He forced her into his van, drove her to a country lane and raped her (four year sentence). At age twenty-eight, following a break up with a girlfriend, he armed himself with a knife, knocked on the door of a house and grabbed a young woman, and in the struggle he cut her hand (eight year sentence for burglary with intent to rape) (*580cf1.4.3).

Previous conviction for raping girls
A man with a significant history of raping and assaulting women: one rape and an indecent assault charge for which he received 7 yrs; two rapes and one indecent assault and assault; and murder for which he got 10 yrs. Similarities in all

offense: the victims were young, and he attempted to restrain them by placing something around their necks. The rapes involved a fifteen year old girl and another seventeen year old; both were babysitting for him and his wife. He is said to be a heavy drinker at the time of the earlier offenses (*210cf1.4.3).

Previous conviction for rape including horrendous physical violence

He went on something of a spree, robbing houses and looking for female occupants. At about 12:30 am, the complainant was at home and asleep in bed when the accused broke into the house. He turned on the light in the hall and this woke the complainant. She went to the top of the stairs and asked him what he was doing. He ordered her to return to the bedroom which she did. He took a frying pan from the kitchen and went into the bedroom. He ordered the complainant to lie down on the bed which she did. He then hit her about the head with the frying pan causing deep lacerations to her head and face. He then ordered her to remove her nightdress which she did. He again struck her with the frying pan causing further injuries. He told her to clean herself up in the bathroom and when she had done this and returned to the bedroom he ordered her to lie down on the bed. He removed his trousers and had sexual intercourse with her. He then ordered her to turn over and he attempted to have intercourse from the rear. He then left the house taking the victim's television with him. A habitual user of drugs; he blames all his sexual offenses on drugs and is unwilling to move beyond this (*1002cf 1.4.2).

Previous Sexual Violence but No Previous Convictions

A number of the men were serious sexual predators with extensive histories of serious sexual violence that were usually not reported or recorded, and thus they had no official history of previous sexual offenses. These were often against intimate partners or other women with whom they were acquainted. As the following examples show, even when these attacks were reported, for various reasons, usually not reported in the files, women felt unable to follow through on their complaints or if they did the perpetrators were not convicted. Historically and still today it is very difficult for women to come forward and report a sexual attack, particularly because they might very well be implicated because of their "routine activities" or because of the way they behaved or dressed. In some countries the public and criminal justice systems are gradually shedding these misconceptions, and there is some hope that in the future these men can be brought to justice early in their violent careers making it possible to challenge their ways of thinking about women and sex, because it seems clear that without such intervention they will not stop their sexual abuse and violence of their own accord. The following examples demonstrate patterns of violent sexual assaults that did not lead to arrest, prosecution, or conviction.

No convictions for sexual violence—but a number of undetected attacks.

Although he had only three previous convictions [none for sexual violence], after his arrest for murder he told medical experts and the police of numerous other offenses which he had committed between February and April of the previous year. Six rapes—his girlfriend, two young girls he had met at a friend's house, three other women. On two occasions he had threatened women with a knife and once with a broken bottle. Other offenses: seven burglaries, eleven muggings— mainly on women. All of these offenses were later confirmed by police to have been committed (*234cf1.4.2).

No convictions for sexual violence—but charged with rape, not convicted
He'd been cleared of raping two women weeks before the murder. Earlier charged with raping his ex-partner but not convicted (*644cf1.4.3).

No convictions for sexual violence—but incidents of sexual assaults
He has had a number of short and longer term relationships, and appeared to be [sexually] normal though he was sexually active from an early age. There are no prior convictions but he related to me an incident involving allegations of indecent assault made by a young woman but not proceeded upon by the police. There is a description of another previous indecent assault accusation from police papers: a 24 year old woman alleges she was grabbed by [perpetrator] from behind, he turned her to face him and lifted her top clothing over her breasts, then bit her right nipple. He pushed her to the ground and onto her back and tried to pull down her knickers and leggings. She struggled free and called the police. She later withdrew the complaint (*725cf1.4.2).

No convictions for sexual violence—but after the murder
he confessed to earlier rapes
The victim of the first rape was a 25 year old married woman who at the time of the offense was eight and one-half months pregnant. The defendant accosted her as she was walking with her dog, dragged her into nearby undergrowth, threatened her with a screwdriver, tied up her dog, forcibly undressed her and then raped her. Second assault a 20 year old woman who was crossing open ground on her way to a railway station was seized by the defendant and told her, "Don't scream. I've got a knife and I'll fucking use it." He pushed her to the ground and started to punch her in the head and face. After his arrest for murder, the defendant admitted the above offenses (*956cf1.4.2).

The following is a case of a vicious sexual predator who was particularly cunning in selecting victims who were unlikely to be able to testify against him because of their mental disabilities.

No convictions for sexual violence, but serious sexual
violence against several women
[During his incarceration in the mental health clinic he] first came to the notice of the police as a result of "wounding with intent" when a 20 year old female mental patient walked into the hospital, she was naked and had the branch of a tree protruding from her vagina. She was taken to the nearby hospital where it was discovered that the branch [measuring 15.5 inches] had penetrated the victim's body to a depth of 11.5 inches, causing serious internal injuries. It was discovered that the accused had been seen with the aggrieved shortly before she received the injuries. He was found not guilty. A year later, a 68 year old patient who suffers from schizophrenia and a speech defect, reported that she had been attacked and

had suffered a serious head injury whilst walking through the underpass that links the two divisions of the hospital. Supposedly found by the accused, the patient has since told staff that the man who "found" her was responsible for causing her injuries. She is, however, totally unable to give evidence against him. On all the occasions that the accused has come to our notice he has always totally denied any wrong-doing. He is, in the police view, a most accomplished liar who is totally resistant to interrogation no matter how long or skillful that interrogation might be. This view is shared by all hospital staff who know him (*998cf1.4.2).

The above narratives graphically illustrate the history of sexual violence in the backgrounds of these men. While some were convicted of rape and/or sexual assault, many were not. In some, this could have been because women were reluctant to follow through on their complaints possibly because they knew the attempt to bring the man to justice might very well not result in a conviction and that they would probably have to endure an assault on their character.

GUILTY AND IN PRISON

Adjustment to the Prison Regime

After conviction and imprisonment, the two challenges facing the offender involve adjusting to life in prison and addressing the offending behavior associated with the murder, which involves cooperating with staff delivering all types of intervention programs. For men convicted of sexual murders, the average tariff was 17 years with a range of 5–30 years. The tariff is the time that must be served before the man can be considered for parole, which means that all of the men will serve a considerable time in prison. Daily life in prison often results in minor infractions of the rules that lead to a discipline report and some kind of action from prison authorities, often the loss of privileges. Most of the sexual murderers (78%) received at least one discipline report which was fairly common to all prisoners, but 33% of them received 10 or more discipline reports which suggests difficulty in adjusting to daily life in prison (Figure 7.3; Appx.IV-Table 7.3). Very few of the sexual murderers were considered model prisoners, some were disruptive in the normal routines of prison life, and a few were regarded as very dangerous even within the highly controlled prison environment.

Sex offenders are usually segregated from other prisoners either by being placed on separate wings within the prison or by being placed in prisons specifically dedicated to sex offenders. Either way, they present specific challenges regarding their place within the penal regime. Sex offenders, particularly pedophiles, may be stigmatized, ostracized, and/or subjected to abuse and/or attack from other prisoners whether they are housed in a protection wing or in a designated prison. In prison, they face numerous challenges in addressing their offense. They must first acknowledge that sex was involved in the murder. Then, they must being willing to participate in offender programs designed to deal with sexual offending and their attitudes, orientations, and behaviors associated with sexual offending. This requires a level of participation that goes well beyond good behavior on the landing and a lack of discipline reports. They cannot just "keep their head down" and cause no problems. Instead, they must be engaged in a project of personal reform based on the willingness to identify themselves as sexual offenders with all of the associated consequences of being identified as such.

But even at the most basic level of simply staying out of trouble and behaving themselves on the landing, only a few (21%) were defined as "model prisoners" who presented no problems to staff or to prison routines. Problems were often associated with their orientations and behaviors relating to woman prison staff.

Model Prisoner
Our working relationship is excellent. He could be considered a "model prisoner" (*1112cf1.4.2).

His behavior as a model prisoner is at odds with the violence perpetrated during the offense (*611cf1.4.2).

Orientations to and Behavior Toward Women Professionals

The definition of a "model prisoner" is largely based on the offenders' adherence to the prison regime. Even though this may be accepted in a general sense, some members of staff look beyond the immediate adherence to the daily routines of the prison and consider wider issues of future danger and risk. Two-fifths (41%) of the sex murderers were defined as unwilling to cooperate with staff who attempt to persuade them to address their offending behavior and related orientations. Additionally, some of the sexual murderers present a distinct threat to women professionals, including members of the custody staff. Within the prison, their orientations to women staff and behavior toward them provide additional evidence regarding the manner in which these men relate to women even within a context in which there is knowledge of their sexual murder and, as such, they might be expected to attempt to manage their behavior accordingly. Some of the men do not appear to attempt to control their behavior even in a context where punishment, such as a loss of privileges, is inevitable.

[Prison Governor Report] Wing staff remark that he is not a control problem but remains extremely deep, keeping his distance from staff and [associating with only] a few selected peers of a similar low profile. I personally would not trust him an inch and would not consider down-grading [to lower category of security] until we get to know him a lot better. His sexual offenses received much media interest and I believe we owe the public, particularly females and staff, a thorough look at him before making radical recommendations—one to watch as far as I am concerned until he comes out of his shell (*911cf1.4.3).

Annoying, Intimidating, and a Danger to Women Staff in Prison

Some men demonstrate their negative orientations to women and their own sense of entitlement with respect to women in their inappropriate behavior toward women prison officers and other women professionals working within the highly controlled and structured environment of the prison. They may view themselves as "ladies men," believe that "all" women are attracted to them, attempt to "flirt" with women staff, and expect them to respond positively. Women staff feel differently.

Making women staff feel uncomfortable

While in custody, pre-sentence, the prison doctor reported he had been told by many female members of staff they were uncomfortable in his presence. They felt intimidated and uncomfortable with his constant compliments—he'd wink at them and constantly stared at them. When questioned about this, he denied it (*601cf1.4.2).

Some behaviors were more direct and intrusive. They involved acts such as touching and sexual displays in the presence of a woman officer. Others involved a sense of possession of a "selected" female member of staff. Attempts to touch and sexual displays illustrate the objectification of the women even in their professional roles within prison. Some men fancied one or more women officers, had favorites, and "thought" themselves into a relationship with a woman member of staff. They might become possessive of the woman and jealous of anyone they viewed as a competitor for her attention, and become angry and resentful if they believed the woman was "unfaithful" to them. Such attitudes and actions to women prison staff strongly parallel those to women on the outside.

Touching women staff

He grabbed a female prison officer's buttock (*617cf1.4.2).

Touching, possessive, and masturbating in front of women staff

Two incidents raise concerns. The first being when he suggested [to a female officer] he demonstrate how he killed his victim, and the second when he attempted to remove a pen from my colleague's breast pocket, touching her breasts as he did so. Perhaps the most regular remark about him has been that "he's got a thing about women." Staff, particularly female staff members, have attempted to help. However, he has then exploited the situation and tended to become jealous and possessive. Thus if another prisoner was selected to accompany his "favorite" on some errand, he would feel hurt and let down and if he feared that his "favorite" was talking about him behind his back he would feel let down and resentful, sometimes resorting to verbal threats but generally just "blanking" the person concerned. There are a number of incidents of him masturbating in front of female officers. More recently he engineered a situation in which a female officer, escorting him to the stores area, returned to find him masturbating. He is unable to relate to people, to just hold ordinary conversations and to experience the ordinary pleasure of social contact. Thus women, ultimately, always come close to being sexual objects, possessions and status symbols and men come close to being threats and rivals. All of the softer human experiences are still largely alien to him. Also assaults on older weaker inmates. After thirteen years in custody he has done little to address his offending behavior, even to the point of declining interviews (*996cf1.4.2).

Other men were aggressive and intimidating in their attempts to undermine the woman officer's authority over them. This might be done with "looks" and a "voice" that suggests threats to her physical safety and/or sexual "innuendo" and "put downs" based on her appearance that are calculated to reduce her authority.

Threats, aggression, and intimidation of women staff

He is verbally aggressive and abusive toward staff—particularly women who were teaching him (*984cf1.4.2).

Some female staff stated that they feel threatened by him. When speaking to staff, he can be quite forceful and at times there is a hint of a latent threat in his voice. As stated previously he does not like being told "NO," and resorts to threats if he thinks this will help. He does little if anything to help himself (*1192cf1.4.2).

A female staff member noted that he avoided eye contact when talking to her, but instead stared at her chest. One month after the interview with me, it was noted he told a staff member "if he had a bullet she would get it" (he was referring to me [female staff psychologist]). He claimed an interest in a female member of staff and indicated that it would be nice if she befriended him and wrote to him. She kept her distance, and reported this. His manner with females is such that almost all our female staff (including very experienced Prison Officers) feel uneasy in his presence. I do not believe this is due to the charges against him (we have all had contact with men in prison who have been involved with extremely violent crimes), but is rather a more instinctive, intuitive reaction which experience has shown, should not be disregarded (*959cf1.4.2).

A few men posed such a high level of danger to the safety of women staff that the prison authorities limited the contact they might have with women officers as well as other women within the prison context including other professionals, visitors, and researchers such as ourselves.

Extreme danger to women staff—following staff and intimidating

On the evening association [recreation], this inmate was following me around the landing, watching my every move. He is very intimidating and will try and get closer and closer. I feel this inmate may have tried to do something given the opportunity. No female staff member should be left alone near him. [Noted in his file]: Special information for staff on "Reception of New Inmates" Form: "Should not be interviewed by lone female members of staff" (*949cf1.4.2).

Extreme danger to women staff—possibly of hostage taking

Even by this prison's standards [highest security] he is regarded as a very dangerous man. There is a strong suspicion that he plans to take one of the female health care staff hostage (*530cf1.4.2).

Extreme danger to women staff—should never be left alone with women staff

He is a grave danger to women, with the increasing number of women who are now employed within our prisons this risk should not be overlooked. He is in need of basic education but should not attend a class in my opinion with a female teacher. Neither should he be alone in the office with a female welfare officer (*998cf1.4.2).

Extremely dangerous, fantasies about raping and murdering a woman member of staff

He clearly stated that he "felt scared about women in prison" and that he had now "come close three or four times to grabbing one and doing what I want."

He then began to physically shake and cry and disclosed that he didn't think that he would ever be able to control himself. He is clearly very distressed by his thoughts and has estimated that he has only *just* managed to prevent himself from acting on them in reality. He explained that he "doesn't want to be a risk to anybody" and has stopped himself from offending in prison against women by thinking of his victim. He is very scared that "one day I may not stop and will carry on." By this he means grabbing a woman, raping her, and then killing and mutilating her. We should assume that he presents a risk to all women. Despite an apparently familiar and benign appearance, he harbors highly distorted beliefs in relation to women and their behavior. In conclusion this information is highly alarming; the inmate is clearly indicating out of his own volition that he presents a very serious and extreme danger to women, even in prison. He is clearly very scared by this situation and states that he feels he has little control over himself despite not wanting to be a danger to others. These disclosures may be seen as a positive development. Other inmates probably present an equal danger, but have not alerted staff to their thoughts. Thus, he can be seen to have in fact "lowered" his risk to some extent by making his disclosures [as a result of the above the prison swung into action to deal with the potential risk] (*1096cf1.4.2).

The examples presented above make very disturbing reading. These are men who clearly have not changed their orientations and behavior toward women and are apparently unwilling and, indeed, unlikely to address these problematic patterns of thinking and behavior. For them, as one of the prison professionals notes, women are primarily sexual objects that might be used in their fantasies or sexual assaults. This is worrying, and it is not surprising that 81% of the sexual murderers were judged a "risk to public safety" and 73% were assessed as "dangerous." Still, the prison professionals must attempt to persuade them to begin the arduous process of change.

Addressing Offending Behavior—From Denial to Responsibility

As shown above, addressing the offending behavior and the attitudes that support it is often extremely difficult and is sometimes judged to be impossible. In order for the offending behavior and murder to be addressed, it must first be acknowledged to have occurred and defined as harmful and unacceptable. To do this, the man must move from denial to responsibility. For most offenders, denial of the murder begins at the start of the legal process and continues even after conviction and imprisonment.

Denial, whether wholesale or partial, may continue for years or may be altered at some time during the sentence. Some may admit to the murder but minimize the violence and reject aspects of it, particularly the sexual components. In addition to denial, minimization of the act and a failure to accept responsibility are common. The ability to "reject" the sexual aspect of the murder is often reinforced by the legal process, whereby the charge of "rape/sexual assault" is not pursued in the murder trial because it is unnecessary to achieve a conviction for murder. In addition, the sexual element of the murder may not be pursued in deference to the family of the victim and/or the reputation of the deceased since defense arguments may seek to implicate the victim even in cases of sexual murder.

Of all the sexual murders, one-half resulted in at least one additional charge such as rape, sexual assault, and robbery, but only 12% resulted in an additional conviction for a sexual offense. For some perpetrators, the lack of a conviction for the sexual component of the murder is used to substantiate their notion that no such element in fact existed within the murder. Thus, they may accept that they committed a murder but deny that there was a sexual component within it. This has implications for the professionals who attempt to work with the offender to get him to focus on the offense, his responsibility for it, and behaviors associated with it, including sexual violence. Denial may be almost complete, or merely modified and never abandoned. Even after conviction and many years in prison, 15% of the men continued to deny that they committed the murder.

Denial

Total denial of the murder
Ten years after conviction, he vehemently denies the index offense, appears absolutely immoveable on this and is unwilling to even discuss it. He shows no insight into his offending behavior (*998cf1.4.2).

Total denial and adamant refusal to accept responsibility for his violence
He minimizes his actions with regard to the rape and murder by denying the murder and maintaining that sex with her was with her consent. His total denial of all offenses and the fact that he sees himself as a victim of racism means that he also displays no insight into any of the [current and previous] sexual offenses he has been charged with. First rape conviction involved striking the victim about the head with a gun and attempted manual strangulation. The murder victim was struck about the face causing her jaw to break and injuries inside her mouth resulting in the bleeding which caused her to suffocate (*922cf1.4.2).

Total denial of the murder and effort to appeal against conviction
He continues to appeal [his conviction] and to claim innocence. [There has been] no work on offending because of denial. He becomes annoyed when discussion about earlier [sex] attacks on women/girls is introduced, and feels he has served his time for them, therefore, they are not relevant (*911.2cf1.4.3).

End of denial and beginning to accept responsibility
So did they do it [convict him] through evidence or how did they decide it was you? And in the end, did you finally say that you did it? No. I denied it all the way through the trial and all the way through my remand, and I admitted it a year after sentencing to my probation officer (*984iv1.4.1).

Initial denial, beginning to accept responsibility—but self-pity
When questioned and confronted with his offense and the need to accept responsibility he becomes agitated and anxious in contrast to his cheery demeanor on the prison wing. [At the time of his conviction] he denied the murder or the sexual assault claiming someone else "did her in" with a car jack and the police found a durex with someone else's semen in it. He is now taking responsibility but the

context within which these issues are framed appears to be one of self-pity rather than concern for the victim. This concerns me. He disputes the sexual element to the murder. He was initially charged with rape and buggery at the time of the murder but these offenses were discharged on committal (*1112cf1.4.2).

Acknowledge Murder but Deny Responsibility by Minimizing and Rationalizing

The next step after varying shades of denial is that of varying shades of minimization and rationalization. Rather than focusing on the notion that the act did not occur, attention is given to the claim that it was not as violent as depicted, or as sexual as depicted, or that there was some reason why it occurred that somehow justifies the act.

Minimizes the severity of the violence in attempt to undermine the prosecution

So you think the police exaggerated the violence and sexual attack in terms of the murder itself? They said it was a violent one. They said she was beaten fifteen times with a china lamp. That can't be true because the china lamp would not stand fifteen blows to a lady's head. I know that for sure. That wasn't mentioned at my trial. They said a lot of things what made it more violent. I think that lamp could stand no more than four on the head at most. And also, you couldn't pick it up with one hand. You have got to pick it up with two hands because of the shape of the lamp. I have done a lot of electric work, you know, I have done a lot of electrics, so I know. So a lot of that information has made it more violent than what it was (*2017iv1.4.1).

Minimizes responsibility by claiming consensual sex and because she was an acquaintance

He accepts he has a history of sexual offending but minimizes offenses by saying he knew the women. "I've never gone out and raped a stranger"—or by saying, "It was consensual sex" (*530cf1.4.2).

No Remorse for the Murder and No Empathy with the Victim

Reform is not possible unless and until the offender moves beyond denial, minimization, and rationalization. Remorse may follow, but even this may be complex and include self-pity, which was relatively common and does not represent genuine remorse for the murder. Some may express little or no remorse for the murder, others may feel pity for their own situation in prison, and some may express a genuine sense of remorse for having committed a murder. Of these men, 51% expressed no remorse for the murder and 69% had no empathy with the victim (Figure 7.3 Appx.IV- Table 7.3).

No remorse and no empathy

Do you regret any of what happened or not? There's only one reason why I feel I wish she wasn't dead [because I am in prison], but if I could have both things, her dead and me outside, I would. I have no real remorse, she's dead (*732iv1.4.2).

He accepts full responsibility but shows no remorse (*580cf1.4.3).

Once he admitted guilt, he says, "it's a shame that she died because I took drugs" rather than "I am ashamed that I caused her to die" (*960cf1.4.2).

[Trial Judge] I formed the view that it was no good in addressing you in expressing the revulsion that I and any other person feel about what went on that night. The central problem that you have is that for that purpose, in a real sense, you are not part of this world. You do not understand what it is that people feel about those circumstances. The revulsion that they feel, the remorse that they would expect [is not present]. But finally I have formed the view that you are potentially a very dangerous person, you would use appalling violence on a vulnerable person if it happened to suit you, and indeed glorying in it (*1108cf1.4.1).

No remorse—self-pity
He described the whole incident in a matter of fact way and recalled little of his prevailing thoughts and feelings except the self protective ones. He expressed some remorse without the appropriate affective component. Outstanding concerns: he has shown a lot of self-pity (*1130cf1.4.3).

The interview with the accused left me with a distinctly detached feeling of a lack of empathy with the victim. He was totally egocentric in his accounts of various events, concerned only with how it might affect future possibilities for his freedom. He never expressed concern for any of the people he victimized. He believed he had earned the right to his freedom. He is potentially very dangerous (*996cf 1.4.2).

His thinking was egocentric, focusing very much on the effect the offense has had on his own life. The only indication of empathy was when he stated, "she was a prostitute, but she didn't deserve to die like that." He showed few signs of remorse or regret and no signs of victim empathy, but he is not a control problem in prison (*1069Cf1.4.3).

Expressions of Empathy and Remorse

Much of the thinking of these men was egocentric and centered only on the impact on themselves of their conviction and imprisonment for murder. Some professionals noted the "complete lack of emotion" when offenders recounted the murder, and one described the account as "spine-chilling." But not all men remained locked in denial and minimization. Some moved beyond egocentrism and associated ways of thinking and began to express regret and genuine empathy and remorse. For a few, this occurred very early in their sentence, but for most it took a considerable period of time and work on the part of prison professionals.

Empathy with the victim
[Four years after conviction] I asked what his feelings are towards the victim and he said he often thinks about her and genuinely regrets what he has done. He went on to say that he recognizes he had a problem, in particular anger control

and realizes there is work to be done before he is released. *[Review 2 yrs later]* He admitted the sexual element of the offense, indicating a significant shift had taken place as he initially claimed no recall of the offense. He has completed stress management and alcohol abuse, and remains motivated to address all of his offending behavior at the first opportunity (*1070cf1.4.2).

Remorse for the murder and empathy with the victim
I consider he is genuinely shocked at what he has done and distressed at having taken a life. When he speaks of the victim, his friend, rather than the person he killed, he displays real affection and care (*1088cf1.4.2).

Remorse because the victim was a woman not a male rival
I mean I've hurt people before, fought people, hurt people, and I've had no remorse whatsoever. I mean that, no remorse whatsoever. I said to the police in my statement, if it had been another pimp or a drug dealer there's no way I would have walked into a police station [reported the murder]. He'd got what he deserved, full stop. There'd have been no remorse, but [here] there was [remorse], quite simply because the person had never hurt me. I just couldn't fathom that in my mind, why did I do this, [she] never hurt me, going out of her way to look after me, you know (*630iv1.4.2).

Remorse slowly emerging
But then afterwards, what puzzles you about your own self is lack of remorse, lack of guilt, you know, but that only lasts for so long. It's like you're numb to it I suppose, or shock or whatever—but it comes! It comes, you know! *Have other people said you should have shown more remorse?* Well, I mean, the problem is that's what they want to see, and as I'm saying—you do feel it (*281iv1.4.2).

REFORM IN PRISON—PROGRAMS, RESISTANCE, AND CHANGE

As previously stated, those convicted of murder are required to address their offending behavior before they can be considered for parole. This may include, for example, alcohol and/or drug abuse programs as well as other related issues.[3] Those convicted of a murder that involved an element of sexual behavior are required to successfully complete programs that specifically address sexual offending. These programs deal with men convicted of sexual offenses against children as well as those against adults. Men may refuse to participate on some or all of the programs for a variety of reasons. They may view them as completely unnecessary or as ineffective in dealing with the issues they define as relevant to their own circumstances and/or they may define them as unrelated to their particular offense. Some men resist everything. Most seem to participate in programs focused on education and general lifestyle issues, but programs focused on sexual offending are resisted by many. As demonstrated above, this may be because they deny that sex was involved in the murder and/or because they do not wish to be defined as a sex offender by prison staff or other inmates. Participation would confirm both to them and to others that sex was, in fact, involved in the murder.

Sexual Offending Treatment Programs (SOTP) are, as the title suggests, specifically designed to deal with sexual offending. These programs were developed in Canada and the United States in the 1980s and introduced into British prisons in the 1990s. Initially, they were designed primarily for pedophiles who had committed sexual offenses against children, and later expanded to included sexual offenses committed against adults.[4] Differing versions of the programs are delivered in some, but not all, British prisons. This means that sexual offenders must be housed in one of the prisons in which an SOTP program is offered in order that they have the opportunity to participate and successfully complete the courses. The programs are based on a cognitive-behavioral model that deals with beliefs, attitudes, and perceptions as related to sexual orientations and behaviors. They are delivered by a range of prison staff, primarily psychologists, but also probation officers and prison officers. Resistance to these particular programs is often very strong and persistent, and some men never acknowledge the sexual element of their crime and as such do not participate in these courses. It is important to consider men's participation on these programs because they demonstrate their orientations to the murder—ranging from complete denial and a refusal to participate to a willingness to deal with their problems and change their behavior. In other words, offenders must engage in the painful process of "remembering" and recounting their violent behavior as an integral part of the difficult journey toward reform.

The following accounts are primarily extracted from our interviews where it was possible to engage men in a discussion about their participation in and assessments of programs. While some men refused to participate in sex offender programs, many had participated in the more general programs, such as Thinking Skills, Alcohol Awareness, Coping Skills, and Drug Abuse. Most responded positively to these and told us they were helpful and made them think about themselves differently. Additionally, based on their experiences men offered critical but useful comments. Some of the main points included that they participated in programs too early in their sentence, the courses were too short, not enough time was spent on problems in their backgrounds, there was no dedicated alcohol abuse program, and there was not enough support for men who revealed during the group work sensitive issues such sexual abuse as a child. One man told us, "When I first came into prison, I had just been "lifed off"; I were like a cabbage, and wasn't thinking straight." He said he could not concentrate on the programs or benefit from them. Another noted that there was plenty of specialist treatment for drug abuse, but not enough help for those with alcohol problems saying, "It's as though the [alcohol] problem doesn't exist." What also stood out in our interviews with the men was their resistance to participating in the SOTP.

We begin with accounts of those who completely rejected or were highly critical of most or all of the programs, especially SOTP, and conclude with men who told us that they had learned important lessons from participating in the programs.

Prison programs viewed as brainwashing
And do you think that actually being in prison has any effect on making you a different person in any way? Controlled, brainwashed, controlled. *How are you brainwashed?* Doing these courses. *What courses are you doing?* At the moment I am on ETS course, Enhanced Thinking Skills. I have done DOTP, that's Drug Offender Treatment Program. I have done Anger Management. *And doing these courses, this is brainwashing you, these courses?* Yeah. *And what are they doing then, this brainwashing?* Trying to change the way you think and if you give the correct answer to something and

actually it is not on their cards, they won't accept it. *What do you mean, they keep trying?* Until you give the answer they have got written on the cards. And they ask you about it time and time again to make sure it is in your head all the time. I give them the right answer back just to get them off my case (*2013iv1.4.2).

"Heal thyself"—rejects programs because he had already reformed himself
What about other people inside like psychologists, probation officers, anyone else, how much contact have you had with people like that, and have they contributed to the change in you that you've told me about? No. No, they tried to tell me, it's over the past two years I've started speaking to them, and they've tried to tell me that I am negative. I say that I'm adamant that I'll never ever commit another violent offense or a sexual offense. *How much impact has probation and psychologists had on you?* None, they haven't, they are very, very negative. They are very, very negative. They say that I say that I'm aware that I've got the capability of this act [murder] because I've committed this act before. I'm capable of doing it again, because once you've already done one, you won't have any reservations about doing this action again. However, I now have free will, I didn't then, or I didn't feel that I did. I now have free will, and I have a moral code. I had no morals then, there were no morals, never had a code in my life, I was never brought up to believe in anything. I just survived. I believe strongly in a moral code and I try to live my life by a moral code, by the Buddhist code: right thought, right word, right action, right deed—the Four Noble Truths. I try to live my life by this, so I know that I am not going to commit, I KNOW that I am not going to commit another sexual offense, another murder, however, I recognise that I'm capable of doing it. I've not had anything to do with your prison service. I've educated myself. I've taught myself this moral code. I've taught myself to meditate, to sit still. I've taught myself to think. I've taught myself to consider other people, all the time try to consider other people (*630iv1.4.2).

Sexual Offender Treatment Program—SOTP

The strongest resistance to program participation was associated with sex offender programs. Men refused to participate because they told us a sexual assault did not occur or they could not remember anything about the murder. Others pointed out they were in a catch-22 position—they did not want to participate because participation would confirm sex was involved in the murder, which they had consistently denied, but they were trapped in a dilemma because they would not be released on parole unless they acknowledged the sexual element of the murder and participated in the SOTP program. Other men participated, but the casefiles indicated that they failed because they did not understand, appreciate, or assimilate the lessons and certainly did not change their orientations.

Deny sexual element of murder so refuses SOTP
[He says the murder was not sexual the evidence says it was and prison officials say he must do SOTP] Well, I have done various programs, anger management, thinking skills and enhanced thinking skills. I wanna get on the SOTP. Well, I don't wanna get on it but they are telling me I have to do SOTP and I am saying I don't have to do it, cos they are saying my crime was sexual cos it was a woman

that I killed so they are saying it was a sexual element and I am saying that it is not. So I can't move forward onto these groups, so I can't go anywhere. *Till you do the SOTP?* Yeah. *And you say you are going to do it or you are not going to do it?* Well, as a lifer I am in a catch 22, so I have to do it, know what I mean? Whether I go on the group and I talk about my background as I am doing, up to the point of when I killed the woman, that's as far as I can go. I can't make up a story and go beyond that. What they want to hear, do you know what I mean. I can only tell them I know what I did. Can't go no further than that (*984iv1.4.1).

Does not want to do SOTP because says he cannot remember doing sex in the murder

They said to me I need to come out of my shell a bit more. I am more worried about the SOTP people because it is a sex offender's course, and what [they say] happened is not what happened. And it is going to be very hard for me to go there, but if I don't do that course I am never going to get out, "Full Stop." If it will help me, fair enough, but how can that course help if I haven't got no memory of doing it? Know what I mean? How is it going to benefit me? But I have got to do it to get out. So I have got to accept what they said at my trial. It happens to a lot of prisoners here. A lot of prisoners in here are innocent of something, but they have got to do it, got to accept it and do it, but what they want me to do is admit to something I did not admit to [at my trial]. But catch 22. What do I do? Sexual thing—do the SOTP course. Go through it, yes, and tell them what happened as far as I can remember. They will say I am lying because in my reports it says. So where do I go from here? *Do you think maybe the course might help you remember?* That's what the course is all about. Maybe something might come up. I don't know. I hope so because I just want to get this nightmare off my head. So I can get on with my sentence. *So basically you need to get on?* I need to get on with it. If they leave it longer, longer, longer, I am not going to remember anything. That's what I am worried about. Then, in my situation—*it won't be no fault of mine*, because I am willing to do any course they want me to but the longer they leave it, the longer I forget because I am forgetting things now. And this is what's worrying me now cos I keep forgetting things (*2017iv1.4.1).

Failed SOTP

He failed the SOTP program because he showed no empathy, rigid thinking, and denial of sexual offending. Has been recommended to go to another prison where they specialize in sexual offenders, but the inmate refuses to go (*1071cf1.4.3).

After some group work [in an SOTP], he stated that he realized that he had raped her; however he has not mentioned the violent and prolonged nature of the assault. He sees women as sexual objects. He stated that his wife was effectively a "legalized prostitute," providing him with sex in return for food and a home. [He] has no idea about consent in a sexual relationship and that it is a shared experience. His views are sexually egocentric and his behavior seems to focus solely on his own sexual gratification. He admitted to being aroused by aggressive sexual intercourse, and a woman psychologist eventually terminated her contact with him because she became concerned that he was becoming aroused while describing the offense to her (*1054cf1.4.3).

Beginning the Process of Change

A few men we interviewed were very positive about the courses and said they helped them change. For some an important part of this process was looking back and thinking through the context and circumstances of the murder, especially their own thinking but also the way the victim must have felt. Others reflected on the significance of their lifestyle, such as an egotistical approach to life that often involved an obsession with obtaining and consuming alcohol.

Learning about blaming women and about blaming the victim
I wanted to shut her up [victim] in case anybody heard her. I was frightened of getting caught. Looking at it now, it was sort of women were always to blame for causing me problems, for hurting me. I think that was due to my experiences with my wife. I only really learned that recently during a group. I've started digging deep into myself. Every time I got hurt there was always a woman involved somewhere. I blamed women for everything. So when the woman woke up and started screaming it made me angry as well. I didn't know which direction to go (*1032iv1.4.3).

From resistance to the Alcohol Awareness course to community educator
I was doing a lot of work when I was at another prison, and I was blackmailed into doing the alcohol course or else I wouldn't get out of prison. So I went on it. It was only like a three day thing. The first time I went on it, I thought it wasn't for me because I wasn't an alcoholic. I had a drink problem, but I wasn't an alcoholic. There was a difference. After two days, I thought I was going to leave until a person stood up and started talking about his past experience with drink. The similarities there of what I'd been through, what he was talking about I'd gone through similar situations. And I thought, yes, it's not alcoholic, it's a drink problem I've got, and I realized that I did have a drink problem. So I put down for the next course again and I went through it, and then I started working with the town Drop-in Centre for four years. Going to colleges round about, schools, probation centers, talking to young kids about my past experience with drink and what it can do to you and how, if you got into trouble, where you'd end up. And I thought, well, I was enjoying it, so I put in for a counseling course so that I can help kids, doing good or something, putting them on the right track, and it went from there. So I put in for the course and I done it for 10 weeks (*642iv1.4.2).

COMPARISONS OF SEX MURDERERS AND MALE-MALE MURDERERS

The qualitative and quantitative evidence across the lifecourse of men who commit a sexual murder indicates that many of them have numerous problems throughout their lives. Adversity in childhood included problematic families, disruptive behavior at home and at school, early onset of offending, and contact with the police and social services. As adults, most of the sexual murderers were under-educated, usually unemployed, and had problems with alcohol. Criminal behavior, contact with the police, and convictions were common. Many had problems with social relationships and particularly those with women. Violent behavior, including violence in general, violence in a previous intimate relationship, and sexual violence both inside and outside domestic relations, characterized the adult lives of many. Overall, the vast majority had some form of sexual problems as well as distorted thinking about women and serious problems in their relationships with them.

Other research on sexual murderers, especially but not exclusively that on serial murderers, has emphasized childhood adversity as a major explanatory factor and suggested that many of their characteristics, particularly those in childhood, differ from those of men in the "normal" population as well as from those of men who commit other types of crime. While accepting that the backgrounds of sexual murderers differ significantly from those of the majority of men in the wider population, we examine more closely the question of if and how they might differ from other types of offenders by comparing various factors across the lifecourse of men who commit a sexual murder with those of men who murder other men.

Comparisons of sexual murderers with male-male murderers reveal many similarities across the lifecourse. A considerable proportion of the men in both groups experienced problems both as children and as adults that involved disruptive and antisocial behavior. The comparisons are shown graphically at the end of this chapter (Figures 7.1, 7.2, and 7.3) and numerically in Appendix IV (Tables 7.1, 7.2, and 7.3). As children, the men in both groups were fairly similar in terms of their families of orientation, childhood experiences, educational achievement, substance abuse, and histories of criminal behavior. As adults, most of the men in both groups were unemployed, but sexual murderers were more likely to be employed (43%) than male-male murderers (28%) (Figure 7.2; Appx.IV-Table 7.2). There was an elevated level of alcohol abuse and criminal behavior in both groups with over 80% of both groups having had at least one previous conviction.

What stands out are factors associated with sexual behavior and relationships with women. While nearly the same proportion of both groups experienced a breakdown in an intimate relationship (MM = 61% vs. SexM = 64%), sexual murderers were significantly more likely than male-male murderers to have physically abused a previous intimate partner (MM = 31% vs. SexM = 44%) and to have sexually abused a previous intimate partner (MM = 4% vs. SexM = 13%). In addition to the figures shown, sexual murderers were more likely to be physically abusing their partner at the time they committed the murder (MM = 25% vs. SexM = 44%), to have had sexual problems as an adult (18% vs. 73%), and to have committed sexual violence against a woman who was not an intimate partner (9% vs. 32%). Although both groups were equally likely to have been convicted for minor assault (41% vs. 48%) or a serious assault (17% vs. 19%), sexual murderers were significantly more likely to have assaulted a woman (MM = 11% vs. SexM = 56%). Previous convictions for serious sexual violence, including rape, were significantly more likely for the sexual murderers (MM = 8% vs. SexM = 21%) (Figure 7.2; Appx.IV-Table 7.2).

The qualitative data suggest a pattern of sexual assaults that go undetected, as well as those that are detected but do not result in an arrest and/or conviction. The qualitative evidence also suggests lifelong problems in relationships with women. As shown in Figure 7.3 at end of chapter and in Appendix IV, Table 7.3, prison professionals were significantly more likely to define sexual murderers as having serious problems with women throughout their adult lives (MM = 18% vs. SexM = 87%). Sex murderers were more likely to lack remorse for the murder (MM = 34% vs. SexM = 51%) and to have no empathy for the victim (MM = 43% vs. SexM = 69%). Within the prison, only a small proportion of both groups were defined as "model prisoners" (MM = 18% vs. SexM = 21%). The behavior and orientations of sexual murderers toward women prison staff, even within the highly controlled environment of the prison, were strong indicators of a continued risk to women should they be released into the community. In that respect, prison professionals were significantly more likely to assess sexual murderers as a potential risk to public safety (MM = 45% vs. SexM = 81%) and to define them as dangerous (MM = 39% vs. SexM = 73%). Although the qualitative and the quantitative evidence suggests many similarities in the lifecourse of male-male murderers and sexual murderers, men who commit a sexual murder are more likely to have strong negative orientations toward women and a history of physical and sexual violence against them.

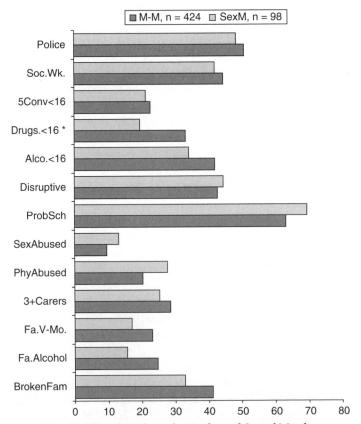

Figure 7.1 SexM—Childhood: Male-Male Murder and Sexual Murder.
* Statistically significant difference.

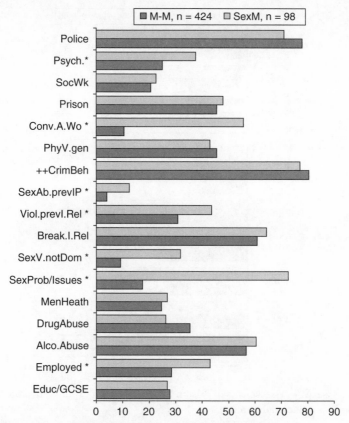

Figure 7.2 SexM—Adulthood: Male-Male Murder and Sexual Murder.
* Statistically significant difference.

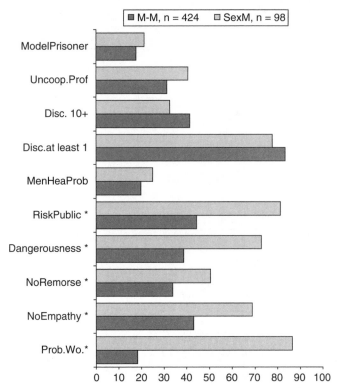

Figure 7.3 SexM—Assessments in Prison: Male-Male Murder and Sexual Murder.
* Statistically significant difference.

PART III

Murder of Older Women

The Knowledge
—Murder of Older Women

It is often stated that the population of the world is rapidly growing older, but this statement must be qualified. Not all the world's populations are growing older. The populations of some of the wealthiest countries in the world, primarily those in the Northern Hemisphere and Western Europe, are growing older, and those over the age of 65 are likely to live longer and to represent a larger proportion of the overall population. In the United States, about 14% of the population is over 65, and this is expected to rise to 19% by 2025.[1] In the United Kingdom, 16% of the population was over 65 in 2012, which is three times what it was in the early 20th century.[2] Life expectancy is generally greater than it was 50 years ago. In the United States, the average life expectancy is 81 for women and 78 for men.[3] In France, Switzerland, and Italy, countries with some of the best life expectancies in Europe, it is 84 for women and the late 70s for men.[4] In the United Kingdom, life expectancy is 81 for women and 77 for men.[5] An illustration of the increase in longevity is provided by the Queen of the United Kingdom who sends a birthday card to every citizen upon their 100th birthday and every birthday thereafter. In 1981, she congratulated 2,420 citizens on reaching the age of 100 or over. In 2012, the Queen sent 12,320 birthday cards to those 100 years of age and over, and 610 of the recipients were at least 105 years old.[6] There has obviously been a dramatic rise in the number of centenarians over a relatively short period of time.

While both life expectancy and the age structures in North America and Europe are changing, it is the population of Japan that may best reflect the future for affluent, industrialized countries of the world. The Japanese population is shrinking and the balance between young and old has already changed dramatically, with people 65+ now constituting about one-quarter of the population and projected to rise to around 35% by 2020, and by 2050 the ratio of the workforce to the elderly is projected to be one-to-one.[7] On average, the Japanese have the longest life expectancy in the world, with an average age of 86 for women and 79 for men. In 2010 about one-third of all Japanese households were occupied by a single person, and elderly single-person households represent 21% of all households, with three out of four occupied by an older woman.[8]

It has been suggested that there may be a need to redefine what constitutes "old age" and who is classified as "elderly." With increasing longevity and improvements in health, the entrance point into the later stages of life is variable. But, for the most part, it is shifting upward with older age requirements for retirement and eligibility for pensions and social security benefits changing, and in some countries men and women work well into their "retirement" years.[9] The population of those over 60 is growing, and women usually live 5 to 7 years longer than men, which means that many issues relating to the older members of society, whether health, social care, poverty, violence, or murder, are disproportionately the issues of older women. In the United States in the 1990s, the ratio of women to men 65 and over was 6:5, but over the age of 85 the ratio was 5:2. Women were also much more likely than men to be living alone (80%) and to be living in poverty.[10] It could be argued that the elderly, particularly those over 75, are some of the most vulnerable individuals in society. But are they more vulnerable to homicide?

National homicide statistics from the United States indicate that the elderly have one of the lowest rates of homicide of any age group. Data from U.S. city, county, state, and national sources suggest that those aged 65 and over constitute between 4% and 8% of all homicides.[11] With the increasing number of the elderly in the population, an increase in the number of homicides in this age group is likely even if the rate of homicide does not change. The rate of homicide of the elderly, for both men and women, has been relatively constant over time, but current projections are contradictory, with some researchers predicting an increase in the rate while others predict a decrease.[12] The murder of older women is rare, and the sexual murder of older women even rarer, but both the numbers and the rates may be underestimated in statistics about crime. For example, intimate partner homicide-suicides may not be included in the compilation of homicide statistics and some of these cases involve older women who are murdered by a husband/male partner before he commits suicide. Although these deaths may be recorded by the coroner, because both individuals are dead, there is no arrest, no charge, and no trial for murder. As such, in some jurisdictions/countries the homicide element of these homicide-suicides may not be recorded.

MURDER OF THE ELDERLY—THE PATTERNS

Research focusing on the murder of the elderly began to emerge in the 1990s as health and medical practitioners turned their attention to this segment of the population. Medical examiners began to report on the homicide of the elderly, including homicide-suicides, as an aspect of the investigations of sudden deaths. In the United States, these investigations were primarily carried out by county medical examiners and coroners relying on autopsies, toxicology reports, and death certificates. For example, one study using county- and statewide data in Alabama, Kentucky, and Indiana, reported that as many as half of the homicidal deaths of an elderly person were the result of gunshot wounds, and fewer cases involved blunt force trauma and asphyxiation.[13] This investigation also revealed a ratio of 3:2 male-to-female deaths among the elderly, which means that for every three male deaths there are two female deaths. Subsequent research using a countywide database from Pennsylvania reported a similar gender ratio but found that the major cause of death was blunt force trauma rather than gunshot wounds.[14] Although social scientists, epidemiologists, and criminologists, primarily in North America, are now investigating the murder of the elderly at the city, state, and national levels, much more research needs to be done in order to gain more knowledge about this type of murder. However, the results that are now available are very consistent. They show that the murder of those age 65 and over continues to represent a relatively small proportion of all homicides, but these murders have some distinct characteristics: There is a gender symmetry of victims, who are almost equally likely to be women as men; the perpetrator is usually a stranger or someone with a minimal acquaintance with the victim; the murders usually take place in the home or place of residence of the victim; and there is little or no history of disputes or conflict between the perpetrator and the victim prior to the murder.

Gender Symmetry of Older Victims of Murder

Gender asymmetry of both perpetrators and victims characterizes homicides of those between the ages of 16 and 64, where most perpetrators are male and 70%–80% of the victims are also male. This changes when the victims are elderly. Although gender asymmetry remains among perpetrators, that is, it is men and not women who kill the elderly, older victims are equally as likely to be women as men. In short, there is near gender symmetry among victims who are elderly. A study based on all homicides in New York City using data from 1990 to 1998 (11,850 cases), revealed that while women accounted for 43% of all older victims, they accounted for only 14% of younger victims (i.e., between ages of 16–64). Elderly victims were likely to be female, white, killed by nonfirearm injuries, and murdered in their own home. This was in sharp contrast to younger victims, who were likely to be male (86%), to be nonwhite (49%), to be shot in the city streets, to have a problem with alcohol, and to be involved in illicit drug use.[15] Other research on elderly victims also reports considerable gender symmetry, with male victims accounting for 49%–68% of all elderly victims.[16]

Comparisons of Older and Younger Victims

Using data from the FBI Homicide Reports, Bachman and Meloy compared the murders of older and younger victims and found several important differences between them.[17] Older victims were more likely than younger victims to be killed by a perpetrator defined as a "known other" or a "stranger" rather than a friend or relative. The "precipitating circumstances" differed for the younger and older age groups, with "other felonies" (mostly thefts) involved in 35% of the murders of the elderly but only 19% of those involving younger victims. Conflicts and arguments preceded 21% of the homicides of the elderly and 39% of younger victims, although the largest category for both age groups was categorized as "other" (41% vs. 44%). A firearm was used to kill 40% of the elderly victims compared with 66% of younger victims. Canadian-based research yielded somewhat similar results with elderly victims more likely than younger victims to be killed in their own home in the context of a "theft-based" assault and to die as a result of a beating and/or strangulation but not from a gunshot wound.[18] The difference in method of killing may be accounted for by the greater use of firearms in criminal acts in the United States than in Canada.

Using the database of homicides in Chicago from 1965 to 1981, Nelson and Huff-Corzine compared homicides of the elderly (65 and older) with those of victims under the age of 65 and found similar patterns to those in other research.[19] Elderly men and women were much more likely than those under 65 to be killed by a stranger in a theft-related homicide. Only 16% of the younger age group, versus 53% of the older age group, were killed in a theft-related murder, and this pattern increased with age. Other research has found similar patterns, with the younger age groups more likely to be killed in homicides related to arguments and confrontations rather than those related to robbery or theft. Among the elderly, the most frequently occurring homicides were those involving a robbery committed in the home, which was much more prevalent than homicides involving some form of conflict.[20]

Using the entire Chicago Homicide Dataset of 27,345 cases collected over a period of 45 years beginning in 1965, Block found that of the 1,486 victims aged 60 and over, 30% (n = 442) were women and 70% were men.[21] This differs from other studies that have found greater symmetry between men and women victims among elderly victims of homicide. However, Block notes that in Chicago, the older victims of homicide were much more likely than younger victims to be killed in a robbery in their own home or at work, and this was particularly likely for women, whose risk appears to increase with age. Contradicting the stereotype of the nonworking, retired person living on a pension, Block found that among those over age 60, men and women were more likely than younger victims to be killed at their place of work.

"Elderly victims were often a proprietor, manager or clerk in a small store," or they worked as a security guard or a cab driver and, as such, were vulnerable to robberies and may have been seen as an "easy mark."[22] In the United States, small shopkeepers and those working in 24-hour gas stations or "quick-stop" convenience stores, whether young or old, often work alone and are in contact with strangers in circumstances that may put them at risk of a robbery and, in some cases, being murdered in the process. In Chicago, older victims were more likely than younger victims to have been strangled/suffocated, clubbed with a "blunt instrument," or beaten with hands, fists, and feet rather than killed with a firearm. When older victims, whether women or men, are assaulted, they are much more likely than younger victims to suffer injuries, to require hospitalization, and to suffer a "lingering death." In addition, Block found that one-quarter of women between the ages 60 and 64 died at the hands of an intimate partner, and a small number were killed in a "familicide." Fox and Levin further note that while the elderly are less likely than the young to be assaulted, they are three times more likely to die when they are.[23]

The Men Who Murder Older Victims

While research on the homicide of older women and men is now expanding, there continues to be very little detailed evidence about the circumstances of these killings and even less about the characteristics of those who commit these murders. One Canadian study of 671 men convicted of homicide between 1988 and 1992 in three "prairie" provinces identified 67 men who had killed an elderly person.[24] The researchers compared the family backgrounds and psychiatric histories of men who killed "elderly" and "nonelderly" victims, and found few differences between them. The men in both groups were about equally likely to have been raised in a family where at least one member of the family had a criminal record and/or a "substance-related" problem. The men in both groups were likely to have a conviction as a juvenile, a conviction for a violent offense as an adult, and to be sporadically employed. Alcohol-related problems and psychiatric morbidity were not apparent in the vast majority of the men in both groups, although one-third were judged to have a "personality disorder." At the time of the homicide, men who murdered the "elderly" were significantly more likely than those who murdered the "nonelderly" to be single (61% vs. 43%), to kill the victim in their own home (67% vs. 32%), to commit murder in the context of a robbery (66% vs. 23%), and to inflict "moderate-to-severe" injuries (82% vs. 56%). About three-quarters of the "nonelderly" but only one-quarter of the "elderly" victims were killed in the context of a "domestic quarrel." Despite these differences, about two-thirds of the offenders in both groups had consumed alcohol at the time of the killing.[25]

Murder by Caregivers

Caregivers sometimes abuse the older person in their care, but few murder them. There is a growing literature about the abuse of the elderly by carers but very little on homicides. Carers may be men or women and include members of the immediate family, especially intimate partners and adult children, and individuals who are employed to look after the older person either in their own home or in a residential home. In one study, the murders of older persons by carers were variously categorized as "homicide by neglect, intentional injury leading to death, and homicide followed by suicide."[26] Using the Centers for Disease Control and Prevention (CDC) Violent Death Reporting System (NVDRS) records of all deaths of an elderly person between 2003 and 2007, 68 incidents were identified that could be classified into one of these three categories. Of those killed by a caregiver, 63% were women killed in their own home. Perpetrators were husbands (31%) or sons (22%), and 35% were killed with a firearm and 25% died of intentional neglect.[27] About two-fifths of these women were between 50 and 79 years of age, and many (49%) were over the age of 80. The researchers conclude that the context of such homicides are complicated and may be "precipitated" by physical illness of the victim or caregiver, mental illness, financial gain, impending crisis, and/or substance abuse of the perpetrator.[28]

HOMICIDE-SUICIDES AMONG THE ELDERLY

Homicides followed by suicide involving the elderly are sometimes described as "mercy killings" and are often judged to have involved a "suicide pact." While it is clear that some of these deaths may be described in this way, emerging evidence challenges the terms "mercy killings" and "suicide pacts" when applied to many of the homicide-suicides among the elderly. The bulk of the studies on homicide-suicides have used medical examiner's records as a source of data. One of the largest, conducted in two regions in Florida, which has a sizable population of the retired elderly, compared 171 cases of homicide-suicide of those over age 55 with those under this age.[29] The study revealed that over three-quarters of the homicide-suicides among the elderly involved the killing of a woman by a male partner. In many cases, jealousy, possessiveness, and separation were apparent, but the researchers concluded that an understanding of these deaths required a consideration of a multiplicity of factors such as alcohol, adverse life events, relationship issues, psychosocial and cultural issues, and "environmental" factors such as the availability of guns.

Drawing on other evidence of homicide-suicide among the elderly in Florida, including police records, media reports, and obituaries from 1999 to 2005, Salari analyzed 225 homicide-suicides resulting in 444 deaths. Most occurred in the home of the victim and were perpetrated by male partners, some of whom were carers, who killed their wife with a firearm. The context usually involved "relationship strife," and intimate partner violence against the woman was present in many of the relationships. In some cases, the homicide victims were "severely isolated" from others.[30]

The evidence regarding homicide-suicides involving older couples consistently suggests that they usually occur in intimate relationships where depression, illness, and other problems are present. They usually involve the murder of a woman by her current or ex-partner; a history of discord, abuse, and sometimes violence; illness of one or both partners; alcohol abuse and suicidal ideation of the perpetrator; and the use of a firearm. The sparse research in this area from Europe and Canada reveals similar patterns: Victims are usually women killed in their own home by an intimate partner or ex-partner. In Europe, women age 65 and over represent approximately 15% of all victims of homicide-suicide.[31]

SEXUAL MURDERS OF OLDER WOMEN

If research on the murder of the elderly is sparse, research focusing on the sexual murders of older women is even more so. Early reports were based on a small number of cases and were usually derived from psychiatric assessments of offenders. Pollack compared men who raped and/or murdered older women age 60 and over (n = 5) with men who sexually assaulted younger women but did not murder them (n = 7). Only two of the men murdered an elderly victim and, as such, the implications of the findings are extremely limited. Briefly, the five men who committed a sexual assault or a sexual murder of an older woman had grown up in a large family, were neighbors of the victim, and the assault was brutal. The two cases of murder involved "gratuitous violence," mutilation of the body, and were "motivated by rage or sadistic intent." For Pollack, sexual rapist/murderers of older women specifically targeted their victims, and he suggested that murders of older women that appeared to be "motiveless" may have been motivated by sex.[32]

While early research on the sexual murder of older women was limited to only a few cases, more recent research is based on larger samples and extends the analysis to include the circumstances of the murder and relevant aspects of the offenders. However, even large datasets extending over several years yield very few cases of the sexual murder of older women. For example, the Chicago Homicide Dataset for 45 years yielded 442 cases of the murder of women aged 60 and over, and only 32 (7%) of these involved sex in the murder. Of these 32 women, approximately 16% were over the age of 80.[33] The Supplementary Homicide Report (SHR) compiled by the FBI for 1976–1999 contained 604 cases of the sexual murder of women age 60 and over. Although this estimate suggests there are very few sexual murders of older women, Safarik, Jarvis, and Nussbaum point out that this may be an underestimate because police and crime-scene investigators sometimes fail to recognize the sexual components of a homicide and/or misclassify the murder.[34] This may also arise because of a restricted definition of sexual violence that may be based only on the act of rape and thus not include other sexual behaviors such as exposure, mutilation, or burning of sexual parts of the body.

Sexual Murders of Older Women—Perpetrators and Circumstances

In order to extend the analysis of the sexual murders of older women, Safarik and colleagues used additional datasets to collect more detailed evidence than that available in the 604 nationally based FBI cases. This yielded 128 cases of the sexual homicide of a women age 60 and older that were committed by 110 perpetrators. These data are presented at length as they provide the most comprehensive assessment to date of the context of the murders, the immediate circumstances, and the details of the offender and victim, including the nature of their relationship and the distance between their residences.[35]

THE PERPETRATORS
The 110 perpetrators had the following characteristics: All were male; the average age was 25, with a wide range between ages 15 and 58; 44% were white, 42% were black, and 13% were Hispanic. Nearly all of the offenders (90%) had at least one criminal conviction, and property and violent offenses were equally present in their criminal histories. Few were employed (30%), and the vast majority of those who did work were in unskilled jobs. Substance abuse, particularly alcohol but also marijuana and cocaine, was almost universal (93%). Although 54% were strangers to the woman they killed, the majority (56%) lived no more than six city blocks from their victim, 30% lived in the same block, and 81% walked to the victim's residence where they committed the murder. About 40% gained entry to the victim's home through unlocked doors or windows, 40% forcibly entered through locked doors or windows, and 20% were "freely admitted" by the victim through some form of deception.[36]

THE VICTIMS
The average age of the women victims was 77, and 86% of them were white. As indicated abover, older women are usually murdered in their own home, and this is even more likely in cases of sexual murder, with 94% of these women killed in their own home. Stability of residency was the norm, with nearly three-quarters of the women having lived in the same neighborhood for 10 or more years, and an additional 14% in the same neighborhood for a period of 4 to 9 years. The researchers note that many of the elderly women lived in what sociologists have termed a "zone of transition," which, in these cases, usually meant a departure of stable working-class families and the arrival of others, many of whom were economically disadvantaged and had problematic backgrounds.

The Relationship Between Perpetrators and Victims

Strangers were overwhelmingly implicated in the killings of older women, whether the murder involved a theft or a sexual attack or both. However, Safari and colleagues note, "Many offenders labeled as strangers may in fact be marginally acquainted with their victims."[37] They suggest that in many of the cases categorized as a "stranger homicide" the victim-offender relationship might best be characterized as "acquaintances," albeit fleeting and/or short-lived. For example, the offender and victim may have passed each other on the street or traveled on the same bus. They may not have spoken or engaged in any sort of exchange, but the offender might have identified the victim as a possible vulnerable target and made an effort to establish where she lived. Other murderers may have previously worked in the victim's house or garden, or carried-out some sort of errand for her. The collection of additional knowledge about such relationships will be important in the ongoing research in this area.

The Murder

The major causes of death were strangulation (63%) and blunt force trauma (38%). The use of a firearm was rare (1%). The perpetrators generally used overwhelming force, what the researchers term a "blitz attack" in gaining access and assaulting the woman. Using two scales, the Homicide Injury Scale and the Injury Severity Score, the researchers concluded that the injuries could be classified as very severe, and many women died from "brutal and excessive injuries." Almost all of the victims (92%) were raped as part of these devastating attacks, and three-quarters of the men also removed the woman's property, such as cash and jewelry, after the murder.[38]

Overall, the evidence from this research contradicts a great deal of speculation about the nature of the sexual aspects within these homicides. Some researchers have suggested that the sexual acts in many murders apparently related to thefts are merely an "afterthought" committed in the context of a burglary. Safarik and colleagues found that in about three-quarters of their cases, the offender did steal something from the residence of the victim, but they defined the theft as an "afterthought" rather than the primary focus of the murder, which they defined as sexual. The main objective was to rape and and assult the victim. Violence was intended and immediate and occurred before the theft. The researchers viewed the primacy of the sexual scenarios as more plausible because they were supported by "third parties, and admissions or confessions to police."[39] As noted in the earlier chapters about sexual murder, the sexual aspects of a murder are sometimes completely ignored in the face of a charge of murder because a sexual charge is not required in order for the legal case of homicide to proceed. When the sexual element is ignored within the criminal justice process, these murders may simply and incorrectly be defined as murders motivated by theft with the consequence that the sexual element of the murder disappears from view.

SERIAL MURDER OF OLDER WOMEN

As stated throughout, mass murders and serial murders are extremely rare but they receive an extraordinary amount of public and media attention both because of the number of individuals killed and also because of the unusual circumstances in which these murders occur. Although multiple murders of any description are rare compared with the enormous number of murders that involve a single victim, the mass murder of older women is extremely unusual in modern times. Older women were once the primary targets of "witch hunts" resulting in the deaths of thousands of women in Europe and America several hundred years ago.[40] However, one of the most notorious cases of the "serial" murder of older women occurred in England in the 1990s, when it was discovered that a local doctor had killed over 200 of his patients over a period of several decades. Eighty percent of his victims were women, and most, although not all, were elderly women. None involved a sexual element. This probably constitutes the largest number of mass killings of older women by a single individual in modern times.

Over many decades, Dr. Harold Shipman killed his elderly patients, mostly women, and managed to conceal the murders under the guise that they had died of an illness that resulted in their death, although he had in fact used lethal injections of a prescription drug to kill them. The murders went undetected for many years primarily because the patients were elderly and unwell and, as such, the deaths did not appear to be suspicious. The doctor signed the death certificates and identified the cause of death as something likely to be viewed as a "normal" cause of death of an elderly person. Thus, the deaths were not viewed as problematic or suspicious. Although he was a respected member of his community, it was discovered during his trial that he had a drug habit and other issues that might have been of relevance. After his conviction and imprisonment for over 200 murders, he committed suicide in prison.[41] His motivations may never be known, but it remains a stark and disturbing fact that his overwhelming choice of murder victim was older women.

SUMMARY

Research about the murder of the elderly is relatively sparse, but the body of knowledge is beginning to expand and would be expected to do so given the changing populations of many countries, where the number of older men and women is increasing and the issues that relate to them are more likely to become matters of public concern. Overall, older individuals are less likely than those who are younger to be murdered or to commit a murder. However, there are some striking findings in the existing research about the murders of the elderly, particularly those relating to the murder of older women.

Among older people who are murdered, women are as likely as men to become the victims. Those who murder the elderly, like those who murder others, are overwhelmingly men, but when they murder an older person, their victims are equally likely to be women as they are to be other men. Although there are more women than men among those over the age of 65, and thus it might be expected that more women in this age group will become the victims of murder, the near gender symmetry among the older victims is more than would be expected if this outcome were simply random. This requires some closer scrutiny in search of a deeper understanding of this pattern and why it might be so.

Existing evidence about the murder of older women indicates that the majority are murdered in their own residence by a stranger in the course of a burglary. When the robbery/murder is in the woman's own home, she is often subjected to severe violence involving blunt force trauma and/or she is smothered or strangled. In the United States, some older women are killed in the context of their employment, such as during a robbery of a convenience store or gas station where they may work alone and late at night. Patterns of employment and retirement vary nationally, and it is not unusual in the United States for women and men to work beyond retirement age and to do so in what might be described as high-risk locations that are open late at night and sometimes 24 hours a day and in places where there is an elevated risk of robbery with a firearm. These conditions are much less prevalent in European countries. In addition, some older women are killed by their male intimate partner in the context of a homicide-suicide, which usually, although not always, involves the use of a firearm. Some of these may best be described as intimate partner murders.[42]

When older women are killed in the context of a sexual attack, it is often at the hands of men who are strangers to them. The perpetrator may live near the woman's home even though they are not personally acquainted, or he may know that an older woman lives in a residence that he targets either for a burglary or a sexual attack, or both. Entrance to the woman's home may be gained through deception, forced entry, or an unlocked door. Strangulation is the usual method of killing, which is not surprising when it occurs in the context of a sexual attack. Guns were rarely used in these murders. The men who commit a sexual murder against an older woman are usually unemployed, are dependent on alcohol and/or drugs, and have a history of offending including property and violent offenses.

Overall, there is a need for much more research about the murder of older women, about the nature and context of these murders, and about the lifecourse of the men who commit them. In the next two chapters, we examine the murder of older women, some of whom were subjected to a sexual attack. Again, we present detailed evidence of the context and circumstances of these murders as well as evidence regarding the backgrounds and ways of thinking of the perpetrators. Given the increasing number of older women (and men) in many countries and the negligible knowledge base regarding these types of murders it very important to analyze the diversity and dynamics of these murders in order to extend existing knowledge about them.

Older Women—The Murder Event

Relationships, Contexts, and Circumstances

In many countries, there is a growing population of the elderly and, with their longer lifespan, women usually make up a greater proportion of this population than men. Although the elderly represent a fairly small minority of the victims of homicide, the number of older people who are murdered is likely to increase with the growing size of this group within the overall population. What happens when men murder older women? Current evidence suggests there are three main recurring circumstances associated with the murder of older women: theft/burglary, sexual murders, and murder followed by suicide. Little is known about the nature, context, and circumstances associated with these murders, and even less is known about the men who perpetrate them. In in this and the next chapter, we use evidence from the Murder Study to examine the murders of older women (age 65 and older) and the men who perpetrate them. This analysis does not include homicide-suicides since these cases were not included in the casefiles, and they do not include older women who were intimate partners since the oldest woman in that category was 56 years of age.

Of the 243 women classified into the three types of murder, 40 (17%) were 65 years of age or older, while only 36 (8%) of the 424 male-male murders were of men aged 65 or older. While the age of 65 does not designate a category of individuals who are necessarily "frail" and thus an easy prey for young burglars, street robbers, and/or those seeking to "tap" an older person for money to buy alcohol, drugs, or other items, they may be perceived as such. Many women over the age of 65 live alone in their own home or reside in sheltered housing or care homes for the elderly and may be thought to have cash or property that could be stolen with relative ease from a person who, by virtue of their age and gender, may be viewed as unlikely to put up much, if any, resistance.

The two main contexts in which men murder older women were almost evenly divided between murders motivated by theft and those that involved a sexual element of some type. The examination of the murder of older women begins with the nature of the relationships between the perpetrators and their victims and considers whether the murder event primarily involved a theft or some form of sexual behavior. This is followed by a consideration of the situations and circumstances in which the murders occur, treatment of the body, and subsequent behavior. Again, perpetrators' accounts provide insight into issues such as denial, rationales, and justifications. Finally, comparisons are made between the murders of older women and male-male murders. Once again, the quantitative data are used to illustrate the main patterns and the qualitative data are used to gain insight into the complexities of the dynamic processes involved.

RELATIONSHIP BETWEEN THE PERPETRATOR AND THE VICTIM

The nature of the relationship between the perpetrator and the victim provides the man with greater legitimate access as an acquaintance and little or none as a stranger, and this may be related to the lethal outcome. If they were strangers, how was contact made? If they were acquainted, what was the nature and duration of the acquaintance and what, if any, relationship might this have to the murder? The nature of the relationships between the perpetrators and the 40 older women victims is shown graphically at the beginning of Appendix V, and included strangers (40%, n = 16) and those who were variously acquainted (60%, n = 24). Those known to one another included short-term acquaintances of 1 day (n = 1) or of several days or longer (n = 6); relatives (n = 5); friends (n = 5); and neighbors (n = 7). In addition, we identified murders that contained any form of sexual attack (53%, n = 21) and those that primarily involved a theft (48%, n = 19). The 19 Theft/Murders were mostly perpetrated by men variously acquainted with the victim (n = 15, 79%) and very few by men who were strangers (n = 4, 21%). By contrast, the 21 Sex/Murders were almost equally divided between men who were acquainted with the victim (n = 9, 43%) and those who were strangers (n = 12, 57%). Murders that involved both theft and sex are categorized as Sex/Murders.

Here, we examine the diversity of these events using the qualitative material in order to illustrate the dynamic interconnection between the perpetrator/victim relationship and the murder as characterized either as Theft/Murder or as Sex/Murder. Theft/Murders of older women usually involved breaking into her home or place of residence, and very few took place on the street or in a public place. Sex/Murders of older women usually involved the perpetrator breaking into the woman's residence and engaging in a sexual act, which varied from disturbing her clothing and displaying her breasts or pubic area to varying levels of sexual assault or rape. A small number of cases did not fit into either category because they did not involve a theft or a sexual attack, but for this analysis they are presented within the category of Theft/Murders.

THEFT/MURDERS OF OLDER WOMEN

Theft/Murders by Relatives and Acquaintances

We begin with Theft/Murders committed by relatives and acquaintances and progress from men with the closest relationship to the woman, such as relatives, to the most distant, such as those who simply live nearby and have only a distant or casual acquaintance. This will be followed by examples of the few cases in which the murder was committed by a stranger.

Relatives and burglary

This 29 year old man killed, by stabbing 10 times, a 79 year woman who was a distant relative during a burglary in her home, and assaulted her 56 year old disabled son who tried to intervene. At 5:00 am, the son woke to hear his mother's screams, and went into her bedroom and recognized the perpetrator. He then tried to get to the front door to get help when the perpetrator attacked him, knocked him out, and fled (*622cf1.2.2). [theft]

He (age 24) murdered a 79 year old relative [also a neighbor] when trying to steal cash from her house (*900cf1.2.2). [theft]

Acquaintances, neighbors, and burglary

The offender (age 21) kills his 70 year old neighbor and family friend. The motive was burglary and he murdered her when she detected and disturbed him (*936cf1.2.2). [theft]

A heavy drinker who murdered his neighbor during a burglary

The offender (age 35) murdered his 73 year old neighbor when trying to burgle her house. He was a heavy drinker and gambler who needed money for his habits and strangled her. He went to the victim's house and was let in by the deceased who was a close friend of his mother's. While the deceased was making him a drink of coffee, he approached her from behind and killed her by manual strangulation. On his own admission, he did this to steal money. After the murder he put on rubber gloves to remove all traces of his visit, and slept two nights in the house with the dead woman's body deliberately placed where it could not be seen from outside. On the third day, he went into a police station and confessed to what he had done (*926cf1.2.2). [theft]

More distant relationships included men who knew the woman in various ways, such as mowing her lawn when he was a child or doing odd jobs as an adult. In many cases, the man knew the woman simply because she lived nearby, but there may have been no direct contact prior to his attempt to steal from her house. These thefts were often to obtain money for alcohol or drugs.

Alcoholic trying to burgle neighbor's house

The perpetrator [a disabled male, aged 40] was a chronic alcoholic who was drunk at the time. He battered an elderly widow (age 67) to death after she discovered him trying to burgle her house during the night. The victim lived alone in the same neighborhood as the perpetrator and his family. He had been babysitting for his sister during the evening [and getting drunk] when he left and went to burgle the widow's house. She died in the neurosurgical unit at the local Hospital (*859cf1.2.2). [theft]

Perpetrator and others commit theft/murder

The 31 year old perpetrator, along with his girlfriend and her sister, attempted to burgle a house occupied by the elderly female victim (age 69), her sister, and a male lodger. The main purpose of the break-in was to obtain the key for a pub that was in the possession of the male lodger who was the manager of the pub. The victim was bludgeoned repeatedly with a table leg (*540cf1.2.2). [theft]

Acquaintance steals woman's car and burgles her house
A 17 year old killed a 74 year old woman, stole from her house and stole her car. At the time of the murder, the perpetrator was living with two other men. He tried to implicate them in the murder, but there was no evidence to support this. Motive: to steal her car, but he can't explain her murder (*570cf1.2.2). [theft]

A few of the thefts were more elaborate and involved some form of deception, fraud, or "business" arrangement that may have involved a more developed plan to obtain money or possessions from the woman.

Brief acquaintance, "business," deception, and murder
The perpetrator (age 37) and the co-accused (age 38) operated a "business" venture targeting elderly people and charging high prices for menial tasks. They killed two elderly sisters in their 70s when disturbed during a robbery of their house. They had previously worked for the sisters and deliberately left a tool so that they would have a reason to return. Upon return, they asked for the tool and then went into the house to see what they could steal. When challenged by the sisters, they set upon them killing one by striking her on the head with an old fashioned flat iron and the other by "staving" in her head and kicking her in the face [she choked on her own blood]. The bones in her face and skull were smashed, and her chest and neck were smashed by jumping on her chest. Then a cushion was placed over her face to make "sure" after one of the co-accused pointed out that she was still alive. The second old lady upon seeing the carnage was also struck a blow to the head with an instrument by one of the men, rendered unconscious, and a cushion placed over her face, and she was suffocated. The house was ransacked but little was taken (*915.1cf1.7.6). [theft]

The following two cases did not involve any form of sexual attack or a direct theft. The first case involved a man who had a long-term acquaintance with the elderly woman he murdered. He claimed that he attacked her (a confused 76 year old widow) because she ridiculed him. The second case involved a son who killed his mother, with whom he lived, after an argument over what to eat for breakfast, but this was done in the context of long-standing disagreements between them and the possibility that he was stealing her pension money.

Long-term acquaintance—no theft—no sex—alleged insult
A 40 year old man killed an elderly, confused widow (age 76). When her husband died, he visited her on a fairly regular basis—doing her shopping, odd jobs etc. He also helped other elderly people, but helped her more often than the others, especially after she became mentally confused after her husband's death. He allegedly killed her because she laughed at his disability. On the day in question, he passed her house and she invited him in. He was in low spirits because his girlfriend had recently left him and his visit from his daughter had come to an end. He says she laughed at the fact that his girlfriend had left him, and because his disability meant he wasn't "much of a catch." He killed her by hitting her on the head with a heavy earthenware jug. He struck her 29 times and stabbed her three times with a kitchen knife. Then he set fire to the room in an attempt to destroy signs of the crime. At first he denied all knowledge to the police, then he admitted hitting her "a couple of times" and setting fire to furniture, but says he can't

remember stabbing her. He later admitted this when confronted with forensic evidence (*625cf1.2.6). [theft]

Son kills mother, a fraught relationship, and he subsequently cashes her pension check

A 41 yr old man kills his 69 year old mother. They lived in the same house, he was her main carer, and apparently she was difficult to live with. There were mounting financial problems partly brought about by her wish to buy and improve the house. On the day of the offense, he recalls getting involved in a "stupid argument" over what to have for breakfast. His mother had insisted that "she knew best." The combinations of his concerns about the possible loss of his job, his health problems, and his mother not listening to him and putting him down by belittling him led to such a buildup of "total frustration" that he picked up a hammer left from some DIY work and struck her on the back of the head. As she lay on the floor he tried for a pulse but became overcome at "seeing someone you loved in pain" and "took his belt and strangled her." On the same day, he took her pension book, forged her signature and cashed it. Sometime later he phoned the family doctor, and the police were contacted. [NB, he had previous convictions for fraud and theft related to his mother's property and had received 1 year probation] (*041cf1.2.7).

Theft/Murders by Strangers

In many cases, the perpetrator and the woman he killed were strangers, but these are not simply random attacks against any stranger he might have attacked. Instead, the men "targeted" a "category" of person known to be vulnerable. When a man breaks into a care home, it is very unlikely that he knows the victim personally, but he knows that the residents are elderly and thus are easy targets for theft or sex or both. He may be indifferent to the gender of his potential victim, but is aware that the usual residents of care homes are "little old ladies." Thus, he is at least vaguely aware that the victim of a "random" attack on such a residence is more likely to be an older woman than an older man. Again, an easier target. Based on the information in the casefiles, it was often apparent from the context that a man described as a "stranger" might very well have known the woman by sight or because he lived nearby.

Stranger—steals and sets house on fire

The perpetrator (age 39) kills by kicking and stamping an 89 year old woman stranger and then sets fire to her house in the course of a burglary (*262cf1.2.2). [theft]

Stranger—intended to steal handbag on the street, followed woman home and murdered her

The perpetrator (age 30) murdered an 81 year old woman. He was on probation at the time, and has a long history of physical and sexual violence against elderly women. [Police Report] I saw the old lady coming out of the Post Office [after obtaining her pension money] and I made up my mind to follow her and snatch her bag if I could. I followed at a good distance but I could see her all the time. She came to a row of houses and went in the front door of one of them. I went around the back. She had taken her hat and coat off. When she saw me in the hall she said, "What do you want? I have got money in the top drawer." I put my hand over her mouth to stop her shouting. I tied a towel around her mouth, and she fell on the floor in the doorway. I tied her hands with another towel and she just went quiet. I was in a right cranky state by then. I just don't know what I'm doing when I'm like that. I ran upstairs and went in the room on the right at the top of the stairs. I don't even know why I did it [the murder] as I had already got £90 in notes from a purse in the top drawer of the sideboard in the living room. I can't remember anything about her after she fell on the floor in the hall (*986cf1.2.6). [theft]

Stranger—burglary of house when drunk and on drugs
[confessed after several years in prison]
I struck her (age 67) with a crow-bar, became frightened and tied her foot to the bed then ran to the top of the stairs and fell down and after some time managed to get up and go out the front door. I was frightened, crying and I walked down the street and saw a phone box and lifted the phone. I tried to phone an ambulance to get help for the lady. Then I went to my mum's house and the police came. (He was intoxicated having taken antidepressant tablets and drunk a full bottle of whisky, some sherry, and cider). [This is his account written in a letter] (*859cf1.2.2). [theft]

SEX/MURDERS OF OLDER WOMEN

The murders of older women that involved sex were almost evenly divided between those perpetrated by an acquaintance (n = 9, 43%) and those perpetrated by a stranger (n = 12, 57%). Of the 21 cases involving a sexual attack, about one-quarter also included a theft and are classified here in terms of the sexual element. We begin with the closest relationships, those perpetrated by relatives and acquaintances.

Sex/Murders by Relatives and Acquaintances

As family members, most men are viewed as "safe" with respect to their female relatives, particularly older ones, and are viewed as guardians and caretakers rather than as potential attackers on mothers, aunts, grandmothers, and others. Only two relatives committed a Sex/Murder and, as such, we begin with the accounts involving friends and neighbors. They reveal the women's trust in the men and his ease of access to her, often facilitated by his performance of odd jobs and the provision of company for women who were alone and lonely.

Friend and near neighbor
The perpetrator (age 44) rapes and kills an 80 year old grandmother in her flat who was described as "sprightly, popular, and, for her age, energetic." He was a friend and near neighbor and had known the victim for a few months and done

odd jobs for her. At first there was nothing immediately suspicious about her death, but the post mortem examinations revealed extensive bruising and that she had had sexual intercourse shortly prior to her death. The perpetrator was interviewed by the police but denied the murder and said he had only seen her on the street. But three days later he left a note with a friend, saying, "I won't be seeing anyone for a long time" (*1000cf1.4.2). [sex]

Sexually assaults, strangles, and cuts the throat of elderly neighbor

A 38 year old man sexually assaults and strangles a female neighbor (age 83). The victim had been strangled manually, her throat was cut, her jaw was fractured and several ribs were broken. She was also seriously sexually assaulted. He was convicted on forensic and fingerprint evidence. The judge described him as "evil" and highly dangerous to the public and to women in particular. In sentencing, he said he would make a whole-life recommendation (*728cf1.4.2). [sex]

Brutal physical and sexual attack on neighbor known since childhood

Earlier in the day, he (age 29) had an argument with his girlfriend and took a cocktail of alcohol and drugs during the evening and sexually abused a fifteen year old girl [which was reported to police and partially thwarted by the girl]. He then broke into the victim's home by kicking open the rear door and brutally attacking his woman neighbor (age 71) whom he had known since the age of 13. She was struck several times with blows of great force in the genital area, rupturing the vaginal wall. He proceeded to disembowel her with his fist through the vaginal/rectal area. A human bite mark was found on the victim's arm which matched his dental record. He was a bit of a "Jack the Lad" about the neighborhood, but was generally liked and known to visit the victim for chats and errands. Most neighbors saw him as friendly and jovial (*913.1cf1.4.2). [sex]

Acquaintance of one day, drunken attack and murder outdoors

The man (age 39) killed a 66 year old woman he had met that day in a pub. In a drunken stupor, he tried to have sex and then brutally killed her. He has a history of alcoholism and blackouts from alcohol and depression. The body was found with a large piece of wood, possibly a table top covering her top half and lying on her back. Her arms were above her head and entangled in her coat and cardigan. Her jeans and knickers were around her right ankle and she still had her right shoe on. She was otherwise naked (*849cf1.4.3). [sex]

Sex/Murders by Strangers

The following are several examples of men breaking into the residences of older women and carrying out brutal attacks related to sexual motivations. Three recount the murders of women living in care homes that were broken into by men who were complete strangers. These murders are particularly horrific because the women were living/residing in a context where they were under the care of others, yet even in these circumstances the men appeared to be determined to break in and carry out a sexual act/attack. The last in this series of accounts is a rare example but provides an illustration of the murder of a very vulnerable older woman who had no home and no carers but was, instead, a homeless older woman living on the streets.

Stranger, drunk, on probation, sex/murder in victim's house

In the early hours of the morning, he (age 22) broke into the house of a widow (age 68) and attacked her in her bedroom, striking her repeatedly about the head, biting her nipple, forcing his fingers into her vagina and then strangling her. There was bruising on both sides of her face and lower jaw and across the throat, also on the inner thighs and vagina which suggested forced sexual abuse. The cause of death was both head injuries and strangulation. In interview, he said that his motive was theft and that he was drunk. He claimed he attacked her only when she began to scream. He was subject to a probation order when this occurred. The victim was described by neighbors as "a friendly old lady who did charitable work." [Forensic Evidence]: Finger and palm prints were found. These were matched with the defendant's that were taken for his previous [sexual] offense for which he was placed on probation. When arrested on the same day, he was found to have a blood level content of 160 mg per 100 ml of blood. In the opinion of the doctor who examined him, it would take eight hours to lose the alcohol from his system, and the doctor suggested that he would not be fit for interview during that period (*1014cf1.4.3). [sex]

Stranger, drunk, sex/murder in a care home for the elderly

The perpetrator (age 32) killed and sexually assaulted a woman age 73 who was a permanent resident of an old peoples' home. On the night of the murder she was taken to her room by two assistants who helped her dress for bed and to enter bed. The perpetrator was found in the home after killing the victim. He smelled of intoxicants and body odor. Post mortem found abrasions in the nose, markings and fresh abrasion to the neck, bruising to the forearm and of the body, bruising in the upper part of the vagina and a split in the posterior wall of the vagina which is consistent with an object of some description being placed in the vagina. Death was by asphyxiation as a result of manual strangulation and an obstruction of the nose and mouth which was compatible with a pillow being pressed over the nose and mouth (*1032cf1.4.3). [sex]

Stranger, attempts to break into several residences in old people's home

He (age 38) was drinking but not drunk and raped and sexually assaulted an elderly female (age 80) after a series of attempts on the same night in a complex of sheltered houses for the elderly. At 12:10 am the perpetrator attempted to gain forced entry to a number of residences in a sheltered housing complex for the elderly. He also attempted to gain admittance by purporting to be a Police Officer. When he failed to gain entry he then went to a fourth residence and gained entry by smashing the rear kitchen window and climbing in. He then went to the bedroom of the premises and viciously attacked the occupant in an attempt to rape her. During the attack, he punched and kicked her about the head and body, stripped her naked, bit her breasts and forced her to have oral sex with him. During the attack, he was disturbed by a Warden attending the premises in response to the distress alarm of the victim. He fled the premises and was arrested nearby. He was interviewed and admitted the offenses. The victim died as a result of her injuries about one month later which included a fractured left cheek bone, severe double fracture of the lower jaw, fracture of her left upper and lower arm and six fractured ribs (*1092cf1.4.3). [sex]

Stranger drunk, broke into old people's home, motive probably sex

The perpetrator (age 24) killed a frail elderly female (age 86) after breaking into an old people's home at night when he was drunk. On New Year's Eve he drank 7–8 bottles of Newcastle Brown Ale and then broke into an old peoples' rest home by climbing onto a balcony and in through the lounge. His motive for breaking in was never clear, but he went up one more floor and into the victim's room. She was battered by four blows with his fist and suffered: a broken cheekbone, jaw, nose and skull fractures and horrific bruising. She was probably sexually assaulted, her dressing gown was raised and there were other indicators. The victim died in hospital 15 days later of pneumonia related to her injuries. He says he had no motivation except curiosity about what was inside an old people's home and just lashed out when he saw something move. He told me specifically that he was *not* angry when he assaulted the victim and that his only motivation was to get away (*897cf1.2.6). [sex]

Two men kill a homeless older woman on the street

The perpetrator (age 19) with one co-accused killed a female (age 65) who they planned to rob and later sexually assaulted. Shortly after midnight, the two accused came upon the deceased in an alleyway leading off one of the main streets. She was a tramp who made a habit of sleeping in parked buses or wherever she could find some shelter. The perpetrator had been drinking vodka on the day of the event, both in the afternoon and evening, smoked cannabis and took some amphetamines. She was dragged down the alley to an area behind a commercial building and thrown to the ground. They gave different accounts of what took place, each seeking to blame the other. It appears that while the co-accused held her down, the perpetrator searched her bags and then her underclothes for money, and stuck his fingers in her vagina. Thereafter, the other accused probably stamped on her abdomen and head causing severe internal injuries. At one stage, she was picked up and swung against a heavy industrial dustbin so that her head struck the metal handle which fractured her skull and penetrated her brain. There were numerous injuries to the head and face generally which had been inflicted with such force that the bone structure of her face was displaced. They made for the house of the co-accused to clean up. The perpetrator then stole a van and they had a joyride in it (*236cf1.4.3). [sex]

Collateral Sex/Murder

The following case is an example of a rare Collateral Sex/Murder. It did not involve a theft or a sexual attack on the older woman who was murdered, but did involve a sexual attack upon her granddaughter who was in her care.

Grandmother murdered trying to protect 19 year old granddaughter who was being raped

The granddaughter (age 19) was woken in the middle of the night by a man who raped and buggered her. He (age 40) then left the room, went downstairs and she says she heard her grandmother (age 80) wailing and gasping. When he returned to her room the noise had stopped. When she started to scream and struggle, he put his hands round her throat and she felt his nails digging into her throat. He raped and buggered her again. The electrical fuse boxes in the cellar had been switched off showing previous knowledge of the house [he had worked in the house]. About four months after the attack and murder, the granddaughter received sexually abusive phone calls and recognized his voice (*640cf1.2.6). [Collateral, Sex/Murder]

Summary of the Types of Relationships Involved in Theft/Murders and Sex/Murders

Delineating the relationships between the men and the older women they murder as strangers or acquaintances and characterizing the murder events in terms of the principle component of theft or sex provides evidence that illustrates the dynamics of these murders.

The qualitative evidence suggests the following:

- The overwhelming majority of murders occurred in the woman's place of residence with acquaintances primarily gaining access through friendship, company, odd jobs, or assistance and strangers breaking into her home in order to steal and/or to commit a sexual attack.
- Many theft/murderers had an ongoing connection with the woman, such as having worked for her or knowing her from the neighborhood, but this was very unusual in the Sex/Murders (42% vs. 5%).
- At the time of the murder, almost all of the men were drinking, most were drunk, and a few were also on drugs.
- Some men appeared to be intent on committing serious violence and murder while others "changed the project" from theft to murder or from a sexual attack to a murder when they thought they would be identified by the victim, she resisted and/or challenged him, or his expectations of the event were somehow thwarted.
- About one-third of all the men who murdered an older woman were angry or in a rage during the murder, but 50% of the theft/murderers were in this emotional state compared to 16% of sex/murderers.
- The sexual assault was opportunistic for a few men but appeared to be the primary purpose of the attack for many.
- The murders were often very brutal and involved far more violence than would be "sufficient" to subdue an older woman for whatever purpose.

The quantitative evidence in Figure 9.1 at the end of the chapter and in Appendix V, Table 9.1, present the evidence regarding the context and circumstances of the 40 murders of older women without regard to whether sex or theft was involved.

Additional quantitative evidence comparing Sex/Murders and Theft/Murders is also presented where relevant in order to further illustrate differences between them. Beginning with a brief description of the perpetrators and victims, the context and circumstances of the murders are examined, including the use of alcohol and drugs prior to the murder, disputes with and/or previous violence against the victim, confrontations during the murder event, time and place, the physical attack, the body, and attempts to avoid detection. Finally, comments by the perpetrator about the murder and events surrounding it are presented in the section "He said."

Context and Circumstances

At the time they committed the murder, the average age of the men was 30 years, ranging from 15 to 49 years, and the average age of the women they murdered was 75 years and ranged from 65 to 89 years. At the time, about 70% of the men were unemployed and were not in an intimate relationship. Most of the men were living on their own, as were most of the women who were widows or single. At the time, 22% of the perpetrators were involved with the police (e.g., arrested for another offense but not in custody), and 19% were on probation and/or under supervision (Figure 9.1; Appx.V-Table 9.1). As shown in the next chapter, nearly two-thirds had previously been in prison. In addition, the quantitative analysis of the murder of women over the age of 80 revealed a significant difference between Theft/Murders and Sex/Murders. Of the 13 women 80 years of age or older, 9 (69%) were the victims of a Sex/Murder and 4 (31%) were the victims of Theft/Murders. This suggests that the men who committed Sex/Murders targeted some of the oldest and most vulnerable of women who were most likely to be without guardians and least likely to have the physical capacity to defend themselves or resist. This is aptly illustrated in the cases of men who attacked women living in sheltered housing or a care home who were often frail and over the age of 80.

Alcohol and Drugs

The context of the murders often involved alcohol and drunkenness of the perpetrators: 53% had been drinking, 37% were drunk, and 19% were using drugs at the time (Figure 9.1; Appx.V-Table 9.1). Sex murderers were significantly more likely than theft murderers to be drinking (70% vs. 33%), drunk (55% vs. 17%), or using drugs (24% vs. 13%). Of the men who were drinking, 31% of sex/murderers had been drinking all day and 45% were drinking 3–6 hours before the murder. None of the theft murderers had been drinking all day, although 50% had been drinking 3–6 hours prior to the murder. For most, this level of consumption would lead to intoxication. Only one woman was drunk, and she had been drinking with the perpetrator. None of the other women had been drinking or taking drugs. Much of the qualitative data illustrates the high level of drinking by the men and the accompanying altered states of thinking and behavior, including perceptions of personal insult and elevated levels of physical and/or sexual aggression. With this level of drunkenness, the woman's defense of her money or property might be viewed through his distorted lens as inappropriate or unacceptable, a challenge to be responded to by "changing the project" from attack to murder, involving great ferocity and the infliction of considerable damage even to the point of murder.

Circumstances at the time of the murder—alcohol

Were you going out a lot [before the offense]? Yeah, probably four times a week. *How much were you drinking?* When I weren't working, probably about 11 pints a night (*1056iv1.4.3).

What had you been drinking in the pub beforehand? I'd been drinking everything and anything. *Everything?* Yes, I'd gone through all the taps [beer] and the optics [alcoholic spirits as served in pubs]. I know I started off drinking lager and Guinness and cider—I'm not sure about the optics—hard alcohol (*304iv1.4.3).

So you were 31 years old at the time [of the murder], living at home with your mother, your aunty, your two kids. Were you drinking then? Yes. I was working morning and nights in the club. *Were you drinking in the club when you were at work?* Yes. *How much were you drinking?* Between 25 to 30 pints of Guinness a day. *Can you drink that much Guinness in a day?* That was during working hours. I used to open the club at 9 in the morning. Then I'd start my drinking. We'd close at 1:00 am the following morning, and we'd go for a drink somewhere. *So you were basically drinking all the time. All the waking hours?* Yes. *You were still able to work?* Yes, it's surprising how you can hide it. I know 25–30 pints sounds a lot, but from 9 o'clock in the morning until 1:00 am the following morning, it only works out about a couple of pints an hour, something like that. I was always good at holding my drink because I started drinking when I was so young. It was only when I started hitting the shorts [spirits] that I'd wind up being drunk. It got to the stage when I needed a drink first thing in the morning, as soon as I got out of bed, just to stop my hands shaking [indicator of alcoholism]. I'd have to have a drink just to get me out of bed, get me on my feet, and get me to work. *And how long had you been drinking this much and were you in that condition?* It started about two and a half years before I committed this offense. It started with the death of my dad. That's when my drinking took off. *But if you're not sleeping?* I've been on three and four day binges without having slept or eaten. Just drank until the pubs closed (*1032iv1.4.3).

Circumstances at the time of the murder—drinking and multidrug use

What were the circumstances of your life at the time of the murder? I'd been out of prison for about a year. *Were you injecting anything?* At the time, I was injecting amphetamines, I even tried injecting LSD. I found that was no good to do intravenously. But I still had a lot of unresolvement in my personal life with women. I couldn't trust women. I was just using them for sex. And they were objects for my own sexual gratification. And I was drug using at the time plus I was living back at the family home. So I was living like this triple life. "No mum, I'm OK, blah, blah, blah. No dad, I'm OK." Then with my mates I was rowdy and fighting. And then at work I was responsible. They were drinkers, whereas my other mates were drug takers, and my family were social drinkers. Then [girlfriend] came back into my life and nearly fucked my head up. My mates were all these Goths, new wave, punk, Nirvana types. They had carrier bags full of these bloody mushrooms. I was working and I wouldn't think anything about forking out for wine, beer, what have you, just sit round their pads, psychedelic, doubling up on these mushrooms (*975iv1.4.3).

Disputes, Previous Violence, and Confrontations

While many male-male and intimate partner murders are preceded by a dispute, only 8% of the murders of older women involved an ongoing dispute between the victim and perpetrator (Figure 9.1; Appx.V-Table 9.1). Clearly, this is related to the fact that many of the murders involved strangers, but even if the man murdered a neighbor or friend, as the qualitative narratives suggest, there was generally no animosity between them. Only 21% of the cases involved a confrontation immediately before the murder. Theft/Murders were more likely than Sex/Murders (33% vs. 9%) to involve a "confrontation" as the woman challenged the intruder, attempted to stop him from stealing her property, or indicated that she knew who he was with the possibility that she would later identify him to the police. Theft/murderers then used serious violence to silence her and/eliminate a potential witness to his burglary. Previous violence by the perpetrators against the victims did not occur and, not surprisingly, there was no previous violence by victims directed at the perpetrators.

THE MURDER EVENT

Time and Place, Physical Attack, and Injuries

The vast majority of the 40 murders occurred in the home of the victim (88%). Outdoor locations were rare. Most of the murders took place between 5 pm and 9 pm (14% Sex/M vs. 26% Theft/M) or between 9 pm and 6 am (68% Sex/M vs. 42% Theft/M), with the remainder between noon and 5 pm. As with the other types of murder, most involved several forms of violence. However, the most common cause of death of older women involved the blunt force trauma usually delivered with bodily violence and in many cases the use of an instrument such as a blunt object (73%) followed by strangulation, choking, or smothering (26%) (Figure 9.1; Appx.V-Table 9.1). In addition, theft murderers were significantly more likely than sex murderers (90% vs. 27%) to use some kind of instrument such as a hammer, iron bar, bottle, brick, or club in the attack on the woman. Kicking, punching, stamping, and multiple stabbing occurred in about a quarter of both types, while strangling/choking and smothering were significantly more likely in Sex/Murders than Theft/Murders (38% vs.11%). Nearly all of the women died within 30 minutes of the attack, 5 or more injuries were inflicted in 83% of the murders, and 10 or more injuries were sustained by many of the women (48%). Again, the number of injuries suggests a sustained attack that was far more ferocious and brutal than would be required to overwhelm an older woman.

The Body After Death, Detection,
and Attempts to Avoid Detection

After the attack, most perpetrators immediately left the woman, who was already dead or dying, and a few engaged in actions meant to avoid detection such as setting fire to the body or her house (Sex/M = 5% vs. Theft/M = 21%). In contrast to the sexual murders of younger women, there were very few reports of sexual acts or mutilation of the body after death. A few of the men simply gave themselves up to the police, and most were apprehended after a standard investigation, with only one-fifth of the cases requiring anything more extensive.

The body after death, what to do with it, and leaving the scene
The clearest memory I have is waking up next to her and I didn't know she was dead. And I was sick because I remember thinking like, smiling to myself—I'm still thinking, you know, that I'm going to have sex and then I realized that she was dead because I touched her face, you know, there was like cold blood on her and I knew it was blood for some reason, it was very black, it was like moonlight. And that's when I came out of that moment of rape—and I was like realizing I'd killed her. *So you had passed out then?* Because at first I was concerned about her and then later I was thinking of hiding the body and panicking, but I couldn't move the body. I felt very weak and I felt sickened, you know, and I sort of left very quickly (*304iv1.4.3).

Attempts to avoid detection
He remembered leaving the scene and hiding for a short while near the bus station before making his way into the garden of a house where he found a bin full of water in which he was able to wash the blood from his face and hands. He took off his jacket, shirt and trousers and hid them in the garden. All these items were heavily stained with blood. This left him in a pair of [under]shorts and a jumper which was also blood stained which he turned inside out. The discarded and hidden clothing was never recovered despite his efforts to lead the officers to the site where he had hidden them (*849cf1.4.3).

After the murder—normal routine and contact with police
So this was the elderly woman you had done some jobs for, how old was she? Eighty, friendly woman, lovely woman. I put the body in a comfortable position, her arm was up here, my mind was working, but the man was up above watching me. I sat up all night smoking and having a drink, and went to work the next day. I think it was that evening when this fellow from the police was doing the normal checks that they do, came to the door and said, "would you mind coming to the police station and giving us some samples." "No problem." So I gave samples of hair, chest hair, pubic hair, having a ball there, laughing and joking. I don't think I had realized then just what I'd done. The next day, I went to the police station. I said, "Can I speak to this detective?" [who had previously interviewed him]. So the guy came out and he said, "what is it?" I said, "it was me that killed" [victim]. "No, we've got somebody for that." [I said], "it was me." He said, "Well, tell me something about it." I went through it stage by stage. He went, "Come on," and that was it. Since then I can piece together how it happened, why it happened, an

apparently motiveless murder. There was no sexual attack, no robbery, nothing. *Was she irritating you at the time?* No, she was a smashing old lady, she was great. One of the friendliest old ladies you could ever meet, I just [clicks his fingers]; they put it down to strangulation, there was all bruising on one side of her neck, it doesn't make sense (*1000iv1.4.2). [sex]

He Says—What Were They Thinking? Perpetrators Accounts of the Murder

At the time, some of the men confessed and took responsibility for the murder, while the accounts of others involved various forms of denial, rationalizations, excuses, and justifications. The specific victim of the murder was not usually blamed, although the justifications and rationales provided by the men sometimes involved a specific woman or women in general who they believed had somehow caused them harm. Some of the men said that the whole thing was inexplicable or an accident. In cases that involved a sexual element, it was often denied in spite of evidence to the contrary. Unlike the sexual murders of younger women, the majority of these men did not suggest that the women consented or initiated any form of sexual contact at the time of the murder, but a few claimed that they had previously had a sexual relationship.

The following examples demonstrate the thinking and actions of men who murder an older woman, either in the context of a theft or a sexual attack. Theft/Murders, as the examples suggest, often involved men attacking a woman after she had interrupted his attempt to steal money or property from her house. Sex/Murders, by contrast were associated with men's effort to subdue the woman before carrying out a sexual act or attack.

He says—theft for drugs, intention to do harm, and anger at women as rationale for murder

Do you think that the motive to break into the house was to get money for drugs? Yes. To get money, primarily for gain. *For gain?* Whether you used it for drugs or drink or going out, whatever. It was the satisfaction of being able to do anything you want because money buys everything. Not finding the money was disillusioning, and it made me *angry* at being thwarted. *So it was frustrating?* And I knew I was going to use violence or create some harm, do some harm. I had no thoughts of killing. *But you knew you'd do violence?* Yes. *So was that in the back of your head or the front?* I didn't know what form it was going to take initially, but when I was in the bedroom I knew I was going to rape that woman. *Did you?* Yes, I knew I was going to exact some revenge on her. It wasn't her [victim]; it was [current girlfriend]; it was [ex-girlfriends]; it was a woman. I think there was a little bit of anger at my mother as well because she'd been very domineering and very controlling. Yeah, but I've always thought, "Why? She's an old woman; that's bloody taboo," but I'd suffered a lot of physical and emotional abuse at home (*975iv1.4.3). [Sex. Stranger]

He says—alcohol, theft, sex, and fear of identification by victim

I think I'd been out in the morning. I think I went to a football match, then all day drinking. I went back to the village, went into the local pub and carried on drinking then I went to a nightclub. *Was that work [job as barman] or were you carrying* *on drinking?* No I was just drinking. At three in the morning, I left the club. Then I think I went to a burger van, and started walking home. Where I live, three or four doors away from me, is a big house. I decided I was going to break into this house. *Had you thought about breaking into this house before?* Not really. So I broke into the house. I went upstairs and was looking through the closet in the bedroom. I heard somebody get out of bed. I heard somebody shouting. I panicked a little bit, punched the person. *Did you have any sense of who it was at the time?* Yeah, I knew it was a woman. I knew that she knew me. *Because you lived near the house?* Yeah. She was on the floor and I ended up strangling her. *What was on your mind?* I think it's more that she knew me and she would contact the police. *How old was she?* I think it was 83, I think. *Were there any sexual things involved?* They said there was, but I've always pleaded not guilty to the sexual part of the crime (*1056iv1.4.3). [NB-The evidence indicated that sex was involved].

He says—odd jobs for older woman, doesn't know what happened—sex/murder

Okay, let's talk about the offense and what was going on in your life. Things were going well. I'd moved into a new block of flats on the ground floor which consisted mainly of old people. I was getting on well with all the residents. One lady in particular, every day when you'd had your lunch [she would say] I need this and that, and you knew rightly it was company she was after. Then it started getting, "can you come and lay a bathroom floor for me?' "a new carpet for my hallway?" If I'd done her a favor, she would say, "There's a fiver." She'd call in every day, and I'd walk over in the evening and we'd go for a walk. So I was sitting in my flat and had a bottle of wine and a few spliffs [marijuana]. I thought, I'll nip down and tell the old lady about my new job because when she comes up, I might be away at work. I went down to tell her, ten minutes later she was dead, just went like that, I don't know what happened (*1000iv1.4.2). [sex]

He says—attempted to disguise it as a burglary in order to explain away the sexual assault

I put my hand over her mouth and carried her to the bed in the same room to make her comfy but I tripped and dumped her on the bed. She was wailing some more, and then I put a pillow over her head. At that point, I meant her no harm. I just wanted to quiet her down. I'm sure I suffocated her with the pillow, her bladder emptied and I ran off. I tried to calm down and think what to do. Decided to make it look like a burglary and that's when things started going wrong. I couldn't perform the burglary. I felt fear and horror. Her eyes seemed to be looking at me accusingly. I tried to cover her eyes by dragging her dress over her face. Her dress snagged on her buttocks and slipped out of my hand. I panicked even more, memories flooded back, I screwed up again. I tried to change fear to anger. I remembered as a kid when some lads raped me, they pissed on me. I tried to do the same but couldn't so I decided to ejaculate. It wasn't easy but I managed it. It didn't do any good. It didn't relieve the emotions surging within me. I was still scared and angry; I wanted to take it out on her. I saw the knife sitting on the chest beside the bed. I'd been using it to try to do the burglary. I dragged her dress right up over her head and attacked her heart with a knife. After seven stabs I stopped, I felt revulsion. I pulled the dress down and stabbed her three or four times. It didn't help, I was still frightened, angry, frustrated, scared. I grabbed the side of the bed and tried to turn it over. She was still looking at me. The body rolled back. I put a pillow on the face and ran. [His version to police] In his statement to police, he tells a slightly different story—knocked back from job, he decided to break into the victim's electric meters, saw her purse on the table and took money. She interrupted him, he pushed her onto the bed, masturbated on her and stabbed her (*648cf1.4.2). [sex]

He says he intended to murder, blames depression and separation from his intimate partner, Sex/Murder

He says he did not intend to kill the victim and that he went to her house to do a burglary but whilst in her bedroom she woke up and started to scream, he grabbed her by the throat and punched her a few times to keep her quiet. She struggled with him; he got into a rage and squeezed her throat harder. When she stopped struggling, he saw blood on her mouth, panicked and ran from the house. He admitted indecently assaulting her but denies rape. [After sentencing] During my [professional] visit to him in July, he disclosed that earlier in the evening of the murder he had watched the victim and her son through a window of their home and decided at that point that he would kill the woman. He told me that he was feeling extremely depressed due to various domestic and social problems [possibly his drinking and his wife's departure] and that he wanted "to be taken away from it all." He went on to state that he would have murdered his partner had he been able to locate her at the time. I think it is likely that his victim experienced the brutality which he actually wanted to inflict upon his partner (*1014cf1.4.3). [sex]

Rare Case of Multiple Murders Including an Older Woman

Serial, spree, and multiple murders are very rare, yet older women are sometimes the victims. The following case involved a spree killing of five individuals including an elderly man and woman, the wealthy employers of a man who worked as their butler, along with three others. He set out to rob and defraud the older couple, and killed them when he was discovered. He and his two accomplices then went on the run and in the end he murdered his accomplices. No sexual attacks were involved in the murders. After these murders, it was discovered that he had previously killed a former prison inmate on a country estate where he was employed because he feared that his plans to steal from his wealthy employer would be revealed.

Household butler and co-accused kill wealthy couple when caught stealing from them, followed by kidnapping and a spree of killings over several days

This is a complex case involving five murders on three separate occasions and in various locations. The perpetrator (age 53), a life-long burglar, fraudster and miscellaneous worker with no history of violence, killed five individuals. The first murder occurred on a large rural estate in Scotland where he was working and engaged in some fraudulent activity relative to his employers. He murdered a man, a former prison mate, who turned up on the estate and threatened to reveal his criminal past to his wealthy employers. He then fled to a large city in

England where he took employment as a butler with a wealthy, elderly couple and engaged in a plot to obtain property by fraud using his wealthy employer's name and bank account [identity theft]. The second murder involved the smothering of the woman employer (age 66) in the flat when she discovered the plot. The three co-conspirators then kidnapped her elderly, senile husband (age 82), bundled him into the back of the car and drove north to Scotland where he was killed some days later. Following this, he killed two co-conspirators whose loyalty he suspected as they were on the run and travelling together after the initial killings. [Secretary of State] The life sentence should mean life. This is one of the very few cases where the facts resemble the most bizarre gangster film in the ruthlessness displayed. In my view he should never be released (*825cf1.2.2). [theft]

COMPARISONS OF MURDERS OF OLDER WOMEN AND MALE-MALE MURDERS

The comparisons of the murders of older women and male-male murders are shown in Figure 9.1 and Appendix V, Table 9.1. At the time of the murder, the perpetrators in both groups were in their late 20s (MM = 27 yrs vs. OWoM = 30 yrs) and the victims were older than themselves (MM = 40 yrs vs. OWoM = 75 yrs). At the time of the murder, a minority of the perpetrators were employed (32% vs. 28%), and most were single (49% vs. 48%) or separated/divorced (18% vs. 23%). With the exception of the age of the victims, there was little or no difference between the two groups with respect to these factors. In both groups, a minority of perpetrators and victims were strangers (31% vs. 40%). Of those who were known to one another, men were most likely to be killed by a male acquaintance (39%) while older women were likely to be murdered by a male acquaintance (18%) or neighbor (18%).

The two groups differed significantly in terms of ongoing disputes between the perpetrator and the victim prior to the murder (MM = 30% vs. OWoM = 8%), confrontations immediately preceding the murder (61% vs. 21%), and previous violence to the victim by the offender (11% vs. 0%) and by the victim to the offender (11% vs. 0%). Anywhere from one-half to two-thirds of the offenders in both groups were drinking at the time of the murder (68% vs. 53%), and many were defined as drunk (49% vs. 37%). Drinking and drunkenness at the time of the murder were relatively common among the male-male victims but almost nonexistent among the older women who were victims (victim drinking, MM = 47% vs. OWoM = 3%) and (victim drunk, 33% vs. 3%). Few of the perpetrators and victims were drinking together at the time of the murder (21% vs. 3%). In short, drinking was an issue for the perpetrators of both types of murder and for the victims of male-male murders but not for the older women who were murdered.

Older women were significantly more likely to be murdered in their own home (MM = 50% vs. OWoM = 88%).Various instruments such as knives, bricks, and bats were commonly used but were more likely in male-male murders (88% vs. 73%). Five or more injuries were also common in both groups but less likely in male-male murders (71% vs. 83%). Strangling, choking, and smothering were significantly more likely to be used in the murders of older women (8% vs. 26%). While more than one perpetrator was involved in a considerable proportion of male-male murders, this rarely occurred in the murder of older women (43% vs. 10%) (Figure 9.1; Appx.V-Table 9.1).

SUMMARY

The relationships between perpetrators and victims were divided almost evenly between strangers and acquaintances and those involving theft or sex. Older women were usually robbed by acquaintances, while they were sexually assaulted both by strangers and by acquaintances. The contexts of the murders of older women usually involved men breaking into a woman's home and attempting to rob her of money or goods and/or to perpetrate a sexual attack against her. Thefts were more likely to be committed by men who were known to the woman and who may have been famil-iar with her house and its contents. For some, access was facilitated through the relationship between the perpetrator and victim, which involved previous contact between them.

Despite the nature of the relationship, and whether the murder involved theft or sex, almost all of the men lived nearby and walked to the woman's residence, where almost all of the murders occurred. Prior disputes between them or previous vio-lence by the man against the woman were extremely rare. When there was a con-frontation at the time of the murder, it usually involved the woman attempting to stop the man from stealing from her or defending herself against a sexual attack, or both. It is at this point that some men appeared to "change the project" from that of theft or sexual assault to that of murder when the woman defied him, chal-lenged him, or in some way thwarted him. Most of the men had been drinking and many were drunk, especially those who committed a sexual murder. As a group, the men who committed a sexual murder were more likely than those who committed a Theft/Murder to be dysfunctional and dissipated in a variety of ways. They were also more likely to kill women who were very old, which suggests that they targeted the most vulnerable of the older women. Almost all of the murders occurred in the home of the victim and were committed in a matter of minutes and without wit-nesses. Strangulation, kicking, beating, and hitting with blunt instruments were common forms of attack and the usual cause of death. There were no reports of fur-ther mutilation of the bodies after death, whether sexual or otherwise.

After the murder, most of the perpetrators left the scene and resumed their normal activities, such as returning to their home or the pub. A few tried to avoid detection by destroying their clothing or altering the scene of the murder. The exculpatory claims of the men included total denial of the murder, a lack of intention to do harm, denial of a sex element, loss of memory, and sometimes a lack of comprehension of what happened or why. Some men were angry, but in the main this was associated with the actual murder and was not some sort of universal anger aimed at all women, although a few men expressed such feelings. Rather, these men were angered when the older women thwarted their efforts to rob or sexually assault them. What stands out for the perpetrators at the time of the murder is a life of unemployment and, for many, a history of chronic intoxication, which was especially true for men who com-mitted a sexual murder. We now turn to a consideration of the lifecourse of the men who murder older women.

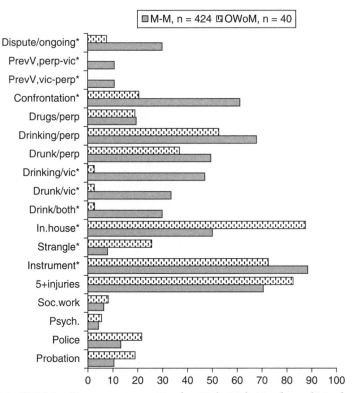

Figure 9.1 OWoM—Circumstances at Murder: Male-Male Murder and Murder of Older Women.
* statistically significant difference.

Murder of Older Women
—Perpetrators

Lifecourse, Orientations, and Cognitions

Who are the men who murder older women? The last chapter focused on the contexts and situations in which older women are murdered. Here the focus is on the lifecourse of the men who committed these murders from childhood to adulthood. Included are their relationships with women, reflections on the murder, behavior in prison, and responses to prison programs oriented to personal change and reform that focus on questions of responsibility for the murder, remorse for the murder, and empathy for the victim. Again, both quantitative and qualitative data are used, and all quotes are identified either as "cf" or "iv" indicating the source from casefiles or interviews. Overall patterns are shown in figures at the end of the chapter and tables in Appendix V. Where relevant, additional evidence is presented in order to provide further details about the differences between the men who murder older women in the context of thefts and those involving a sexual element. Sex/Murders and Theft/Murders of older women are compared in order to identify differences between them. Finally, all 40 cases of men who murder older women are examined together and compared with the 424 cases of murder in which men murder other men.

LIFECOURSE—CHILDHOOD

As stated previously, children live their lives in the home, school, and community, with varied treatment and success in each. The early years present numerous social and developmental challenges and difficulties for all children, and evidence suggests that experiences in childhood have a profound effect on adult life chances, personalities, and behavior. The analysis begins with issues relating to the family of origin and caretakers, and follows with the performance of the child at school and behavior within that context.

Family of Origin and Caretakers

The family of origin of men who murder older women included parents with a broken relationship (44%), a father violent to their mother (31%), a father who abused alcohol

(21%), and a father who had at least one previous conviction (20%). In addition, some experienced three or more changes in caretakers (23%) and/or were taken into care (18%). Many families had contact with the police (50%) and social services (42%), and some with psychologists or psychiatrists (26%), probation (22%), and healthcare (20%) (Figure 10.1; Appx.V-Table 10.1). A criminal conviction of their father/male carer was significantly more likely among sex/murderers than theft/murderers (30% vs. 7%).

We begin with families of origin that were more conventional and experienced fewer problems, and these are followed by examples of those whose experiences were more problematic. The illustrations of problematic circumstances in childhood and adulthood are more numerous than those that are less problematic. This is done in order to present the broad nature and complexity of the problems experienced by some of the men and not to suggest the prevalence of such problems. Most of the men were born to parents who were married (92%), and nearly two-thirds spent most of their childhood in families that remained intact.

Conventional, unproblematic, and happy family
His father was a post office worker. He had one brother and remembers a happy childhood. He liked school, and represented it in football and tennis. He left school at 14, at which time his parents separated and his father entered the Army. When he was 20, his mother remarried (*825cf1.2.2). [sex]

Mixed relationships with mother, father, and sister
There was always food on the table, we got what we needed, but there was never anything to spare. *How about your relationship with the people in your family, how did you get on with your mother?* She's dead now. We were very close when she was alive. *But [as you said] she was fed up with you for being arrested [as a child].* But I can understand that, it didn't mean we weren't close, even then. She was disabled. She just couldn't look after me. I kept getting in trouble all the time. *And how about your father, how did you get on with him?* Now, I get on great with him, but there was always a lot of conflict when I was young. *Your sister? Very close? Who would you say was the most important person to you in your childhood?* My sister. We were very close (*979cf1.2.2). [theft]

However, where problems did exist, they were often complex in nature and sometimes affected several members of the family including fathers, mothers, and siblings. For example, when alcohol was a problem, usually but not always for the father, it was often accompanied by violence against his mother.

Violence and deaths within the family
He is the youngest of seven children, born in Malaysia while his father was in the military. Violence was a common occurrence in the home (although mostly directed at other family members). When he was about 11 years old, his father died of a brain hemorrhage following a drunken brawl with his daughter's boyfriend. His mother died while he was in prison on a previous sentence, and his brother committed suicide during the same sentence. He began offending when young. Most of the offenses were for violence and he has a history of sexual violence (*849cf1.4.3). [sex]

Childhood family, alcohol problems of his father and siblings
Did anybody have any problems with alcohol when you were growing up? Yes, my dad and one of my brothers and one of my sisters. I don't think they were diagnosed as alcoholics but I believe that eventually one sister had a drink problem, then the next sister—the younger one down—started drinking more. One of the brothers, the one who was in the Royal Navy, he used to drink a lot. At first it wasn't a problem but as he got older it also ruined his life because he could have been an instructor, a deep sea diver but he used to drink (*304iv1.4.3). [sex]

Problems within the family, many stepfathers, and violence against his mother
He has no knowledge of his biological father who separated from his mother in early childhood. He was brought up by his mother who co-habited with three different step-fathers. He described his mother as a heavy drinker and tells me she received convictions for shoplifting. He tells me he witnessed domestic violence [against his mother] during childhood and had difficulties in his relationships with stepfathers, especially in early adolescence. He recounts assaulting and being assaulted by his various step-fathers. He had numerous truancies (*1014cf1.4.3). [sex]

As children, some of the boys were violent within their family of origin. The violence was usually directed at their parents and siblings and sometimes included destroying the house and property.

His use of aggression and violence in his family of origin
He had a fairly ordinary family home, both parents working, one sibling, but a lot of parental discord (although no evidence of violence). At age 10–12, emotional difficulties began and he became a very disturbed child: truanted, ran away from home, stole from parents, and trashed the family home with friends, some violence by him to his mother, a bully and aggressive at school. An unhappy home; and personality difficulties reinforced each other. He saw lots of family/child therapists and psychiatrists, had few friends, loved animals, and had a poor work record (*658cf1.2.2). [sex]

Violence by Father Against Mother

One of the frequent problems was the use of violence by his father against his mother. This was often chronic and characterized much of family life throughout childhood.

Strict father, alcohol, and intimate partner violence
He came from a hardworking family, was third out of seven siblings. All of his four brothers are employed in good occupations and none have a criminal record. His memories of his early life are hazy but not particularly happy. He recalls difficulty in learning to read and write and in the end it was his father who taught him. His father appears to have been a traditionally strict and punitive parent with the mother taking a softer and more caring approach. He also recalls difficulties in his parent's marriage caused by excessive drinking on the part of his father which resulted in

physical violence being meted out on his mother. This memory has affected his relationship with his father and he does not feel close to him (*1092cf1.4.3). [sex]

Father violent to mother and mother's resilience
Did your father ever hit your mother? Yes. How often? I'm not sure, but it seemed like once a week. He never did it sober. I think it upset her emotionally, a lot. I mean she was probably caught, she was trapped; she was terrified. She was frightened of him? Yes, yes. I mean, like, she'd got all the children, you know, she had very old fashioned ideas as well—once you're married, you know, that's it. I mean that doesn't work today—quite rightly—if it doesn't work, leave. But then it was very "vowful"—"for better or for worse," you know, and she was like that, where really, she should have left him. She should have left him, but I suppose she saw the nice side of him as well. But I don't think she ever forgave him, I don't think she ever forgave men in general. Did you see any of the violence, or much of the violence? Yes. I saw it frequently. How did that affect you? Well, it used to make me feel upset and angry. Normally when it happened there was only the two of us, me and my brother—the one that died—and he was like a year and a half older than me and we would try and wrestle him off. He stabbed him [his father] once with a little potato knife and that stopped him. I mean it didn't cause a serious wound, but it stopped him (*304iv1.4.3). [sex]

Father violent to mother and mother hit back
When you were a kid how did it make you feel when your mother hit your father? Was it always he was hitting her and she hit him back or what? [His father was regularly violent to his mother]. It was never a case that she'd just start laying into him or anything. It was just fighting. And was this usually when he was hitting her? Yes. She'd never pre-empt [initiate] it. (*979iv1.2.2). [theft]

School

As boys, most had problems at school (71%), and nearly half (46%) were disruptive at school and many were frequent truants. A few spent time in a Special School (13%) for learning difficulties, and 8% spent some time in residence in an institution for disruptive children.

Happy at school and relatively conventional childhood
Defendant was born in a small town and was the younger of two children. He attended school regularly, had a happy childhood with no family history of mental illness, criminality or alcoholism. He enjoyed school though [school reports suggest] he was not the keenest of scholars but he managed well academically and mixed well socially but truanted to some extent towards the end of his schooling. He eventually left at the age of 15 without qualifications (*926cf1.2.2). [theft]

School—poor performance and rarely attended
How did you get on with your school work? Not too good, I wasn't the brightest of pupils. It wasn't until I left school that I actually learnt to read properly. So were you playing truant a lot before you went to Borstal, or not very much? There were

sometimes when I didn't go at all. I used to go in the morning, get my mark [for attendance], and come out. And go back in the afternoon period, get my mark again, and then come out again (*1032iv1.4.3). [sex]

Problems of the Child, Alcohol, Drugs, and Early Offending

Before the age of 13, 20% had at least one conviction, and thus could be categorized as early-onset offenders. By the age of 16, about one-fifth (21%) had five or more convictions, with 23% having committed a serious violent offense and a few (6%) having committed a sexual offense. In addition, sex/murderers were significantly more likely than theft/murderers to have committed offenses involving serious physical violence (37% vs. 6%) and sexual assault (19% vs. 00%), and were much more likely to abuse alcohol (63% vs. 27%) and/or drugs (20% vs. 6%). By age 16, a quarter (26%) of all the men who murdered older women had been incarcerated in a criminal justice institution for juveniles, but this was significantly more likely for sex/murderers than theft/murderers (32% vs. 6%). Overall, the evidence in Figure 10.1 at the end of the chapter in Appendix V, Table 10.1, indicate that many of the men were identified as having problems with alcohol abuse when they were children (45%), and some also had problems with drug abuse (14%). Only one of the men was reported to have been violent to animals. Substance abuse and theft were often linked, as shown below.

Alcohol problems of the child and the parents
My dad was a heavy drinker. My mum was an alcoholic up until I was 21. *So both your father and your mother were heavy drinkers?* Yes. *And you, when did you start?* I started drinking when I was 14. *Was it a problem then or not a problem?* It was a problem because I was stealing to finance the drinking. *So the alcohol wasn't so much the problem at that point, it was the stealing or was the alcohol also the problem?* I liked my alcohol, it gave me courage. It made me "Jack-the-Lad." *Even at the age of 14, drink was a problem?* Yes. That's why I was stealing, to get money to go out to buy my drink (*1032iv1.4.3). [sex]

Drug abuse as a child
In the end, you were addicted to heroin, but what age did you start taking drugs and what drugs were you taking? I was 13. I started off on solvents, smoked a bit of cannabis, then progressed. *What age were you when you moved on to heroin, heavier drugs?* I suppose I was about 15. That's when I first came across it. I wasn't a regular user then. *Regular use, when was that?* About 17. *On a daily basis?* Yes. *How many times a day?* Depending on how much I could get, just as often as possible. *Was heroin your drug of choice? Did you take cocaine?* I have done, but it wasn't on a regular basis. I smoked crack, but I wouldn't say that was a regular thing. *Did you take anything else on a regular basis?* Yes, ecstasy, weekly. *Any legal drugs, anti-depressants, barbiturates, sleeping pills?* Yes, now and again. Tamazepan, diazepam, magadon, that sort of thing. *Did it matter to you what it was, did you choose certain things that you liked more than others or did you just take anything that was on the go?* No, it wasn't quite like that. Obviously heroin, but if I couldn't get heroin I'd have a bang with anything. I preferred downers [but] whatever I could get (*979iv1.2.2). [theft]

Frequent Offending and Incarceration

As boys, some were prolific offenders and were incarcerated in institutions of young offenders such as Boys Homes and Borstals. The first two cases cited below are a continuation of the cases cited above. They involve boys with alcohol and drug problem who continued to offend over several years during their childhood and adolescence and were eventually incarcerated.

Frequent thefts for alcohol
Up to the age of 16, were you ever in trouble with the police? Yes, always stealing, thefts, burglaries, and then the arson. *So in terms of the thefts and burglaries, were there quite a few of these?* When I was 15, I went to court on 21 charges of burglary, theft. There were still a few more on top of that but I can't remember exactly. (*1032cf1.4.3). [sex]

Frequent thefts for drugs
You say you were in trouble quite a few times before the age of 16? I got to the stage where I'd be getting arrested once every couple of weeks or so. Petty things: stealing, stealing cars, stealing from shops. *Were you drinking then?* No. *Taking drugs?* Yes. I was a heroin addict. (*979iv1.2.2). [theft]

Youth incarceration—Boys Home
He committed a number of offenses as a juvenile "which resulted in him being sent to a Boys Home which he left when he was 15 years old" (*1092cf1.4.3). [sex]

Reform school—for problem behavior—a fighter and early offender
Were you ever bullied at school? No. *Ever get into fights at school?* All the time. *You mentioned earlier you went to reform school, what for?* Breaking-and-entering. *And how old were you when you went there?* I think I was twelve (*206iv1.4.2). [sex]

Even at an early age, some of the boys had already begun to "specialize" in offending against the elderly.

Theft from the elderly
His first conviction (age 13) was for burglary of his local community care centre [for the elderly] plus two attempted burglaries. His next recorded conviction was for burglary involving an elderly woman in her house (*1014cf1.4.3). [sex]

Physical and/or Sexual Abuse of the Child and Sexual Offending by the Child

As children, one-fifth had been physically abused (20.0%) and just over one-tenth had been sexually abused (11%) (Figure 10.1; Appx.V-Table 10.1). Importantly, sex/murderers were significantly more likely than theft/murderers to have been sexually abused (19% vs. 00%). Across the entire group, those who were physically abused in childhood, most were victimized by their birth- or stepfather, and only one was victimized by their birth mother. Most of the men who were sexually abused were the victims of their father and/or stepfather. As children, very few (7%) were identified as having problematic sexual behavior, with even fewer (6%) having committed a sexual offense, usually against another child.

Physical and sexual abuse at boarding school

And would you say you were quite happy at school? No. *No, why is that?* I got bullied an awful lot and being separated from my family, being in a place I didn't know was difficult [boarding school]. *Was it?* Very, there was a lot of sexual abuse. There was a lot of beating and I'm not talking about from the boys. The brothers, they're like priests but they're not. *I hope you don't mind me asking but were you sexually abused as a boy?* Yeah, by the brothers. *How long did that go on for?* Three years. *What kind of affect do you think it had on you?* I've never told my family or anything like that. Nobody knew anything until I told this member of [prison] staff and you [interviewer]. I'm trying to be very, very honest with you. *I know, and I appreciate that and I really think that it's difficult?* It's more difficult than you imagine. *Yeah, I'm sure it is. Do you mind if I ask another couple of questions about it?* No, go on. *Okay, was it happening to other boys?* Uhuh. There was one Brother [names him] that started it off as part of the punishment. He'd make you pull your pajama bottoms down and he'd make you bend over and put your palms down to the bottom of the bath then he would nip you while more or less admiring your backside. *And did it go on from there? I mean was there actual penetration?* No, there was not really any penetration. It was always just you fondled him or he fondled you or he gave you a kiss. That's as far as I know that it ever went, I don't know about some of the other one's but that's all that ever happened with me. *Did you ever talk about it amongst yourselves?* No, no. Nobody ever said anything. Not that I was ever aware of, no. *Yeah, what kind of atmosphere was there then?* Tense, it was not a happy school, not the way I'd always pictured a boarding school, like on television (*294iv1.2.2). [theft]

Sexual abuse and sexual offenses

Psychiatric reports refer to a childhood of poverty and physical and sexual abuse within the family. He self reports leaving school at 15, low attainment, with violence inside and outside the home as a way of life followed by the use of LSD and amphetamines. He states he was sexually abused by his older brother at age six. At age 10, he was discovered attempting intercourse with his niece. During his teen years, he reports masturbatory fantasies centered on buggering young boys but also fantasies about females which included aggressive sex (*1041cf1.4.3). [sex]

LIFECOURSE—ADULTHOOD

Adult Circumstances and Employment

Men who murdered older women were generally undereducated, with 67% leaving school before age 16 and only 25% obtaining any qualifications. Additionally, leaving school with no qualifications was significantly more likely among sex/murderers (91%) than theft/murderers (56%). Across both types, only 26% were usually employed, the majority had problems with alcohol (62%), and a minority abused drugs (24%) (Figure 10.2; Appx.V-Table 10.2). The following examples illustrate the various work patterns of the men that ranged from fairly steady employment to more sporadic patterns that may have included substantial periods of unemployment.

Vocational training and good worker
He was employed as an apprentice fitter in a local steel mill, and eventually obtained an Ordinary National Certificate in Engineering [applied]. He worked steadily in the steel industry from this point onwards, and was mostly described as a good worker although he did lose some time through illness and was dismissed from one job for excessive lunchtime drinking. Then he worked as a bar steward. Once again, he was described as a good worker, timekeeper and attendee (*926cf1.2.2). [theft]

Employed and unemployed
He worked steadily as a kitchen porter for the first 8–10 years of his employed life and then he was infrequently employed. At the time of the offense he was unemployed (*1092cf1.4.3). [sex]

Poor worker
And the reasons for changing these jobs? Well I was sacked on all of them really. And why was that? Various reasons. Stealing [on the job]. Not turning up for work (*979iv 1.2.2). [theft]

Youth employment scheme, employed, and unemployed
He left school at age 16, was unemployed and then on a Youth Employment Scheme as a motorcycle mechanic. He was unemployed for six months until he went to work on a training course with the Prince Charles Trust. During his time with the Trust, he had two placements in Old People's Homes in two different cities. However, he failed to complete the 43 week training course. He then worked as a security guard but left work and has remained unemployed ever since [about 3 years]. He has three previous offenses [burglary and criminal damage] but no violent offenses and was never in prison (*897Cf1.2.6). [theft]

Alcohol and Drugs

As adults, the majority had serious problems with alcohol that often began in childhood. For many, alcohol became the center of their daily life. Fewer had problems with drugs, and some had problems with both.

Alcohol to excess
He has had numerous charges associated with alcohol, and at the time of the murder his drinking was completely out of control. He was consuming vast amounts of spirits, was sometimes amnesic after a night's drinking, irrational and bad tempered when in drink, and pre-occupied with the control and supply of alcohol. He tended to drink in a solitary way, avoiding social contact. His GP [doctor] was concerned about his use of alcohol and depression. He was totally apathetic

during the police interview and was adamant that he did not cause the injuries that resulted in the victim's death. On the face of it, his behavior is that of a man totally disinhibited by the effects of alcohol, short of cash and looking for an opportunistic target (*859cf1.2.2). [theft]

Numerous jobs lost because of alcohol

What kinds of jobs did you do? Just manual labouring jobs. *Did you do various ones?* I worked on building sites. I was on the railway. I worked in pubs and clubs, evenings and afternoons. If I didn't have a day job, I'd work in the afternoons. *What was your main job?* Working in pubs and clubs. *And when you left these other jobs, what was the reason for that?* Alcohol. *And did you usually work, or did you have periods when you weren't working, when you were unemployed?* I usually worked (*1032iv1.4.3). [sex]

Problems with alcohol and gambling

He admitted to being a heavy drinker, and at one stage was drinking 12–14 pints of beer a day with added spirits. However he tells me his level of alcohol consumption had decreased at the time of the offense. He was drinking large amounts of alcohol only on the day he received his Social Security [welfare] money. He also admitted that whatever money was left after a day of drinking he would gamble on the horses and one armed bandits [slot machines] (*926cf1.2.2). [theft]

Alcohol and drugs to excess

I think we've talked enough about alcohol and drugs but just to check, were you drinking every day? Yes. *How much?* Not every day, it was more towards the weekends. *How much would you say, at the weekends, you were drinking per day?* Friday night, drunk till you dropped really, until the pub closed and you couldn't get any more. And then it started again Saturday afternoon and Saturday night. At the time it was the 11 till 3 pm closing time, and 6 till 11 pm closing time. *And were you doing drugs at the same time?* Yes. Smoking cannabis, mushrooms, amphetamines and things. *But latterly was it more the drink, before you came in here, or was it a combination? Were you doing amphetamines and. . .?* The amphetamines tapered off more in favor of mushrooms because they were free. You could just go and pick them. *When you did the crime, you talked about you had a lot of drink, do you think it was also a drug thing going on at the time?* No. Initially, I did use the drugs as an excuse—I was out of my head, I didn't know what I was doing because I didn't have sufficient emotional or intelligent maturity to see what I was doing or why I was doing it. Impulsivity—just acting on the spur of the moment (*975iv1.4.3). [sex]

Mental Health

About one-third of the men (35%) had mental health problems that involved contact with psychologists and/or psychiatrists (Figure 10.2; Appx.V-Table 10.2). Although not shown in the figures, 20% of all of the men who murdered older women had been "sectioned," that is, involuntarily committed to a mental institution. It is possible to be sectioned for mental illness, criminal behavior, and/or extreme episodes associated with alcohol or drug abuse.[1] Overall, 51% had sexual problems of various types with a greater likelihood among sex/murderers than theft/murderers (76% vs. 22%).

Orientations to and Relationships with Women

The casefiles and interviews contained many comments about women and relationships with them. Some had fairly good relationships with women in general and with women partners. However, many of the men believed that women were disreputable and exploited men. Primarily, they saw them as objects of sexual conquest. These views were usually expressed without reflection on their own character or behavior. As shown in Figure 10.3 and in Appendix V, Table 10.3, 62% of the men had problems in their relationships with women.

Feelings of inadequacy and anger about relationships with women
You've said yourself that you are a sex offender and you've talked a lot about the different things that you've been involved in, all involving young women and girls, and I just wanted to ask you what that was about? I suppose if I'm honest with myself it was inadequacy, could I pull [attract women]? Was I still acceptable? Was I still on a par that was acceptable to that sector? Do you know what I mean? *I'm not sure.* It was my feelings of not being good enough, and then the rejection making me angry. Does that answer it? *Maybe. I suppose the other thing that I have picked up is that you seem to speak disparagingly about women, about your wife, your girlfriends.* I don't mean to put them down as such. I'm reflecting, this is about me, how the issue has affected me. Don't get me wrong. I knew my wife from when I was six years old and I hit her head with a fucking brick. She went beyond my needs. This is her words not mine. I obviously loved the woman. I wouldn't have been with her for so long. I wouldn't come back out of jail each time and go back to her. But, I suppose I relied on her because she took the dominant role. *So you were quite dependent on her in some ways?* Yes. Do you understand what I mean? That's the inadequacy, I always was like that. I don't know, because I felt the inadequacy and that's what I reflect on, my inadequacy in all the relationships (*206iv1.4.2). [sex] [NB: In interview, he spoke extensively and graphically, even pornographically, about the "despicable" sexual behavior of women and, at the same time, boasted about his own sexual conquests.]

Bad experiences with women partners
Then I get the other one. I met her five months after [the breakup with another girlfriend], dried me out of money completely, and I was going to lose my house. *Yeah?* So that's when I took to kill myself—I couldn't take much more of it. The last six months, my bank account was going dry. She was using me just like this other one did. She said she was going to have a child. We moved but it didn't happen [the child]. *Yeah?* She left me; she went away for a weekend, came back and gave me an hour's notice, change of mind, moving back with my husband. And I have just sold my house to move because of her. I had to cancel it because she gave me an hour's notice. So I had, like, one day's notice before Christmas, then an hour's notice (*1000iv1.4.2). [sex]

Women as sexual conquests

Was there violence in any of your relationships? No, none whatsoever. I didn't force myself on any [other women], and the strange thing is why did I need to rape this woman [age 79]. Why did I need to force myself on her sexually because I never had any trouble with any girls and relationships? My mum's phone would be ringing off the hook, is [he] in, where is he, can I contact him? I was very promiscuous. There were three or four relationships at the same time [he names four women], and they all didn't know about each other, oh God! (*975iv1.4.3). [sex]

Previous Physical and/or Sexual Violence Against Women

Of the 40 men who murdered an older woman, 39% had a history of violence in general, which included violence against other men, and 29% of the men had committed some form of sexual violence outside of an intimate relationship. It should be noted that these assaults did not necessarily result in arrests or convictions (Figure 10.2; Appx.V-Table 10.2). In addition to the figures shown, various comparisons were made between the men who murdered an older woman in the context of a theft and those who murdered in the context of a sexual attack. Previous incidents of physical violence against others, outside of intimate relationships, was more likely among those who committed a Sex/Murder (47%) than those who committed a Theft/Murder (29%). Previous incidents of sexual violence were also more likely among those who committed a Sex/Murder (44%) than those who committed a Theft/Murder (13%).

Numerous sexual offenses and prison but no recognition of responsibility or need to change

[His comments in interview]: *You've been in and out of prison for most of your life, what for?* This last twenty years have all been sex offenses. *They've all been sex offenses? No burglaries, thefts or whatever?* No. Indecent assault on my daughter, that was the first sex offense [15 years ago], then with my wife, on a rape conviction. Come out after that, then a four year sentence—two years and eight months I done. After being out for nearly eleven weeks or something [I was] done for attempted rape on my daughter's friend. Then, the next one was indecent assault, and then she [his intimate partner] put me in the frame for [sexual assault of] the grand daughter and herself, and that all came to nothing. But, I mean, for the first sex conviction I got four years for rape. Three years later, I got seven years for attempted rape, then when I came out I got three years for indecent assault. And until I get proper help with it, I'll always be angry about it. I see guys here who's done more horrific crimes than me (*206iv1.4.2). [sex]

[Information from his Casefile]: His criminal history charts an ominous graduation over 35 years from petty offending through violence against the person to an escalating series of violent sexual offenses which began 15 years ago and culminated most recently in the murder of an 85 year old woman whom he also sexually assaulted. It is clear that there is a sadistic element to his assaults. He has a tendency to minimize his offences. He claims that hard drug use contributes to some of his offenses, and it may be pertinent to note that he is currently displaying strong resistance to the drug testing initiative [despite having spent some time in a therapeutic institution for serious offenders] (*206cf1.4.2). [sex]

Lifelong history of sexual offending against women and girls
At age 26, he was convicted of gross indecency and sodomy, and received a Hospital Order under the Mental Health Act. At age 36, he was sentenced to one year in prison for Indecent Assault on a 12 year old girl. She was pulled to the ground, he put his hand over her mouth then put his hand inside her trousers and his finger in her vagina. A passer-by raised the alarm. At age 44, he received an eight year sentence for Indecent Assault on a 79 year old woman. He was the care-taker of the accommodation where she lived. She sustained vaginal injury and bruising to the legs and face. He did not participate in the SOTP program dur-ing this sentence. Despite a lengthy history of extremely serious sexual and vio-lent offences against boys, girls and elderly women [NB: all vulnerable groups] such behavior has not been challenged in a structured setting. This is of primary importance in setting future targets (*1041cf1.4.3). [sex]

Lifelong history of sexual offending against older women
All the premises attacked by the perpetrator were old people's homes with female occupants [for which he had previous convictions]. The attacks carried out by the defendant were sexually motivated and are consistent with the previous attacks he has made on elderly women for which he has received substantial prison sen-tences. He had been sentenced to life ten years earlier for an attack on a 72 year old woman but the sentence was reduced to eight years on appeal. After being released, he was sentenced to 10 years for burglary, wounding and rape. The mur-der and rape [index offense] were committed in the same bungalow where he had committed a sexual attack against another elderly woman (*1092cf1.4.3). [sex]

Physical and Sexual Violence to Intimate Partners

Of the men who murdered an older woman, 35% had never had an intimate relation-ship. Of those who had ever been in an intimate relationships, most (71%) had experi-enced a separation, divorce, or break-up of some type. Within their previous intimate relationships, some were known to have been physically violent (39%) or sexually violent (4%), although such violence was rarely reported (Figures 10.2 and 10.3; Appx.V-Tables 10.2 and 10.3). Of all 40 men, 62% were defined by profession-als as "having problems with women," and this was even more likely among those who committed a Sex/Murder than those who committed a Theft/Murder (81% vs. 39%).

Violence to intimate partner and blaming her
for his murder of an older woman
The women in his life, mother and his co-habitants, report that he had physi-cally assaulted them quite severely. After leaving prison, he received a probation order for setting his partner's flat on fire. A few months later, he was rearrested for assaulting his wife after she had told him of infidelities she had committed

with different partners during his previous custody [his account of her behavior]. [Probation Report] On several occasions he has blamed her [his partner] behavior for "pushing him" into hitting her. For example, he described her as "dirty, untidy, unhygienic, lazy, adulterous and unable to care for their child adequately." On a recent visit after sentencing he expressed bitterness towards his partner for causing his homelessness [forced him out because of his violence] and voiced a perceived link between that predicament and his need to burgle the house where he committed the murder (*1014cf1.4.3) [sex]

Previous Convictions

Across the whole group, 84% of the 40 men who murdered an older woman had a history of persistent criminal behavior, 90% had at least one previous conviction, 63% had five or more previous convictions, and 63% had previously been in prison. Convictions for physical violence included minor assault (33%) and serious physical assault (8%). In addition, 18% had committed at least one serious sexual assault including rape. Of those with a previous conviction for assault, 60% of the men had usually assaulted a woman (Figure 10.2; Appx.V-Table 10.2). Significantly, one-third of the sex/murderers had one or more convictions for serious sexual assault and/or rape while only one man among the theft/murderers had such a conviction (33% vs. 5%). In addition, sex/murderers were more likely than theft/murderers to have served at least one prison sentence (76% vs. 47%). Most of the following accounts of previous convictions focus on sexual offending.

Lifelong offender—numerous convictions including sexual assaults on girls and women

His first offense was at the age of fifteen for which he was cautioned. After serving time in a Borstal and being released, he was found guilty at the Crown Court [superior court] of rape, with one offense of indecent assault taken into account, and received a sentence of four and one-half years imprisonment. Upon release, he appeared again before the Crown Court, and was convicted of rape, robbery with violence and indecent assault for which he received concurrent sentences of eight years, seven years and two years respectively. At the age 21, he was convicted of another rape and served three years. The circumstances of this last offense were that late at night he attacked a 71 year old woman as she was walking home down a quiet street. He dragged her into a back alley, pushed her to the ground and pulled her scarf tightly round her face so that she had difficulty breathing. He then removed her shoes, ripped off her under clothes, indecently assaulted her and raped her twice. Having done so, he took out her false teeth and put his penis in her mouth before ripping a necklace from her neck and running off with her handbag. He served six years for robbery, indecent assault and rape, and was released despite police advice to the contrary (*986cf1.2.6). [theft]

Numerous convictions for sexual and physical violence against women

[Previous offense was for rape] He and his brother raped a woman on the way home from the pub. He admits regarding women in a very low light, seeing them as providing him with sexual gratification and very little else. He has more recently refined this view to incorporate feelings of anger created when his first serious relationship ended, interpreting the rape as being related to the anger and distress over this failed relationship. After release from one of his prison terms, he began to experience anxiety attacks and used drink to give him courage. [Ten years ago], he stole a pensioner's handbag and pushed her to the ground. He had been drinking prior to the offence and admits that this was designed to give him the courage to commit an offence [sentenced to three years]. Whilst on home leave from prison, he was convicted of assaults when he entered a house armed with a knife and during an altercation injured a woman and her seven year old daughter [9 year sentence subsequently reduced to 3 years]. Within days of release from a sentence [for sexual assault], he was arrested for rape but was acquitted after several months on remand. For the next year, he avoided offending, but with domestic problems with his new partner his drinking increased and the relationship came to an end. He met another woman and after a bout of drinking, and following her comments which he felt implied she "used men," he struck her with a claw hammer causing a fractured skull, fractured arm, broken nose, and severe lacerations requiring 45 stitches (*849cf1.4.3). [sex]

Many convictions for sexual and physical violence and judged a lethal danger to women

[Judge] His numerous previous convictions for grave sexual offences involving women of various ages were characterized by strangling and/or choking the victims into submission. I have no doubt that the offense was sexually motivated. The gravity of his offending has escalated over the past ten years and I regard him as a lethal danger to any female who becomes acquainted with him, and in my judgment this will remain the position for many years to come (*882cf1.4.2). [sex]

GUILTY AND IN PRISON—TWO CHALLENGES

Adjustment to the Prison Regime and Behavior to Women Staff

Upon being convicted for murder, all of the men received sentences with tariffs ranging from 12 to 25 years. The average tariff was 15 years. It is notable that about one-third of the sex/murderers and none of the theft/murderers received a tariff of over 18 years. Once in prison, the men face the dual challenges of adapting to the prison regime and addressing their offending behavior. Both challenges were particularly difficult for the men who murdered an older woman whether the murder occurred in the context of a theft or of a sexual attack.

In prison, only one man was defined as a "model prisoner," 75% had at least one discipline report, and 45% had 10 or more. Just over one-third (36%) were defined as having mental health problems (Figure 10.3; Appx.V-Table 10.3). Many of the men (48%) refused to cooperate with prison professionals, and a few had particular problems with respect to women staff.

Sexual advances to female staff in prison and a continued risk

In view of his recent worrying infatuation with a nurse and his inappropriate sexual advances to her and other female members of staff he must still be regarded as a risk to the public and release or transfer to open conditions is out of the question (*986cf1.2.6). [theft]

Addressing Offending Behavior—From Denial to Responsibility

As with the other types of murder, denial is common, beginning at the outset of the legal process and sometimes continuing after conviction and imprisonment. Denial may be complete or partial, and may continue for years. Complete denial may be because of the inability to face the enormity of the murder, shame about its content, or a solid belief that he was falsely convicted. Complete denial may be followed by varying levels of minimization, including notions such as "it was not really very violent," or "it did not involve a sexual element," or "something else was to blame" or "someone else was to blame." Even after several years in prison, 18% of the men continued to deny the murder.

Continued denial—a continued risk to women and to himself
[Probation Report] He denies involvement in the murder, his alibi is that he was in the center of the city at the time and that it is a case of mistaken identity—he claims his brother did it (*728cf1.4.2). [sex]

Total denial, no remorse, no empathy
The perpetrator is in total denial, expresses no remorse and lacks empathy. He remains a high risk because of this murder and his criminal life style. He had a previous conviction at the age of 15 for an indecent assault on a 12 year old girl which he claims is irrelevant to the present offense (*915.1cf1.7.6). [theft]

Persistent denial after decades in prison
No mental illnesses but I still feel that he represents a significant risk, particularly in view of his inability and unwillingness to look at the level of his offending [Ten Year Review]. It was unanimously agreed that he could not be recommended for release. He showed no signs of being constructive or positive about his future and it was felt that there was a good deal of underlying aggression and he was considered still too dangerous for release [Eight years later]. No ongoing offense work has been undertaken whilst in prison due in the main to his continued denial. In raising the matter of the offense, I was somewhat taken aback when he informed me that he was in fact innocent. He maintains that there was no proof of his guilt and that he was coerced into signing statements and "fitted up by the police." But he had now decided, at the age of 52, that he did not want to get out of prison (*986cf1.2.6). [theft]

No Remorse for the Murder and No Empathy with the Victim

A minority expressed remorse for the murder and sympathy for the victim, but the majority did not, with 51% expressing no remorse and 71% having no empathy. Accordingly, 70% were defined as a risk to public safety, and 67% were deemed to raise concerns about "dangerousness" (Figure 10.3; Appx.V-Table 10.3). In addition to the figures shown and as stated earlier, sex/murderers were significantly more likely than theft/murderers to be defined as having problems with women (81% vs. 39%), to have no empathy with the victim (85% vs. 56%), to be defined as dangerous (86% vs. 44%), and to be a risk to public safety (91% vs. 47%). The process of change may begin with total denial and a lack of remorse and empathy but, with time, one or more of these sentiments may be altered for a variety of reasons that may or may not be directed toward positive changes in sentiment. The following accounts illustrate this progression.

Continued denial of responsibility, placing blame elsewhere, and limited remorse

In my view, he has little genuine insight into his overall behavioral problems. He still tends to put most of the responsibility for his offending upon his drug and alcohol abuse, his traumatic upbringing and the perceived short comings of his [intimate] partner rather than fully accepting his personal culpability in the decision to indecently assault and murder the victim. He expresses some remorse but I think his feelings reflect his understanding of society's attitude towards his behavior rather than genuine, insightful empathy for the victim. Additionally, at the time of this report, he was still claiming his wife [she was not the murder victim] was a compulsive liar and that he did not have violent sex with her (*1014cf1.4.3). [sex]

No remorse for murder, no empathy for the victim, dehumanizing description of the victim, man of limited intellect

[Review board, several years after sentencing] He said he was not angry when he assaulted the victim, and that his only motivation was to get away. When pressed about his feelings towards the victim he became quiet and responded reluctantly. His description of the victim (a frail 86 year old woman) is dehumanizing and to some extent degrading. He talks about the victim as "her" or "she" and in other reports I note that he referred to her as "something." When asked specifically about how the victim was attacked and what he felt as he struck the blows he did not respond. I also asked him about the victim's state of partial undress. He became very agitated at this point and insisted that he did not undress her. I pointed out to him that he stated he could remember almost nothing of what occurred, and yet he was sure that he had not removed her clothing. I told him I found this inconsistent. He reiterated that he had not removed her clothing. In summary, I believe that his attitude toward the victim is very underdeveloped. He seems to regard her in a very impersonal way. His expressions of remorse are shallow and centre on feelings of disgust towards himself. He feels very little apparent sympathy for the victim or the victim's family. Of note is the fact that when I asked him if he might murder again once released he replied after a lengthy pause, "Yes, I think I would." He could not expand on why he said this (*897cf.1.2.6). [theft]

From lack of remorse to some change after 10 years but continued concerns about risk

He initially refused to talk about his offense, but he seems to be talking about it now, and that is where I have to express my concern with this man. He does like talking about the offense, in fact, he relished it. He expressed remorse and shame, but I do suspect that this is paying lip service to the system. I don't think he is genuinely remorseful at all. Ten years after his sentence he finally goes onto the SOTP program. The feedback from the tutors on the SOTP has been extremely positive, and I believe he has also completed Alcohol Awareness, Anger Management, Social Skills, and the core Sex Offender Programs. Although reports indicate excellent progress, last year a woman psychologist reported that he will talk about his offense but "severely minimizes the amount of violence used." He also has a tendency to blame a concoction of prescribed drugs and alcohol for his offending behavior (*1092cf1.4.3). [sex]

Over time, some of the men begin to develop a fuller understanding of the murder and their own responsibility for it. With this growing recognition about themselves and their behavior may also come a growing sense of the person they killed as well as that of others.

Empathy, self-awareness, and shame developed over time

Was she [the victim] older as well? Yes, she was 70-bloody-9, 79, which made it even more despicable for me. I'm able to talk about it now, but I've had years and years of soul searching and shame and guilt. There were times when I just wouldn't, I wouldn't have come on this interview with you because I couldn't face my own shame. And it still hurts now, I still feel shameful, but it's past. That's how I look at it. I can't undo the past, I can only try and make sense of it. I think it [anger and rage] had just built up as a consequence of failed relationships. [It meant] me continually blaming them and not looking at my own actions, my own behavior. I mean, one of the things she [former girlfriend] said to me that [was important] was when I said, "why did you go with him" [her new partner]? And she said, "for the first time in years, I've been able to laugh." I was stunned because I was such a self-centered, egotistical little shit that I couldn't see myself. *And you think she was fair in what she said or was it just. . .?* Oh I couldn't accept anybody's point of view. I didn't consider anyone else's feelings other than my own. I was self-centered, selfish, and arrogant. If you didn't like it, "bollocks, fuck off." Really, I was very rude and arrogant (*975iv1.4.3). [sex]

REFORM IN PRISON—PROGRAMS, RESISTANCE, AND CHANGE

As stated previously, those convicted of murder cannot be considered for release until they have successfully addressed both the offense and behaviors associated with it. This involves prison programs that deal with life skills, thinking skills, problems associated with alcohol and drugs, and those associated with sexual offending. The SOTP, Sexual Offender Treatment Program, is required for all those convicted of a murder that contained a sexual element, which applies to about half of the men who murdered an older woman. Generally, there is strong resistance to participating in the SOTP program, because it means that the man is identified as a sexual offender, which has implications for where the sentence is served, including the particular prison and specific wings within prisons (i.e., segregated and under protection). Participation in the program requires not only that the man deal with the murder but also with sexual elements of the murder. In these cases, this means addressing the fact that he sexually attacked an older woman. For some, resistance is absolute.

Unwilling to deal with the offending behavior and a continued risk

[Probation Report] He poses the highest degree of risk of physical and sexual harm to women and children, and is himself at some risk from self harm by suicidal action and assault from other inmates. His family and personal history suggests he may not survive this sentence. Even at this very early stage, it can sadly be predicted that without a substantial change in openness about his offenses and recognition of his sexually violent problem the degree of risk is unlikely to diminish other than by reason of his physical deterioration (*1041cf1.4.3). [sex]

Beginning the Process of Change—SOTP

When asked to reflect on the prison programs, including SOTP, some reflected on specific issues relating to programs in general—their content, duration, confidentiality, and additional support following group work—and their effectiveness in changing attitudes and behaviors. Below, we cite two men at length.

Pornography and changing attitudes to women and sex

What about the work that you've done on the SOTP? Was that constructive? I'll do everything I can to change while I'm in prison. In my last sentence, I served six years [for rape] and I was smoking cannabis every night and had a big collection of girlie magazines. It was childish, immature, because I used to have them categorized: blondes, brunettes, red heads, tall, small, big breasted, small, nice legs, etc. *Was that something that you used a lot of, pornographic magazines?* Yes, but not hard core ones. But that was seeing women as sex objects, you know, I was looking at these pictures of breasts and legs. So I was just seeing women as sex objects which is what they were portraying in the magazines. But I was on the SOTP and it made me realize because of what I've done, especially to [name of his murder victim] as well as the hammer attack [earlier attack on a girlfriend], you know, my feelings of revulsion towards it—someone like me. *So do you think your attitudes towards women have changed?* Oh, yeah, definitely because I've stopped the girlie magazines. *What made you change your attitude?* I would say the thoughts going on the SOTP. Because of the offenses I've committed, I've got to move away from seeing women as sex objects but it's difficult because sex should mean something in a loving relationship. I haven't got that! I haven't had that for five years, and I may never have that again. *And how does that make you feel?* Like a sense of love is avoiding me because to have a sexual fantasy, it's not a loving act, it never can be. You are thinking the thoughts of someone else [the pornographer]. All I've done is cleansed the thoughts I used to have. I've gentled the nature of the sex drive, and that [task] has still got to be ongoing (*304iv1.4.3).

The same man continues:

SOTP and learning to reflect on and understand empathy

There were times when I felt that the psychology was going too far, and now I feel stronger that I've turned the corner [with a successful sentencing review]. It's like during the SOTP, you're trapped in the same thoughts that you had when you were committing the offense. And all the emotions you go through, they're different from what the actual victim feels, and no way to the same intensity, but you feel most of the emotions victims go through in a different way. It's that "feeling of a word" that was a very good insight for me because I could mouth a word very, very easily but when you have the "feeling of it," it's different all together (*304iv1.4.3).

Another man spoke at length about SOTP and other issues related to the nature and delivery of programs in prison.

SOTP—facilitating insight and empathy and other issues about prison programs

What about the SOTP? The SOTP, I don't think it's run long enough. I don't think they go into your childhood enough. I think the group I was on, with the children and that [pedophiles], I think it was run pretty good. *Did you make the decision to do the groups?* Yeah. At first I wasn't too keen about going, and then I just thought, yeah, I'll do it. They went into your childhood a little bit but I don't think they go into it deep enough. *What do you think was the most useful aspect of the program for you?* I think realising what I'd done wrong, how my life was going. I think it made me respect people more and help people more. It made me think how my victim could have felt, how my family felt, all kinds of stuff. *Do you think you'd already started thinking about that stuff or did that bring it up?* That brought it up. *Have these lessons been important for prison? Have any of these ideas helped you in prison?* Yeah. *How so?* I think my attitude as well, like towards officers and other cons. I mean some of the officers have a dig at you now and again to see how you react. I just ignore them now. I don't bite or anything. I mean, I might have done before, before I came to prison. *What are these digs about?* Oh they just wind you up about all kinds of things really. I mean, some of the officers call inmates "nonces" [pedophiles] and stuff, they shouldn't do stuff like that (*1056iv1.4.3). [sex]

Men raised other issues about the programs including the view that the alcohol and other programs were too short and some were introduced too early in the sentence when men were not yet ready to take in the content because they were still adjusting to being in prison. For those who had experienced sexual abuse as children or as adults, there was a fear that revealing this within the groups might be revealed to others within the prison, including prison officers and other inmates, and that this would become a problem for the men when they returned to the landing (prison wing). Finally, the men reflected on prison programs and on their future.

Prison programs, personal change, and the future

In terms of prison programs, what programs have you done? Drug offender treatment program. *Anything else?* Enhanced thinking skills. *Have these been helpful to you at all?* Yes. *In what way?* I'm not as impulsive I don't think. *What sort of things would you like to do when you leave prison?* Try and get back to leading a normal life. *Meaning? What's normal?* Job, place to live, a relationship, do normal things (*979iv.1.2.2). [theft]

COMPARISONS OF MEN WHO MURDER OLDER WOMEN AND MALE-MALE MURDERERS

Men who murder older women are compared with men who murdered other men across the lifecourse including numerous factors in childhood, in adulthood, and in prison. These are shown graphically in the figures at the end of the chapter and numerically in the tables in Appendix V. In childhood (Figure 10.1; Appx.V-Table 10.1), only one factor yields a statistically significant difference between the two groups, with drug abuse before the age of 16 more likely among male-male murderers than men who murder older women (MM = 33% vs. OWoM = 14%). Overall, the childhood experiences of both groups could be characterized as problematic with just under half coming from broken homes, about one-quarter with a father who was an alcoholic, and a similar proportion whose father used violence against their mother and whose family had contact with police and social work. Still fewer lived with three or more carers during childhood and/or were in some form of care, which included foster care families as well as care homes. For both groups, a large proportion experienced problems in school and were disruptive. About half of both groups abused alcohol before the age of 16 and about one-third had five or more convictions before the age of 16. About one-fifth of both groups were physically abused as children, and fewer were sexually abused.

As adults (Figure 10.2; Appx.V-Table 10.2), a majority of the men in both groups were undereducated and chronically unemployed, abused alcohol, and experienced a breakdown in an intimate relationship. The vast majority were characterized by persistent criminal behavior, contact with the police, and convictions. Although at least one prison sentence was common for both groups, this was significantly more likely for those who murdered an older woman (MM = 45% vs. OWoM = 63%). The greatest differences between the two groups included sexual problems or issues (18% vs. 51%) and sexual violence outside a domestic relationship (9% vs. 29%). For those convicted of an assault, a woman was more likely to be the usual victim among those who murdered an older woman (11% vs. 60%), and these men were also more likely to have a previous conviction for a sexual assault (8% vs. 18%).

Life in prison included adapting to the prison regime and addressing offending behavior (Figure 10.3; Appx.V-Table 10.3). Across almost all of the relevant factors, men who murdered older woman were significantly more likely to do less well, to have problems, and to cause problems. Specifically, they were almost never defined as model prisoners, and they were less likely to cooperate with prison professionals across the regime as well as in the treatment programs (MM = 31% vs. OWoM = 48%). Professional judgments included problems with women (18% vs. 62%), lack of remorse (34% vs. 51%), lack of empathy (43% vs. 71%), a risk to the public (45% vs. 70%), and dangerousness (39% vs. 67%). All of these differences were statistically significant. Overall, the comparisons with male-male murderers suggest that men who murder older women are more likely to have problems in relationships with women and to "specialize" in violence against women and less likely to feel remorse for the murder and have empathy for their victim.

SUMMARY

The 40 men who murdered an older woman were initially classified in terms of whether the murder primarily involved a theft (n = 21) or a sexual attack (n = 19) and whether the perpetrator and victim were strangers or acquainted. The murders that involved a theft were more likely to be committed by men who were acquainted with the woman they robbed and killed, while those involving a sexual attack were more likely to be committed by a man who was a stranger to the woman he killed. When all of the 40 men are examined together, both the qualitative and the quantitative findings reveal significant problems across the lifecourse.

As children, they were likely to have numerous problems, including parents or caretakers who were themselves beset by problems that often required the intervention of police, social workers, and others. As children, they were likely to fail at school, to be disruptive, to abuse alcohol before age 16, and to leave school without qualifications. A minority were physically and/or sexually abused. A few began offending very young and had numerous convictions, and a substantial minority spent time in a criminal justice institution. As adults, the majority were usually unemployed, abused alcohol and/or drugs, and were persistent offenders. Their relationships with women were problematic. Some never had an intimate relationship and others had numerous problematic ones that may have included physical violence against their woman partner.

For those who had a previous conviction for assault, the victim was usually a woman. About one-fifth had a previous conviction for a sexual assault, but the qualitative material suggests that many more had previously committed some form of sexual assault that did not result in any form of legal action. This was most likely among those who committed a sexual murder. The lives of the sex/murderers were punctuated by sexual problems and sexual offending, and they killed the oldest and most vulnerable of the older women. Within prison, only one of the 40 men was described as a model prisoner, three-quarters had more than one discipline report, and nearly half had 10 or more. Nearly half of the men were described as uncooperative with professionals, and over one-third had mental health problems. In brief, the lives of the men who murder older women could best be characterized as dysfunctional, chaotic, dissipated by alcohol, and sometimes by drugs.

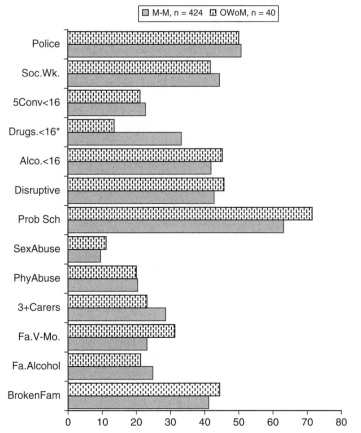

Figure 10.1 OWoM—Childhood: Male-Male Murder and Murder of Older Women.
* Statistically significant difference.

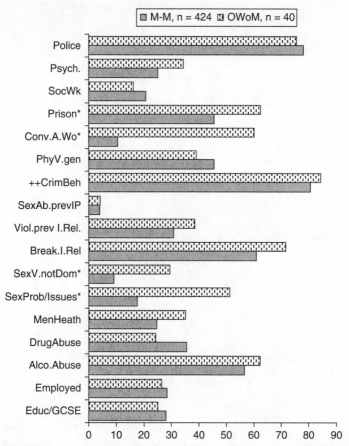

Figure 10.2 OWoM—Adulthood: Male-Male Murder and Murder of Older Women. * statistically significant difference.

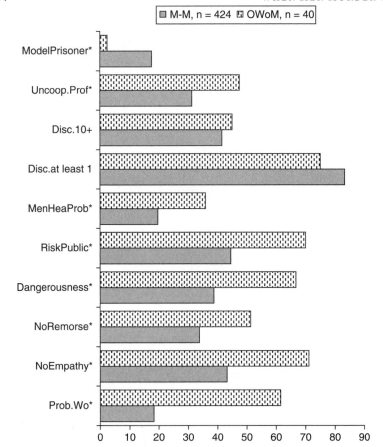

Figure 10.3 OWoM—Assessments in Prison: Male-Male Murder and Murder of Older Women.

* Statistically significant difference.

When Men Murder Women

Comparisons and Conclusions

As stated in chapter 1, the Murder Study was designed to investigate all types of murder committed by and against men, women, and children, and to do so in a way that would expand knowledge about the act of murder, the situations and circumstances in which it occurs, and the men and women who commit this most extreme act of violence. Gathering intensive and extensive evidence about all types of murder not only allows for a fuller understanding of homicide in general but also makes it possible to consider how different types of murder might vary both in terms of the individual characteristics of those who commit murder and in terms of the particular situations and circumstances in which they do so.

Most homicides are committed by men who kill other men, and this is reflected in the information about homicide reported at a national level. As such, statistics about homicide more closely reflect patterns associated with homicides that involve only men and not those that involve women either as victims or as offenders. While this is particularly the case in countries with very high rates of homicide, it also affects national reports in countries with lower rates. Even in these countries, figures about homicide and the general characterizations about it are shaped by murders committed by men against other men. Depending on the country, anywhere from 20% to 40% of all homicides are committed by men against women, and it is essential to disaggregate homicide data by gender if we are to learn more about the murder of women. It is also essential to compare different types of murders if we are to go beyond explanations of homicide that are generally based on murders that involve only men. The contexts and circumstances associated with different types of murder need to be explored. In addition, findings about the murder of women need to be compared with those about the murder of men not only to consider how they may differ but also to learn how they may be alike. Only then is it possible to more fully consider if gender really matters and, if so, to delineate some of the main factors that seem to make a difference.

In order to distinguish what, if anything, might differentiate acts of murder committed by men who kill other men from those in which men murder women, it is not sufficient to simply disaggregate murder based on gender alone. Although the examination of all male-male murders and all male-female murders is an improvement over simply examining all murders together without distinguishing between them in any way, it isn't enough. More needs to be known, and it is important to ask if there are any real or important differences among the murders of women that would be lost if this approach were followed. For us, the answer required still further disaggregation of the murders of women by men in an effort to seek additional knowledge and further understanding of the different contexts in which women are murdered.

Although the Murder Study was designed to explore all types of murder, here we focused only on those perpetrated by men against women and identified three main types: the murder of intimate partners (n = 105), sexual murders (n = 98), and the murder of older women (n = 40). For each type, we have examined the relationships between the male perpetrators and their women victims, the situations and circumstances at the time of the murder, and the lifecourse of the men who commit each type of murder. Detailed findings about each type have been presented in the previous three parts along with comparisons of murders committed by men against other men.

COMPARING FOUR TYPES OF MURDER

Here, we draw all of these comparisons together, consider them as a whole, reflect on the overall characterizations of the different types, and consider their similarities and differences. The four types of murder include the three types of male-female murders and the male-male murders. As in the earlier parts, the comparisons across the four types examine both the murder events and the lifecourse of the perpetrators from childhood to adulthood and in prison. The purpose is not to reiterate the specific findings already presented in each of the three parts but, rather, to provide an overview of some of the main patterns associated with all of the 667 murders examined throughout. These comparisons assist in considering what, if anything, might distinguish murders in which the victims are women rather than men. We briefly revisit each of the three types of murder of women in order to emphasize the important and/or unique aspects of each before returning to the four-way comparisons of the behavior of men in prison and their responses to the efforts to assist them in addressing their offending behavior. Finally, we discuss existing efforts within the community to identify and respond to men who use physical and/or sexual violence against women. These include various forms of risk assessment and intervention programs for sex offenders and intimate partner abusers.

The four-way comparisons presented in figures at the end of the chapter include the nature of relationships between perpetrators and victims (Figure 11.1), the circumstances at the time of the murder (Figure 11.2), childhood (Figure 11.3), adulthood (Figure 11.4), and behavior and professional assessments in prison (Figures 11.5). Although it can be a bit mesmerizing to consider all four comparisons together, it is important to ask how each type compares in order to extend knowledge beyond the separate two-way comparisons made in the earlier parts about each of the three types of murder of women. At this point, it is only possible to provide an overview of some of the general characterizations across the four types of murder, before considering final observations about each type. The discussions of each type will be reversed, beginning with the murder of older women, followed by sexual murders, and ending with the murder of intimate partners. The four-way comparisons begin with the lifecourse.

The Lifecourse of the Perpetrators: Comparisons of Four Types of Murder

In the main, the vast majority of men in all four groups had similar life experiences, characterized by serious antisocial and criminal behavior and, for many, the use of violence (Figure 11.3). Whether they murdered a woman or another man, many grew up in families that experienced considerable assistance/intervention from social services and/or criminal justice. A considerable minority grew up with a father who abused alcohol, was convicted of criminal offenses, and used violence against his mother. Around the same proportions were physically abused, and a few were sexually abused. Many had serious problems at school and were disruptive, and the qualitative material suggests this was more extensive and intense for men who committed sexual murder, including those who committed a sexual murder of an older woman. Alcohol abuse in childhood/adolescence was quite common in the backgrounds of men who murdered other men, sex/murderers, and the murderers of older women. Although not shown in the figures, around two-fifths of all four groups were early-onset offenders, having been "convicted" of a crime before the age of 13, and about one-quarter was incarcerated before the age of 16. This profile aptly fits the experiences of men who murder other men, sex/murderers, and the murderers of older women. Yet, as Figure 11.3 and the relevant tables in the appendices show, this summary of childhood experiences does not generally describe the group of men who murdered intimate partners. Around one-quarter of these men did not experience adversity in childhood. They grew up in relatively conventional families and had no prior convictions before committing the murder.

As shown in Figure 11.4, there are many similarities in the adult lives of the men across the four types of murder. The majority left school early and failed to achieve educational qualifications, and chronic or sporadic unemployment was the norm in all types. Alcohol abuse was common to all, but least likely among the group of men who murdered an intimate partner. A breakup of at least one intimate relationship was very common to all. The men in all four types, with the exception of a minority of the intimate partner murderers (IPMurderers), were very likely to have been known to the police and to have engaged in persistent criminal behavior. Many had served at least one prison sentence, though this was more likely for the men who murdered older women and, again, less likely for IPMurderers. Sex/murderers and men who sexually murdered an older woman were much more likely than the men in the other groups to be judged to have a sexual problem and to have committed a sexual assault outside of an intimate relationship. Although not shown, they were also more likely to have been convicted of a serious sexual assault. In contrast to the others, men who murdered an intimate partner were more likely to have been violent in a previous relationship. A small proportion of IPMurderers and sex/murderers had committed sexual violence against an intimate partner. Considering all four types, of those with a conviction for assault, men who murdered women were much more likely than men who murdered other men to have been convicted of assaulting a woman.

The evidence presented throughout this book consistently shows that the backgrounds of the men who murder women are in many respects similar to those of men who murder other men. However, there are important differences, and this is especially the case of IPMurderers. As shown in Figure 11.4, in most comparisons the group of men who murdered an intimate partner stands apart from those who commit other types of murder. As a group, the IPMurderers were more likely to have obtained educational qualifications and to be regularly employed and less likely to abuse alcohol or drugs and to engage in persistent criminal behavior. But a considerable proportion was likely to have experienced a broken relationship, to use violence against a previous intimate partner, and to be convicted of an assault in which the victim was a woman (although this was similar for sex/murderers and slightly more likely among men who murdered older women). By contrast, the men who murdered other men rarely had convictions for assault that involved women victims.[1] In brief, men who murder other men seem to specialize in violence against men, while those who murder women are more likely to specialize in using violence against women. Those who murder intimate partners are set apart in many ways that suggest more conventionality in the backgrounds of a reasonable proportion of these men, although they also specialize in the use of violence against women. The men who murder older women and those who commit sexual murders also appear to specialize in the use of violence against women but, in contrast to IPMurderers, they were far less likely to have profiles that suggest an otherwise relatively conventional lifestyle.

The Murder Event—Comparisons of Four Types of Murder

Comparisons of the type of relationships between perpetrators and victims across all four types indicate that both men and women were more likely to be murdered by those known to them than by a stranger. Obviously, all intimate partners were known to one another. However, the majority of male-male murders, sexual murders, and the murders of older women involved those who were acquainted/related in some way, and a minority involved those who were strangers (Figure 11.1).

In the overview of circumstances at the time of the murder and the murder event, a few comparisons stand out (Figure 11.2). Ongoing disputes, most of considerable duration, preceded the vast majority of intimate partner murders and a reasonable proportion of male on male murders, but were nearly nonexistent in the other two types. Previous violence to the victim prior to the murder was very common in the murder of intimate partners but unusual in the other three types of murder. Confrontations immediately preceding the murder were very likely in intimate partner murders and male-male murders, but less likely in sexual murders, and very rare in the murders of older women. With the exception of IPMurderers, about one-half of the men were intoxicated at the time of the murder (Figure 11.2).

Within the murder events, many men used their body, hands, and feet to attack the woman or man they killed. A considerable proportion of all four groups used an "instrument" such as a blunt object, knife, or ligature to commit the murder, although the use of a knife or blunt object was most likely to occur in murders between males. The use of a firearm was extremely rare. What distinguished the murders of women was the use of a ligature and strangulation in all three types. Older women were often suffocated. Across all four groups, about two-thirds of the men inflicted five or more injuries on their victim, and this was most likely in the murder of older women. Although not shown in the figures, about two-thirds of the IPMurderers were angry or in a rage during the murder, and this was also very likely for men who committed a theft/murder of an older woman. Most murders took place in the home of the victim, particularly the murder of older women and intimate partners, although the majority of sexual murders and those between men also took place in the home or place of residence of the victim.

These and other comparisons lend support to the importance of disaggregating homicides by gender in order to gain more adequate and meaningful evidence not only about those committed against women but also about those committed against men. The further disaggregation of the murders of women into the three types identified in the Murder Study has yielded important knowledge and insights that would not be possible if these murders had not been considered separately. Similar statements might equally be made about a deeper study of other types of murder not considered here, such as the killing of children, murders committed by women, and murders committed by individuals who are themselves children or adolescents. In addition, the study of murders between men would also seem to warrant an examination of the different types contained within this overall group. These are important issues to be undertaken in other studies, and the findings from the comparisons of the four types of murder suggest that there is much to be gained from an approach that involves a deeper examination of homicide events and perpetrators when they are divided by type of murder and compared across types.

Some broad and general conclusions can be drawn from these findings. The men who commit murder are, for the most part, disadvantaged economically, educationally, and socially. Many abuse substances, particularly alcohol, and generally have few, failed, or unstable personal relationships. Most have histories of previous offending, and the type of previous offenses are often precursors of the type of murder they eventually commit. That is, most men who murder men have histories of offending against other men, while most men who murder women have histories of offending against women. Even more specifically, most men who commit a sexual murder have previously committed sexual violence against women, and most men who murder an intimate partner have previously committed violence against this or another woman partner, including those with no previous convictions for these or any other offenses. In short, men who murder women tend to "specialize" in perpetrating violence against women. We now return to the three types of murder of women for a brief overview of each.

When Men Murder Older Women

The cases of men who murdered a woman age 65 or over were divided almost evenly between those that primarily involved a theft and those that included a sexual element/attack of some type that ranged from disturbing clothing and uncovering sexual parts of the body to rape. Almost all of the murders, whether involving theft or sex, occurred in the home or residence of the women. Generally, the murders that involved sex were committed by strangers, while those that involved a theft were committed by men known to the women including acquaintances, neighbors, friends, or relatives. The majority of the men were unemployed, lived on their own, and were not in an intimate relationship, and many were on remand (bail) or probation for another offense, sometimes of a sexual nature.

The older women who were killed appear to have been selected because of their "extra" vulnerability of being both older and a woman. Are older women more vulnerable than older men? Existing research indicates that men are the usual victims of murders involving those who are young. By contrast, women and men are almost equally likely to be the victim when the murder involves the killing of person over the age of 60.

In the Murder Study, older women age 65 and over represented 17% (n = 243) of all women victims—men of the same age represented 9% of the 424 male victims. On this basis we might assume that women are indeed more likely to be targeted as they are seen as more vulnerable and an easy target. This is illustrated by the fact that the sex/murderers of older women were much more likely than the theft/murderers to have killed women over the age of 80. The qualitative materials demonstrate this pattern. Some of the sex murderers specifically targeted a very elderly woman or a location housing such women, for example, a care home and, often in a drunken stupor, attacked and sexually assaulted these very vulnerable women.

The vast majority of the men broke into the home of an older woman who lived near his own place of residence with the intention of committing a burglary, a sex attack, or both, but not usually with a clear intention to kill. On the day of the murder, many of the men had been drinking and were drunk. Of those who committed a Sex/Murder, about three-quarters had been drinking, half of them were drunk, and about one-third of them had been drinking all day. Of those who committed a Theft/Murder, about one-third had been drinking, and two-fifths of them were drunk, although none of them had been drinking all day. Alcohol was the substance of "choice" for most, although some were polysubstance abusers, especially those who committed a sexual act within the murder. Serious problems with alcohol and a pattern of all-day drinking were common. Long-standing problems of substance abuse may have played a part in the sex/murderer's choice of the most vulnerable women who were over the age of 80, possibly because they believed that the oldest of the old would be the easiest to overwhelm and the least able to resist. Of all the women who were murdered, older women were the most likely to be bludgeoned to death.

Theft/murderers of older women were often motivated by the need for money or goods that could be exchanged for alcohol and/or drugs, whereas sex/murderers were usually driven by sexual motives that were filtered through a haze of intoxication. Very few of the men were angry at the time of the murder, although some reported becoming angry in response to the women who confronted them, resisted them, and/or indicated that they knew who they were and might report them. Women who caught men "in the act," were often surprised and frightened and sometimes remonstrated with them. The qualitative accounts demonstrate men's anger when women objected to their intrusion into her home and the theft of her possessions. Men apparently found such resistance offensive and acted to silence the woman with brutal force. Men's anger was not usually reported in cases involving the sexual murder of older women.

Violence was often used to silence the victim or eliminate a potential witness to a burglary or a sexual assault. These actions constituted a dynamic process that evolved from a theft and/or a sexual attack to an encounter that included extreme forms of physical violence. Such reactions illustrate the lack of consequential thinking among these men. When caught in the act of stealing from the home of a woman who knows or recognizes him, he could flee and risk a possible conviction for burglary but, instead, he murders her in an effort to avoid a charge of theft, which, in turn, results in a life sentence for murder rather than a possible conviction for a lesser offense. This lack of consequential thinking occurred with great regularity in these cases.

Men who murdered older woman were typically living on their own, had difficulty in relationships with women, had problems with alcohol and/or drugs, and were intoxicated at the time of the murder, which usually involved strangulation and/or injuries caused by kicking and punching with hands and feet. The dynamic of "changing the project" from a theft or a sexual attack to the act of murder was apparent in cases when a man broke into a woman's residence, was met with resistance, and responded with a ferocious and sometimes frenzied attack that killed her.

When Men Murder Women for Sex

Men who committed a sexual murder of a woman under the age of 65 were usually younger than their victim, unemployed, single or separated/divorced, and living on their own. Most of the men and women were acquainted, although many were strangers. The type of relationship between the perpetrator and the victim affected the nature of his access to her. For those who were strangers, men had no "legitimate" form of social access to the woman that might be used as a route to obtaining sex from her. As such, he used immediate force, violence, and/or subterfuge in order to gain sexual access. Social access was not a problem for men who were acquainted, but this did not imply sexual access, which still had to be "negotiated" and/or forced. Although sexual access was not a problem with respect to women who were working as prostitutes, other issues still had to be negotiated. Even when physical violence was not "necessary" in order to gain sexual access to the woman, many men nonetheless used immediate and excessive force.

Across all types of relationships, the main methods of killing involved strangulation, beating with hands and feet, and bludgeoning with various instruments. Although some research indicates that greater violence is used when the victim is a stranger, evidence from the Murder Study suggests little difference between the type of relationship and the number of injuries inflicted during the murder. Indeed, some of the murders of acquaintances were among the most prolonged and brutal because they took place in the home of the victim, which allowed the man time to carry out a prolonged attack. By contrast, men who murdered women in more public settings usually did not have an extended amount of time but, instead, had to subdue and silence the woman quickly in order to sexually assault and murder her before being discovered by others. The prospect of discovery in a public location was often avoided by attacking women in outdoor locations that were deserted, which reduced the chance of discovery.

In sexual murders, ongoing disputes between the victim and offender were rare, as were previous incidents of violence to the victim. Confrontations associated with sexual murder were highly circumstantial, as women attempted to repulse the aggressive sexual demands of the murderer and/or attempted to defend themselves against his violent actions. These altercations were not linked to long-term conflicts associated with such things as jealousy, possessiveness, or other issues but are, instead, more accurately defined as acts of self-defense in response to an attack. Most women were killed in their own home or place of residence, although women

who were strangers, including those working as prostitutes, were often killed in isolated locations. Sex/murderers were likely to be drinking and drunk at the time as
was a minority of the victims. While alcohol was not the "cause" of this violence,
as some perpetrators suggest, it may have played a role in the sexual attack and the
murder, as the poor judgments of the men transformed the woman's sociability
into an agreement to sex. However, alcohol was not necessary to induce this type
of thinking, because most of the men, whether drunk or sober, were not interested
in women's feelings and concerns. The murders were usually over in minutes. A few
involved prolonged sexual violence and/or physical torture, but this was rare. About
one-fifth of the men carried out further acts against the woman's body after death,
which included sex, mutilation, and/or dismembering of the body. Sex after death
and sexual mutilation were uncommon.

The vast majority of these men set out to obtain sex. Some imagined the sex would
be "consensual," others anticipated using violence to obtain sex, and a few "fantasized" a brutal killing involving sadistic violence and/or mutilation of the body. For
a few, the murder began with a sexual attack that was opportunistic. For others, it
appeared that the men "changed the project" from the original intent of obtaining
sex to the use of brutal force when they were met with resistance from the woman
and/or when they were unable to perform sexually. Either way, the man blamed the
woman and shifted from the task of forcing sex on her to one of killing her in order
to punish her for her resistance or for his sexual failure. These men were accustomed
to using physical and/or sexual violence against women, and, as such, each of their
sexual encounters would have been charged with the potential for intimidation,
aggression, and violence. Before the murder, a few of the men were involved in a
series of sexual and physical attacks on women over a relatively short period of time
in which the murder was the last of these attacks.

Other research has emphasized the importance of anger before and during a
sexual murder. About one-third of these men claimed to be angry during the sexual
murder and, like men who murdered an intimate partner, some appeared to be in a
constant state of anger. In the main, anger was primarily situational. When women
rebuffed men, refused their sexual advances, or thwarted their intentions, men
became angry and used severe violence in retaliation. In a few cases, the anger was
associated with a woman other than the one they killed or with women in general.
In some of these cases, the men indicated that if they had had the opportunity,
they would have killed the woman who "caused" their anger. A few claimed they
were angry because a woman working as a prostitute ridiculed or laughed at them
because of a sexual problem such as impotence. Such accounts seem implausible,
particularly as women who work as prostitutes know the potential for violence
among their clients and are unlikely to behave in such a reckless and dangerous
manner. Again, intoxication leading to misjudgments and faulty interpretations
may have played a role in the men's behavior or the accounts simply serve as post
hoc rationalizations.

Women working as prostitutes in a commercial relationship with men buying
sex constituted a considerable proportion of the victims of sexual murder, especially those killed by men who were strangers. Sex workers are frequent victims of
male violence, and it seems that some of the men who murdered prostitutes during
a commercial transaction were intent not only on obtaining sex but also on carrying out serious violence against the woman. Sex workers usually attempt to assess

the potential danger of "clients," but this is far from foolproof. Assessments of the "dangerousness" of clients are usually made on the street and in difficult circumstances. These judgments may be affected by the pharmacological effects of alcohol and/or drugs that reduce the ability to recognize warning signs, but intoxication was no more likely among the sex workers than among the other victims of sexual murder.

Only a few of the sexual attacks corresponded to the descriptions of the sadistic violent fantasizer found in the serial killer literature and some accounts of sexual murderers. The typical sex murderer found in the Murder Study was a man in his late 20s or early 30s who had a history of sexual and/or physical violence against women and was intent on obtaining sex from a woman who could have been a stranger or an acquaintance. If the woman refused or resisted sex, he was prepared to use violence in order to overcome her resistance and to obtain sex without regard for the consequences even to the point of murder. Other cases involved men with fixed intentions from the outset that were focused not only on obtaining sex but also on using violence in the act of doing so. A very few cases involved men who, from the outset, intended to commit both a violent sexual assault and a murder.

When Men Murder Intimate Partners

The average age of the husbands, cohabitants, or boyfriends who murdered their women partners was 34, and the average age of the women was 31. Most of the men were undereducated and unemployed or underemployed, although a minority had some educational qualifications and were steadily employed. Many had a history of previous convictions, violence to a previous intimate partner, and one or more failed relationships. One-quarter of the men had personal and demographic characteristics that were relatively conventional, and this is reflected in the overall averages for the entire group. The majority had ongoing disputes with their woman partner and had previously used violence against her, and there was a confrontation at the time of the murder. The majority of the men were not drunk at the time of the murder, and almost none of the women were. The overwhelming majority of the murders occurred in the home. Women were beaten, strangled, and bludgeoned, and some were stabbed; firearms were rarely used.

It is men's orientations to and assumptions about the appropriate behavior of women, their sense of entitlement over women, and the need to uphold their own moral universe that led to the murder of the vast majority of women partners. For these men, women partners should not be able to act independently of their wishes and demands. This included attempts to terminate failing relationships, even those that were extremely violent, to live on their own, or to establish a relationship with a new partner. Almost all of the relationships involved long-term conflicts and disputes often regarding the man's possessiveness and jealousy. These were heightened when the woman threatened to end the relationship, attempted to leave, or had actually done so. Conflicts leading to violence are not restricted to possessiveness and jealousy but are also associated with various aspects of daily life that involve male privilege and authority including issues about money, domestic work, and the care and custody of children.

A common assumption is that the murder of an intimate partner usually, if not always, constitutes an incremental shift or slip from a nonlethal to a lethal outcome that simply reflects more of the same rather than something different. Evidence presented here leads to skepticism regarding this interpretation. The IPMurderers were some of the most determined of all the murderers. Many had a fixed firm intention to kill their partner. For many, this usually occurred in the context of attempts to cajole, persuade, and violently coerce the woman to remain in the relationship or return to it. As such, the intimate partner murders often involved a dynamic process involving men "changing the project" from one of attempting to keep or reclaim their partner to one fixed on her death. A minority of these men were not using violence against their partner before they killed her, but, once made, their decision to annihilate her was just as determined as that of the men who had been inflicting violence on their partner before they murdered her. As is usually the case with those who perpetrate violence, these men often saw themselves as victims who had been wronged and, as such, were embittered and indignant. They viewed themselves as acting in a moral universe wherein their anger and violence was appropriate and justified. Anger, even rage, constituted the background for many of the men for whom these emotions were omnipresent and all consuming. In their view, their partner deserved to be killed, and this was vividly expressed in their justifications, denial of culpability, and blaming of the victim. Similar processes were clearly evident in the majority of collateral murders reported here.

An important "discovery" in the Murder Study was the type and number of collateral murders that occurred in the context of intimate partner conflicts (n = 62). The intensive methods of the Murder Study enabled us to identify the murders of others such as, children, relatives, friends, and new partners that were related to intimate partner conflicts. These were acts of revenge against those who attempted to protect the women, such as friends and relatives, and against new partners when new relationships were established. Children were usually killed as an act of revenge with the intention of inflicting maximum pain on the woman. These collateral murders increase the overall number of those killed in the context of intimate partner conflicts and underscores the nature and intensity of thinking that shapes the clear and focused intention to kill the woman partner, and if not her then someone near and dear to her as a means of inflicting pain on her. Future research should be alert to these and other types of collateral murders and collect evidence about their nature and prevalence.

A few of the men who murdered their partner not only perpetrated physical violence but also carried out a sexual attack. Boyfriends were more likely than husbands and cohabitants to have committed sexual violence within the murder. This might relate to the shorter length of such relationships and/or their more tenuous nature. In that sense, these murders may be similar to the sexual murders committed by an acquaintance, and, as such, there may be a blending and/or blurring of the categorization of these cases. For example, it could be that some of these men were serious sexual predators who established a boyfriend/girlfriend relationship solely or primarily for the purpose of obtaining sex or sexual attacks, or that a sexual attack was more likely to occur when the murderer was a boyfriend because the relationship was more tenuous. Either way, this needs to be more fully explored.

Men who murder an intimate partner were the most intent on committing murder. For them, "changing the project" usually did not involve a shift of actions or intentions within the context of the murder event itself but, instead, involved a shift of intentions in advance of the murder. The notion "If I can't have you, no one can" frequently applied as men decided to kill the woman partner who had left him, was in the act of doing so, or was believed to be ready and willing to do so. In contrast to the other two types of murder, these men were the most concerted and focused in their intention to kill the woman who no longer belonged to them, and some of these men were also willing to kill others as an act of revenge against the woman partner.

In Prison—Behavior and Professional Assessments

All of the murderers were in prison when we interviewed them and/or collected information from their casefiles. All were sentenced to life, and many had received a substantial tariff of many years. In Figure 11.5, the four types of murder are compared in terms of how the men adapted to prison regimes and their reactions to prison programs oriented to working with them to deal with their offending behavior and ways of thinking.

Within the prison regime, men are judged in terms of the frequency and nature of issues relating to discipline with the most cooperative often defined as "model prisoners" who posed few problems to the daily running of the prison. A few points stand out. IPMurderers were most likely to be defined as model prisoners and least likely to have discipline reports. Men who murdered older women and those who committed a sexual murder were least likely to be viewed as "model prisoners"; less likely to cooperate with professionals, particularly those running various programs; and most likely to be judged as dangerous and a risk to public safety should they be released. Male-male murderers and IPMurderers were least likely to be defined as experiencing mental health problems. The men who murdered older women were most likely to be assessed as having mental health problems, which may reflect a greater prevalence of mental health problems within this group prior to the murder and incarceration. As the qualitative materials illustrate, the behavior of the sex/murderers in prison constituted a unique form of dangerousness. Some of them were unwilling or unable to control their sexual predilections and behaviors in the presence of women prison officers and other women staff. This points to continuing problems among this group of men that represent unique risks for women staff and presents numerous challenges for all those who work with them.

The men were challenged to take responsibility for the murder. An integral part of these efforts involved questions of remorse for the murder and empathy with the victim. While levels of empathy and remorse might fluctuate for individual men, at the time of the study there were important differences among the four types of murderers. Although a considerable proportion of all types expressed little to no remorse, this was much more apparent for the men who murdered older women and the sex/murderers. The foundational aspect of these expressions is the nature of the men's orientations to and relationships with women, and prison staff judged the vast majority of the men who murdered a woman as "having problems with" women. As noted throughout, these assessments were not merely based on what men did and said in prison but also on the wealth of information about their behavior prior to imprisonment. Indeed, our interviews and reading of the casefiles led us to similar conclusions. Men who murdered other men were much less likely to be judged to have problems with women. It is possible that selection bias played a part in these assessments. Since these men murdered a woman, they may be more likely to be defined as having problems with women. Even if this was so, the magnitude of the differences was such that the differences would appear to be real rather than an artifact of selection bias.

Changing Violent Men

While in prison, the men are required to engage in their own reformation. Yet, as the evidence presented throughout suggests, many find it difficult or impossible to confront their actions and take responsibility for the murder even when assisted in doing so. One of the major goals of prison programs is the prevention of another murder and other types of violent crime. Very few men who are imprisoned for murder and serve a prison sentence commit another murder after release. Of the 424 men who murdered another man, seven (2.1%) were serving a sentence for a second homicide. Of the 243 men who murdered a woman, nine (3.7%) were serving a sentence for a second homicide. These levels parallel findings from other countries.[2] For homicide offenders, the risk of committing another murder is low but the risk of committing another violent offense is higher than would be expected in the general population. Comparative rates of recidivism among offenders released after serving a sentence for another type of offense are mixed, with some research indicating greater prevalence for both property and violent offenses among homicide offenders and some finding the reverse. However, one of the most consistent findings is that the risk of reoffending for all types of crime decreases with age. Offenders released after serving long sentences for committing a homicide are usually older than other released offenders, and this might account for the reports of lower levels of offending among this group. In other words, maturation diminishes risk.

The probability of convicted murderers committing another homicide after their release is low. However, the objective while in prison is a reduction in the potential for committing violence and other crimes upon release by reducing or eliminating the problems associated with these acts. The question is, will these men embark on this work and will it actually help them reduce their risk to others? As the evidence has shown, this is an arduous task.

Denial, minimization, and deflection of responsibility were serious problems among the men included in this study. While many may eventually take on the task of working to change their orientations toward themselves, their violence, and the victim as well as the attendant ways of thinking and behavior, such as abuse of alcohol, the commitment usually ebbs and flows. Additionally, most of these men had histories of violence against women and serious anti-social behavior and some had been convicted of previous violence against women. Yet, punishments, including imprisonment and for a few participation on intervention programs did not deter them. On the basis of the evidence reported here and other research it is clear that the way forward in attempts to confront violence against women and deal with dangerous men is meaningful sanctions coupled with challenges to their behavior and ways of thinking through program participation.

Cognitive-Behavioral Programs for Offenders

Following the lead of the Canadian prison system, the English and Scottish prison services have created various intervention programs for offenders. As discussed in earlier chapters, these are based on "cognitive-behavioral" principles that aim to challenge the way offenders think and behave, because their thinking about themselves and their relationships with others are often at the core of their offending behavior. The strongest, probably most important strand of development in these types of interventions has emerged from work with sex offenders, particularly pedophiles.[3] Cognitive-behavioral interventions designed for sex offenders, wherever they are delivered, have similar components. Marshall, one of the most influential academic and therapeutic professionals in the field, has outlined the most important components of these programs whether delivered in prison or the community.[4] For example, they should address problems of denial and minimization, empathy, cognitive distortions, problems in relationships and sociability, and substance use and abuse. Predictably, sex offender programs should address various sexual problems deemed to be associated with sexual offending.

In dealing with sex offenders, Marshall recommends a number of procedures that are reflected in the evidence presented here. Initially, it is important to determine sex offenders' levels of denial, minimization, and sense of responsibility for their actions. This is crucial in the process of risk assessment and "reform." The process of intervention usually begins by asking the offender to provide an account of the offense and the context in which it occurred, and this has been shown in the narratives presented about each of the three types of murder. Of utmost importance is challenging the offender's accounts and ways of thinking. According to Marshall, offenders frequently represent themselves in an exculpatory manner and "many outright deny they have committed an offense."[5] Much of the literature suggests that challenging offenders requires considerable skill and professional judgment because some offenders profess "remarkably pro-social views" that are at variance with their behavior as reported by others. Offenders generally have poor social skills, and, as the evidence presented here suggests, this is especially the case in their relationships with women.

A second strand of work with men who use violence against women is firmly embedded in community efforts to end intimate partner violence against women that began in Britain and the United States in the 1970s.[6] Efforts to deal with this violence began with the provision of refuges and shelters for abused women and challenges to social and legal systems to alter their responses to this problem. Following this, programs for abusers were developed primarily in conjunction with the battered women's movement in the United States as a part of the overall effort to end violence against women. This had at its core a commitment to protecting women by dealing with the men who used violence against them. These early interventions for abusers, particularly the Duluth program model developed by Ellen Pence and Michael Paymar and the work of David Adams and colleagues at Emerge in Boston, have influenced the development of abuser programs throughout the world.[7] The first European programs began in Scotland with CHANGE and the Lothian Domestic Violence Probation Project and later developed in England and Wales.[8] Abuser programs conceive of men's violence against women as learned and purposeful behavior that involves the decision to use violence in order to achieve some desired outcome. They are based on the principle that the best way to deal with the violence and associated behaviors is to get men into programs that challenge their use of violence and ways of thinking about women that are associated with it. While some abuser programs focus on men who volunteer to participate, others are linked with the criminal justice system and require arrest, conviction, and mandatory participation in an abuser program as an aspect of sentencing. Abuser programs are now well established particularly in the United States, Great Britain, Canada, Australia, and various European countries.

EVALUATIONS OF PROGRAMS FOR OFFENDERS AND RISK ASSESSMENT

There has been a great deal of controversy about the effectiveness of programs for sex offenders and for abusers of intimate partners. There is now a growing body of evidence suggesting that these interventions can be effective with certain types of sex offenders, with the greatest resistance to programs among men who have committed rape.[9] Fewer evaluations of programs for abusers have been conducted and the evidence is also mixed, yet some results indicate that they may reduce the abusive and violent acts of certain types of men.[10] However, to our knowledge there are no programs in British prisons dedicated solely to dealing with those who commit a sexual murder or kill an intimate partner.

In addition to offender programs, the assessment of risk and danger are becoming more common. The most developed approaches to risk assessment come from the work with sex offenders, particularly in Canada. Two types of risks are assessed, static and dynamic.[11] Focusing on sex offenders, particularly pedophiles, Hanson has distilled a number of static risks, such as sexual interest in children, prior sexual offenses, stranger victims, early onset of sex offending, and single never married. Dynamic risk factors include poor intimacy skills, no intimate relationships, attitudes tolerant of sexual assault, an inability or unwillingness to delay (sexual) gratification, and negative peer influences.[12] In contrast to non–sex offenders, these men lack empathy for women, prefer sex in "uncommitted relationships," that is, sex without intimacy, and derive little satisfaction from relationships with an intimate partner. Although these men may endorse prosocial remarks that sex offending is wrong, they nonetheless continue to "provide justifications and excuses that mitigate the seriousness of their own crimes."[13] The egocentric demands of sex offenders are paramount, and those who refuse to participate in intervention programs or fail to complete them are more likely to repeat their sexual crimes. In this study, the sex/murderers, including those who murdered older women, exhibited many of the same risk factors highlighted by Hanson prior to the murder.

The literature on risk factors and risk assessment associated with violence against intimate partners is not as extensive as the work with sex offenders. Women's advocates such as Barbara Hart in the United States were among the first to stress the importance of assisting women to assess the dangers they faced in their relationships with violent men. This approach to risk assessment originated within the battered women's movement and was meant to be used by women to assess the risks posed by their abusive partners. This has now grown and expanded to include the use of risk assessment by those working on abuser programs and is now widely used within criminal justice systems, particularly in the United States. There are a number of risk assessment tools now in use by various organizations and agencies with a focus on nonlethal violence and abuse. The Danger Assessment tool was developed by Campbell and her colleagues in order to assess the risk of homicide among intimate partner abusers.[14] The 15-item list of potential risks is to be used by women in conjunction with a calendar in order to enhance their own assessments of risk and danger. The major risk factors include previous threats to use a weapon (firearm), threats to kill, choking, violent and constant jealousy, forced sex, a gun in the house, and increasing severity of physical violence. Other important factors include intense controlling behavior and the man's use of illicit drugs and being drunk every day or almost every day. Most of these risk factors were found in the cases of intimate partner murder reported here. Risk assessment must not be viewed as an outcome in its own right nor as a static indicator of risk and danger. Instead, it should be viewed as one element in the management of violent offenders within the context of a dynamic process in which violence may escalate and even turn to murder.

When Men Murder Women

Efforts to improve the safety of women, to challenge men who commit sexual and physical violence against women, punish wrongdoing, and work to prevent it occurring in the first place are of the utmost importance. Throughout the last quarter of the twentieth century, first in the most prosperous North American, Northern European, and Antipodean countries, social movements developed to attempt to improve the safety of women and their children. In Great Britain groups such as Rape Crisis and Women's Aid provided advice, support, and shelter for women who had been physically abused by their partners and/or sexually assaulted. This is now a worldwide movement, and violence against women including the murder of women is now recognized by the UN, WHO, UNESCO, and the European Union as a significant problem requiring immediate and meaningful action. In many ways the perceptions of violence against women have been transformed from a view that it was appropriate, legitimate, and inevitable to one that sees it as the opposite: never appropriate nor legitimate nor inevitable. For those who have lived and worked to end violence against women in this transformative era, the world seems a better place, yet women are still raped and murdered. They are still assaulted and murdered by intimate partners, and older women are still being attacked in their homes and murdered. In some countries, the perpetrator can do this with impunity. *When Men Murder Women* is a contribution to the knowledge of when and why this happens, and a contribution to what is known about the men who murder women. It adds to the knowledge base on which it is possible to create social changes and interventions aimed at improving the lives and safety of women and holding men accountable for their violent actions.

Throughout we have asked the questions, What happens when men murder women? Who are the men who murder women? and How do these murders compare to those in which men murder other men? These and other questions have been addressed in the examination of the murder of intimate partners, sexual murders, and the murder of older women. Evidence from casefiles and interviews have been used to examine murder events and the lifecourse of the men who perpetrate them. The focus on the murder event includes the nature of the relationship between the man and the woman he murders, the situations and circumstances associated with the murder, the nature of attack and injuries, subsequent treatment of the body after death, and actions to avoid detection. The nature and type of relationships between the men and the women they murder provides the contexts in which men have more or less access to women, hold differing notions about their own entitlements, and constitute the platforms for exercising authority, power, and control, and meting out punishments including violence and sometimes murder. The focus on the lifecourse of the perpetrators explores their backgrounds as children and their lifestyles as adults, including education, employment, substance abuse, criminal behavior, and violence against women including present and previous women partners. Chronic alcohol abuse was a serious problem for some, and most of the men specialized in using violence against women. Once convicted and imprisoned, their behavior within the prison regime ranged from "model prisoners" with few discipline problems to men who were uncooperative and disruptive. All murderers are required to participate in intervention programs designed to address various aspects of their offending behavior and to assist them in developing personal insights, a sense of responsibility for their actions, remorse for the murder, and empathy with the victim. This was done with varying degree of success.

The amount, quality, and level of detailed information held in the casefiles about each case of murder and gathered in the interviews has not only allowed for an expansion of knowledge about each of the three main types of murder explored throughout but also facilitated the discovery of several subtypes. These include the collateral murders associated with intimate partner conflict and the sex/murders and theft/murders of older women. Although the murders of women constitute a considerable proportion of all murders, they have often been ignored, inappropriately conceptualized, or simply overlaid with a template designed to explain murders committed by men against other men. The evidence presented here demonstrates that another template is required if we are to gain a better and fuller understanding of when men murder women. This fuller examination allows for more enhanced concepts and theoretical developments that highlight the central importance of gender and the nature of the relationships between women and men in understanding and explaining when and why men commit the ultimate act of violence against women.

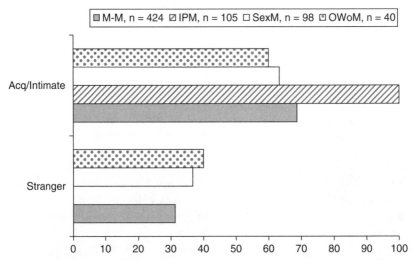

Figure 11.1 Four Types of Murder—Relationships: Between Perpetrators and Victims; Strangers and All Acquaintances/Intimates (%).

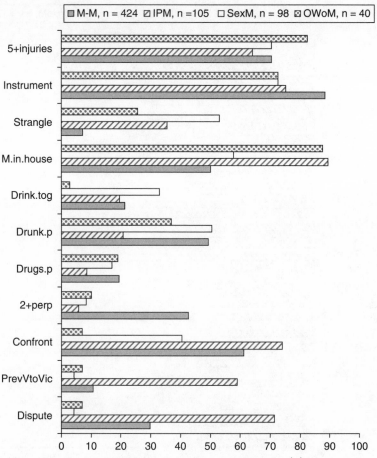

Figure 11.2 Four Types of Murder—Circumstances at Murder (%).

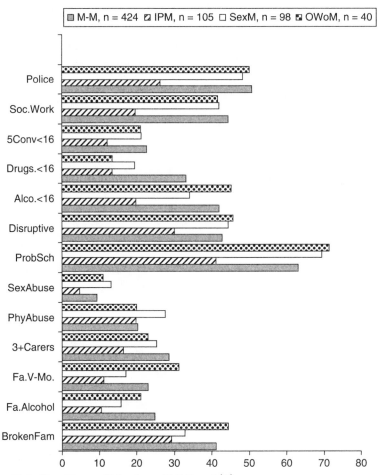

Figure 11.3 Four Types of Murder—Childhood (%).

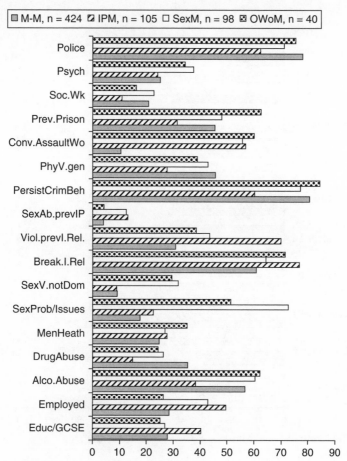

Figure 11.4 Four Types of Murder—Adulthood (%).

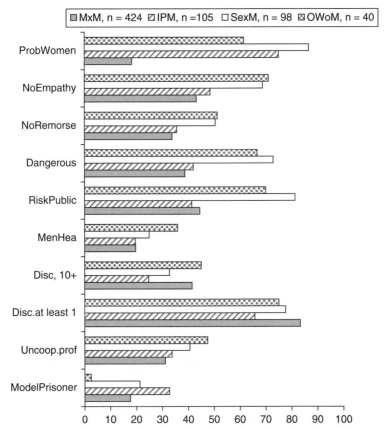

Figure 11.5 Four Types of Murder—Assessments in Prison (%).

MURDER STUDY—DATA COLLECTION AND ANALYSIS

Casefiles and Interviews—Data Collection,
Variable Specification, and Nodes

DATA COLLECTION—CASEFILES
DATA COLLECTION—INTERVIEWS
DATA ANALYSIS (quantitative data)—VARIABLE SPECIFICATION for SPSS
DATA ANALYSIS (qualitative data)—qsr.NUDIST NODES

I.1. Casefiles—Data collection instrument and codebook for SPSS (contents only, pages color-coded, 440+ specific items not shown)
I.2. Interview Schedule—Cover Page (contents only—specific items not shown)
I.3. Casefiles—Variable Specification for SPSS
I.4. Nud*ist/QSR—Nodes/Categories (for Qualitative Data from Casefiles and Interviews)

I.1. CASEFILES—DATA COLLECTION INSTRUMENT AND CODEBOOK FOR SPSS (LIST OF CONTENTS ONLY)

Contents of Data Collection Instrument and Codebook for SPSS

-	**Codebook, 52 pages, 400+ variables for SPSS, color-coded by topic as below***	
B	(green)	Background details (personal identifiers) (employment)
E	(white)	Murder Event (inc. victim info)
L	(yellow)	Legal process (of murder), Convictions as adult and previous offenses
P	(white)	Prison, Parole, ~Training programs, Violence in prison
S	(blue)	School, Family of Origin, and Childhood (inc. abuse as child)
R	(cream)	Adult relationship(s) (inc. viol. to partner/s, children, others)
Z	(pink)	Substance/Alcohol problems, Professionals involved as adult

*codebook containing all variables not shown

I.2. INTERVIEW SCHEDULE—COVER PAGE (INCLUDING LIST OF TOPICS FOR INTERVIEW)

-Tape-recorded and transcribed into Word documents, then coded and transferred to Nud*ist/qsr for analysis of qualitative data (see nudist nodes below)

National Study*

Principle Investigators: Professor Russell Dobash, Professor Rebecca Dobash, Criminology, School of Law, University of Manchester

Senior Researchers: Dr. Kate Cavanagh and Dr. Ruth Lewis,

Research Location: University of Manchester

Date _____, Interviewer: _____, Location _____

Interview I.D. [e.g.,RD001] _____, Prison Number _____, Casefile I.D. _____

GENERAL DETAILS --
- = Current Location
- = Individual Background (ethnicity, religion, marital status, children, employment, education)

CHILDHOOD ---
- = and Family Background (parents/carers, siblings)
- = and Family Issues (problems, police contact)
- = History of Family Arguments and Violence (FatherViol./MotherViol./OtherViol.)
- = Childhood Discipline (discipline, violence, sexual abuse)
- = Previous Offenses (as child, as adult)

THE EVENT [MURDER] ---
- = Circumstances Prior to Event (living arrangements, etc.)
- = The Day of the Event
- = The Event
- = Immediately After the Event (reaction to arrest, conviction, and imprisonment)

ADULT LIFE AND RELATIONSHIPS --
- = Social Network
- = Alcohol
- = Drugs
- = Relationship(s) with Intimate Partner(s)
- = Own Children)
- = Violence to Partner(s) [over time]

ATTITUDES AND PERCEPTIONS --
- = Images of Self
- = Attitudes Toward Others (elderly, weak, gay, women, vulnerable)

PRISON AND PRISON PROGRAMS ---
- = Prison—behaviour and adjustment
- = Programs and Counselling

OBSERVATIONS ABOUT INTERVIEW—[researcher's impressions] ....

---

*Specific items not shown

I.3. VARIABLE SPECIFICATION FOR SPSS

*CHILDHOOD (Before Age 16) (variable specification)

Variable	Definition
Problems of parents and family:	
Broken relationship	Parents divorce/separate
Alcohol abuse by father	Chronic alcoholism or binge drinking
Criminal record father	At least one conviction of father
Family dysfunction	Professionals interviews with offender &/or family
Poverty	Living conditions and/or chronic unemployment of caretakers
Father violent to mother	Usually reported by the murderer
Disrupted caretaking:	
3+ changes in caretakers	3 or more changes in caretakers
In care as child	In care = foster, adopted, or care institution at least once
Abused as child:	
Physically abused	Physical abuse of reportable nature, not "ordinary" chastisement
Sexually abused	Sexual abuse, mostly intrusive
Problems of the child:	
Problems at school	Aggression & fighting, but mostly persistent truancy/ absconding
Disruptive behavior (pre-13)	Unruly, aggressive beh. at home &/or school before age 13
Sexual problems	Identified by parents and/or authorities (e.g., school, GPs/family doctors)
Mental health problems	Identified by authorities (school, GPs/family doctors)
Alcohol abuse	Not mere drinking, consumption beyond casual usage
Drug abuse	Not mere incident but steady use
Suicide attempt	Serious attempt at suicide
Violence and criminal justice:	
Onset of offending pre-13	Criminal behavior, e.g., larceny, assault, not "antisocial" acts
Serious violence as child	Beyond playground fights—Violence to peers, siblings, parents, teachers, and others
5+ convictions	5 or more convictions before age 16
CJ institution (ever)	Incarceration for offending before age 16
CJ institution (6+mos)	Incarceration for 6 or more months
Involvement of professionals with family during childhood:	
Social services	Social work with anyone in family
Medical services	Medical services to family, more than common, minor ailments
Psychology/psychiatric	Psychological/psychiatric services for anyone in family
Police	Police intervention in family, usually father of offender
Probation services	Probation of anyone in family

*ADULTHOOD (variable specification for SPSS)

Variable	Definition
Education and employment:	
Ethnicity	As recorded in case file
GCSE* or above	Educated to GCSE (age16) or above
A level or above	Secondary school or above, but rarely more than secondary school
Regularly employed	Includes only those regularly employed
White collar job	Dept. Employment categories = clerical, managerial, & professional
Problems as adult:	
Alcohol abuse	Chronic alcohol abuse—ID by offender, his family, professionals
Drug abuse	Persistent drug use—ID by offender, his family, professionals
Mental health problems	Identified by professionals
Poverty as an adult	Relative but serious economic disadvantage
Suicide attempt	Serious attempt, not including attempts during current sentence
Sexual violence/aggression	Sexual violence and/or aggression
Intimate Relationships:	
Breakdown of intimate relationship/s	Breakdown of marriage or cohabitating relationship/s
Violence in previous relationship	Assessed after murder by:—police, previous partners, witnesses, reports in Casefiles
Problems with women	Probs. in orientations to/rel. with women ID by professionals
Criminal behavior:	
Persistent criminal behavior	Many convictions also unrecorded crimes, e.g., domestic violence
At least 1 previous conviction	Identified through police/court records
5+ convictions	Number of convictions (official records), not times in court
Previous prison	At least one previous prison sentence
Violence, general, not domestic violence:	
Physical violence in general (not domestic violence.)	ID through offending and/or convict/s for violence (not domestic violence)
Conviction for minor assault	As in English and Scottish Law
Conviction for serious assault	As in English and Scottish Law
Professionals involved as adult:	
Social services	Social work involved with perpetrator
Medical Health	Medical Health services to perpetrator
Psychological/psychiatric	Psychological/psychiatric service to perpetrator
Police	Police involved with perpetrator
Probation	Probation of perpetrator
Type murder:	MM, IPM, SexM, OWoM [male-male; Intimate Partner Murder, SexMurder, Murder of Older Women
Age at time of murder	age at murder

* GCSE = General Certificate of Standard Education obtained through national exam at age 16.

*CIRCUMSTANCES AT TIME OF MURDER AND MURDER EVENT

Variable	Definition
Perpetrator at time of murder:	
Employed at time of murder	Employed at time of murder
Relationship at time of murder:	
Married	married
Cohabiting	permanent relationship involving co-residence
Serious rel, not co-residing	serious boyfriend/girlfriend, not residing together usually a sexual relationship
Separated at time of murder	previous partners, now separated
Conflict and violence in relationship:	
Ongoing dispute between perp and victim	Dispute/conflict of some duration
Previous viol.—perpetrator to victim	Info from relatives, friends, neighbors, victim's coworkers
Prevous viol.—victim.to.perpetrator	(account solely from perp. not usually accepted without corroboration)
Circumstances at murder event:	
Confrontation-before murder	Recorded in police records of interviews w/ offender & others
Jealousy/possessive	As above
Separated	As above
Drinking/drugs at murder	As above + forensic report
Drugs (offender) at murder	As above + forensic report
Professionals involved as adult:	
Social services	Social work involved with perpetrator
Medical	Health services to perpetrator
Psychiatric/psychological	Psych/psychiatric service to perpetrator
Police	Police involved with perpetrator
Probation	Probation of perpetrator
Alcohol and/or Drugs:	
Drinking (offender)	had been drinking but not drunk
Drunk (offender)	drunk
Drinking (victim)	had been drinking but not drunk
Drunk (victim)	drunk
Location and method of killing:	
In/near house of vic. &/or perp.	House, lawn, nearby street
Strangle	
Instrument used	usually club, brick, bat, or knife (rarely a gun)
Five or more injuries	five or more injuries in murder
Sexual attack in murder	murder contained a sexual element
Responses during and after murder:	
Emotion—anger/rage reported by murderer	

*IN PRISON-BEHAVIOR OF OFFENDER AND PROFESSIONAL ASSESSMENTS

Variable	Definition
Behavior in prison:	
"Model" prisoner	Settled, cooperates with staff, assoc. with inmates, participates on progs., few/no discipline probs.
Ever on discipline report	report for infraction of prison rules
Ten or more discipline reports	10+ reports for infraction of prison rules
Assessments of professionals:	
Mental health problems	assessed by medical &/or psych. staff
Reports-at risk of self-harm	as above
Concern-risk to public safety	assessed by prison, psychology, probation staff, & parole review panels
Concern-dangerousness	as above
Offender orientation to victim & murder	as above
No remorse for murder	Assessed throughout prison sentence in interviews with prison, psychology, & probation staff
No empathy with victim	as above
Problems with women	as above + earlier assessments by others [as above]

I.4. NUD*IST/QSR—NODES/CATEGORIES (QUALITATIVE DATA FROM CASEFILES AND INTERVIEWS)

-*Casefiles: text typed into Word documents, then coded and converted to Nud*ist/ qsr Nodes,*
-*Interviews: tape-recorded, typed into Word documents, then coded and converted to Nodes*

NODES—Main Nodes (whole numbers in bold) followed by sub-nodes (further sub-nodes not specified)

(1).....................**/Murder Type**..
(1 1)...................**/Murder Type/Male Offender-intimate partner victim**
(1 1 1)   /Murder Type/M-intimate/Intimate
(1 1 2)   /Murder Type/M-intimate/Collateral
(1 1 3)   /Murder Type/M-intimate/Contract
(1 1 4)   /Murder Type/M-intimate/Family
(1 1 5)   /Murder Type/M-intimate/Same Sex
(1 2).................. **/Murder Type/Male Offender-other victim**
(1 2 1)   /Murder Type/M-other/Alcohol-drugs
(1 2 2)   /Murder Type/M-other/Property
(1 2 3)   /Murder Type/M-other/Public Order
(1 2 4)   /Murder Type/M-other/Public Order Gangs groups
(1 2 5)   /Murder Type/M-other/Business
(1 2 6)   /Murder Type/M-other/Elderly
(1 2 7)   /Murder Type/M-other/Relative
(1 2 8)   /Murder Type/M-other/ friend.acquaintance.neighbor
(1 2 9)   /Murder Type/M-other/Contract
(1 3).................. **/Murder Type/Male Offender-child victim**
(1 3 1)   /Murder Type/M-child/Intimate
(1 3 2)   /Murder Type/M-child/ friend.acquaintance.neighbor
(1 3 3)   /Murder Type/M-child/Stranger
(1 3 4)   /Murder Type/M-child/Sex-intimate
(1 3 5)   /Murder Type/M-child/Sex-friend.acquaintance.neighbor
(1 3 6)   /Murder Type/M-child/Sex-strangers
(1 4).................. **/Murder Type/Male Offender-sexual murder**
(1 4 1)   /Murder Type/M-sex/Heterosexual-intimate
(1 4 2)   /Murder Type/M-sex/Heterosexual-friend.acquaintance.
(1 4 3)   /Murder Type/M-sex/Heterosexual-stranger
(1 4 4)   /Murder Type/M-sex/Same Sex-male-male
(1 5)   /Murder Type/M-misc
(1 6)...................**/Murder Type/Female Offender-intimate partner victim**
(1 6 1)   /Murder Type/F-intimate/Intimate
(1 6 2)   /Murder Type/F-intimate/Collateral
(1 6 3)   /Murder Type/F-intimate/Contract
(1 6 4)   /Murder Type/F-intimate/Family

(1 6 5)   /Murder Type/F-intimate/Same Sex
(1 7)....................../Murder Type/Female Offender—other victim
(1 7 1)   /Murder Type/F—other/Alcohol.drugs
(1 7 2)   /Murder Type/F—other/Property
(1 7 3)   /Murder Type/F—other/Public   Order
(1 7 4)   /Murder Type/F—other/Public Order-gangs
(1 7 5)   /Murder Type/F—other/Business
(1 7 6)   /Murder Type/F—other/Elderly
(1 7 7)   /Murder Type/F—other/Relative
(1 7 8)   /Murder Type/F—other/Contract
(1 8)....................../Murder Type/Female Offender-child victim
(1 8 1)   /Murder Type/F-child/Intimate
(1 8 2)   /Murder Type/F-child/ friend.acquaintance.neighbor
(1 8 3)   /Murder Type/F-child/Stranger
(1 8 4)   /Murder Type/F-child/Sex-intimate
(1 8 5)   /Murder Type/F-child/Sex-friend.acquaintance.neighbor
(1 8 6)   /Murder Type/F-child/Sex-stranger
(1 9)....................../Murder Type/F-sex
(1 9 1)   /Murder Type/F-sex/Heterosexual-familial
(1 9 2)   /Murder Type/F-sex/Heterosexual-friend.acquaintance.neighbor
(1 9 3)   /Murder Type/F-sex/Heterosexual—stranger
(1 9 4)   /Murder Type/F-sex/Same Sex
(1 10)   /Murder Type/F-misc
(2)....................../base data...
(2 1)................. /base data/Perpetrator gender
(2 1 1)   /base data/Perp gender/male
(2 1 2)   /base data/Perp gender/female
(2 2)   /base data/Perp age
(2 2 1)   /base data/Perp age/0-15 yrs
(2 2 2)   /base data/Perp age/16-19
(2 2 3)   /base data/Perp age/20-24
(2 2 4)   /base data/Perp age/25-29
(2 2 5)   /base data/Perp age/30-39
(2 2 6)   /base data/Perp age/40-49
(2 2 7)   /base data/Perp age/50-59
(2 2 8)   /base data/Perp age/60-69
(2 2 9)   /base data/Perp age/70-79
(2 2 10)   /base data/Perp age/80+
(2 3)..................../base data/Victim gender
(2 3 1)   /base data/Vic gender/male
(2 3 2)   /base data/Vic gender/female vic
(2 4)..................../base data/Victim age
(2 4 1)   /base data/Vic age/0-15
(2 4 2)   /base data/Vic age/16-19

(2 4 3)	/base data/Vic age/20-24
(2 4 4)	/base data/Vic age/25-29
(2 4 5)	/base data/Vic age/30-39
(2 4 6)	/base data/Vic age/40-49
(2 4 7)	/base data/Vic age/50-59
(2 4 8)	/base data/Vic age/60-69
(2 4 9)	/base data/Vic age/70-79
(2 4 10)	/base data/Vic age/80+
(2 5)	/base data/Data source
(2 5 1)	/base data/Data source/Casefile
(2 5 2)	/base data/Data source/Interviews
(3)....................**/One liners**......**(brief description of each case)**........................
(4-9)	/Blank
(10)....................**/Childhood**...
(10 1)	/Childhood/Living Arrangements; Rels with Parents-Family-Others
(10 2)	/Childhood/Problems & Responses to them
(10 3)	/Childhood/Description of person-personality
(11)....................**/Adulthood**...
(11 1)	/Adulthood/Relationships, family, friends
(11 2)	/Adulthood/Problems & Responses to them
(11 3)	/Adulthood/Description of person-personality
(12)....................**/Sexual Identity-practices [Child-Adult]**.............................
(12 1)	/Sexual Identity-practices [Child-Adult]/Orientation
(13)....................**/Alcohol-drugs**...
(13 1)	/Alcohol-drugs/Child
(13 2)	/Alcohol-drugs/Adulthood
(14)....................**/Previous Physical Violence [behavior & offending]**.................
(14 1)	/Previous Phys. Violence [beh. & offending]/CHILD Perp
(14 2)	/Previous Phys. Violence [beh. & offending]/ADULT Perp
(14 3)	/Previous Phys. Violence [beh. & offending]/orientations, attitudes
(15)....................**/Previous Sexual Violence [behavior & offending]**.....................
(15 1)	/Previous Sexual Violence [beh. & offending]/CHILD Perp
(15 2)	/Previous Sexual Violence [beh. & offending]/ADULT Perp
(15 3)	/Previous Sexual Violence [beh. & offending]/orientations, attitudes
(16)....................**/Previous Other-Property Crime [behavior & offending]**........
(16 1)	/Previous Other-Property Crime [beh. & offending]/CHILD Perp
(16 2)	/Previous Other-Property Crime [beh. & offending]/ADULT Perp
(16 3)	/Previous Other-Property Crime [beh. & offending]/orientations, attitudes
(17)....................**/Murder—context**..
(17 1)	/Murder—context/Context-Immediate Circumstances

(18)...................../**Murder—event**..

(18 1)   /Murder—event/Immediately After

(18 2)   /Murder—event/Explanations, Motivations, Why Kill

(19)...................../**Perpetrator-Victim Relationship**..

(20)...................../**Victim [Personal Characteristics]**..

(21)...................../**Murder, Orientations-Reflections**...

(21 1)   /Murder, Orientations-Reflections/by Others

(22)...................../**Murder, Legal Processes**...

(23)......................**Prison**..

(23 1)   /Prison/Drink-Drugs

(23 2)   /Prison/Violence

(23 3)   /Prison/Other Problems

(23 4)   /Prison/Programs, Training, Education

(23 5)   /Prison/Staff-Officers

(24)...................../**Professional Evaluation from**..

(24 1)   / Psychiatry

(24 2)   / Psychology

(24 3)   / Social Work

(24 4)   / Legal

(24 5)   / Prison

(24 6)   / Probation

(24 7)   / Medical

(25)...................../**Orientations about Other Groups & People**................................

MURDER STUDY—CASEFILES

II.1 Casefiles—Achieved Sample of All Murders, n = 866 (786 male perpetrators and 80 female perpetrators)

II.2 Casefiles—All Murders of Women by Men (n = 271)

II.3 Casefiles—Three Types of Murder of Women by Men, n = 243: Intimate Partner (n = 105), Sexual Murder (n = 98), Murder of Older Women (n = 40)

II.1 CASEFILES—ACHIEVED SAMPLE OF ALL MURDERS, N = 866

786 Male Perpetrators and 80 Female Perpetrators

	Male Perpetrators	Female perpetrators	Total
Victims:	..	..	..
Male-adult >16 yrs	424**	43	467
Male child <16 yrs	36	5	41
...			
Female-adult >16 yrs	271***	24	296
Female-child <16 yrs	55	3	58
TOTAL	786*	75 + (5 missing data)	866

Note: Comparison of the achieved sample of the Casefile data-set and the national Homicide Index for England/Wales (which includes both Murder and Manslaughter) indicates similar patterns between the variables that can be compared, e.g., age, gender, and relationship.

* 786 male perpetrators includes 612 from England/Wales and 174 from Scotland.
**All Men Who Murder Men (n = 424)
*** All Men Who Murder Women (n = 271)

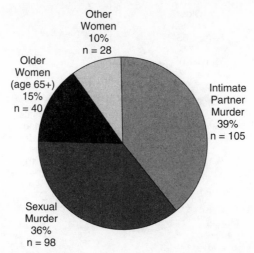

Appx.III-Figure 2.2 Casefiles—All Women Murdered by Men, Total, n = 271*

II.2 CASEFILES—ALL WOMEN MURDERED BY MEN, TOTAL, N = 271

Intimate Partner Murder, n = 105; Sexual Murder, n = 98; Murder of Older Women, n = 40; Total, n = 243

Twenty-eight women were not included because they were not an intimate partner, there was no sexual attack in the murder, or they were not over age 65.

Details of 28 women not included in the three types:

  Twelve Intimate Partner Collaterals (IPC), women under age 65 and with no sex in the murder (three friends/acq./protectors and nine relatives/protectors inc. mothers, sisters, mothers-in-law)
  Sixteen women under age 65 and with no sex in the murder (10 short acquaintances; 4 neighbors/friends; and 2 business acquaintances)

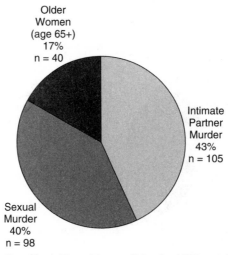

Older
Women
(age 65+)
17%
n = 40

Intimate
Partner
Murder
43%
n = 105

Sexual
Murder
40%
n = 98

Appx.II-Figure 2.3 Casefiles—Three Types of Murder of Women by Men, Total, n = 243* — (in Ch.1 & Appx.II)

II.3 CASEFILES—THREE TYPES OF MURDER OF WOMEN BY MEN, TOTAL, N = 243*

Three Types of Murder of Women by Men: Intimate Partner Murder (n = 105); Sexual Murder (n = 98); Older Women (n = 40), Total n = 243*.

* Twenty-eight women were not included because they did not fit into the three types in Figure II.2.

APPENDIX III

INTIMATE PARTNER MURDER (IPM)
(for chapters 3–4)

MALE-MALE AND INTIMATE PARTNER MURDER

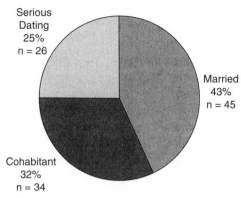

Appx.III-Figure 3.0 IPM—Relationship Between Perpetrators and Victims.

Appx.III-Table 3.1 IPM—Circumstances at Murder: Male-Male and
                       Intimate Partner Murder

Circumstances at Time of Murder	MM n = 424 (%)	IPM n = 105 (%)	P Value	Odds Ratio
Age & Employment at Murder				
Offender mean age at murder (range)*	26.9 yrs	34.2 yrs	.000	NA
Victim mean age at murder (range)**	40.1 yrs	31.3 yrs	.000	NA
Employed at time of murder	32.2%	48.5%	.002	1.994
Perpetrator—Relationship at Murder				
Single	48.8	NA	–	–
Married	10.8	43	–	–
Cohabiting	15.2	32	–	–
Dating/not coresiding	6.7	25	–	–
Separated/divorced***	18.1	[see note]	–	–
Viol. in rel. at time of murder^^	26.1	61.6	.000	6.069
Perp.-Victim Rel. at Murder (MM only)				
Stranger	31.3	NA	–	–
Acquaintance	38.9	NA	–	–
Neighbor	3.8	NA	–	–
Friend	15.0	NA	–	–
Relative	9.0	NA	–	–
Same Sex Intimate Rel, (MM only)	3.0	NA	–	–
Circumstances at Murder				
Conflict/Viol Between Offender & Victim				
Ongoing dispute—offender & victim	29.8	71.4	.000	5.853
Previous violence, *offender* to victim	10.6	59.0	.000	11.726
Previous violence, *victim* to offender	10.6	5.9	.159	.535
Confrontation immediately before M.	61.1	74.0	.016	1.836
More than one perpetrator	42.7	5.8	.000	.082
More than one adult victim	5.9	3.9	.377	.618
Drinking/Drugs at Murder				
Drugs (offender)	19.4	8.4	.007	.362
Drinking (offender)	67.8	40.6	.000	.329
Drunk (offender)	49.4	20.8	.000	.272
Drinking (victim)	47.0	24.7	.000	.375
Drunk (victim)	33.4	11.3	.000	.255
Offender & victim drinking together	21.4	19.6	.695	.916
Location & Method of Killing				
In or near house of victim	50.0	89.4	.000	8.415
Strangle/choke/smother	7.1	35.6	.000	6.771
Instrument used^^^	88.4	75.2	.001	.415
Five or more injuries	70.5	64.2	.178	.735

(continued)

Appx.III-Table 3.1 CONTINUED

Circumstances at Time of Murder	MM n = 424 (%)	IPM n = 105 (%)	P Value	Odds Ratio
Prof. Involved at Time of Murder				
Social Services	6.3	9.2	.301	1.521
Medical	3.4	2.0	.496	.596
Psychiatric/psychological	4.2	2.0	.280	.451
Police	13.2	11.1	.622	.840
Probation	10.4	5.1	.093	.449

* two tailed t test (perpetrator- age range MM = 14–69 yrs; IPM = 17–54 yrs)

** two tailed t test (victim- age range MM = 16–90 yrs; IPM = 16–56 yrs)

*** note: main type of rel. shown (marr/cohab/boy-girlFriend) but 37% of them were sep./div. at time of murder

^^ n=41/157 & 61/89

^^^ mostly ligatures, blunt instruments, clubs, knives, and very rarely guns

Appx.III-Table 4.1 IPM—CHILDHOOD: MALE-MALE AND INTIMATE
PARTNER MURDER

Problems in Childhood (pre-16)	MM n = 424 (%)	IPM n = 105 (%)	P Value	Odds Ratio
Problems of Parents & Family				
Broken relationship	41.2	29.3	.040	.597
Alcohol abuse by father	24.8	10.6	.005	.361
Criminal record of father	16.2	4.6	.005	.249
Poverty/disadvantage of family	18.2	11.2	.124	.575
Father violent to mother	23.1	11.3	.023	.431
Disrupted Caretaking				
3+ changes in carers	28.6	16.5	.015	.494
In care as child	23.2	12.5	.022	.474
Abused as a Child				
Physically abused	20.4	19.8	.943	.978
Sexually abused	9.5	4.7	.151	.466
Problems of the Child				
Problems at school	63.1	41.2	.000	.409
Disruptive behavior (pre-16)	42.8	30.1	.030	.569
Sexual problems (pre-16)	5.7	1.2	.078	.195
Mental health problems	13.4	12.8	.877	.948
Alcohol abuse (pre-16)	41.9	19.8	.000	.342
Drug abuse	33.2	13.5	.000	.315
Violence & Criminal Justice				
Onset of offending (pre-13)	20.7	12.7	.068	.560
Serious violence (pre-16)	15.5	9.0	.130	.551
Sexual violence (pre-16)	3.1	3.4	.758	1.228
Violence to animals as child	1.7	2.2	.721	1.341
5+ Convictions (pre-16)	22.7	12.2	.063	.540
Criminal justice institution (ever)	26.7	12.9	.008	.434
Involve Professional with Family				
Social services	44.4	19.6	.000	.304
Medical	16.7	14.3	.574	.831
Psychological/ Psychiatric	26.6	16.5	.045	.545
Police	50.7	26.4	.000	.353
Probation	24.9	16.5	.088	.594

Appx.III-Table 4.2 IPM—Adulthood: Male-Male and Intimate
Partner Murder

Adult Lifecourse	MM n = 424 (%)	IPM n = 105 (%)	P Value	Odds Ratio
Ethnicity*				
White/Anglo/European	89.9	87.4	.459	.779
Afro-Caribbean	5.2	5.8	.792	1.133
Asian, Indian subcontinent	3.5	5.8	.285	1.691
Education & Employment				
Left school before 16	56.6	50.5	.304	.795
GCSE** or above	27.9	40.2	.016	1.736
A level or higher (high school)	5.1	14.7	.001	3.218
Usually employed	28.4	49.5	.000	2.451
Problems as Adult				
Alcohol abuse	56.6	38.2	.001	.477
Drug abuse	35.4	14.9	.000	.316
Mental health problems	24.6	27.7	.513	1.179
Poverty(disadvantage) as adult	18.2	9.7	.044	.475
Sexual problems/issues	17.5	22.5	.235	1.378
Sexual violence/not domestic	9.1	8.9	.966	1.018
Family dysfunction as adult	25.7	34.0	.116	1.474
Intimate Relationships				
Breakdown of intimate rel(s)	60.8	76.8	.003	2.143
Viol. in previous intimate rel(s)***	30.8	69.8	.000	5.151
Sex abuse to prev. int. partner/s^^	4.0	13.1	.004	3.633
Criminal Behavior				
Persistent criminal behavior	80.5	60.2	.000	.370
Physical violence in general	45.5	27.7	.002	.456
At least 1 prev. conv. (all off.) #	85.0	76.0	.031	.566
5+ convictions (all offenses)	67.1	45.2	.000	.403
At least one conviction for:				
Minor assault (physical)	40.9	31.7	.089	.674
Serious assault (physical)	17.1	13.5	.369	.754
Serious sex assault (inc. rape)	7.7	2.9	.078	.355
If prev. conv. for assault (physical):				
Usual victim a woman	10.5	56.8	.000	11.156
Previous Prison	45.4	31.4	.010	.546
Professionals Involved as Adult				
Social Services	20.7	10.9	.028	.461
Medical	21.7	23.5	.691	1.113

(continued)

Appx.III-Table 4.2 CONTINUED

Adult Lifecourse	MM n = 424 (%)	IPM n = 105 (%)	P Value	Odds Ratio
Psychiatric/psychological	25.0	24.0	.802	.935
Sectioned/mandatory mental health	5.4	2.9	.291	.522
Police	77.9	62.4	.022	.475
Probation	33.8	21.4	.015	.524

* Numbers from other ethnic backgrounds are small and are not reported here
** GCSE— Gen. Certificate of Std. Educ., obtained through national examination at age 16
*** n=73/273 & 67/96
^^ n=9/225 & 11/84
# Aver. number of prev. convictions= MM = 17 prev.conv.; IPM = 10 prev.conv. (two tailed t test p = .001).

Appx.III-Table 4.3 IPM—Assessments in Prison: Male-Male
and Intimate Partner Murder

Behavior & Professional Assessments	MM n = 424 (%)	IPM n = 105 (%)	P Value	Odds Ratio
Behavior in prison				
Model prisoner	17.6	32.7	.001	2.281
Uncooperative w/ professionals	31.3	33.7	.679	1.103
Discipline report, at least one	83.3	65.7	.000	.384
Discipline reports, 10 or more	41.5	24.8	.002	.466
Assessments of professionals in prison				
Mental health problems	19.7	19.6	.999	1.000
Concern about risk to public safety	44.5	41.4	.596	.887
Concern about "dangerousness"	38.7	42.0	.560	1.141
Orientation to the victim and murder				
No remorse for murder	33.8	35.6	.719	1.069
No empathy with victim	43.2	48.5	.347	1.233
Problems with women	18.3	75.0	.000	13.479

APPENDIX IV

SEXUAL MURDER (SexM)

(for chapters 6–7)

MALE-MALE AND SEXUAL MURDER

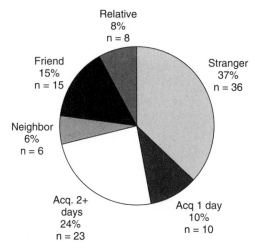

Appx.IV-**Figure 6.0**   SexM—Relationship Between Perpetrators and Victims.

Appx.IV-Table 6.1 SEXM—CIRCUMSTANCES AT MURDER: MALE-MALE
AND SEXUAL MURDER

Circumstances at Time of Murder	MM n = 424 (%)	SexM n = 98 (%)	P Value	Odds Ratio
Age & Employment at Murder				
Offender mean age at murder (range)*	26.9 yrs	29.2 yrs	.021	NA
Victim mean age at murder (range)**	40.1 yrs	31.4 yrs	.000	NA
Employed at time of murder	32.2%	44.8%	.020	1.771
Perpetrator—Relationship at Murder				
Single	48.4	40.8	.174	.734
Married	10.8	17.3	.076	1.726
Cohabiting	15.2	15.3	.975	1.010
Dating/not coresiding	6.7	4.1	.326	.588
Separated/divorced	18.1	21.4	.444	1.236
Viol. in int. rel. at time of murder	26.1 (n = 41/157)	46.0 (n = 21/46)	.002	2.472
Perpetrator-Victim, Rel. at Murder				
Stranger	31.3	36.7	.285	1.284
Acquaintance	38.9	33.7	.335	.797
Neighbor	3.8	6.1	.297	1.663
Friend	15.3	15.3	.995	.998
Relative	9.0	6.1	.362	.662
Same Sex Intimate Rel, (MM only)	3.0	NA		
Circumstances at murder				
Conflict/Viol. Between Offender & Victim				
Ongoing dispute between offender & victim	29.8	4.1	.000	.100
Previous violence, *offender* to victim	10.6	4.1	.047	.361
Previous violence, *victim* to offender	10.6	1.0	.003	.087
Confrontation immediately before M.	61.1	40.4	.000	.431
More than one perpetrator	42.7	8.2	.000	.119
More than one adult victim	5.9	10.3	.117	1.834
Drinking/Drugs at Murder				
Drugs (offender)	19.4	16.9	.582	.843
Drinking (offender)	67.8	74.2	.229	1.367
Drunk (offender)	49.4	50.5	.839	1.048
Drinking (victim)	47.0	44.6	.694	.908
Drunk (victim)	33.4	30.1	.564	.858
Offender & victim drinking together	21.4	33.0	.018	1.602

(continued)

Appx.IV-Table 6.1 CONTINUED

Circumstances at Time of Murder	MM n = 424 (%)	SexM n = 98 (%)	P Value	Odds Ratio
Location & Method of Killing				
In or near house of victim	50.0	57.7	.169	1.366
Strangle/choke/smother	7.1	53.1	.000	14.846
Instrument used***	88.4	72.6	.000	.350
Five or more injuries	70.5	70.4	.983	.995
Prof. Involved at Time of Murder				
Social Services	6.3	4.3	.473	.674
Medical	3.4	4.3	.655	1.297
Psychiatric/psychological	4.2	7.6	.167	1.894
Police	13.2	9.8	.368	.710
Probation	10.4	14.1	.301	1.423

* two tailed t test (perpetrator—age range MM = 14–69 yrs; SexM = 15–51 yrs)
** two tailed t test (victim—age range MM = 16–90 yrs; SexM = 16–64 yrs)
*** mostly ligatures, blunt instruments, clubs, knives, and very rarely involved guns

Appx.IV-Table 7.1 SEXM—CHILDHOOD: MALE-MALE AND SEXUAL MURDER

Problems in Childhood (pre16)	MM n = 424 (%)	SexM n = 98 (%)	P Value	Odds Ratio
Problems of Parents & Family				
Broken relationship	41.2	32.9	.150	.694
Alcohol abuse by father	24.8	15.7	.077	.564
Criminal record of father	16.2	17.1	.854	1.062
Poverty/disadvantage of family	18.2	13.3	.283	.686
Father violent to mother	23.1	17.1	.261	.688
Disrupted Caretaking				
3+ changes in carers	28.6	25.3	.510	.842
In care as child	23.2	18.5	.326	.750
Abused as Child				
Physically abused	20.4	27.7	.147	1.496
Sexually abused	9.5	13.1	.326	1.438
Problems of the Child				
Problems at school	63.1	69.4	.275	1.327
Disruptive behavior (pre-16)	42.8	44.4	.789	1.068
Sexual Problems (pre-16)	5.7	11.7	.056	2.930
Mental health problems	13.4	18.6	.215	1.477
Alcohol abuse (pre -16)	41.9	34.1	.192	.718
Drug abuse	33.2	19.5	.013	.488
Violence & Criminal Justice				
Onset of offending (pre-13)	20.7	19.6	.802	.931
Serious violence (pre-16)	15.5	22.9	.103	1.622
Sexual violence (pre-16)	3.1	7.4	.068	2.524
Violence to animals as child	1.7	2.4	NA	NA
5+ Convictions (pre-16)	22.7	21.3	.762	.919
Criminal justice institution (ever)	26.7	25.3	.773	.927
Involve Professional with Family				
Social services	44.4	42.0	.684	.907
Medical	16.7	17.0	.940	1.024
Psychological/ Psychiatric	26.6	32.2	.293	1.311
Police	50.7	48.3	.690	.910
Probation	24.9	31.0	.244	1.355

Appx.IV-Table 7.2 SᴇxM—Aᴅᴜʟᴛʜᴏᴏᴅ: Mᴀʟᴇ-Mᴀʟᴇ ᴀɴᴅ Sᴇxᴜᴀʟ Mᴜʀᴅᴇʀᴇʀ

Adult Lifecourse	MM n = 424 (%)	SexM n = 98 (%)	P Value	Odds Ratio
Ethnicity*				
White/Anglo/European	89.9	92.9	.363	1.467
Afro-Caribbean	5.2	6.1	.712	1.192
Asian, Indian subcontinent	3.5	1.0	.193	.281
Education & Employment	–	–	–	–
Left school before 16	56.6	52.6	.477	.851
GCSE** or above	27.9	26.8	.826	.946
A level or higher (high school)	5.1	8.2	.228	1.674
Usually employed	28.4	42.9	.008	1.893
Problems as Adult	–	–	–	–
Alcohol abuse	56.6	60.3	.448	1.117
Drug abuse	35.4	26.3	.071	.653
Mental health problems	24.6	26.9	.650	1.126
Poverty (disadvantage) as adult	18.2	7.1	.012	.341
Sexual problems/issues	17.5	72.6	.000	12.497
Sexual violence/not domestic	9.1	31.8	.000	4.670
Family dysfunction as adult	25.7	26.9	.822	1.061
Intimate Relationships	–	–	–	–
Breakdown of intimate relationship(s)	60.8	64.3	.562	1.158
Viol in previous intimate rel.***	30.8	43.5	.050	1.760
Sex abuse to prev. intimate partner/s^^	4.0	12.5	.011	3.413
Criminal Behavior	–	–	–	–
Persistent criminal behavior	80.5	77.1	.447	.812
Physical violence in general	45.5	42.9	.652	.899
At least 1 prev.conv. (all offenses) #	85.0	79.6	.187	.687
5+ convictions (all offenses)	67.1	64.3	.589	.881
At least one conviction for:	–	–	–	<>
Minor assault (physical)	40.9	37.8	.566	.876
Serious assault (physical)	17.1	19.4	.601	1.162
Sexual assault (inc. rape)	7.7	21.4	.000	3.247
If prev. conv. for assault (physical):	–	–	–	–
Usual victim a woman	10.5	55.6	.000	10.625
Previous Prison	45.4	47.9	.661	1.105
Professionals Involved as Adult	–	–	–	–
Social Services	20.7	22.7	.675	1.127
Medical	21.7	22.2	.907	1.034
Psychiatric/psychological	25.0	37.5	.018	1.800
Sectioned/mandatory mental health	5.4	11.3	.021	2.207
Police	77.9	71.0	.154	.693
Probation	33.8	41.8	.153	1.406

* Numbers from other ethnic backgrounds are small and are not reported here
** GCSE—Gen. Certificate of Std. Educ., obtained through national examination at age 16
*** n=73/237 & 30/69
^^ n=9/225 & 11/64
#Average number of previous convictions = MM = 17 prev.convictions; SexM = 16 prev.convictions. (2 tailed t test p = ns)

Appx.IV-Table 7.3 SexM—Assessments in Prison: Male-Male
and Sexual Murder

Behavior & Professional Assessments	MM Murder n = 424 (%)	Sex Murder n = 98 (%)	P Value	Odds Ratio
Behavior in prison				
Model prisoner	17.6	21.3	.405	1.266
Uncooperative w/ professionals	31.3	40.6	.083	1.499
Discipline report, at least 1	83.3	77.6	.184	.695
Discipline reports, 10 or more	41.5	32.7	.107	.683
Assessments of professionals in prison	–	–	–	–
Mental health problems	19.7	25.0	.245	1.363
Concern about risk to public safety	44.5	81.3	.000	5.411
Concern about "dangerousness"	38.7	72.9	.000	4.270
Orientation to the victim and murder	–	–	–	–
No remorse for murder	33.8	50.5	.002	1.737
No Empathy with victim	43.2	68.8	.000	2.895
Problems with women	18.3	86.6	.000	28.944

APPENDIX V

MURDER OF OLDER WOMEN (OWoM)

(for chapters 9–10)

MALE-MALE & MURDER OF OLDER WOMEN

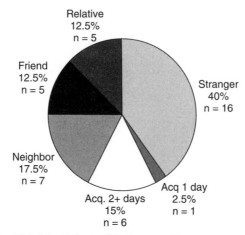

Appx.V-Figure 9.0 OWoM—Relationship Between Perpetrators and Victims.

Appx.V-Table 9.1 OWoM—Circumstances at Murder: Male-Male and Murder of Older Women

Circumstances at Time of Murder	MM n = 424 (%)	OWoM n = 40 (%)	P Value	Odds Ratio
Age & Employment at Murder				
Offender mean age at murder (range)*	26.9yrs	29.8yrs	.058	NA
Victim mean age at murder (range)**	40.1yrs	74.6yrs	NA	NA
Employed at time of murder	32.2%	27.5%	.532	.794
Perpetrator—Relationship at Murder				
Single	48.8	47.5	.911	.964
Married	10.8	15.0	.433	1.443
Cohabiting	15.2	7.5	.184	1.159
Dating/not coresiding	6.7	7.5	.815	1.159
Separated/divorced	18.1	22.5	.500	1.308
Viol. in intimate rel. at time of murder***	26.1	23.5	.071	2.493
Perpetrator-Victim, Rel. at Murder				
Stranger	31.3	40.0	.232	1.429
Acq.	38.9	17.5	.007	.330
Neighbor	3.8	17.5	.000	5.383
Friend	15.3	12.5	.625	.785
Relative	9.0	12.5	.467	1.444
Same Sex Intimate Rel, (MM only)	3.0	NA		
Circumstances at Murder				
Conflict/Viol. Between Offender & Vic.				
Ongoing dispute—offender & victim	29.8	7.5	.003	.190
Previous violence, *offender* to victim	10.6	0.0	.030	.903
Previous violence, *victim* to offender	10.6	0.0	.030	.903
Confrontation immediately before M.	61.1	20.5	.000	.165
More than one perpetrator	42.7	10.0	.000	.149
More than one adult victim	5.9	2.5	.590	.407
Drinking/Drugs at Murder				
Drugs (offender)	19.4	18.9	.963	.980
Drinking (offender)	67.8	52.6	.058	.526
Drunk (offender)	49.4	36.8	.141	.599
Drinking (victim)	47.0	2.6	.000	.030
Drunk (victim)	33.4	2.6	.000	.052
Offender & victim drinking together	21.4	2.7	.006	.112
Location & Method of Killing				
In or near house of victim	50.0	87.5	.000	7.000
Strangle/choke/smother	7.8	25.6	.000	4.052
Instrument used^^	88.4	72.5	.005	.349
Five or more injuries	70.5	82.5	.105	1.984
Prof. Involved at Time of Murder				
Social Services	6.3	8.1	.666	1.316
Medical	3.4	8.1	.154	2.505
Psychiatric/psychological	4.2	5.4	.727	1.307
Police	13.2	21.6	.134	1.880
Probation	10.4	18.9	.117	2.007

* two tailed t test (perpetrator- age range MM = 14-69yrs; OlderWomen = 15-49yrs)

** two tailed t test (victim- age range MM = 16-90yrs; OlderWomen = 65-89yrs)

*** n=41/157 & 8/17

^^ mostly ligatures, blunt instruments, clubs, knives, no guns were used in OWoMs

Appx.V-Table 10.1 OWoM—CHILDHOOD: MALE-MALE AND MURDER
OF OLDER WOMEN

Problems in Childhood (pre-16)	MM n = 424 (%)	OWoM n = 40 (%)	P value	Odds ratio
Problems of Parents & Family				
Broken relationship	41.2	44.4	.723	1.133
Alcohol abuse by father	24.8	21.2	.662	.824
Criminal record of father	16.2	20.0	.547	1.308
Poverty/disadvantage of family	18.2	11.4	.309	.576
Father violent to mother	23.1	31.3	.286	1.537
Disrupted Caretaking				
3+ changes in carers	28.6	23.1	.469	.751
In care as child	23.2	18.4	.513	.753
Abused as Child				
Physically abused	20.4	20.0	.974	.986
Sexually abused	9.5	11.1	.761	1.186
Problems of the Child (pre-16)				
Problems at school	63.1	71.4	.316	1.475
Disruptive behavior (pre-16)	42.8	45.7	.738	1.126
Sexual problems	5.7	6.5	.867	1.136
Mental health problems	13.4	11.8	.811	.876
Alcohol abuse	41.9	45.2	.720	1.145
Drug abuse	33.2	13.5	.014	.315
Violence & Criminal Justice (pre-16)				
Onset of offending (pre-13)	20.7	20.0	.930	.964
Serious violence	15.5	22.9	.263	1.608
Sexual violence	3.1	5.7	.409	1.901
Violence to animals as child	1.7	0.0	NA	NA
5+ Convictions (pre-16)	22.7	21.1	.828	.914
Criminal justice institution (ever)	26.7	25.6	.965	1.017
Involve Professional w/Family				
Social services	44.4	41.7	.775	.904
Medical	16.7	20.0	.631	1.238
Psychological/Psychiatric	26.6	25.7	.925	.963
Police	50.7	50.0	.939	.974
Probation	24.9	21.6	.669	.837

NB: serious physical health problem MM = 8.5%, OWoM = 18.9%, P = .039, Odds = 2.503

Appx.V-Table 10.2 OWoM—Adulthood: Male-Male and Murder
of Older Women

Adult Lifecourse	MM n = 424 (%)	OWoM n = 40 (%)	P Value	Odds Ratio
Ethnicity*				
White/Anglo/European	89.9	87.5	.647	.794
Afro-Carribbean	5.2	7.5	.541	1.474
Asian, Indian –subcontinent	3.5	2.5	.727	.696
Education & Employment				
Left school before 16	56.6	66.7	.225	1.471
GCSE** or above	27.9	25.0	.681	.855
A level or higher (high school)	5.1	0.0	.241	.907
Usually employed	28.4	26.3	.773	.895
Problems as Adult				
Alcohol abuse	56.6	62.2	.500	1.269
Drug abuse	35.4	24.3	.189	.596
Mental health problems	24.6	35.1	.167	1.648
Poverty (disadvantage) as adult	18.2	3.1	.029	.144
Sexual problems/issues	17.5	51.3	.000	4.937
Sexual violence/not domestic	9.1	29.4	.000	4.153
Family dysfunction as adult	25.7	28.6	.729	1.146
Intimate Relationships				
Breakdown of intimate relationship(s)	60.8	71.4	.285	1.584
Viol in previous intimate rel.***	30.8	38.5	.433	1.396
Sex abuse to prev. intimate partner/s^^	4.0	4.2	.975	1.034
Criminal Behavior				
Persistent criminal behavior	80.5	84.2	.574	1.296
Physical violence in general	45.5	38.9	.468	.772
At least 1 prev.conv.(all offenses)#	85.0	90.0	.388	1.594
5+ convictions (all offenses)	67.1	62.5	.565	.821
At least one conviction for:	–	–	–	–
Minor assault (physical)	40.9	32.5	.316	.703
Serious assault (physical)	17.1	7.5	.112	.389
Serious sex assault (inc. rape)	7.7	17.5	.037	2.512
If previous conviction for physical assault:	–	–	–	–
Usual victim a woman	10.5	60.0	.000	13.730
Previous Prison	45.4	62.5	.039	2.004
Professionals Involved as Adult				
Social Services	20.7	16.2	.532	.749
Medical	21.7	27.0	.464	1.331
Psychiatric/psychological	25.0	34.3	.237	1.554
Sectioned/mandatory mental health	5.4	20.5	.000	4.457
Police	77.9	75.4	.766	.887
Probation	33.8	43.2	.244	1.500

* Numbers from other ethnic backgrounds are small and are not reported here
** GCSE—Gen. Certificate of Std. Educ., obtained through national examination at age 16
*** n=73/237 & 10/26
^^ n=9/225 & 1/25
#Average number of previous convictions = MM = 17; OlderWo = 16 prev.convictions.
(2 tailed t test p = ns).

Appx.V-Table 10.3 OWoM—ASSESSMENTS IN PRISON: MALE-MALE AND
MURDER OF OLDER WOMEN

Behavior & Professional Assessments	MM n = 424 (%)	OWoM n = 40 (%)	P Value	Odds Ratio
Behavior in prison				
Model prisoner	17.6	2.5	.013	.119
Uncooperative w/ professionals	31.3	47.5	.034	2.014
Discipline report, at least one	83.3	75.0	.194	.607
Discipline reports, 10 or more	41.5	45.0	.644	1.166
Assessments of professionals in prison	–	–	–	–
Mental health problems	19.7	35.9	.018	2.275
Concern about risk to public safety	44.5	70.0	.002	2.888
Concern about "dangerousness"	38.7	66.7	.001	3.179
Orientation to the victim and murder	–	–	–	–
No remorse for murder	33.8	51.3	.029	1.929
No empathy with victim	43.2	71.1	.001	3.235
Problems with women	18.3	61.5	.000	7.123

CHAPTER 1

1. Smith M.D. & Zahn, 1999; Liem & Pridemore, 2013; UNODC, United Nations Office of Drugs and Crime, 2013:13.
2. UNODC, 2011.
3. Verkko, Veli, 1951, cited in Kivivuori, Savolainen, & Danielsson, 2013:96.
4. For France, see Mucchielli, 2012; For England/Wales, see Soothill & Francis, 2013. NB: the figure for the United Kingdom in Table 1.1 includes Scotland as well as England/Wales.
5. Federal Bureau of Investigation, 2012, Table 13, "Murder Circumstances."
6. Wolfgang, 1957; Wolfgang & Ferracuti, 1967.
7. Smit, de Jong, & Bijleveld, 2013; Marshall, I.H. & Summers, 2013.
8. Smit, de Jong, & Bijleveld, 2013.
9. Riedel, 1999.
10. Langford, Isaac, & Kabat, 1998; Riedel, 1999; Flewelling & Williams, 1999.
11. Langford et al., 1998.
12. Langford et al., 1998.
13. Federal Bureau of Investigation, 2012.
14. Soothill & Frances, 2012.
15. Paulozzi et al., 2004.
16. Kivivuori, Savolainen, & Danielsson, 2013. See also, Smith, M.D. & Zahn, 1999; Heitmeyer & Hagan, 2003.
17. Messner & Rosenfeld, 1999.
18. For the United States, see Liebow, 1967; Anderson, 1990. For male culture and violence in societies in South America and Latin America and a Latino culture in the United States, see Descola, 1996; Lancaster, 1992; Bourgois, 1995. For Europe, see Spierenburg, 1998.
19. Corzine, Huff-Corzine, & Whitt, 1999.
20. Wolfgang, 1957.
21. Luckenbill, 1977.
22. Luckenbill, 1977:183.
23. For a critical assessment of "victim precipitation," see Dobash, R. E., & Dobash, 1984; Rock, 1998. See also Polk & Ranson (1991), who question the applicability of this perspective to the killing of children, and Jurik & Winn, 1990; Jurik & Gregware, 1992, on homicides by women.

24. Soothill et al., 2002; Reaves, 2006.
25. Parker & Averhahn, 1999.
26. Bye, 2013:240.
27. Bye, 2013:240.
28. For classic statements, see Moffitt, 1993; Farrington & Loeber, 2000; Laub & Sampson, 2003.
29. Dobash, R. P., et al., 2007.
30. Dobash, R. P., et al., 2007.
31. Silverman & Kennedy, 1987.
32. Polk, 1994:20–21.
33. Polk, 1994:20–21.
34. Toch, 1969.
35. Sykes & Matza, 1957; Bandura, 1991; Dobash & Dobash, 2011.
36. Wilbanks, 1982:151; Wilson, 1993a:5, 1993b.
37. Toch, 1969; Chimbos, 1978.
38. For 1980s research on the murder of women, see Daly & Wilson, 1988; Block, 1988; Mercy & Saltzman, 1989.
39. For 1990s commentary and research on the murder of women, see Gartner, 1990; Jurik & Winn, 1990; Radford & Russell, 1992; Campbell, 1992; Browne & Williams, 1993; Polk, 1994; Websdale, 1999.
40. Dobash, R. E., & Dobash, 2004; Brookman, 2005; Adams, 2007.
41. Dobash, R. E., & Dobash, 1979: Appendix C: "The Study," 250–261.
42. For example, see Dobash, R. E., & Dobash, 1992; Schlesinger et al., 1992; Dobash, R. P., Carnie, & Waterhouse, 1993; Dobash, R. P., et al., 1999; Dobash, R. P., et al., 2000.
43. Dobash, R. E., & Dobash, 1979:26–29; Dobash, R. P., & Dobash, 1983; Dobash, R. E. & Dobash,1998.
44. Weber, 1949:67–79.
45. For recent attempts at constructing general theories of violence see the volume edited by Eisner & Karstedt, 2009.
46. For the legal aspects of a "life sentence" for "murder," see Ashworth & Mitchell, 2000; Padfield, 2002.
47. See Parole Board, 2008, for information about parole. For offender programs, see HM Prison Service, 2014.
48. Ashworth & Mitchell, 2000.
49. For further details, see Lewis, et al., 2003; Dobash, R. P., et al., 2004:589–590. Comparisons of the intensive casefile dataset and the extensive Homicide Index indicated that they are similar in terms of variables that can be compared which increases confidence in the generalizability of findings from the casefiles. Comparisons of the casefile dataset for men with each of 5years (1991–1995) of the Homicide Index for England/Wales (including figures for both murder and manslaughter) reveal many similarities (see Cotton, 2003). The period 1991–1995 was selected for comparison because the vast majority of the murders in the casefile dataset occurred during or before those years. For details see Dobash, R. E., et al. 2007.
50. www.qsrinternational.com; Richards, 2006.
51. Lewis et al., 2003.
52. For findings about the murder of children from the Murder Study, see Cavanagh, Dobash, & Dobash, 2005, 2007.

Chapter 2

1. Jones, 1980; Browne, 1987; Jurick & Winn, 1990.
2. See Martin, 1976; Dobash, R. E. & Dobash, 1979, 1992; Russell, 1992; Schechter, 1982; Pence & Paymar, 1983.
3. Cooper & Smith, E. L. 2011.
4. Violence Policy Center, 2011.
5. Violence Policy Center, 2000, 2011:6.
6. Violence Policy Center, 2011.
7. Cooper & Smith, E.L., 2011; Soothill & Francis, 2013.
8. Soothill & Francis, 2013; see Miles, 2012, for a discussion of the limitations of the Homicide Index, England/Wales on estimates of alcohol abuse among homicide offenders.
9. Liem & Pridemore, 2013.
10. Marshall, I. H., & Summers, 2013; Smit, de Jong, & Bijleveld, 2013.
11. For various countries, see for example—Netherlands, Gampat & Liem, 2013; Finland, Lehti & Kivivuori, 2013; Germany, Birkel & Dern, 2013; Sweden, Granath, 2013; and Switzerland, Markwalder, & Killias, 2013.
12. Stockl et al., 2013.
13. Wallace, 1986; Daly & Wilson, 1988a; Johnson & Chisholm, 1989; Carcash, 1998; Violence Policy Center, 2011.
14. Daly and Wilson, 1988a.
15. Wilson & Daly, 1992.
16. Wilson & Daly, 1992; Websdale, 1999.
17. Fox & Zawitz, 2007.
18. Dugan, Nagin, & Rosenfeld, 1999, 2003.
19. Wilson, Johnson, & Daly, 1995; Wilson & Daly, 1998.
20. Shackelford & Mouzos, 2005.
21. Dawson & Gartner, 1998; Johnson & Hotton, 2003; Miethe & Regoeczi, 2004.
22. Dawson & Gartner, 1998.
23. Dobash, R. E., et al., 2007, Table 3.
24. Dawson & Gartner, 1998; Brownridge & Halli, 2002; Shackelford & Mouzos, 2005.
25. Dobash, R. E., et al., 2007.
26. Wilson, Johnson & Daly, 1995; Wilson & Daly, 1998.
27. James, B. & Daly, 2012.
28. Wilson & Daly, 1998.
29. James, B. & Daly, 2012.
30. See for example Dobash, R. E., & Dobash, 1979; Dobash, R. P., et al., 2000; for an overview, see Basile & Black, 2011.
31. Daly & Wilson, 1988a.
32. Daly, Wilson, & Weghorst, 1982; Daly & Wilson, 1988a, 1988b.
33. For an overview, see Wilson & Daly, 1998:199–230.
34. Daly & Wilson, 1988a:296.
35. Polk, 1994.
36. Chimbos, 1978, 1998; Wallace, 1986; Polk & Ranson, 1991; Dobash, R. E., & Dobash, 2011; Goussinsky & Yassour-Borochowitz, 2012.
37. Campbell, 1992.
38. Websdale, 1999.
39. Adams, 2007.

40. Dobash, R. E., et al., 2007.

41. Wilson & Daly, 1993, 1998; Dawson & Gartner, 1998; Campbell et al., 2003; Campbell et al., 2007.

42. Campbell et al., 2003; Campbell et al., 2007; See also Moracco, Runyan, & Butts, 1998; Smith, P.H., Moracco, & Butts, 1998.

43. Campbell et al., 2003; Campbell et al., 2007. On the significance of guns, see Kellerman et al., 1993.

44. Sharps et al., 2003.

45. Thomas, Dichter, & Matejkowski, 2011:302.

46. Carcash & James, M. 1998.

47. Dobash, R. E., et al. 2007:13, 14.

48. Block & Christakos, 1995; Moracco et al., 1998; Thomas, Dichter, & Matejkowski, 2011:302.

49. Dobash, R. E., & Dobash, 2009:202.

50. For a review of literature, see Dobash, R. E., & Dobash, 2009, 2011.

51. For South Africa see Mathews et al., 2004; for Australia and the United States, see Shackelford & Mouzos, 2005; for the United States, see Campbell et al., 2007.

52. Dobash, R. P., et al., 2004; Dobash, R. E., et al., 2007; Dobash, R. E., & Dobash, 2009.

53. Dobash, R. E., & Dobash, 2009.

54. Weizmann-Henelius et al., 2012.

55. Adams, 2007.

56. Adams, 2007:109.

57. Echeburua, Fernandez-Montalvo, & Amor, 2003.

58. Thomas, Dichter, & Matejkowski, 2011:291, 304.

59. Langford, Isaac, & Kabat, 1998:357.

60. Harbor House, 2008.

61. Cavanagh, Dobash, & Dobash, 2007:731.

62. Lee, 2009:9.

63. Dobash, R. E., & Dobash, 2012.

64. Liem & Oberwittler, 2013:198.

65. Logan et al., 2008.

66. Logan et al., 2008.

67. Koziol-Mclain et al., 2006; Banks, Sklar, & Bauer, 2008; Barber et al., 2008.

68. West, 1965.

69. Liem & Oberwittler, 2013:206. For parasuicides see Liem, Hengeveld, & Koenraadt, 2009.

70. Liem & Oberwittler, 2013:211.

71. Liem & Oberwittler, 2013:204.

72. Roberts, K., et al., 2010. This paper also includes a comprehensive review of studies of homicide-suicides carried out in other countries.

73. Liem et al., 2011:74, Table 5. Firearm ownership is relatively high in Switzerland (28% of households) because every male must serve in the military and their rifles are kept at home during and sometimes after their time in the military. By contrast, only 5% of the Dutch population possesses a gun. Cited in Liem et al., 2011:71.

74. Liem, et al., 2011:75.

75. Wilson & Daly, 1995; Daly & Wilson, 1998:216–217; Liem, et al., 2013:351.

76. Liem & Oberwittler, 2013:207.

77. Liem, et al., 2013:351.

78. Daly & Wilson, 1988a, 1988b; Wilson, Johnson, & Daly, 1995.

79. Wilson & Daly, 1998:225–266.
80. Wilson & Daly, 1998:226.
81. Websdale, 2010: Chapters 4 &5.

CHAPTER 3
1. For further findings on type of relationship and intimate partner murder see, Dobash, R. E., et al., 2007.
2. See Dobash, R. E., et al., 2007:16, and Tables 1 and 3.
3. Dobash, R. E., & Dobash, 2011.
4. See Wilson & Daly, 1998:206–207, cited in Dobash, R. E., & Dobash, 2011; Goussinsky & Yassour-Borochowitz, 2012.
5. See Cavanagh, Dobash, & Dobash, 2007; Dobash, R. E., & Dobash, 2012.

CHAPTER 4
1. Dobash, R. E., & Dobash, 2009.
2. Dobash, R. E., & Dobash, 2009.
3. Dobash, R. E., & Dobash, 2009.

CHAPTER 5
1. Burgess et al., 1986; Ressler et al., 1986.
2. Proulx, Cusson, & Beauregard, 2007:9–28.
3. Ressler et al., 1986.
4. Myers et al., 1993. Some criminologists suggest the numbers may have been higher.
5. Proulx, Cusson, & Beauregard, 2007.
6. Cusson, 2007:1.
7. For popular accounts see Evans & Skinner, 2004; Werner, 2012.
8. Myers et al., 1993.
9. Greenall, 2011.
10. Weinshel & Calet 1972, cited in Myers et al., 1993.
11. Schlesinger, 2007:1, cited in Greenall, 2011.
12. Groth, Burgess, & Holmstrom, 1977; Burgess et al., 1986:252.
13. For useful reviews of this literature see, Chan & Heide, 2009; Carter & Hollin, 2010; Greenall, 2011.
14. Burgess et al., 1986:266.
15. Burgess et al., 1986:264.
16. Burgess et al., 1986:258.
17. Burgess et al., 1986:264.
18. Burgess et al., 1986:266
19. Burgess et al., 1986.
20. Numerous typologies have been proposed, and Kerr and colleagues have suggested four general approaches: pragmatic, such as crime scene–derived organized/dis-organized types; theory led, primarily based on psychodynamic assumptions; clinical, emerging from work with offenders including, for example, the catathymic (based on emotions such as anger) and the compulsive; and statistically derived approaches that rely on methods such as "cluster analysis" to develop types. Kerr, Beech, & Murphy, 2012.
21. For early examples see Ressler et al., 1986; Ressler, Burgess, & Douglas, 1988.
22. See Kerr, Beech, & Murphy, 2012, for a useful discussion of different approaches to definitions.

23. Roberts, J. V. & Grossman, 1993; Kong et al., 2003.

24. Meloy, 2000; Chicago estimates calculated from Block, 2013:174, Table 4.

25. Lemard & Hemenway, 2006.

26. Francis & Soothill, 2000; Francis et al., 2004.

27. Abrahams, et al., 2008.

28. Beech, Fisher, & Ward, 2005:1366.

29. Keppel & Walter, 1999:35.

30. Porter et al., 2003.

31. Porter et al., 2003:460.

32. Smith, S. G., Basile, & Karch, 2011.

33. Chan & Heide, 2009.

34. Holmes & De Burger, 1988.

35. Chan & Heide, 2009.

36. Carter & Hollin, 2010.

37. For a variety of definitions of sexual murder, see Ressler, Burgess, & Douglas, 1988:xiii; Douglas et al., 1992:132; Kerr et al., 2013.

38. Carter & Hollin, 2010:26, see also Meloy, 2000.

39. Flowers, 2001, in Greenall, 2011:2; Cusson, 2007: 1; Schlesinger, 2007; summarizing the conventional view of sex murders: Langevin et al., 1988; Douglas et al., 1992.

40. Folino, 2000.

41. Burgess et al., 1986; Groth et al., 1977.

42. Milsom, Beech, & Webster, 2003.

43. Nicole & Proulx, 2007.

44. Nicole & Proulx, 2007:34, Table 2.1.

45. Grubin, 1994:626–627.

46. Grubin, 1994:626–627.

47. Langevin et al., 1988; Langevin, 2003.

48. Oliver et al., 2007:162.

49. Oliver et al., 2007:167.

50. See Bunting, 2005, for an extensive review of the research literature that found no more than 5% of sex abusers of children were females.

51. Nicole & Proulx, 2007.

52. Nicole & Proulx, 2007:37.

53. Grubin, 1994.

54. Nicole & Proulx, 2007:39, Table 2.4.

55. Oliver et al., 2007:166–167.

56. Brittain, 1970.

57. Grubin, 1994:628.

58. See Myers et al., 1993; Proulx & Sauvetre, 2007:52, for a review.

59. Hare, 1991.

60. Proulx & Sauvetre, 2007:52–53.

61. Porter et al., 2003.

62. Proulx & Sauvetre, 2007.

63. Carter & Hollin, 2010.

64. Cusson, 2007.

65. Oliver et al., 2007.

66. Grubin, 1994.

67. Roberts, J. V. & Grossman, 1993.

68. Abrahams et al., 2008:133–134.
69. Grubin, 1994:627.
70. Oliver et al., 2007:170–171.
71. Oliver et al., 2007:170, Table 10.4.
72. See Safarik, Jarvis, & Nussbaum, 2002, and chapters in Part III, "The Murder of Older Women."
73. Oliver et al., 2007:166, Table 10.1.
74. Grubin, 1994:627.
75. Chene & Cusson, 2007:72.
76. Chene & Cusson, 2007:79, Figure 4.2.
77. Chene & Cusson, 2007:80.
78. Chene & Cusson, 2007:85.
79. Chan & Heide, 2009:50; see Carter & Hollin, 2010:42–43 for similar conclusions.

CHAPTER 6
1. Barnard, 1993; Barnard, McKeaganey, & Leyland, 1993; Farley & Barkan, 1998; see Dudek, 2001, for a review.

CHAPTER 7
1. For classic statements see Moffit, 1993; D'Unger et al., 1998; Laub & Sampson, 2003.
2. Farrington, 2003; Loeber & Stouthamer-Loeber, 1998; Moffitt, 1997; Wikstrom et al., 2013.
3. See HM Prison Service, 2014, for a brief description of all offender programs currently operating in prisons in England/Wales.
4. Marshall, W. L., & Laws, 2003; See Brown, 2005, for a comprehensive review.

CHAPTER 8
1. US Census Bureau, 2014.
2. UK Office for National Statistics, 2014.
3. US Bureau of Census, 2014.
4. OECDi Library, 2014.
5. OECDi Library, 2014.
6. Guardian, 2013, September 28:5.
7. Statistics Bureau of Japan, 2011.
8. Statistics Bureau of Japan, 2011.
9. For a discussion of the shifting definitions of old age, see Addington, 2013.
10. U.S. Census Bureau, 1995.
11. See Krienert & Walsh 2010; Block, 2013 Riedel, 2013, for reviews.
12. Safarik, Jarvis, & Nussbaum, 2002; Chu & Kraus, 2004; Block, 2013.
13. Falzon & Davies, 1998; Shields, Hunsaker, D. & Hunsaker, J. 2004.
14. Koehler, Shakir, & Omalu, 2006.
15. Abrams et al., 2007.
16. Chu & Kraus, 2004.
17. Bachman & Meloy, 2008.
18. Kennedy & Silverman, 1990.
19. Nelson & Huff-Corzine, 1998. The Homicide in Chicago Database is the largest and most comprehensive ongoing study of homicides anywhere in the world.
20. See Nelson & Huff-Corzine, 1998, for an excellent overview of this evidence.
21. Block, 2013:174, calculated from Table 4.

22. Block, 2013:177.
23. Fox & Levin, 1991; Trojan & Krull, 2012.
24. Ahmed & Menzies, 2002.
25. Ahmed & Menzies, 2002.
26. Karch & Nunn, 2011.
27. Karch & Nunn, 2011.
28. Karch & Nunn, 2011; see also Jordan et al., 2010.
29. Cohen, Llorent, & Esidorfer, 1998. See also Copeland, 1986.
30. Salari, 2007.
31. For Europe, see Liem & Oberwittler, 2012:209; For Canada, see Bourget, Gagne, & Whitehurst, 2010.
32. Pollack, 1988. Earlier research on the sexual assault of elderly women, concluded that rape and murder are about power, anger, or both, which are expressed as an urge to punish, dominate, and control the victim. See Groth, Burgess, & Holmstrom, 1977.
33. Block, 2013:174, calculated from Table 4. The number of older women killed in a sexual murder reported here differs somewhat from the numbers reported in the article because we have included two categories of homicide syndrome: "sexual assault" and "both sexual assault and instrumental". The 16% is an estimate because the data reported in Table 4 and the relevant text are difficult to reconcile, but it seems clear that this is an appropriate approximation.
34. Safarik, Jarvis, & Nussbaum, 2002.
35. Safarik, Jarvis, & Nussbaum, 2002.
36. Safarik, Jarvis, & Nussbaum, 2002.
37. Safarik, Jarvis, & Nussbaum, 2002:516.
38. Safarik, Jarvis, & Nussbaum, 2002:515.
39. Safarik, Jarvis, & Nussbaum, 2002.
40. See Larner, 2000; Sharpe, 2001, for useful overviews of the persecution of men and women for witchcraft in Europe. Although it is clear that men were condemned as witches, women, often older women, were much more likely to be persecuted in the context of fears of women's sexuality and patriarchal power. An excellent exhibition at the National Galleries of Scotland in 2013, Witches and Wicked Bodies, demonstrated the diverse and even subverted ways the pictorial representations of witches evolved from the Renaissance to the present day. Most importantly a major theme in these representations is the "sensational" activities such as "attendance at Sabbaths and their enthusiastic engagement in 'diabolical pacts,' both of which were thought to have involved them in lascivious sexual practices." Of course, it is women, including older women, depicted as engaging in such practices. The powerful catalog that accompanied the exhibition makes an important contribution to the knowledge base on witchcraft in Europe: Petherbridge, 2013, the quote is from page 9.
41. White & Richie, 2004; Home Secretary, 2007.
42. Liem & Oberwittler, 2013:201.

CHAPTER 10

1. See Royal College of Psychiatrists, 2014, for details. In Britain, being "sectioned" refers to section 136 of the Mental Health Act 1983 that specifies when an individual appears mentally disturbed in a public place, they can be detained involuntarily

to be assessed in a "place of safety," which is meant to be a mental health unit. From the Murder Study, men detained involuntarily under the Mental Health Act included male-male murderers (5%), intimate partner murderers (3%), sexual murderers (9%), and murderers of older women (20%).

CHAPTER 11

1. See Dobash, R. E. & Dobash, 2009.
2. Liem, 2013.
3. For important reviews and overviews about sexual offenders and their treatment, although not about sex/murderers, see Marshall, W. L., Laws, & Barbaree, 1990 (a classic); Hollin, 2001; Brown, 2005; Beech, Craig, & Browne, 2009.
4. Marshall, W. L., 1999.
5. Marshall, W. L., 1999. For a discussion of dealing with denial among intimate partner abusers in the context of group therapy, see Partanen, Wahlstrom, & Holma, 2006.
6. For an account of the development of abuser programs in the United States, see Gondolf, 2002. For an overview of abuser programs in the United Kingdom, see Dobash, R. E., & Dobash, 1992.
7. For early statements of the Duluth model see Pence, 1983; & Pence & Paymar, 1993. For a tribute to Ellen Pence and her enormous contribution to the global development of work with abusers, see Dobash, R. E., & Dobash, 2010, and the entire volume of *Violence Against Women* in which this article appears.
8. For a discussion of the content and organization of these programs especially in the United Kingdom, see Dobash, R. P., et al., 2000.
9. Brown, 2005, chapters 7–9.
10. Dobash, R. E., et al., 2000; Gondolf, 2002; Tolman & Edleson, 2011.
11. See Hanson, 2001, for the most succinct yet thorough discussion of these risk factors.
12. Hanson, 2001:89.
13. Hanson, 2001:90.
14. Campbell et al., 2003; Campbell et al., 2014.

REFERENCES

Abrahams, N., Martin, L. J., Jewkes, R., Mathews, S., Vetten, L., & Lombard, C. (2008). The epidemiology and pathology of suspected rape homicide in South Africa. *Forensic Science International, 178*, 132–138.

Abrams, R. C., Leon, A. C., Tardiff, K., Marzuk, P. M., & Sutherland, K. (2007). "Gray murder": Characteristics of elderly compared with nonelderly homicide victims in New York City. *American Journal of Public Health, 97*, 1666–1670.

Adams, D. (2007). *Why do they kill?: Men who murder their intimate partners.* Nashville, TN: Vanderbilt University Press.

Addington, L. A. (2013). Who you calling old?: Measuring "elderly" and what it means for homicide research. *Homicide Studies, 17*, 134–153.

Ahmed, A. G., & Menzies, R. P. (2002). Homicide in the Canadian prairies: Elderly and nonelderly killings. *Canadian Journal of Psychiatry, 47*, 875–879.

Anderson, E. (1990). *Streetwise: Race, class, and change in an urban community.* Chicago, IL: University of Chicago Press.

Ashworth, A., & Mitchell, B. (2000). Introduction. In A. Ashworth & B. Mitchell (Eds.), *Rethinking English homicide law* (pp. 1–20). Oxford, UK: Oxford University Press.

Bachman, R., & Meloy, M. (2008). The epidemiology of violence against the elderly: Implications for primary and secondary prevention. *Journal of Contemporary Criminal Justice, 24*, 186–197.

Bandura, A. (1991). Social cognitive theory of moral thought and action. In W. M. Kurtines & J. L. Gewirtz (Eds.), *Handbook of moral behavior and development* (pp. 45–103). Hillsdale, NJ: Erlbaum.

Banks, L., Crandall, C., Sklar, D., & Bauer, M. (2008). A comparison of intimate partner homicide to intimate partner homicide-suicide. *Violence Against Women, 14*, 1065–1078.

Barber, C. W., Azrael, D., Hemenway, D., Olson, L. M., Nie, C. W., Schaechter, J., & Walsh, S. (2008). Suicides and suicide attempts following homicide. *Homicide Studies, 12*(3), 285–297.

Barnard, M. A. (1993). Violence and vulnerability: Conditions of work for streetworking prostitutes. *Sociology of Health & Illness, 15*, 683–705.

Barnard, M. A., McKeganey, N. P., & Leyland, A. H. (1993). Risk behaviours among male clients of female prostitutes. *British Medical Journal, 307*, 361–362.

Basile, K. C., & Black, M. C. (2011). Intimate partner violence against women. In C. M. Renzetti, J. L. Edleson, & R. K. Bergen (Eds.), *Sourcebook on violence against women* (2nd ed., pp. 111–131). Thousand Oaks, CA: Sage.

Beech, A., Fisher, D., & Ward, T. (2005). Sexual murderers' implicit theories. *Journal of Interpersonal Violence, 20,* 1366–1389.

Beech, A. R., Craig, L. A., & Browne, K. D. (Eds.). (2009). *Treatment of sex offenders: A handbook.* Chichester, UK: Wiley-Blackwell.

Birkel, B., & Dern, H. (2013). Homicide in Germany. In M. C. A. Liem & W. A. Pridemore (Eds.), *Handbook of European homicide research: Patterns, explanations, and country studies* (pp. 313–328). New York, NY: Springer Science.

Block, C. R. (1988). *Homicide in Chicago.* Chicago, IL: Loyola University of Chicago.

Block, C. R. (2013). Homicide against or by the elderly in Chicago, 1965–2000. *Homicide Studies, 17,* 154–183. (Originally published online 8 March 2013.)

Block, C. R., & Christakos, A. (1995). Intimate partner homicide in Chicago over 29 years. *Crime and Delinquency, 41,* 496–526.

Bourget, D., Gagne, P., & Whitehurst, L. (2010). Domestic homicide and homicide-suicide: The older offender. *Journal of the American Academy of Psychiatry & the Law, 38,* 305–311.

Bourgois, P. (1995). *In search of respect: Selling crack in el Barrio.* Cambridge, UK: Cambridge University Press.

Brittain, R. P. (1970). The sadistic murderer. *Medicine, Science, & the Law, 10,* 198–207.

Brookman, F. (2005). *Understanding homicide.* Thousand Oaks, CA.: Sage.

Brown, S. (2005). *Treating sex offenders: An introduction to sex offender treatment programmes.* Cullompton, UK: Willan.

Browne, A. (1987). *When battered women kill.* New York: Free Press, Collier Macmillan.

Browne, A., & Williams, K. R. (1993). Gender, intimacy, and lethal violence: Trends from 1976 through 1987. *Gender & Society, 7,* 78–98.

Brownridge, D. A., & Halli, S. S. (2002). Understanding male partner violence against cohabiting and married women: An empirical investigation with a synthesized model. *Journal of Family Violence, 17,* 341–361.

Bunting, L. (2005). *Females who sexually offend against children: Responses of the child protection and criminal justice systems.* NSPCC Policy Practice Research Series. London: NSPCC.

Burgess, A. W., Hartman, C. R., Ressler, R. K., Douglas, J. E., & McCormack, A. (1986). Sexual homicide: A motivational model. *Journal of Interpersonal Violence, 1*(3), 251–272.

Bye, E. K. (2013). Alcohol and homicide in Europe. In M. C. A. Liem & W. A. Pridemore (Eds.), *Handbook of European homicide research: Patterns, explanations, and country studies* (pp. 231–246). New York, NY: Springer Science.

Campbell, J. C. (1992). "If I can't have you, no one can": Power and control in homicide of female partners. In J. Radford & D. E. H. Russell (Eds.), *Femicide: The politics of woman killing* (pp. 99–113). New York, NY: Twayne.

Campbell, J. C., Glass, N., Sharps, P. W., Laughon, K., & Bloom, T. (2007). Intimate partner homicide: Review and implications of research and policy. *Trauma, Violence & Abuse, 8,* 246–269.

Campbell, J. C., Webster, D., Koziol-McLain, J., Block, C. R., Campbell, D., Curry, M. A.,... Laughon, K. (2003). Risk factors for femicide in abusive relationships: Results from a multi-site case control study. *American Journal of Public Health, 93,* 139–152.

Campbell, J. C., Webster, D., Koziol-McLain, J., Block, C. R., Campbell, D., Curry, M. A., . . . Wilt, S. A. (2014). Assessing risk factors for intimate partner homicide. *National Institute of Justice Journal, 250,* 14–19.

Carcash, C., & James, M. (1998). Homicide between intimate partners in Australia. *Trends & Issues in Crime and Criminal Justice, 90*. Canberra: Australian Institute of Criminology. Retrieved from: http://www.aic.gov

Carter, A. J., & Hollin, C. R. (2010). Characteristics of non-serial sexual homicide offenders: A review. *Psychology, Crime & Law, 16*, 25–45.

Cavanagh, K., Dobash, R. E., & Dobash, R. P. (2005). Men who murder children inside and outside the family. *British Journal of Social Work, 35*, 667–688.

Cavanagh, K., Dobash, R. E., & Dobash, R. P. (2007). The murder of children by fathers in the context of child abuse. *Child Abuse & Neglect, 31*, 731–746.

Chan, H. C., & Heide, K. M. (2009). Sexual homicide: A synthesis of the literature. *Trauma, Violence & Abuse, 10*, 31–54.

Chene, S., & Cusson, M. (2007). Sexual murderers and sexual aggressors: Intention and situation. In J. Proulx, E. Beauregard, M. Cusson, & A. Nicole (Eds.), *Sexual murderers: A comparative analysis and new perspectives* (pp. 71–86). Chichester, UK: Wiley.

Chimbos, P. D. (1978). *Marital violence: A study of inter-spousal homicide.* San Francisco: R & E.

Chimbos, P. D. (1998). Spousal homicides in contemporary Greece. *International Journal of Comparative Sociology, 39*(2), 213–223.

Chu, L. D., & Kraus, J. F. (2004). Predicting fatal assault among the elderly using the national incident-based reporting system crime data. *Homicide Studies, 8*, 71–95.

Cohen, D., Llorente, M., & Eisdorfer, C. (1998). Homicide-suicide in older persons. *American Journal of Psychiatry, 155*, 390–396.

Cooper, A., & Smith, E. L. (2011). *Homicide trends in the United States, 1980–2008.* U.S. Department of Justice, Bureau of Justice Statistics. Available at: http://bjs.ojp.usdoj.gov/content/pub/pdf/htus8008.pdf

Copeland, A. R. (1986). Homicide among the elderly: The metro Dade county experience, 1979–1983. *Medical Science Law, 26*, 259–262.

Corzine, J., Huff-Corzine, L., & Whitt, H. P. (1999). Cultural and subcultural theories of homicide. In M. D. Smith & M. A. Zahn (Eds.), *Homicide: A sourcebook of social research* (pp. 42–57). Thousand Oaks, CA: Sage.

Cusson, M. (2007). Introduction. In J. Proulx, E. Beauregard, M. Cusson, & A. Nicole (Eds.), *Sexual murderers: A comparative analysis and new perspectives* (pp. 1–5). Chichester, UK: Wiley.

Cotton, J. (2003). Homicide. In C. Flood-Page & J. Taylor (Eds.), Crime in England and Wales 2001/2002:Supplementary volume (pp. 1–27). London: Home Office Statistical Bulletin.

Daly, M., & Wilson, M. (1988a). *Homicide.* New York: Aldine de Gruyter.

Daly, M., & Wilson, M. (1988b). Evolutionary social psychology and family homicide. *Science, 242*, 519–524.

Daly, M., Wilson, M., & Weghorst, S. J. (1982). Male sexual jealousy. *Ethology & Sociobiology, 3*, 11–27.

Dawson, R., & Gartner, R. (1998). Differences in the characteristics of intimate femicides: The role of relationship state and relationship status. *Homicide Studies, 2*, 378–399.

Descola, P. (1996). *The spears of twilight: Life and death in the Amazon jungle.* London: HarperCollins.

Dobash, R. E., & Dobash, R. P. (1979). *Violence against wives: A case against the patriarchy.* New York, NY, & London, UK: Free Press & Open Books.

Dobash, R. E., & Dobash, R. P. (1984). The nature and antecedents of violent events. *British Journal of Criminology, 24*, 269–288.

Dobash, R. E., & Dobash, R. P. (1992). *Women, violence and social change*. London: Routledge.

Dobash, R. E., & Dobash, R. P. (1998). Violent men and violent contexts. In R. E. Dobash, & R. P. Dobash (Eds.), *Rethinking violence against women* (pp. 141–168). Newbury, CA: Sage.

Dobash, R. E., & Dobash, R. P. (2009). Out of the blue: Men who murder an intimate partner. *Feminist Criminology, 4*, 194–225.

Dobash, R. E., & Dobash, R. P. (2010). Ellen Pence appreciation: Letters from Britain and Europe. *Violence Against Women, 16*, 1054–1054.

Dobash, R. E., & Dobash, R. P. (2011). What were they thinking?: Men who murder an intimate partner. *Violence Against Women, 17*, 111–134.

Dobash, R. E., & Dobash, R. P. (2012). Who died?: Murder of others in the context of intimate partner conflict. *Violence Against Women, 18*, 662–671.

Dobash, R. E., Dobash, R. P., Cavanagh, K., & Medina-Ariza, J. J. (2007). Lethal and non-lethal violence against an intimate partner: Comparing male murderers with non-lethal abusers. *Violence Against Women, 13*(4), 1–27.

Dobash, R. P., Carnie, J., & Waterhouse, L. (1993). Child sexual abusers: Recognition and response. In L. Waterhouse (Ed.), *Child abuse and child abusers: Protection and prevention* (pp. 113–135). London & Philadelphia: Kingsley.

Dobash, R. P., & Dobash, R. E. (1983). The context-specific approach. In D. Finkelhor, R. J. Gelles, G. T. Hotaling, & M. A. Straus (Eds.), *The dark side of families* (pp. 261–276). Beverly Hills, CA: Sage.

Dobash, R. P., & Dobash, R. E. (2004). Women's violence to men in intimate relationships: Working on a puzzle. *British Journal of Criminology, 44*, 324–349.

Dobash, R. P., Dobash, R. E., Cavanagh, K., & Lewis, R. (2000). *Changing violent men*. Thousand Oaks, CA: Sage.

Dobash, R. P., Dobash, R. E., Cavanagh, K., & Lewis, R. (2004). Not an ordinary killer—just an ordinary guy: When men murder an intimate woman partner. *Violence Against Women, 10*, 577–605.

Dobash, R. P., Dobash, R. E., Cavanagh, K., Smith, D., & Medina-Ariza, J. J. (2007). Onset of offending and life course among men convicted of murder. *Homicide Studies, 11*(4), 243–271.

Dobash, R. P., Monaghan, L., Dobash, R. E., & Bloor, M. (1999). Bodybuilding, steroids and violence: Is there a connection? In P. Carlen & R. Morgan (Eds.), *Crime unlimited: Questions for the 21st century* (pp. 166–190). London: Macmillan.

Douglas, J. E., Burgess, A. W., Burgess, A. G., & Ressler, R. K. (1992). *Crime classification manual*. New York, NY: Lexington Books.

Dudek, J. A. (2001). *When silenced voices speak: An exploratory study of prostitute homicide*. Unpublished Ph.D. dissertation, Hanemann University, Philadelphia.

Dugan, L., Nagin, D. S., & Rosenfeld, R. (1999). Explaining the decline in intimate partner homicide. *Homicide Studies, 3*(3), 187–214.

Dugan, L., Nagin, D. S., & Rosenfeld, R. (2003). Do domestic violence services save lives? *National Institute of Justice Journal Studies, 250*, 20–25.

D'Unger, A. V., Land, K. C., McCall, P. L., & Nagin, D. S. (1998). Early predictors of latent classes of delinquent criminal careers: Results from a mixed Poisson regression analyses of the London, Philadelphia and Racine cohorts studies. *American Journal of Sociology, 103*, 1593–1630.

Echeburua, E., Fernandez-Montalvo, J., & Amor, P. J. (2003). Psychopathological profile of men convicted of gender violence: A study in the prisons of Spain. *Journal of Interpersonal Violence, 18,* 798–812.

Eisner, M., & Karstedt, S. (Eds.). (2009). Focus: General theory of violence. *International Journal of Conflict and Violence, 3,* 3–142.

Evans, S. P., & Skinner, K. (2004). *Jack the Ripper: Letters from Hell.* Stroud, Gloucestershire, UK: Sutton.

Falzon, A. L., & Davis, G. G. (1998). A 15 year retrospective review of homicide in the elderly. *Journal of Forensic Sciences, 43*(2), 371–374.

Farley, M., & Barkan, H. (1998). Prostitution, violence, and posttraumatic stress disorder. *Women & Health, 27,* 37–49.

Farrington, D. P. (2003). Key results from the first forty years of the Cambridge study in delinquent development. In T. Thornberry & M. Krohn (Eds.), *Taking stock of delinquency: An overview of findings from contemporary longitudinal studies* (pp. 137–183). New York, NY: Kluwer.

Farrington, D. P., & Loeber, R. (2000). Epidemiology of juvenile violence. *Child & Adolescent Psychiatric Clinics of North America, 9,* 733–748.

Federal Bureau of Investigation. (2012). "Table 13: Murder circumstances." In *Crime in the United States: Uniform crime reports, supplemental homicide reports.* Washington, DC: Government Printing Office.

Flewelling, R. L., & Williams, K. R, (1999). Categorizing homicides: The use of disaggregated data in homicide research, In M. D. Smith & M. A. Zahn (Eds.), *Homicide: A sourcebook of social research* (pp. 96–106). Thousand Oaks, CA: Sage

Flowers, R. B. (2001). Sex crimes, predators, perpetrators, prostitutes, and victims: An examination of sexual criminality and victimization. Springfield, IL: Thomas.

Folino, J. O. (2000). Sexual homicides and their classification according to motivation: A report from Argentina. *International Journal of Offender Therapy & Comparative Criminology, 44,* 740–750.

Fox, J. A., & Levin, J. (1991). Homicide against the elderly: A research note. *Criminology, 29,* 317–327.

Fox, J. A., & Zawitz, M. W. (2007). *Homicide trends in the US: Intimate homicide.* Washington, DC: Bureau of Justice Statistics.

Francis, B., & Soothill, K. (2000). Does sex offending lead to homicide? *Journal of Forensic Psychiatry, 11,* 49–61.

Francis, B., Barry, J., Bowater, R., Miller, N., Soothill, K., & Ackerley, E. (2004). *Using homicide data to assist murder investigations.* London, UK: Home Office Online Report 26/04.

Ganpat, S. M., & Liem, M. C. A. (2013). Homicide in the Netherlands. In M. C. A. Liem & W. A. Pridemore (Eds.), *Handbook of European homicide research: Patterns, explanations, and country studies* (pp. 329–341). New York, NY: Springer Science.

Gartner, R. (1990). The victims of homicide: A temporal and cross-national comparison. *American Sociological Review, 55,* 92–106.

Gondolf, E. W. (2002). *Batterer intervention systems: Issues, outcomes and recommendations.* Thousand Oaks, CA: Sage.

Goussinsky, R., & Yassour-Borochowitz, D., (2012). "I killed her, but I never laid a finger on her"—A phenomenological difference between wife-killing and wife-battering. *Aggression & Violent Behavior, 17,* 553–564.

Granath, S. (2013). Homicide in Sweden. In M. C. A. Liem & W. A. Pridemore (Eds.), *Handbook of European homicide research: Patterns, explanations, and country studies* (pp. 405–419). New York, NY: Springer Science.

Greenall, P. V. (2011). Understanding sexual homicide. *Journal of Sexual Aggression.* Advance online publication. doi:10.1080/13552600.2011.596287

Groth, A. N., Burgess, A. W., & Holmstrom, L. L. (1977). Rape: Power, anger, and sexuality. *American Journal of Psychiatry, 134,* 1239–1243.

Grubin, D. (1994). Sexual murder. *British Journal of Psychiatry, 165,* 624–629.

Guardian. (2013, September 28). Growth of the "oldest old." *The Guardian,* p. 5.

Hanson, R. K. (2001). Sex offender risk assessment. In C. Hollin (Ed.), *Handbook of offender assessment and treatment* (pp. 85–96). Chichester, UK: Wiley.

Harbor House. (2008). *Domestic violence also kills random victims.* Available at: http://www.harborhousefl.com/index

Hare, R. D. (1991). *The Hare psychopathy checklist—revised.* North Tonawanda, NY: Multi-Health Systems.

Heitmeyer, J. H. W. & Hagan, J. (Eds.). (2003). *International Handbook of Violence Research.* London, UK: Kluwer.

HM Prison Service (2014). *Justice: Offender behaviour programmes (OBPs).* Retrieved May 1, 2014, from: www.justice.gov.uk/offenders/before-after-release/obp

Hollin, C. (Ed.). (2001). *Handbook of offender assessment and treatment.* Chichester, UK: Wiley.

Holmes, R. M., & De Burger, J. (1988). *Serial murder.* Newbury Park, CA: Sage.

Home Secretary. (2007). *Learning from tragedy, keeping patients safe.* London, UK: Stationery Office. Available at: https://www.gov.uk/government/data/file/228886/7014.pdf.

James, B., & Daly, M. (2012). Cohabitation is no longer associated with elevated spousal homicide rates in the United States. *Homicide Studies, 16*(4), 393–403.

Johnson, H., & Chisholm, P. (1989). Family homicide. In *Canadian social trends* (Vol. 14, pp. 17–28). Ottawa: Statistics Canada.

Johnson, H., & Hotton, T. (2003). Losing control: Homicide risk in estranged and intact intimate relationships. *Homicide Studies, 7,* 58–84.

Jones, A. (1980). *Women who kill.* New York: Fawcett Columbine.

Jordan, C. E., Pritchard, A. J., Duckett, D., Wilcox, P., Corey, T., & Combest, M. (2010). Relationship and injury trends in the homicide of women across the life span: A research note. *Homicide Studies, 14,* 181–192.

Jurik, N. C., & Gregware, P. (1992). A method for murder: The study of homicides by women. *Social Problems, 4,* 179–201.

Jurik, N. C., & Winn, R. (1990). Gender and homicide: A comparison of men and women who kill. *Violence & Victims, 5,* 227–242.

Karch, D., & Nunn, K. C. (2011). Characteristics of elderly and other vulnerable adult victims of homicide by a caregiver: National violent death reporting system—17 U.S. States, 2003–2007. *Journal of Interpersonal Violence, 26,* 137–157.

Kellerman, A. L., Rivara, F. P., Rushforth, N. B., Banton, J. G., Reay, D. T., Francisco, J. T.,... Somes, G. (1993). Gun ownership as a risk factor for homicide in the home. *New England Journal of Medicine, 329,* 1084–1091.

Kennedy, L. W., & Silverman, R. A. (1990). The elderly victim of homicide: An application of routine activity theory. *Sociological Quarterly, 31,* 305–317.

Keppel, R. A., & Walter, R. (1999). Profiling killers: A revised classification model for understanding sexual murder. *International Journal of Offender Therapy & Comparative Criminology, 46,* 417–437.

Kerr, K. J., Beech, A. R., & Murphy, D. (2013). Sexual homicide: Definition, motivation and comparison with other forms of sexual offending. *Aggression & Violent Behavior*, *18*, 1–10.

Kivivuori, J., Savolainen, J., & Danielsson, P. (2013). Theory and explanation in contemporary European homicide research. In M. C. A. Liem & W. A. Pridemore (Eds.), *Handbook of European homicide research* (pp. 95–109). New York, NY: Springer Science.

Koehler, S. A., Shakir, A. M., & Omalu, B. I. (2006). Cause of death among elder homicide victims: A 10-year medical examiner review. *Journal of Forensic Nursing*, *2*, 199–203.

Kong, R., Johnson, H., Beattie, S., & Cardillo, A. (2003). Sexual offences in Canada. *Juristat*, *23*(6). Canadian Center for Justice Statistics.

Koziol-Mclain, J., Webster, D., McFarlane, J., Block, C. R., Ulrich, Y., Glass, N., & Campbell, J. C. (2006). Risk factors for femicide-suicide in abusive relationships: Results from a multisite case control study. *Violence & Victims*, *21*, 3–21.

Krienert, J. L., & Walsh, J. A. (2010). Eldercide: A gendered examination of elderly homicide in the United States, 2000–2005. *Homicide Studies*, *14*(1), 52–71.

Lancaster, R. N. (1992). *Life is hard: Machismo, danger, and the intimacy of power in Nicaragua*. Berkeley: University of California Press.

Langevin, R. (2003). A study of the psychosexual characteristics of sex killers: Can we identify them before it is too late? *International Journal of Offender Therapy & Comparative Criminology*, *47*, 366–382.

Langevin, R., Ben-Aron, M. H., Wright, P., Marchese, V., & Handy, L. (1988). The sex killer. *Annals of Sex Research*, *1*, 263–301.

Langford, L., Isaac, N., & Kabat, S. (1998). Homicides related to intimate partner violence in Massachusetts: Examining case ascertainment and validity of the SHR. *Homicide Studies*, *2*, 353–377.

Larner, C. (2000). *Enemies of God: The witch-hunt in Scotland*. Edinburgh, Scotland: John Donald.

Laub, J. H., & Sampson, R. J. (2003). *Shared beginnings, divergent lives: Delinquent boys to age 70*. Cambridge, MA: Cambridge University Press.

Lee, N. L. (2009). *Family and intimate partner homicide*. Richmond: Virginia Department of Health, Chief Examiner.

Lehti, M., & Kivivuori, J. (2013). Homicide in Finland. In M. C. A. Liem & W. A. Pridemore (Eds.), *Handbook of European homicide research: Patterns, explanations, and country studies* (pp. 391–404). New York, NY: Springer Science.

Lemard, G., & Hemenway, D. (2006). Violence in Jamaica: An analysis of homicides 1998–2002. *Injury Prevention*, *12*, 15–18.

Lewis, R., Dobash, R. E., Dobash, R. P., & Cavanagh, K. (2003). Researching homicide: Methodological issues in the exploration of lethal violence. In R. M. Lee & E. A. Stanko (Eds.), *Researching violence: Essays in methodology and method*. London, UK: Routledge.

Liebow, E. (1967). *Tally's corner: A study of negro streetcorner men*. Boston, MA: Little, Brown.

Liem, M. C. A. (2013). Homicide offender recidivism: A review of the literature. *Aggression & Violent Behavior*, *18*, 19–25.

Liem, M. C. A., Barber, C., Markwalder, N., Killias, M., & Nieuwbeerta, P. (2011). Homicide-suicide and other violent deaths: An international comparison. *Forensic Science International*, *207*, 70–76.

Liem, M. C. A., Hengeveld, M. W., & Koenraadt, R. (2009). Domestic homicide followed by parasuicide. *International Journal of Offender Therapy & Comparative Criminology, 53*(5), 497–516.

Liem, M. C. A., & Oberwittler, D. (2013). Homicide followed by suicide in Europe. In M. C. A. Liem & W. A. Pridemore (Eds.), *Handbook of European homicide research: Patterns, explanations, and country studies* (pp. 197–215). New York, NY: Springer Science.

Liem, M. C. A., & Pridemore, W. A. (Eds.). (2013). *Handbook of European homicide research: Patterns, explanations and country studies.* New York, NY: Springer Science.

Loeber, R., & Stouthamer-Loeber, M. (1998). Development of juvenile aggression and violence: Some common misconceptions and controversies. *American Psychologists, 53*, 242–259.

Logan, J., Hill, H. A., Black, M. L., Crosby, A. E., Karch, D. L., Barnes, J. D., & Lubell, K. M. (2008). Characteristics of perpetrators in homicide-followed-by-suicide incidents: National violent death reporting system—17 US states, 2003–2005. *American Journal of Epidemiology, 168*(9), 1056–1064.

Luckenbill, D. F. (1977). Criminal homicide as a situated tansaction. *Social Problems, 25*, 176–186.

Markwalder, N., & Killias, M. (2013). Homicide in Switzerland. In M. C. A. Liem & W. A. Pridemore (Eds.), *Handbook of European homicide research: Patterns, explanations, and country studies* (pp. 343–354). New York, NY: Springer Science.

Marshall, I. H., & Summers, D. L. (2013). Contemporary differences in rates and trends of homicide among European nations. In M. C. A. Liem & W. A. Pridemore (Eds.), *Handbook of European homicide research: Patterns, explanations, and country studies* (pp. 39–69). New York, NY: Springer Science.

Marshall, W. L. (1999). Current status of North American assessment and treatment programs for sexual offenders. *Journal of Interpersonal Violence, 14*, 221–239.

Marshall, W. L., & Laws, D. R. (2003). A brief history of behavioral and cognitive behavioral approaches to sexual offender treatment: Part 2. The modern era, *Sexual Abuse: A Journal of Research & Treatment, 15*, 93–120.

Marshall, W. L., Laws, D. R., & Barbee, H. E. (Eds.). (1990). *Handbook of sexual assault: Issues, theories and treatment of the offender.* New York: Plenum.

Martin, D. (1976). *Battered wives.* San Francisco, CA: Glide.

Mathews, S., Abrahams, N., Martin, L. J., Vetten, L., van der Merwe, L., & Jewkes, R. (2004). *"Every six hours a woman is killed by her intimate partner": A national study of female homicide in South Africa.* MRC Policy Brief, No. 5, June.

Meloy, J. R. (2000). The nature and dynamics of sexual homicide. *Aggression & Violent Behavior, 5*, 1–22.

Mercy, J. A., & Saltzman, L. E. (1989). Fatal violence among spouses in the United. States. *American Journal of Public Health, 79*, 595–599.

Messner, S. F., & Rosenfeld, F. (1999). Social structure and homicide: Theory and research. In M. D. Smith & M. A. Zahn (Eds.), *Homicide: A sourcebook of social research* (pp. 27–41). Thousand Oaks, CA: Sage.

Miethe, T. D., & Regoeczi, W. C. (2004). *Rethinking homicide: Exploring the structure and process underlying deadly situations.* New York, NY: Cambridge University Press.

Miles, C. (2012). Intoxication and homicide: A context-specific approach. *British Journal of Criminology, 52*, 870–888.

Milsom, J., Beech, A. R., & Webster, S. D. (2003). Emotional loneliness in sexual murderers: A qualitative analysis. *Sexual Abuse: A Journal of Research & Treatment, 15,* 285–296.

Moffitt, T. E. (1993). "Life course-persistent" and "adolescence-limited" anti-social behaviour: A developmental taxonomy. *Psychological Review, 100,* 674–701.

Moffitt, T. E. (1997). Adolescence-limited and life course-persistent offending: A complementary pair of development theories. In T. P. Thornberry (Ed.), *Developmental theories of crime and delinquency* (pp. 11–54). New York, NY: Transaction.

Moracco, K. E., Runyan, C. W., & Butts, J. D. (1998). Femicide in North Carolina, 1991–1993: A statewide study of patterns and precursors. *Homicide Studies, 2,* 422–446.

Mucchielli, L. (2013). Homicides in contemporary France. In M. C. A. Liem & W. A. Pridemore (Eds.), *Handbook of European homicide research: Patterns, explanations, and country studies* (pp. 301–312). New York, NY: Springer Science.

Myers, W. C., Reccoppa, L., Burton, K., & McElory, R. (1993). Malignant sex and aggression: An overview of serial sexual homicide. *Bulletin of the American Academy of Psychiatry Law, 21,* 435–451.

Nelson, C., & Huff-Corzine, L. (1998). Strangers in the night: An application of the life-style routine activities approach to elderly homicide victimization. *Homicide Studies, 2*(2), 130–159.

Nicole, A., & Proulx, J. (2007). Sexual murderer and sexual aggressors: Developmental paths and criminal history. In In J. Proulx, E. Beauregard, M. Cusson, & A. Nicole (Eds.), *Sexual murderers: A comparative analysis and new perspectives* (pp. 29–50). Chichester, UK: Wiley.

OECDiLibrary (2014). OECD Factbook 2011-2012 Economic, Environmental and Social Statistics, assessed 2014 at http://dx.doi.org/10.1787/factbook-2011-en.

Oliver, C. J., Beech, A. R., Fisher, D., & Beckett, R. (2007). A comparison of rapists and sexual murderers on demographic and selected psychometric measures. In J. Proulx, E. Beauregard, M. Cusson, & A. Nicole (Eds.), *Sexual murderers: A comparative analysis and new perspectives* (pp. 159–173). Chichester, UK: Wiley.

Padfield, N. (2002). *Beyond the tariff: Human rights and the release of life sentence prisoners.* Cullampton, UK: Willan.

Parker, R. N. Averhahn., K. (1999). Drugs, alcohol, and homicide: Issues in theory and research. In M. D. Smith & Zahn, M. A. (Eds.), *Homicide: A sourcebook of social research* (pp. 176–191). Thousand Oaks, CA: Sage.

Parole Board. (2008). Prisoners and families: Information about sentence, tariff & applying for life licence. London, UK: Parole Board for England and Wales.

Partanen, T., Wahlstrom, J., & Holma, J., (2006). Loss of self-control as excuse in group-therapy conversations for intimately violent men. *Communication & Medicine, 3*(2):171–183.

Paulozzi, L. J., Mercy, J., Frazier, L., & Annest, J. L. (2004). CDC's national violent death reporting system: Background and methodology. *Injury Prevention, 10,* 47–52.

Pence, E., & Paymar, M. (1993). *Power and control: Tactics of men who batter.* New York, NY: Springer.

Pence, E., & Paymar, M. (1983). The Duluth domestic abuse intervention project. *Hamline Law Review, 6*(2), 247–6275.

Petherbridge, D., & Trustees of the National Galleries of Scotland. (2013). *Witches and wicked bodies.* Edinburgh, Scotland: NGS Publishing.

Polk, K. (1994). *When men kill: Scenarios of masculine violence*. New York, NY: Cambridge University Press.

Polk, K., & Ranson, D. (1991). The role of gender in intimate homicide. *Australian & New Zealand Journal of Criminology, 24*, 15–24.

Pollock, N. L. (1988). Sexual assault of older women. *Annals of Sex Research, 1*, 523–532.

Porter, S., Woodworth, M., Earle, J., Drugge, J., & Boer, D. (2003). Characteristics of sexual homicides committed by psychopathic and nonpsychopathic offenders. *Law and Human Behavior, 27*, 459–470.

Proulx, J., & Sauvetre, N. (2007). Sexual murderers and sexual aggressors: Psychopathological considerations. In J. Proulx, E. Beauregard, M. Cusson, & A. Nicole (Eds.), *Sexual murderers: A comparative analysis and new perspectives* (pp. 51–69). Chichester, UK: Wiley.

Proulx, J., Cusson, M., & Beauregard, E. (2007). Sexual murder: Definitions, epidemiology and theories. In J. Proulx, E. Beauregard, M. Cusson, & A. Nicole (Eds.), *Sexual murderers: A comparative analysis and new perspectives* (pp. 9–28). Chichester, UK: Wiley.

Proulx, J., Beauregard, E., Cusson, M., & Nicole, A. (Eds.). (2007). *Sexual murderers: A comparative analysis and new perspectives*. Chichester, UK: Wiley.

QSR/NVivo (ND). QSR International. Available at: www.qsrinternational.com

Radford, J., & Russell, D. E. H. (Eds.). (1992). *Femicide: The politics of woman killing*. New York, NY: Twayne.

Reaves, B. (2006). *Violent felons in large urban counties: State court processing statistics, 1990–2002*. Special Report, Bureau of Justice Statistics. Washington, DC: U.S. Department of Justice.

Ressler, R. K., Burgess, A. W., & Douglas, J. E. (1988). *Sexual homicide: Patterns and motive*. New York, NY: Free Press.

Ressler, R. K., Burgess, A. W., Hartman, C. R., Douglas, J. E., & McCormack, A. (1986). Murderers who rape and mutilate. *Journal of Interpersonal Violence, 1*, 273–287.

Richards, L. (2006). *Handling qualitative data: An introduction*. Thousand Oaks, CA: Sage.

Riedel, M. (1999). Sources of homicide data: A review and comparison. In M. D. Smith & M. A. Zahn (Eds.), *Homicide: A sourcebook of social research* (pp. 75–95). Thousand Oaks, CA: Sage.

Riedel, M. (2013). Special issue on elderly homicide: An introduction. *Homicide Studies, 17*, 123–133.

Roberts, K., Wassenaar, D., Canetto, S. S., & Pillay, A. (2010). Homicide-suicide in Durban, South africa. *Journal of Interpersonal Violence, 25*(5), 877–899.

Roberts, J. V., & Grossman, M. G. (1993). Sexual homicide in Canada: A descriptive analysis. *Annals of Sex Research, 6*, 5–25.

Rock, P. (1988). Murderers, victims and "survivors": The social construction of deviance. *British Journal of Criminology, 38*, 185–200.

Royal College of Psychiatrists. (2014). *Being sectioned (in England and Wales)*. Accessed May 2014 from: http://www.rcpsych.ac.uk/healthadvice/problemsdisorders/beingsectionedengland.aspx

Russell, D. E. H. (1992). Femicide: The murder of wives. In J. Radford & D. E. H. Russell (Eds.), *Femicide: The politics of woman killing* (pp. 286–299). New York, NY: Twayne.

Russell, D. E. H., & Harmes, R. A. (Eds.). (2001). *Femicide in global perspective*. New York, NY, & London, UK: Columbia University, Teachers College Press.

Safarik, M. E., Jarvis, J. P., & Nussbaum, K. E. (2002). Sexual homicide of elderly females: Linking offender characteristics to victim and crime scene attributes. *Journal of Interpersonal Violence, 17,* 500–525.

Salari, S. (2007). Patterns of intimate partner homicide suicide in later life: Strategies for prevention. *Clinical Interventions in Aging, 2,* 441–452.

Sampson, J. H., & Laub, R. J. (2003). Shared beginnings, divergent lives: Delinquent boys to age 70. Cambridge, MA, & London, UK: Harvard University Press.

Schechter, S. (1982). *Women and male violence.* Boston, MA: South End.

Schlesinger, L. B. (2007). Sexual homicide: Differentiating catathymic and compulsive murders. *Aggression & Violent Behavior, 12,* 242–256.

Schlesinger, P., Dobash, R. E., Dobash, R. P., & Weaver, C. K. (1992). Women viewing violence. London, UK: British Film Institute, and Bloomington: Indiana University Press.

Shackelford, T. K., & Mouzos, J. (2005). Partner killing by men in cohabiting and marital relationships: A comparative, cross-national analysis of data from Australia and the United States. *Journal of Interpersonal Violence, 20,* 1310–1324.

Sharpe, J. (2001). *Witchcraft in early modern England.* New York: Pearson Education.

Sharps, P., Campbell, J. C., Campbell, D., Gary, F., & Webster, D. (2003). Risky mix: Drinking, drug use and homicide. *National Institute of Justice Journal, 250,* 8–13.

Shields, L., Hunsaker, D., & Hunsaker, J. (2004). Abuse and neglect: A ten-year review of mortality and morbidity in our elderly in a large metropolitan area. *Journal of Forensic Sciences, 49,* 1–6.

Silverman, R. A., & Kennedy, L. W. (1987). Relational distance and homicide: The role of the stranger. *Journal of Criminal Law and Criminology, 78,* 272–308.

Smit, P. R., de Jong, R. R., & Bijleveld, C. J. H. (2013). Homicide data in Europe: Definitions, sources, and statistics. In M. C. A. Liem & W. A. Pridemore (Eds.), *Handbook of European homicide research: Patterns, explanations, and country studies* (pp. 5–23). New York, NY: Springer Science.

Smith, S. G., Basile, K. C., & Karch, D. (2011). Sexual homicide and sexual violence-associated homicide: Findings from the national violent death reporting system. *Homicide Studies, 15,* 132–153.

Smith, P. H., Moracco, K. E., & Butts, J. D. (1998). Partner homicide in context: A population based perspective. *Homicide Studies, 2,* 400–421.

Smith, M. D., & Zahn, M. A. (Eds.). (1999). *Homicide: A sourcebook of social research.* Thousand Oaks, CA: Sage.

Soothill, K., & Francis, B. (2013). Homicide in England and Wales. In M. C. A. Liem & W. A. Pridemore (Eds.), *Handbook of European homicide research: Patterns, explanations, and country studies* (pp. 287–300). New York, NY: Springer Science.

Soothill, K. Francis, F., Ackerley, E., & Fligelstone, R. (2002). *Murder and serious sexual assault: What criminal histories can reveal.* Police Research Series, Paper 144. London, UK: Home Office.

Spierenburg, P. (1998). Masculinity, violence, and honor: An introduction. In P. Spierenburg (Ed.), *Men and violence: Gender, honor, and rituals in modern Europe and America* (pp. 1–36). Columbus: Ohio State University Press.

Statistics Bureau of Japan. (2011). *2010 Japan Census, Population over 65 by sex and household.* Accessed May 2014 at: http://www.stat.go.jp/english/data/kokusei/pdf/20111026.pdf

Stockl, H., Devries, K., Rotstein, A., Abrahams, N., Campbell, J., Watts, C., & Garcia Moreno, C. (2013). The global prevalence of intimate partner homicide: A systematic review. *Lancet, 382,* 859–865.

Sykes, D., & Matza, D. (1957). Techniques of neutralization: A theory of delinquency. *American Sociological Review, 22*, 664–670.

Thomas, K. A, Dichter, M. E., & Matejkowski, J. (2011). Intimate versus non-intimate partner murder: A comparison of offender and situational characteristics. *Homicide Studies, 15*, 291–311.

Toch, H. (1969). *Violent men*. Chicago, IL: Aldine.

Tolman, R. M., Edleson, J. L., & Bergen, R. K. (2011). Intervening with men for violence prevention. In C. M. Renzetti, J. L. Edleson, & R. K. Bergen (Eds.), *Sourcebook on violence against women* (2nd ed., pp. 351–365). Thousand Oaks, CA: Sage.

Trojan, C., & Krull, A. C. (2012).Variations in wounding by relationship intimacy in homicide cases. *Journal of Interpersonal Violence, 27*, 2869–2888.

UK National Statistics. (2014). *Publication hub: Population estimates/projections. Life expectancies/mortality rates*. Retrieved from http://webarchive.nationalarchives.gov.uk/20140721132900/http://www.statistics.gov.uk/hub/population/population-change/population-estimates

US Census Bureau. (1995). *Statistical brief: Sixty-five plus in the US*. Retrieved from: http://www.census.gov/population/socdemo/statbriefs/agebrief.html

US Census Bureau. (2014). Retrieved May 2014 from: http://www.census.gov/population/projections/files/summary/NP2012-T3C.xls

UNODC, United Nations Office of Drugs and Crime. (2013). *Global Study on Homicide 2013*. Retrieved November 2014 from http://www.unodc.org/documents/gsh/pdfs/2014_GLOBAL_HOMICIDE_BOOK_web.pdf.

UNODC, United Nations Office of Drugs and Crime. (2011). *Global Study on Homicide 2011*. Retrieved April, 2013 from: http://www.unodc.org/documents/data-andanalysis/statistics/Homicide/Globa_study_on_homicide_2011_web.pdf.

Verkko, V. (1951). *Homicides and suicides in Finland and their dependence on national character*. Copenhagen: G. F. C. Gads Fortag.

Violence Policy Center. (2000). *When men murder women: An analysis of 1998 homicide*. Retrieved from: http://www.vpc.org/studies/dv3cont.htm

Violence Policy Center. (2011). *When men murder women: An analysis of 2009 homicide data*. Retrieved from: http://www.vpc.org/studies/wmmw2011.pdf.

Wallace, A. (1986). *Homicide: The social reality*. Sydney, Australia: New South Wales Bureau of Crime and Statistics.

Weber, M. (1949). *The methodology of the social sciences* (E. Shils & H. A. Finch, Eds. & Trans.). New York, NY: Free Press.

Websdale, N. (1999). *Understanding domestic homicide*. Boston, MA: Northeastern University Press.

Websdale, N. (2010). Familicidal hearts: The emotional styles of 2011 killers. New York, NY: Oxford University Press.

Weinshel, E., & Calet, V. (1972). On certain neurotic equivalents of necrophilia. *International Journal of Psychoanalysis, 53*, 67–75.

Weizmann-Henelius, G., Matti Grönroos, L., Putkonen, H., Eronen, M., Lindberg, N., & Häkkänen-Nyholm, H. (2012). Gender-specific risk factors for intimate partner homicide: A nationwide register-based study. *Journal of Interpersonal Violence, 27*, 1519–1539.

Werner, A. (2012). *Jack the Ripper and the East End*. London, UK: Chatto & Windus.

West, D. J. (1965). *Murder followed by suicide*. Cambridge, MA: Harvard University Press.

White, B., & Ritchie, J. (2004). *Prescription for murder: The true story of Harold Shipman*. London, UK: TimeWarner Books.

Wikstrom, P.-O. H., Oberwittler, K., Treiber, K., & Hardie, B. (2013). *Breaking rules: The social and situational dynamics of young people's urban crime.* Oxford, UK: Oxford University Press.

Wilbanks, W. (1982). Murdered women and women who murder: A critique of the literature. In N. H. Rafter & E. A. Stanko (Eds.), *Judge, lawyer, victim, thief: Women, gender roles, and criminal justice.* Boston, MA: Northeastern University Press.

Wilson, A. V. (1993a). Introduction. In A. V. Wilson (Ed.), *Homicide: The victim/offender connection* (pp. 1–19). Cincinnati, OH: Anderson.

Wilson, A. V. (Ed.). (1993b). *Homicide: The victim/offender connection.* Cincinnati, OH: Anderson.

Wilson, M., & Daly, M. (1992). Till death us do part. In J. Radford, & D. E. H. Russell (Eds.), *Femicide: The politics of woman killing.* New York, NY: Twayne.

Wilson, M., & Daly, M. (1993). Spousal homicide risk and estrangement. *Violence & Victims, 8,* 3–16.

Wilson, M., & Daly, M. (1995). Familicide: The killing of spouses and children. *Aggressive Behavior, 21,* 275–291.

Wilson, M., & Daly, M. (1998). Lethal and nonlethal violence against wives and the evolutionary psychology of male sexual proprietariness. In R. E. Dobash & R. P. Dobash (Eds.), *Rethinking violence against women* (pp. 199–230). Thousand Oaks, CA: Sage.

Wilson, M., Johnson, H., & Daly, M. (1995). Lethal and non-lethal violence against wives. *Canadian Journal of Criminology, 37,* 331–362.

Wolfgang, M. (1957). Victim precipitated criminal homicide. *Journal of Criminal Law, Criminology, & Police Science, 48,* 1–11.

Wolfgang, M. E., & Ferracuti, F. (1967). *The subculture of violence.* London, UK: Tavistock.

SUBJECT INDEX

employment, *See* lifecourse of
    offenders—adulthood.
England/Wales, *See* homicide, national
    data and studies; murder of women,
    national data and studies [by country]
European Countries, *See* homicide,
    national data and studies; murder
    of women, national data and
    studies [by country]
explanations, *See* theories, concepts,
    explanations and conceptual
    frameworks

familicide, 4, 23, 31, 33–4, *See also*
    murder of women, types of
family, *See* lifecourse of offenders—
    childhood, carers, family of
    orientation, parents
family of orientation, *See* lifecourse
    of offenders—childhood, carers,
    family of orientation, parents
fantasy, *See* murder of
    women—murder event
father violent to mother, *See* lifecourse
    of offenders—childhood, carers,
    family of orientation, parents
FBI, Federal Bureau of Investigation,
    Uniform Crime Reporting Program
    of the FBI. *See also* homicide; murder
    of women, national data and studies
    [by country]
fatality reviews, *See* homicide research,
    fatality reviews
femicide, 10, *See* murder of women
filicide (child murder), 32, *See also*
    collateral murders/killings,
    familicide
firearms, 24, 32–3, 49, 51, 64, 143, 192,
    193, 195, 196, 197, 200, 253, 284,
    292, 299
friend, *See* murder of women; relationships
    between perpetrators and victims
gender, 1, 2, 4–5, 7–8, 10, 12, 20, 25, 31,
    59, 99, 109, 119–20, 148, 192–3,
    199, 201, 205, 245, 249, 260
girlfriend, *See* murder of women,
    murder event; relationship between
    perpetrators and victims
guns, *See* firearms

"he says" (what were they thinking?) 57–8,
    139–41, 145–7, 215–7
Hispanics, 24
Homicide Indexes (UK), *See* murder of
    women, national data and studies
    [by country]
homicide, national data, 2–6, 8, 22,
    24–5, 33
    disaggregation of, 4–5
    proportion of male and female
        perpetrators and victims, 2–4
    rates of, 2–4
    See also murder of women,
        national data and studies
        [by country]
homicide, research by type
    academic studies, 4, 23, *See also*
        murder of women, national data
        and studies [by country]
    case studies, 6–7
    fatality reviews, 6
    national data, 4–6, 23,
        See also murder of women,
        national data and studies
        [by country]
homicide-suicide, 23, 31–3, 192, 195–6,
    200, 201

injuries, *See* murder of
    women—murder event
interactional perspectives, *See* concepts,
    explanations, and conceptual
    frameworks
interventions, *See* lifecourse of
    offenders—prison assessments;
    programs for offenders in the
    community
interview schedule, *See* Appendix II,
    Murder Study
interviews, *See* Murder Study
intimate partner murder, 23–104, Ax:
    281–8

jealousy, *See* murder of women—
    murder event, possessiveness and
    jealousy
justifications and rationalizations, 2, 10,
    19, 37, 57, 117, 121, 145, 202, 215,
    258, 84